Adobe®

Photoshop® Elements 7

① ② ③ ④ ⑤ ⑥ ⑦ **on Demand**

Steve Johnson
Perspection, Inc.

Kate Binder

Que® Que Publishing, 800 East 96th Street, Indianapolis, IN 46240 USA

Adobe® Photoshop® Elements 7 On Demand

Library of Congress Cataloging-in-Publication Data is on file

ISBN-10 0-7897-3931-3

ISBN-13 978-0-789-73931-5

Printed and bound in the United States of America

First Printing: December 2008

11 10 09 08   4 3 2 1

Que Publishing offers excellent discounts on this book when ordered in quantity for bulk purchases or special sales.

For information, please contact: U.S. Corporate and Government Sales

    1-800-382-3419 or corpsales@pearsontechgroup.com

For sales outside the U.S., please contact: International Sales

    1-317-428-3341 or International@pearsontechgroup.com

Publisher
Paul Boger

Associate Publisher
Greg Wiegand

Acquisitions Editor
Laura Norman

Managing Editor
Steve Johnson

Authors
Steve Johnson
Kate Binder (update)

Technical Editor
Kate Binder

Page Layout
Beth Teyler

Interior Designers
Steve Johnson
Marian Hartsough

Photographs
Tracy Teyler
Holly Johnson

Indexer
Katherine Stimson

Proofreader
Holly Johnson

Team Coordinator
Cindy Teeters

Acknowledgements

Perspection, Inc.

Adobe Photoshop Elements 7 On Demand has been created by the professional trainers and writers at Perspection, Inc. to the standards you've come to expect from Que publishing. Together, we are pleased to present this training book.

Perspection, Inc. is a software training company committed to providing information and training to help people use software more effectively in order to communicate, make decisions, and solve problems. Perspection writes and produces software training books, and develops multimedia and web-based training. Since 1991, we have written more than 100 computer books, with several bestsellers to our credit, and sold over 5 million books.

This book incorporates Perspection's training expertise to ensure that you'll receive the maximum return on your time. You'll focus on the tasks and skills that increase productivity while working at your own pace and convenience.

We invite you to visit the Perspection web site at:

www.perspection.com

Acknowledgements

The task of creating any book requires the talents of many hard-working people pulling together to meet impossible deadlines and untold stresses. We'd like to thank the outstanding team responsible for making this book possible: the writers, Steve Johnson and Kate Binder (for the update); the technical editor, Kate Binder; the production editor, Beth Teyler; proofreader, Holly Johnson; and the indexer, Katherine Stimson.

At Que publishing, we'd like to thank Greg Wiegand and Laura Norman for the opportunity to undertake this project, Cindy Teeters for administrative support, and Sandra Schroeder for your production expertise and support.

Perspection

About The Authors

Steve Johnson has written more than 50 books on a variety of computer software, including Adobe Photoshop CS4 and CS3, Adobe Flash CS4 and CS3, Dreamweaver CS4 and CS3, Microsoft Office 2007 and 2003, Microsoft Windows Vista and XP, Microsoft Office 2008 for the Macintosh, and Apple Mac OS X Leopard. In 1991, after working for Apple Computer and Microsoft, Steve founded Perspection, Inc., which writes and produces software training. When he is not staying up late writing, he enjoys playing golf, gardening, and spending time with his wife, Holly, and three children, JP, Brett, and Hannah. Steve and his family live in Pleasanton, California, but can also be found visiting family all over the western United States.

Kate Binder has mastered Photoshop and several other graphics programs over the past 20 years and is starting to feel quite old. She still enjoys tinkering with photos and does so at every opportunity. (It's much more entertaining than doing actual work.) When she can be found working, Kate is most likely to be doing magazine or book production, creating ebooks for major publishers, or writing books like this one. Books Kate has written or cowritten include *Sams Teach Yourself Adobe Photoshop Elements 6 in 24 Hours* (Sams, 2008), *The iMac Portable Genius* (Wiley, 2008), *Easy Mac OS X Leopard* (Que, 2007), *Sams Teach Yourself Adobe Photoshop CS4 in 24 Hours* (Sams, 2008), *Easy Adobe Photoshop Elements 4* (Que, 2005). Kate lives in an old house in New Hampshire with her husband, journalist Don Fluckinger, and assorted children, greyhounds, cats, and (she's pretty sure) a mouse under the dryer. Kate's Website is http://www.prospecthillpub.com.

We Want To Hear From You!

As the reader of this book, *you* are our most important critic and commentator. We value your opinion and want to know what we're doing right, what we could do better, what areas you'd like to see us publish in, and any other words of wisdom you're willing to pass our way.

As an associate publisher for Que, I welcome your comments. You can email or write me directly to let me know what you did or didn't like about this book—as well as what we can do to make our books better.

Please note that I cannot help you with technical problems related to the topic of this book. We do have a User Services group, however, where I will forward specific technical questions related to the book.

When you write, please be sure to include this book's title and author as well as your name, email address, and phone number. I will carefully review your comments and share them with the author and editors who worked on the book.

Email: feedback@quepublishing.com

Mail: Greg Wiegand
         Que Publishing
         800 East 96th Street
         Indianapolis, IN 46240 USA

For more information about this book or another Que title, visit our web site at *informit.com/register*. Type the ISBN (excluding hyphens) or the title of a book in the Search field to find the page you're looking for.

Contents

Introduction

Welcome to *Adobe Photoshop Elements 7 On Demand*, a visual quick reference book that shows you how to work efficiently with Photoshop Elements 7. This book provides complete coverage of basic to advanced Photoshop Elements skills.

How This Book Works

You don't have to read this book in any particular order. We've designed the book so that you can jump in, get the information you need, and jump out. However, the book does follow a logical progression from simple tasks to more complex ones. Each task is presented on no more than two facing pages, which lets you focus on a single task without having to turn the page. To find the information that you need, just look up the task in the table of contents or index, and turn to the page listed. Read the task introduction, follow the step-by-step instructions in the left column along with screen illustrations in the right column, and you're done.

What's New

If you're searching for what's new in Photoshop Elements 7, just look for the icon: **New!**. The new icon appears in the table of contents and throughout this book so you can quickly and easily identify a new or improved feature in Photoshop Elements 7. A complete description of each new feature appears in the New Features guide in the back of this book.

Keyboard Shortcuts

Most menu commands have a keyboard equivalent, such as Ctrl+P, as a quicker alternative to using the mouse. A complete list of keyboard shortcuts is available in the back of this book and on the Web at *www.perspection.com*.

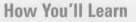

How You'll Learn

How This Book Works

What's New

Keyboard Shortcuts

Step-by-Step Instructions

Real World Examples

Workshops

Get More on the Web

Step-by-Step Instructions

This book provides concise step-by-step instructions that show you "how" to accomplish a task. Each set of instructions includes illustrations that directly correspond to the easy-to-read steps. Also included in the text are time-savers, tables, and sidebars to help you work more efficiently or to teach you more in-depth information. A "Did You Know?" provides tips and techniques to help you work smarter, while a "See Also" leads you to other parts of the book containing related information about the task.

Easy-to-follow introductions focus on a single concept.

Illustrations match the numbered steps.

Numbered steps guide you through each task.

See Also points you to related information in the book.

Did You Know? alerts you to tips, techniques and related information.

Real World Examples

This book uses real world examples files to give you a context in which to use the task. By using the example files, you won't waste time looking for or creating sample files. You get a start file and a result file, so you can compare your work. Not every topic needs an example file, such as changing options, so we provide a complete list of the example files used through out the book. The example files that you need for project tasks along with a complete file list are available on the Web at *www.perspection.com*.

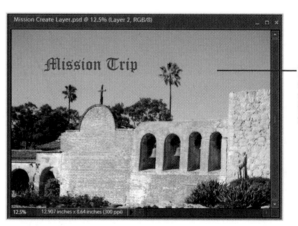

Real world examples help you apply what you've learned to other tasks.

Workshops

This book shows you how to put together the individual step-by-step tasks into in-depth projects with the Workshops. You start each project with a sample file, work through the steps, and then compare your results with project results file at the end. The Workshops in the back of this book and associated files are available on the Web at *www.perspection.com*.

Workshops

Introduction

The Workshop is all about being creative and thinking outside of the box. These workshops will help your right-brain soar, while making your left-brain happy; by explaining why things work the way they do. Exploring the possibilities is great fun; however, always stay grounded with knowledge of how things work. Knowledge is power.

Getting and Using the Project Files

Each project in the Workshop includes a start file to help you get started with the project, and a final file to provide you with the results so you can see how well you accomplished the task.

Before you can use the project files, you need to download them from the web. You can access the files at *www.perspection.com*. After you download the files from the web, uncompress the files into a folder on your hard drive to which you have easy access from Photoshop Elements.

Project 1: Creating a Sketch from Scratch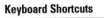

Skills and Tools: Multiple Layers, Gaussian Blur, and Blending Modes

Photoshop Elements has a ton of filters. In fact, there are 105 filters located under the Filters menu. Filters perform a wealth of special-effects operations; everything from artistic, distort, and even sketch effects, and while filters are very creative, and fun to use, there is a limit to what they can do. For example, Photoshop Elements has no less than 14 Sketch filters, and while they do creative things to an image they can't do everything. What if you want to create what looks like a sketch effect and none of the sketch filters do what you want? If you don't know how to do things from scratch, you're stuck with the limitations of the filters. The technique you are about to learn will not only let you create an awesome sketch effect, but will give you a better understanding of how blending modes work with multiple layers. There are a lot of steps to this process; however, the end result is more than worth the effort. In addition, if this process seems familiar, they are; many of the steps used in the sharpening workshop are similar to this effect, until you get to the end.

The Project

In this project, you'll take a photograph and through the judicious use of multiple layers, and blending modes convert it into a beautiful colorized sketch. There are a lot of steps in this workshop, but the final results are more than worth the journey.

499

The **Workshop** walks you through in-depth projects to help you put Photoshop Elements to work.

Get More on the Web

In addition to the information in this book, you can also get more information on the Web to help you get up to speed faster with Photoshop Elements 7. Some of the information includes:

Transition Helpers

◆ **Only New Features.**
Download and print the new features list as a quick and easy guide.

Productivity Tools

◆ **Keyboard Shortcuts.**
Download a list of keyboard shortcuts to learn faster ways to get the job done.

Keyboard Shortcuts

Adobe Photoshop Elements 7

Adobe Photoshop Elements is a powerful program with many commands, which sometimes can be time consuming to access. Most menu commands have a keyboard equivalent, known as a **keyboard shortcut**, as a quicker alternative to using the mouse. For example, if you want to open a new document in the Editor in Photoshop Elements, you click the File menu, point to New, and then click Blank File, or you can abandon the mouse and press Ctrl+N to use shortcut keys. Using shortcut keys reduces the use of the mouse and speeds up operations. If a command on a menu includes a keyboard reference, known as a keyboard shortcut, to the right of the command name, you can perform the action by pressing and holding the first key, and then pressing the second key to perform the command quickly. In some cases, a keyboard shortcut uses three keys. Simply press and hold the first two keys, and then press the third key. Keyboard shortcuts provide an alternative to using the mouse and make it easy to perform repetitive commands.

Keyboard Shortcuts	
Command	**Shortcut**
PHOTOSHOP ELEMENTS 7	
Shortcuts for the Organizer	
Navigating	
Move selection up/down/left/right	Up Arrow/Down Arrow/Left Arrow/Right Arrow
Move up without changing selection	Page Up
Move down without changing selection	Page Down
Select first item and scroll view to it. (In Date view, selects first item in Year, Month, or Day view	Home
Select last item and scroll view to it. (In Date view, selects last item in Year, Month, or Day view	End
Select multiple contiguous items	Shift + Up Arrow/Down Arrow/Left Arrow/Right Arrow
Show full-sized thumbnail of selected photo	Enter

517

Additional content is available on the Web.

More Content

◆ **Photographs.** Download photographs and other graphics to use in your Photoshop Elements documents.

◆ **More Content.** Download new content developed after publication.

You can access these additional resources on the Web at *www.perspection.com.*

Photographs help you use Photoshop Elements to get work done.

Getting Started with Photoshop Elements 7

Introduction

Adobe Photoshop Elements 7 is a photo image enhancement program that runs seamlessly on the Windows platforms. Photoshop Elements 7 provides a new streamlined interface yet also contains many of the powerful features found in Photoshop CS4.

Creative artists from Hollywood, brochure designers, as well as casual users turn to Photoshop Elements for its easy of use and proven ability to create special effects and image composites; however, Photoshop Elements' ability to manipulate digital images, restore photographs, as well as create digital artwork from scratch, has made it a popular choice in the digital industry. When it comes to digital photography, Photoshop Elements is literally the best the computer industry has to offer.

Photoshop Elements accepts images created with any digital camera, or traditional photographic film images, converted to the digital format through the use of a scanner. Once an image is opened in Photoshop Elements, the designer can manipulate the image thousands of ways, everything from color correction, reducing dust and scratches in an old image, to removing a tree, or adding a missing friend.

What You'll Do

Install Photoshop Elements

Launch Photoshop Elements

Use the Welcome Screen

View the Workspaces

Choose Commands

Switch Between the Organizer and Editor

Work with the Task Pane in the Organizer

Work with Bins in the Editor

Work with Palettes

Move Palettes

Work with Editor Tools

Undo and Redo an Action

Get Online Information

Get Help While You Work

Check for Updates and Patches

Exit Photoshop Elements

Installing Photoshop Elements

To perform a standard program install, insert the Photoshop Elements 7 installation disc into the drive on your computer or download the software online and start the setup program, and follow the onscreen instructions. Make sure to have your serial number handy because you'll be asked to enter it during the installation process. If you're updating from a previous version of Photoshop Elements, you'll be required to verify the older version by instructing Photoshop where on your hard drive the old version exists, or by inserting the previous version's install disk. Adobe, in an attempt to thwart software piracy, now requires online or phone activation of the program. The process can be postponed for 30 days. However, at the end of 30 days, the Photoshop Elements program will shut down if it has not been properly activated. You can't blame Adobe for attempting to protect their products, since some surveys suggest there are more pirated versions of Photoshop than those purchased.

Prepare to Install Photoshop Elements 7 for Windows

1. Refer to the table to make sure your computer meets the minimum system requirements.

See Also

See "Managing Catalogs" on page 58 for information on selecting a catalog from a previous version of Photoshop Elements or Photo Album.

Photoshop Elements 7 System Requirements

Hardware/Software	Minimum (Recommended)
Computer Processor	Intel Pentium 4, Pentium M, or Centrino 2 GHz (or compatible) processor
Operating System	Microsoft Windows XP SP2 or Vista
Hard Drive	1.5 GB of available space
Available RAM	1 GB
Video Card	16-bit color
Monitor Resolution	1024 x 768 at 96 dpi or less
Display driver	Microsoft DirectX 9 compatible
CD-ROM drive	Any type
Web features	Microsoft Internet Explorer 6 or 7 or Mozilla Firefox 1.5 through 3.x

Install Photoshop Elements 7 for Windows

1 Close any other Adobe programs open on your computer.

2 Insert the Photoshop Elements disc into your DVD drive, or download the software online to your hard disk.

3 If necessary, double-click the DVD icon or open the folder with the downloaded software, and then double-click the set up icon.

4 Follow the onscreen instructions to install, register, and activate the program.

IMPORTANT *Photoshop Elements requires you to activate the program in order to use it. Activation (using the Internet or by phone) must be accomplished within 30 days of installation, or Photoshop Elements will cease to function. You are not required to register the program. If you decide to register, you receive installation support, notifications of updates, and other services from Adobe.*

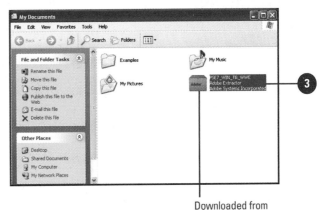

Downloaded from the Adobe web site

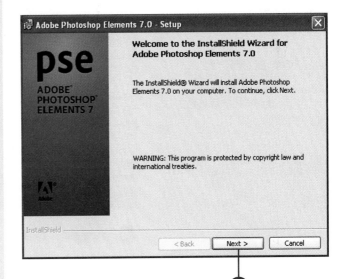

Did You Know?

You can also use Photoshop Elements on the Macintosh. Adobe Photoshop Elements 6.0 is currently available on the Macintosh. Check the Adobe web site at *www.adobe.com* for more details about the latest version.

Launching Photoshop Elements

You can launch Photoshop Elements like any other program. When you launch Photoshop Elements, a Welcome Screen dialog box appears, displaying easy access buttons to organize, edit, create, or share your photos. When you click one of the buttons, the Photoshop Elements Editor or Organizer workspace appears with options you need to work with images. After you dismiss the Welcome Screen dialog box on first use, the Adobe Updater Preferences dialog box appears, asking you to select options to update Photoshop Elements and other Adobe related software. If you want to access the Adobe Updater Preferences dialog box later, you can use the Updates command on the Help menu.

Launch Photoshop Elements 7

1. Click **Start** on the taskbar.

2. Point to **All Programs**.

3. Click **Adobe Photoshop Elements 7.0**.

4. In the Welcome Screen, click a button to work on photos.

5. If the Adobe Updater dialog box appears, follow the instructions to complete the update.

6. If a dialog box appears, asking you to set up the Organizer, click **Yes** to specify the location where your photos and other media reside, or click **No** to set up the Organizer later.

Did You Know?

You can create and use a keyboard shortcut to start Photoshop. Click Start on the taskbar, point to All Programs, right-click Adobe Photoshop Elements 7.0, and then click Properties. In the Shortcut Key box, type or press any letter, number, or function key, such as P, to which Windows adds CTRL+ALT, and then click OK. In Windows, press the shortcut you defined (Ctrl+Alt+P) to start Photoshop Elements.

For Your Information

Using Adobe Updater Preferences

The Adobe Updater Preferences dialog box allows you to set update options for installed Adobe products, such as Photoshop, Adobe Bridge, Adobe Help Center, and Adobe Stock Photos. When you select the Automatically Check For Adobe Updates check box, you can select options to automatically download or ask before performing the download. See "Checking for Updates and Patches" on page 22 for information on using the Adobe Updater Preferences dialog box.

Using the Welcome Screen

The Welcome Screen dialog box appears when you launch Photoshop Elements or you click the Welcome Screen button on the Shortcuts bar in the Organizer or Editor. The Welcome Screen displays easy access buttons to organize, edit, create, or share your photos. When you click one of the buttons, the Photoshop Elements Editor or Organizer workspace appears with options you need to work with images. You can also click buttons on the Welcome Screen to create a new Photoshop.com account or sign in to your existing account.

Use the Welcome Screen

 Launch Photoshop Elements or click the **Welcome Screen** button on the shortcuts bar.

② To access the Photoshop Elements window with specific options, click one of the following buttons:

♦ Organize. Displays the Organizer window with the Organize tab on the task pane.

♦ Edit. Displays the Editor window with the Edit tab on the task pane.

♦ Create. Displays the Organizer window with th e Organize tab on the task pane.

♦ Share. Displays the Organizer window with the Share tab on the task pane.

③ To activate a membership in Adobe's new Photoshop.com web site, choose one of the following options:

♦ Sign in. If you already have a Photoshop.com account, enter your user name and password and click **Sign In.**

♦ Create an account. If you haven't signed up for Photoshop.com and you want to use its features, click **Join Now!** to set up your free account.

① Welcome Screen button

Welcome screen

Viewing the Workspaces

Photoshop Elements provides two work-spaces—the Organizer and Editor—in a compact user interface with a dark background that is intended to make it easier to work with your photos. The **Organizer** allows you to find, organize, and share your photos and media files, while the **Editor** allows you to create and edit photos. The Organizer and Editor include a tab-based layout with tabs for Organize, Fix, Create, and Share to help with organization and reduce clutter.

After you import your photos, media clips, and PDF files into the Organizer, you can find, view, and share them. The Photo Browser displays all the files in the Organizer using different thumbnail size views, which you can sort by date, keywords (which includes People, Places, and Events), or other options using the Organize tab in the Task pane. If you can't locate a file, you can use the Search box (**New!**) or the Find menu to search for files by filename, caption, history, media type, and

Organizer Workspace

Welcome Screen button
Displays the Welcome Screen dialog box.

Menu/Shortcuts bar
Displays menus and buttons to execute tasks.

Display button
Displays a menu of views.

Navigation/ adjustment buttons
Displays and rotates images.

Search box
Searches photo collection based on search terms you enter.

Editor button
Displays a menu to open the Editor.

Task pane
Displays tabs with access to palettes and buttons.

Status bar
Displays the number of items selected and contained in the Photo Browser.

Photo Browser
Displays your photos, media files, and projects.

details, also known as **metadata**, which describes how and when and by who a particular set of data was collected, or how the data is formatted.

If you want to fix an image, you can use the Fix tab in the Organizer to open the image in Editor, or open the image file directly in Editor. The Editor provides three ways to create and edit images: Full Edit, Quick Fix, and Guided Edit. If you want to add special effects to an image, Full Edit provides the most con-

trol. If you want to quickly fix or alter an image, Quick Fix works the best. If you are not sure where to start to edit an image, Guided Edit walks you through the process for making different image alterations.

After you have fixed an image or two, you can use the Create or Share tab in the Organizer or Editor to create or share different types of projects, such as a photo book, calendar, collage, online gallery, slide show, greeting card, CD/DVD jacket, and more.

Editor Workspace

Welcome Screen button
Displays the Welcome
Screen dialog box.

Menu/Shortcuts bar
Displays menus and
buttons to execute tasks.

Organizer button
Displays a menu to
open the Organizer.

Options bar
Displays
options for
the selected
tool.

Toolbox
Provides
tools for
editing
images.

Workspace buttons
Move
between
different
editor modes.

Palettes
Help you
monitor and
modify
images.

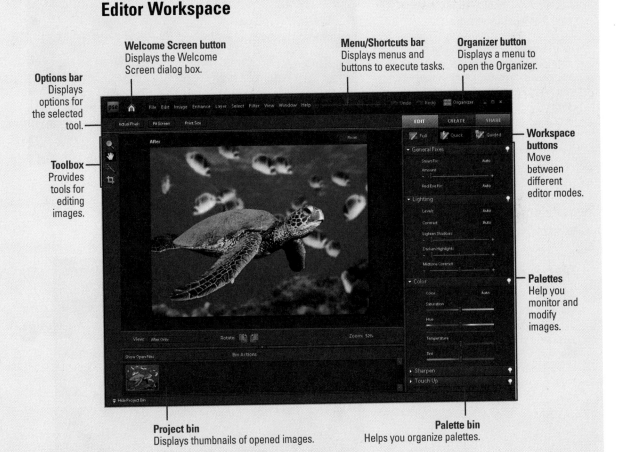

Project bin
Displays thumbnails of opened images.

Palette bin
Helps you organize palettes.

Choosing Commands

In the Organizer and Editor, commands are organized in groups on the menu bar. Next to the menu bar is the shortcuts bar, which displays frequently used buttons—such as Undo, Redo, Minimize, Restore, and Close—that you may be already familiar with from other Windows programs. In addition to menu commands and buttons, you can also open a **context menu**, also known as a shortcut menu, with a group of related commands by right-clicking a program element.

Choose a Command from a Menu

1. Click a menu name on the menu bar.

2. Click the command you want.

   If the command is followed by an arrow, point to the arrow to see a list of related options, and then click the option you want.

   TIMESAVER *You can use a shortcut key to choose a command. Press and hold down the first key and then press the second key. For example, press and hold the Ctrl key and then press S (or Ctrl+S) to select the Save command.*

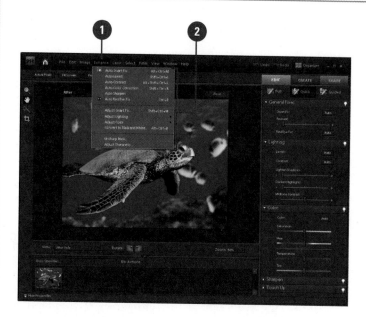

Choose a Command from a Context Menu

1. Right-click an object (a tool, selection, or palette).

2. Click a command on the shortcut menu. If the command is followed by an arrow, point to the command to see a list of related options, and then click the option you want.

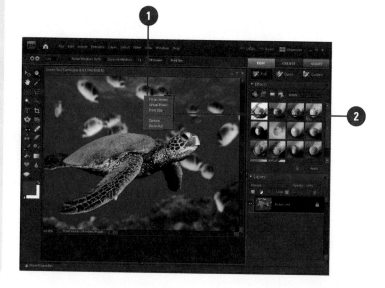

Switching Between the Organizer and Editor

After you launch Photoshop Elements in either the Organizer or Editor window, you can quickly switch between the two workspaces. In the Organizer, you can use the Editor button to open an image in the Editor workspace in one of the three edit modes: Quick Fix, Full Edit, or Guided Edit. In the Editor, you can use the Organizer button to open the Organizer workspace. Some buttons on tabs in the Editor or the Organizer open the other workspace. For example, the Slide Show button on the Create tab in the Editor opens the Organizer.

Switch Between the Organizer and Editor

◆ **Switch to Organizer.** In the Editor, use one of the following methods:

  ◆ **Organizer button.** Click the **Organizer** button.

  ◆ **Tab buttons.** Some buttons on tabs in the Editor, such as the Slide Show button on the Create tab, open the Organizer.

◆ **Switch to Editor.** In the Organizer, use one of the following methods:

  ◆ **Editor button.** Click the **Editor** button, and then **Quick Fix**, **Full Edit**, or **Guided Edit**.

  ◆ **Tab buttons.** Some buttons on tabs in the Organizer, such as the Quick Fix button on the Fix tab, open the selected image in the Editor.

Tab buttons   Organizer button

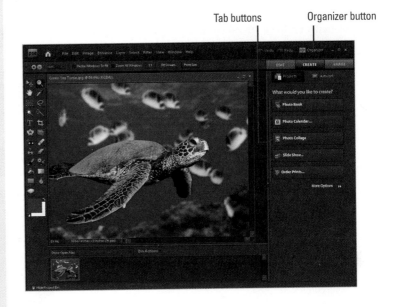

Tab buttons   Editor button

Working with the Task Pane in the Organizer

In the Organizer, a task pane appears on the right side of the Photo Browser as a separate window. The task pane displays various tabs for each of the main photo tasks: Organize, Fix, Create, and Share. If you need a larger work area, you can use the Window menu or the Show/Hide Task Pane button on the border edge to hide the task pane, or drag the task pane border edge to resize it. Some tabs in the task pane, such as the Organize tab, are divided into sections, known as palettes. Some palettes are always appear on the task pane, such as Albums and Keyword Tags, while other palettes are removable, such as Quick Share and Properties.

Work with the Task Pane in the Organizer

◆ **Show the Task Pane.** It appears by default on the right side of the Photo Browser. Click the **Window** menu, and then click **Show Task Pane**.

> **TIMESAVER** *Click the Show/Hide Task Pane button to show or hide the task pane.*

◆ **Hide the Task Pane.** Click the **Window** menu, and then click **Hide Task Pane**.

◆ **Resize the Task Pane.** Point to the task pane border edge until the pointer changes to double arrows, then drag the edge to resize it.

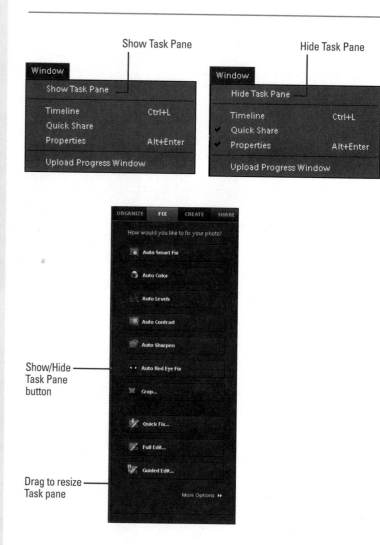

Show Task Pane

Hide Task Pane

Show/Hide Task Pane button

Drag to resize Task pane

Working with Bins in the Editor

In the Editor, Photoshop Elements uses the bins—Palette and Project—to make it easier to select options and work with photos. The Palette Bin organizes and stores related options into individual palettes, while the Project Bin displays thumbnails of open photos. By default, the Palette Bin appears along the right side of the Editor workspace, while the Project Bin appears at the bottom of the workspace. If you need a larger work area, you can use several different methods to hide a bin, or drag the bin border edge to resize it.

Work with the Bins in the Editor

◆ **Show the Palette Bin.** Click the **Show/Hide Palette Bin** button (at the left edge of the palette bin), or click the **Window** menu, and then click **Palette Bin**.

◆ **Hide the Palette Bin.** Click the **Show/Hide Palette Bin** button (at the left edge of the palette bin), or click the **Window** menu, and then click **Palette Bin**.

◆ **Show the Project Bin.** Click the **Show Project Bin** button (at the bottom of the project bin), or click the **Window** menu, and then click **Project Bin**.

◆ **Hide the Project Bin.** Click the **Hide Project Bin** button (at the bottom of the project bin), or click the **Window** menu, and then click **Project Bin**.

TIMESAVER *Click the Adjust Project Bin Size button to show or hide the project bin.*

◆ **Resize a Bin.** Point to a bin border edge or a dotted-line bar between palettes until the pointer changes to double arrows, then drag the edge to resize it.

Show/hide Palette Bin   Show/hide Project Bin

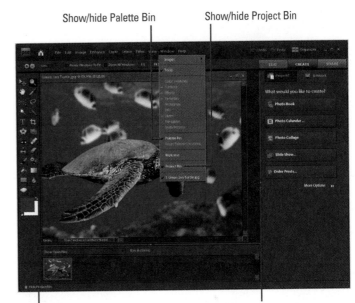

Hide/show Project Bin   Hide/show Palette Bin

Working with Palettes

Palettes appear in both the Organizer and Editor and give you easy access to many task specific commands and operations from general fixes to color control. A palette appears with a header, which includes the Open/Close arrow button, palette title and other varying options, such as the More and Close buttons. You can use the Window menu or click a Open arrow button to display a palette, and then select options on the palette or choose palette specific commands from the More menu or other available buttons to perform actions. Instead of continually moving, resizing, or opening and closing windows, you can use the Open/Close arrow button (triangle) to the left of the palette name to collapse or expand individual palettes to save space.

Show and Hide a Palette

 Click the **Window** menu.

2 Click a palette name, such as Quick Share or Properties in the Organizer, or Color Swatches, Layers, Navigator, or Tools in the Editor (Full Edit).

TIMESAVER *To close a panel, click the Close button (x) on the palette or the tab you want to close. This only works on undocked palettes.*

See Also

See "Moving Palettes" on page 14 for information on docking palettes (putting them into the Palette Bin) and undocking them (taking them out of the Palette Bin).

Palettes on Window menu

Click to reset Palette locations

Collapse and Expand a Palette

1 To collapse or expand a palette, click the **Open/Close** arrow button (triangle) on the header of the palette.

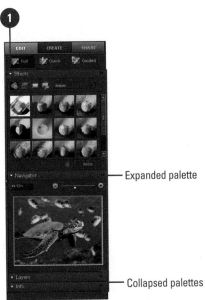

Expanded palette

Collapsed palettes

Use the Palette More Options Menu

1 In the Editor, open or expand a palette to display it.

2 Click the **More Options** button (double triangle or More text) on the right side of the palette header bar.

◆ **More Options button.** The More Options button appears as a double triangle when the palette is attached to the Palette Bin. It appears as text (More) when the palette is detached from the Palette Bin.

3 Click a command from the list (commands vary depending on the palette).

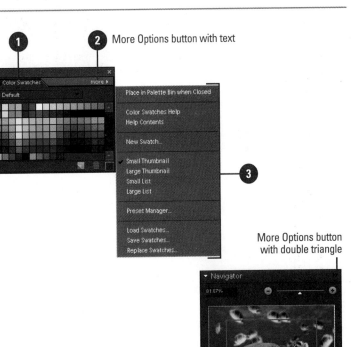

More Options button with text

More Options button with double triangle

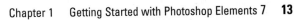

Moving Palettes

If a palette is not located in a position that you prefer, you can move it to another location. You can attach and detach, also known as dock and undock, palettes in the Palette Bin (in the Editor on the Edit/Full tab). When you drag a palette's header bar out of the Palette Bin, the palette detaches and appears in a separate window group. When you detach a palette, you can also drag it into an existing window group, where the palettes appear as tabs. When you drag a detached palette's tab to the Palette Bin, the palette re-attaches. When you move palettes, they remain as you left them until you reset or change them. In the task pane of the Organizer, you can dock and undock the Properties palette, which works differently than the palettes in the Editor.

Detach a Palette in the Editor

1. In the Editor (Edit/Full tab), open or expand a palette to display it.

2. Drag the palette header bar out of the Palette Bin or window group.

3. Drop it onto the Photoshop Elements window.

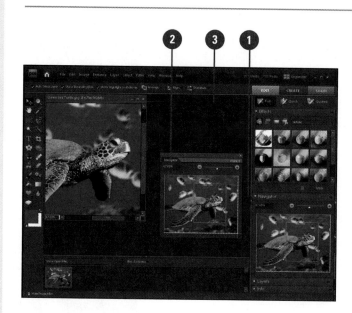

Attach a Palette in the Editor

1. In the Editor (Edit/Full tab), open or expand a palette to display it.

2. Drag the palette header bar into the Palette Bin or another window group.

   ◆ You can also click the **More** button in the palette header bar, click **Place In Palette Bin when Closed**, and then click the **Close** button (x) in the palette.

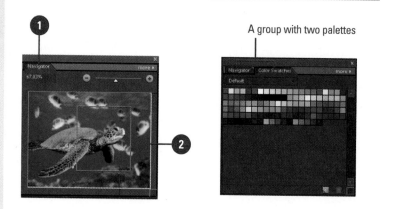

A group with two palettes

Undock or Dock Properties Palette in the Organizer

1. In the Organizer, open or expand the Properties palette.

2. Use one of the following commands.

   ◆ **Undock.** Click the **Undock Properties Panel** button on the right side of the palette header bar.

   ◆ **Dock.** Click the **Dock To Organizer Pane** button on the right side of the palette header bar.

Did You Know?

You can move a palette within a Palette Bin. In the Editor (Edit/Full tab), drag the palette header bar within the Palette Bin.

You can reset palettes to default positions. In the Editor (Edit/Full tab), click the Window menu, and then click Reset Palette Locations.

Click to undock Properties panel

Click to dock Properties panel

Working with Editor Tools

Photoshop Elements has an abundance of tools; located in the toolbox of the Editor workspace, they give a photo editor tremendous control over any creative designing problems that may crop up. For example, the toolbox contains eight selection tools (you can never have enough selection tools), 11 painting or shape tools, 4 type tools, and 12 tools dedicated to restoring and manipulating old images. Add to that mix the sampling and and view tools, and you have a total of 48 dedicated tools. When you work on an image, it's important to know what tools are available, and how they help in achieving your design goals. The Editor likes to save space, so it consolidates similar tools under one button. To access multiple tools, click and hold on any toolbox button that contains a small black triangle, located in the lower-right corner of

the tool button. Take a moment to explore the toolbox in the Editor workspace and get to know the tools.

The toolbox contains the tools needed to work through any job, but it's not necessary to click on a tool to access a tool. Simply using a letter of the alphabet can access all of Photoshop Elements' tools. For example, pressing the V key, switches to the Move tool, and pressing the W key, switches to the Magic Wand tool. In addition, if a tool has more than one version, such as the Eraser tools, pressing the Shift key, along with the tool's shortcut lets you cycle through all of the tool's versions. You can point to a tool to display a tool tip with the tool's name and shortcut key or you can refer to Adobe Photoshop Elements Keyboard Shortcuts (available for download on the web at

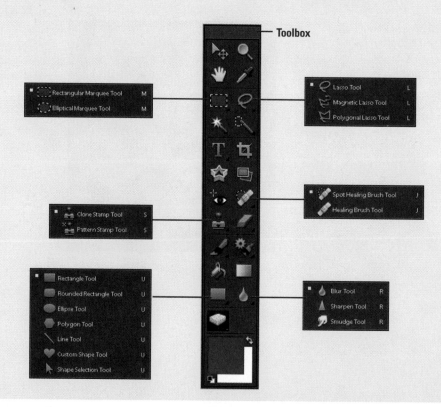

www.perspection.com) for more information on all the letter assignments for the various tools. To really get efficient in Photoshop, you need to learn to use both hands. Use one hand for your mouse, and the other on the keyboard to make quick changes of tools and options. Think of playing Photoshop Elements, like a piano—use both hands.

Using the Options Bar

The Options bar in the Editor workspace displays the options for the currently selected tool. If you are working with the Marquee tools, options such as Feather, Mode, Width, and Height appear. When working with Brushes, tool options such as Brush size, Mode, Opacity, Style, Limits, and Tolerance appear. The Options bar for the Airbrush and Paintbrush tools shows some of the Brushes options, but also includes Flow. The Pencil tool shows Auto Erase, along with the standard Brushes options, while the standard Shape tool includes Fill Pixels, Geometry, Blending Modes, Opacity, and Anti-alias. The important thing to remember is that the Options bar is customized based on the tool you have selected.

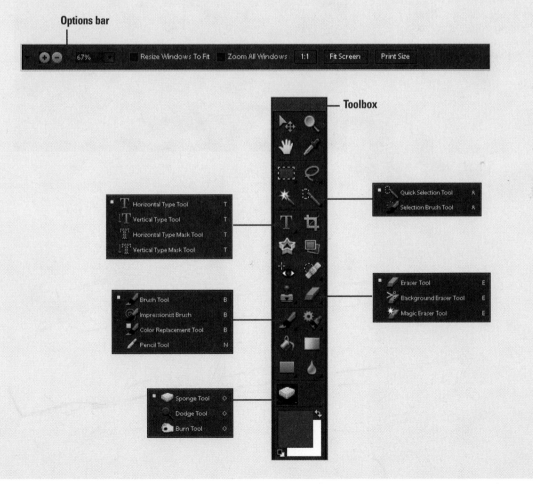

Options bar

Toolbox

Undoing and Redoing an Action

You may realize you've made a mistake shortly after completing an action or a task. The Undo feature lets you "take back" one or more previous actions, including data you entered, edits you made, or commands you selected. For example, if you were to apply the Graphic Pen filter and then didn't like the results, you could undo the filter instead of having to start over with a untouched image. A few moments later, if you decide that you like the filter's results after all, you could use the Redo feature to restore its effects.

Undo, Redo, or Cancel an Action

◆ **Undo an Action.** Click the **Undo** button on the shortcuts bar or click the **Edit** menu and then click **Undo** to undo the last action you completed.

> **TIMESAVER** *Press Ctrl+Z to undo an action.*

◆ **Redo an Action.** Click the **Redo** button on the shortcuts bar or click the **Edit** menu and then click **Redo** to restore your last undone action.

> **TIMESAVER** *Press Ctrl+Y to undo an action.*

◆ **Cancel an Action.** Hold down the Esc key until the action is cancelled.

Edit menu

Undo/Redo buttons

Getting Online Information

If you want to find out more about Photoshop Elements, you can go to several helpful Adobe web pages directly from Photoshop Elements. You can select commands on the Help menu to visit the Adobe product support centers page, the Adobe Photoshop Elements 7 product page, or the Adobe Idea Gallery page in your default browser. The Online Support command provides support information about Photoshop Elements, which includes top issues, recent documentation, and installation instructions. You can also search the Photoshop Elements Knowledgebase. The Photoshop Elements Online command provides information on Photoshop Elements along with related products and services. Finally, the Online Learning Resources command provides access to the Adobe Idea Gallery web page with great ideas, examples, and videos.

Get Online Information from Adobe

1. Launch Adobe Photoshop Elements, if necessary.

2. Click the **Help** menu.

3. Click any of the following:

   ◆ **Online Support.** Click to display the Adobe product support centers page.

   Click **Adobe Photoshop Elements** to see the program's support pages.

   ◆ **Photoshop Elements Online.** Click to display the Adobe Photoshop Elements 7 product page.

   ◆ **Online Learning Resources.** Click to display the Adobe Idea Gallery page where you can get ideas, see examples, and watch videos.

   IMPORTANT *Accessing this online information requires a computer with a connection to the Internet.*

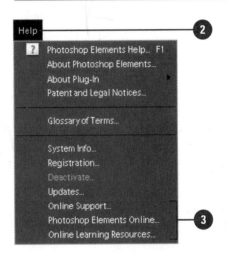

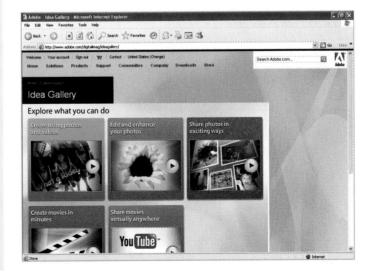

Getting Help While You Work

Working in Photoshop Elements can be a rewarding experience, but it can also be frustrating when you're looking for that specific piece of information to complete a project. Adobe understands how important it is to have access to information quickly, so they created the Adobe Help Center with different types of help options on the web (**New!**). You can also download a PDF version of the Photoshop Elements 7 help files, which you can view when you're not connected to the Internet or even print.

Get Program Help

1. Click the **Help** menu, and then click **Photoshop Elements Help**.

   If you have an Internet connection, the Adobe Photoshop Elements 7 Help and Support page opens in your browser. Click **Photoshop Elements Online Help** to open the Photoshop Elements documentation page.

2. Use the **Expand** (Plus sign) or **Collapse** (Minus sign) indicators and links to select the appropriate topic on the left, and view the corresponding help information on the right. If available, click links, such as *Tell me more...* to get additional information.

3. If you can't find the help topic you need, click in the **Search** box, type in a specific piece of information to search, and press Enter.

4. To view a printable PDF version of the Photoshop Elements manual, click the **PDF** link at the top of the page.

5. When you're done reading about your help topic, click the **Close** button in your browser.

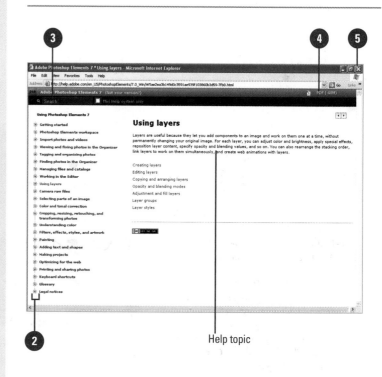

Help topic

Get Troubleshooting Help

① Click the **Help** menu, and then click **Photoshop Elements Help**.

If you have an Internet connection, the Adobe Photoshop Elements 7 Help and Support page opens in your browser. Click **Photoshop Elements Support Center** to open the Photoshop Elements documentation page.

② Click **Top issues, Recent documents,** or **Installation help** to see a list of common problems that users encounter.

③ If you can't find the topic you need, click in the **Search** box, type in a specific piece of information to search, click **Search**, and then click a heading link on the Search Results page.

④ Click a link to view the help information and then click any related links to other help topics.

⑤ To return to the Search Results page, click the **Back** button in your Browser window as needed.

⑥ When you're done reading about your help topic, click the **Close** button in your browser.

Did You Know?

You can find definitions for terms in Photoshop Elements. Click the Help menu, and then click Glossary of Terms (requires an Internet connection) to display the Adobe Resource Center web site, where you can select terms under the Glossary section in the left pane to display definitions.

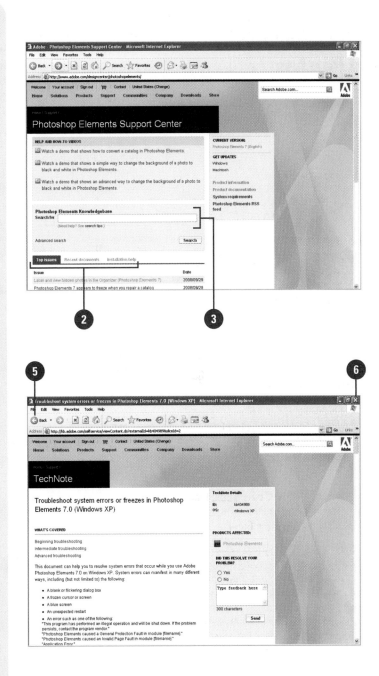

Checking for Updates and Patches

As time passes, Photoshop Elements—like any other program—will change. There are two types of changes to an program: updates and patches. Updates are enhancements to a program such as a new feature, option, or command. Patches are fixes for problems discovered after the public release of the program. The good news is that both updates and patches are free and self-installing. Adobe gives you two ways to check for changes. You can check on your own from the Adobe web site, or directly through the Adobe Updater. The Adobe Updater Preferences dialog box allows you to set update options for Photoshop Elements and other installed Adobe products. You can set the update preferences to check for updates monthly and automatically download them or ask before performing the download.

Check for Updates Directly from the Internet

1 Open your Internet browser.

2 Go to the following web address: *www.adobe.com/downloads/ updates/*

3 Click the list arrow, and then click **Photoshop Elements - Windows**.

4 Click **Go**.

Any updates or patches appear in a list headed by the version of Photoshop Elements for which they were created.

5 Follow the onscreen instructions to download and install the software.

> **IMPORTANT** *Checking on your own requires a computer with a connection to the Internet. Since some of the updates can be rather large, it's recommended you have high-speed access; 56k is good, DSL or cable modem is better.*

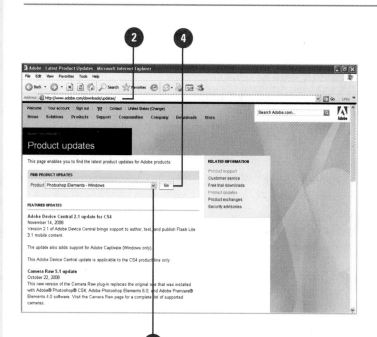

Check for Updates from the Help Menu

 1 Launch Adobe Photoshop Elements, if necessary.

2 Click the **Help** menu, and then click **Updates**.

Photoshop Elements automatically connects you to the Internet, and checks for updates. If there are any updates available, Adobe downloads and installs them.

IMPORTANT *Remember, these files can be quite large. So, if you're running with a slow Internet connection speed, you might want to perform downloading files at a low traffic time. Also, by making sure you don't have other programs running, you can maximize your system's resources for the downloading of files.*

When the check or download is complete, the Adobe Updater dialog box opens.

3 To change Adobe Updater preferences, click **Preferences**, select the **Automatically Check For Updates** check box, select the time interval and update options you want, and then click **OK**.

4 Click **Quit**.

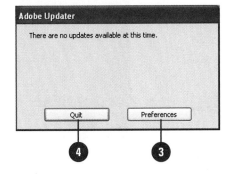

Select to update an application.

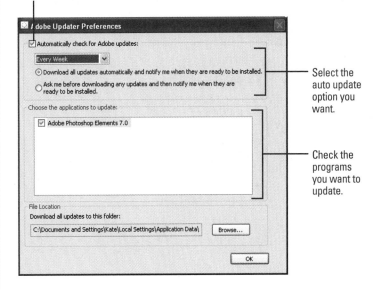

Select the auto update option you want.

Check the programs you want to update.

Exiting Photoshop Elements

When you finish working with your photos and media in Photoshop Elements, it's time to exit the program. When you want to exit Photoshop Elements, you need to exit both the Editor and Organizer workspace windows. Exiting one doesn't automatically exit the other. You'll want to make sure that all of your documents have been properly saved and closed before you exit Photoshop Elements. Photoshop Elements performs a bit of memory management, saves the current location of the palettes and toolboxes, and then quits.

Exit Photoshop Elements

 In the Editor or Organizer, click the **File** menu.

 Click **Exit**.

> **TIMESAVER** *Click the Close button on the program window or press Ctrl+Q to exit Photoshop Elements. You can also double-click the Photoshop Elements icon in the upper-left corner of the window.*

If necessary, click **Yes** to save your changes.

Photoshop Elements closes and you are brought back to your desktop.

Click to exit Photoshop Elements

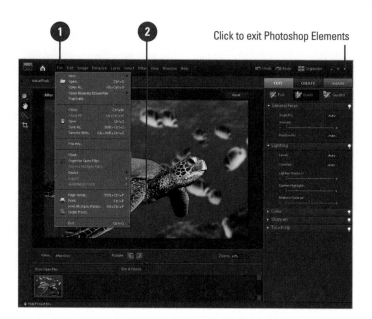

Customizing the Way You Work in the Organizer

Introduction

The best way to customize the way you work in the Organizer is to set the options in Photoshop Elements preferences. Photoshop Elements preferences serve several purposes. They help customize the program to your particular designing style, and they help you make it easier to manage and locate photos in the Organizer.

In Files preferences, you can set file import settings to specify how you want Photoshop Elements to import and manage image files from different sources. If you have a digital camera or card reader, you can set preferences for downloading photos from the hardware devices. In addition to using a digital camera or card reader to import photos into the Organizer, you can also specify a folder on your computer from which to import photos from your mobile phone. When you download photos into the Organizer, Photoshop Elements uses the Adobe Photo Downloader (APD) dialog box. You can set preferences for the automatic or manual use of the APD dialog box to search for and download photos.

If you like using Folder Location or Date view, you can select an option to display all the photos grouped by folder (the default) or only show the files in the selected folder in Folder Location view, or select the holidays most relevant to you and create custom events in Date view. In Keyword Tags and Album preferences, you can set options for manual sorting, keyword tag display icons, and tag searching, either faster or more accurate.

In Adobe Partner Services preferences, you can set options to check for new service updates, Adobe promotions, product support updates, and other third party services. When you want to share your photos and projects, Sharing preferences provide you with options to select the e-mail client you want to use to share photos and projects via an e-mail message.

What You'll Do

Set General Photo Browser Preferences

Modify Files Preferences

Set Folder Location View Preferences

Set Editing Preferences

Set Camera or Card Reader Preferences

Set Scanner Preferences

Set Date View Preferences

Set Keyword Tags and Albums Preferences

Set E-mail Sharing Preferences

Set Adobe Partner Services Preferences

Setting General Photo Browser Preferences

General preferences in the Organizer help you configure some common features for changing the appearance of the user interface (**New!**) and viewing photos in the Photo Browser. Specifying whether to display photos from oldest to newest or from newest to oldest, as well as how to display the date format are available in General preferences. Other options, such as allowing photos to resize past 100%, showing both matching and closely matching search results, using the current system font instead of the one specified by the application or showing fade transitions, can all be turned on or off in the options area. If you have hidden a dialog box by selecting the Don't Show Again check box, you can reset all the warning dialog boxes so they appear again.

Set General Photo Browser Options

1. In the Organizer, click the **Edit** menu, and then point to **Preferences**.

2. Click **General**.

3. Select the Appearance options (**New!**) you want to use:

   ◆ **User Interface Brightness.** Drag to specify the brightness of the user interface.

   ◆ **Changes Affect Grid Brightness.** Select to use the User Interface Brightness setting for the grid brightness.

   ◆ **Reset Brightness.** Click to reset the brightness to the default setting.

4. Click the **Print Sizes** list arrow, and then select a default value of inches or centimeter/millimeters for print.

5. Click the **Show Oldest First within Each Day** (default) or **Show Newest First within Each Day** option.

6. Click the **MM/DD/YYYY** (default) or **DD/MM/YYYY** option.

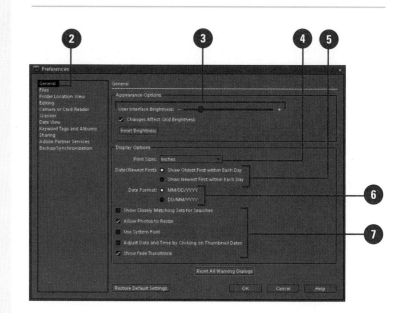

⑦ Select the various options you want to use:

◆ **Show Closely Matching Sets for Searches.** Select to show both matching and closely matching search results.

◆ **Allow Photos to Resize.** Select to scale photos past 100% up to the maximum size of the available space (default).

◆ **Use System Font.** Select to use the current system font instead of the one specified by the application.

◆ **Adjust Date and Time by Clicking on Thumbnail Dates.** Select to click on dates in the Photo Browser to adjust dates.

◆ **Show Fade Transitions.** Select to show fade transition in the Photo Browser (default)

⑧ To display all warning dialog boxes hidden by selecting the Don't Show Again check box, click **Reset All Warning Dialogs**.

⑨ To reset default settings, click **Restore Default Settings**.

⑩ Click **OK**.

Did You Know?

You can access Organizer preferences from the Editor. In the Editor, click the Edit menu, point to Preferences, and then click Organize & Share.

Modifying Files Preferences

When you take a photo with your digital camera, the image file includes additional information besides the photo, know as **metadata**. The metadata for a photo typically includes the date and time, shutter speed and aperture, and camera model. In addition to the default metadata, you can add your own custom metadata to an image file too. When most digital cameras take and save a photo and its metadata, they typically use the **EXIF (Exchange Image File)** image file format, a standard for exchanging data between camera and software. If an image file includes a Digimarc watermark, Photoshop Elements displays copyright information in the title bar and adds it to the File Info dialog box. In Files preferences in the Organizer, you can set file import settings to specify how you want Photoshop Elements to import and manage image files from different sources.

Modify Files Options

1. In the Organizer, click the **Edit** menu, and then point to **Preferences**.

2. Click **Files**.

3. Select the File options you want to use:

   ◆ **Use "Last Modified" Date if EXIF Date is Not Found.** Select to use file last modified date for photos without an EXIF date (default). Deselect to leave the date unknown.

   ◆ **Import EXIF Caption.** Select to to import EXIF captions from files if available (default). Deselect to delete the caption information.

   ◆ **Automatically Search for and Reconnect Missing Files.** Select to automatically search for and reconnect missing files (default).

   ◆ **Enable Multisession Burning to CD/DVD.** Select to enable multisessions burning to CD/DVD, which allows you to copy files to a disc multiple times to maximize the use of the CD/DVD.

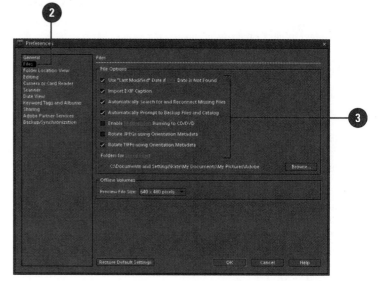

- ◆ **Rotate JPEGs using Orientation Metadata.** Select to speed up the rotate of JPEGs in the Photo Browser by using low resolution thumbnails. Deselect to use high resolution thumbnails.

- ◆ **Rotate TIFFs using Orientation Metadata.** Select to speed up the rotate of TIFFs in the Photo Browser by using low resolution thumbnails (default). Deselect to use high resolution thumbnails.

④ To select a location for projects and other saved files, click **Browse**, select a folder, and then click **OK**.

⑤ Click the **Preview File Sizes** list arrow, and then select a preview screen size when storing photos offline.

⑥ Click **OK**.

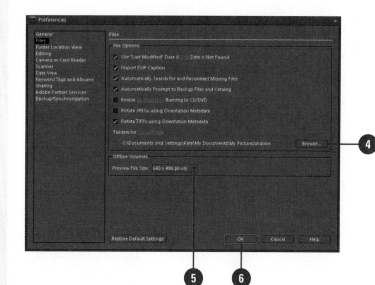

Setting Folder Location View Preferences

Folder Location view in the Organizer displays the Photo Browser in two panes, or split screen. A folder hierarchy pane appears on the left side and an image thumbnail panel on the right side. The folder hierarchy panel displays a tree structure of the folders on your computer, while the image thumbnail pane displays the photos on your computer. In Folder Location View preferences, you can select an option to display all the photos grouped by folder (the default) or only show the files in the selected folder.

Set Folder Location View Options

1. In the Organizer, click the **Edit** menu, and then point to **Preferences**.

2. Click **Folder Location View**.

3. Select the one of the following Show Files options: **All Files Grouped By Folder** or **Only Files in the Selected Folder**.

4. Click **OK**.

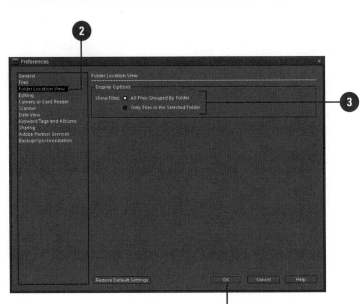

Setting Editing Preferences

If you have another photo editing application, such as Adobe Photoshop, installed on your computer that contains additional editing tools, you can access the application from the Edit menu in the Organizer to edit a photo. In Editing preferences, you can select an option to enable a supplementary editing application and then choose the application you want to appear on the Edit menu. The command on the Edit menu appears as Edit with *application name*. If you selected Photoshop, for example, the command appears as Edit with Photoshop.

Set Editing Options

1. In the Organizer, click the **Edit** menu, and then point to **Preferences**.

2. Click **Editing**.

3. Select the **Use a Supplementary Editing Application** check box to use an additional application for editing photos.

4. Click **Browse**, select the application, and then click **Open**.

5. Click **OK**.

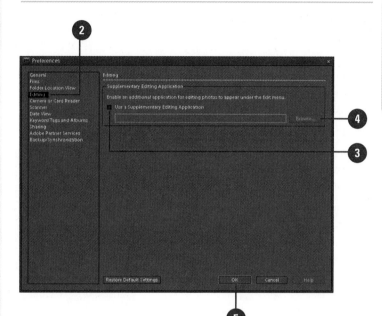

Setting Camera or Card Reader Preferences

A **digital camera** is a camera that takes digital photographs. A small memory card inserted into a digital camera stores the photos you shoot. A **card reader** is a portable hardware device attached to your computer in which you insert the card from the digital camera to download photos into Photoshop Elements. Camera or Card Reader preferences in the Organizer allows you to set options for downloading photos from a digital camera or card reader. When you download photos from a camera, card reader, or mobile phone, Photoshop Elements uses the **Adobe Photo Downloader** (APD) dialog box. In Camera or Card Reader preferences, you can set options for the automatic or manual use of the APD dialog box to search for and download photos. In addition, you can set options to automatically fix red eyes, suggest the use of photo stacks, and use the group custom name as a keyword tag for the imported photos.

Set Camera or Card Reader Options

1. In the Organizer, click the **Edit** menu, and then point to **Preferences**.

2. Click **Camera or Card Reader**.

3. To select a location for camera or card reader files, click **Browse**, select a folder, and then click **OK**.

4. Select the File options you want to use:

   ◆ **Automatically Fix Red Eyes.** Select to automatically fix red eye on import (default).

   ◆ **Automatically Suggest Photo Stacks.** Select to automatically suggest photo stacks on import.

   ◆ **Make 'Group Custom Name' a Keyword Tag.** Select to use the group custom name specified in the APD as a keyword tag.

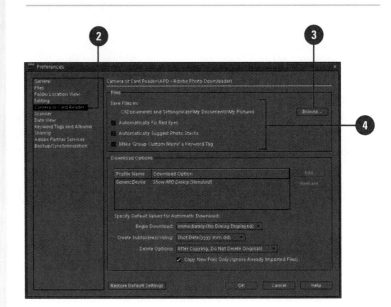

5 To select an APD dialog box or other APD options, select a download profile for a particular device, click **Edit**, click the **Download Options** list arrow, select an option, and then click **OK**.

    ◆ Remove. Select a current download option, and then click **Remove**.

6 If you selected the Auto Launch Adobe Photo Downloader on Device Connect check box, select the Download options to specify default values for automatic download:

    ◆ **Begin Download.** Select an option to specify how to automatically download files.

    ◆ **Create Subfolder(s) Using.** Select to create a subfolder using the selected date format.

    ◆ **Delete Options.** Select an option to specify how to automatically delete files.

    ◆ **Copy New Files Only (Ignore Already Imported Files).** Select to copy new files and ignore already imported ones (default).

7 Click **OK**.

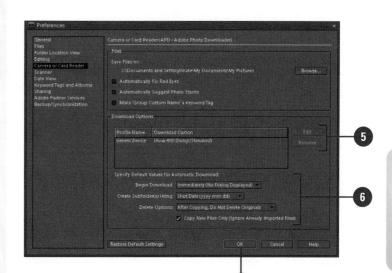

Setting Scanner Preferences

If you have a scanner attached to your computer, you can scan a photo print to create a digital photo file on your computer. Scanner preferences in the Organizer allow you to select options related to the scanner hardware and scanned photo file. In Scanner preferences, you can select the scanner hardware device attached to your computer you want to use, specify the file type and related quality setting for the scanned photo file, and select the folder location where to store it on your computer. In addition to selecting scanner options, you can also set options to automatically fix red eyes for the scanned photos.

Set Scanner Options

1. In the Organizer, click the **Edit** menu, and then point to **Preferences**.

2. Click **Scanner**.

3. Select the Import options you want to use:

   - **Scanner.** Select a scanner attached to your computer or network.

   - **Save As.** Specify the file type in which to save scanner files, and then set a related quality level, if available.

     The higher the quality level, the higher the file size.

   - **Automatically Fix Red Eyes.** Select to automatically fix red eye on import (default).

4. To select a location for scanner files, click **Browse**, select a folder, and then click **OK**.

5. Click **OK**.

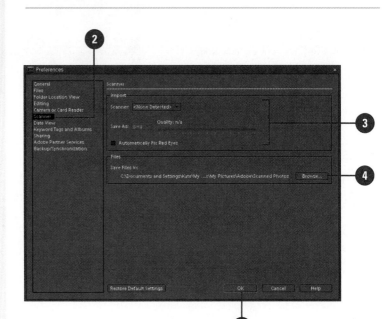

Setting Date View Preferences

Date view allows you to view and locate photos based on a certain day, month, or year. In Date view, you can keep track of recurring standard events, such as holidays, and custom event, such as birthdays, as well as add personalized notes to any day. In Date View preferences, you can select the holidays most relevant to you and create custom events. Depending on your preference, you can use Monday or Sunday as the first day of the week.

Set Date View Options

1. In the Organizer, click the **Edit** menu, and then point to **Preferences**.

2. Click **Date View**.

3. Select the **Use Monday as first day of the week** check box to use Monday as the start of the week or deselect to use Sunday as the start of the week.

4. Select the check boxes next to the holidays you want to use in Date view.

   ◆ **Select All and Deselect All.** Click to select all or deselect all the check boxes.

5. Use the following options to specify and work with events.

   ◆ **New.** Click to create a new event, which includes the date and frequency.

   ◆ **Edit.** Select an existing event, and then click to modify it.

   ◆ **Delete.** Select an existing event, and then click to remove it.

6. Click **OK**.

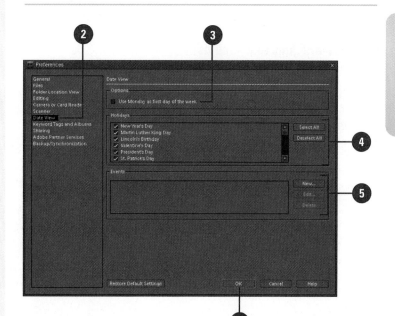

Setting Keyword Tags and Albums Preferences

A **keyword tag** is an information label that a program or you create and attach to photos to make them easier to locate. You can create your own custom tags with information important to you and attach multiple tags to the same photo for improved organization. An **album** is a group of photos organized into a collection. Each photo in an album is numbered to make it easier to sort and view. An album is useful for organizing images in photo albums and slide shows. In Keyword Tags and Album preferences, you can set options for manual sorting, keyword tag display icons, and tag searching, either faster or more accurate.

Set Keyword Tags and Albums Options

1 In the Organizer, click the **Edit** menu, and then point to **Preferences**.

2 Click **Keyword Tags and Albums**.

3 Select the **Manual** or **Alphabetical** option for the following Sorting options:

◆ **Categories.** A group of photos organized by keyword tags, such as People.

◆ **Sub-Categories.** A subgroup of photos within a category organized by keyword tags, such as Family under the People category.

◆ **Keyword Tags.** A custom tag under any category or subcategory to organize photos.

◆ **Album Groups.** A group of albums.

◆ **Albums.** A group of photos you want to view together.

4 Select the Keyword Tag Name icon display option you want.

5 Select the **Faster Searching** or **More Accurate Searching** option for face tagging.

6 Click **OK**.

Setting E-mail
Sharing Preferences

Sharing preferences in the Organizer provide you with options to select the e-mail client—such as Windows Mail (Vista), Outlook Express (XP), Microsoft Outlook, or Adobe E-mail Service—you want to use to share photos and projects via an e-mail message. If you don't have an e-mail client with an account, you can use the Adobe E-mail service to select an e-mail message directly from Photoshop Elements. If you make changes to photo captions, you can select the Write E-mail captions to catalog option to have Photoshop Elements automatically update e-mail captions in the catalog.

Set E-mail Sharing Options

① In the Organizer, click the **Edit** menu, and then point to **Preferences**.

② Click **Sharing**.

③ Click the **E-mail Client** list arrow, and then select an e-mail client program.

 ◆ **Windows Mail.** Select as the default on Windows Vista.

 ◆ **Outlook Express.** Select as the default on Windows XP.

 ◆ **Microsoft Outlook.** Select as the default when installed along with Microsoft Office.

 ◆ **Adobe E-mail Service.** Select to e-mail directly from Photoshop Elements.

④ Select the **Write E-mail captions to catalog** check box to update changes to photo captions in Photo Mail (HTML) to the catalog.

⑤ Click **OK**.

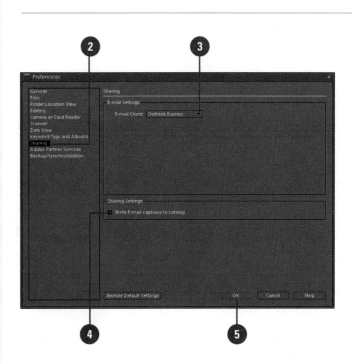

Setting Adobe Partner Services Preferences

Photoshop Elements uses Adobe Photoshop Services, such as the Kodak EasyShare Gallery, to provide access to additional online services. You can use these services in Photoshop Elements to send photos and create projects, such as a Photo Collage. The Adobe Photoshop Services are updated from time to time. In Adobe Partner Services preferences, you can set options to check for new service updates, Adobe promotions, product support updates, and other third party services. You can set options to automatically or manually check for services and to be notified when changes occur for specific types services. After you set your Adobe Partner Services options, you can access notification and updates by using the View Notification button or Envelope button on the Status bar in the Organizer workspace.

Set Adobe Partner Services Options

1. In the Organizer, click the **Edit** menu, and then point to **Preferences**.

2. Click **Adobe Partner Services**.

3. Select the Check for Services options you want to use:

   ◆ **Automatically check for services.** Select to automatically check for Adobe partner services.

      ◆ Click **Refresh** to manually check for new services. If new services become available, a dialog box appears.

   ◆ **Notify me about Service Updates.** Select to let you know about service updates.

   ◆ **Notify me about Adobe Promotions.** Select to let you know about Adobe promotions.

   ◆ **Notify me about Product Support Notifications.** Select to let you know about product support information.

   ◆ **Notify me about Third Party Services.** Select to let you know about related third party services.

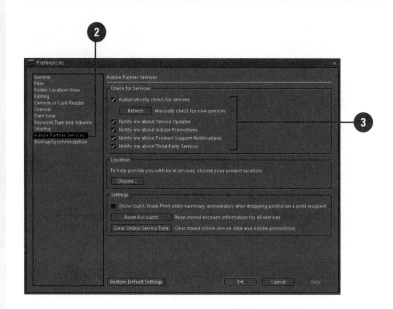

4 To select a location for local services, click **Choose**, select a country location, and then click **OK**.

5 Select the Settings options you want to use:

- ◆ **Show Quick Share Print order summary immediately after dropping photos on a print recipient.** Select to complete an order in one step using the Quick Share palette.

- ◆ **Reset Accounts.** Click to reset stored account information for all services.

- ◆ **Clear Online Service Data.** Click to clear stored online service data and Adobe promotions.

6 Click **OK**.

7 After you set your Adobe Partner Services options, you can access notifications and updates by using either of the following buttons:

- ◆ **View Notification.** Click the button (Mailbox icon) on the Status bar at the bottom of the Organizer window to view available notifications, updates, and services. In the Notifications window, select a notification, and then click **View**, or select an update or service, and then click **Run**.

- ◆ **Envelope.** Click the button (Envelope icon) on the Status bar at the bottom of the Organizer window to view available notification, update, or service in the Status bar.

IMPORTANT *You need to be connected to the Internet in order to get service notifications and updates.*

Importing Photos into the Organizer

3

Introduction

Before you can start using Photoshop Elements to edit photos and create projects, you need to import your photos and other media files into one or more catalogs. A catalog is a way to reference files on your computer or other storage device without moving them. Think of a catalog as a database of links to your photos and media files. The catalog links keep track of the photo's location, file format, attached tags, and date. A catalog can reference all the media you have on your computer or a subset of folders. Typically, users create a single catalog for all the media files on their computer. However, you can create more than one for different purposes, such as one catalog for work-related photos and media files, and another one for personal use.

You create a catalog by starting Photoshop Elements for the first time, and then clicking Yes in the Setup Organizer dialog box, or by using commands—such as From Camera or Card Reader, From Scanner, or From Files and Folders—on the Get Photos and Videos submenu on the File menu. After you have Photoshop Elements create a catalog, you can start to use the Organizer to manage, search, and fix photos and other media files.

What You'll Do

Specify Watched Folders

Import Tags Attached to Photos

Get Photos from Files and Folders

Get Photos by Searching

Get Photos from a CD or DVD

Get Photos from a Cameras or Card Reader

Get Photos from a Scanner

Get Photos from a Mobile Phone

Get Photos from a Video in the Editor

Add Photos to the Organizer from the Editor

Create and Open a Catalog

Manage Catalogs

Move Files in a Catalog

Delete Files from a Catalog

Back Up a Catalog

Restore a Catalog Backup

Specifying Watched Folders

A watched folder is a folder location on your computer that Organizer automatically checks for photos to add to the Organizer workspace. By default, your My Pictures (XP) or Pictures (Vista) folder is always watched. If you have photos and other media files in other locations, you can add them to the watched folder list. If you no longer want to watch a folder, you can quickly remove it from the list. In addition, you can also set options to watch all sub-folders within a watched folder, and to specify how you want to add new files found in the watched folders, either by notification or automatically.

Add Folders to the Watched Folders List

① In the Organizer, click the **File** menu, and then click **Watch Folders**.

② Click **Add**.

③ Navigate to and select the folder you want to add to the watched folders list.

④ Click **OK**.

The folder name appears in the Folders To Watch list.

⑤ Click **OK**.

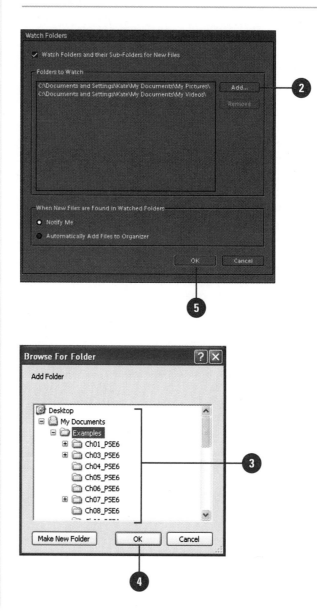

Remove Folders from the Watched Folders List

1. In the Organizer, click the **File** menu, and then click **Watch Folders**.

2. Select the watched folder you want to remove.

3. Click **Remove**.

   The folder is removed from the list.

4. Click **OK**.

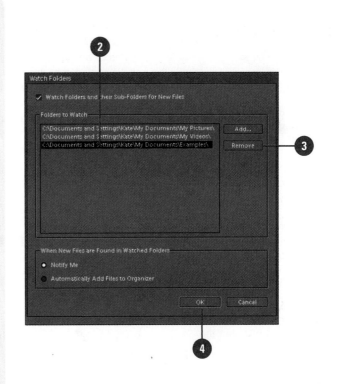

Change Watch Folders Settings

1. In the Organizer, click the **File** menu, and then click **Watch Folders**.

2. Select the **Watch Folders and their Sub-Folders for New Files** check box to watch all sub-folders in the specified watch folders.

3. Select the **Notify Me** or **Automatically Add Files to Organizer** option to specify how you want to add new files found in the watch folders.

4. Click **OK**.

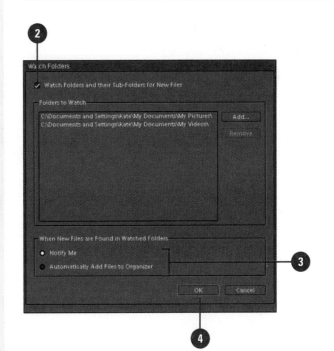

Importing Tags Attached to Photos

A keyword tag, also known as a tag, is an information label that is attached to photos to make them easier to locate. Some tags are automatically attached to a file when you create it, such as name and size, while custom tags are manually attached by the user. You can create your own custom tags with information important to you and attach multiple tags to the same photo for improved organization. When you import photos that already contain tags, you can specify whether you want to retain, rename, delete or remap them. When you import a new tag from an imported photo, it appears in the Keyword Tags palette, where you can apply it to other photos.

Import Tags Attached to Photos

1 In the Organizer, click the **File** menu, and then point to **Get Photos and Videos**.

2 Click any of the commands on the submenu to get files.

3 Select the options you want, and then click the button to start the import process, such as Get Photos.

If an imported photo included one or more tags, the Import Attached Keyword Tags dialog box appears.

4 Select the tags you want to import. If a tag has an asterisk (*), a tag with the same name already exists in the Tags palette.

The tags not selected are removed from the photos during the import process.

5 Click **OK**.

Navigate to the Import location

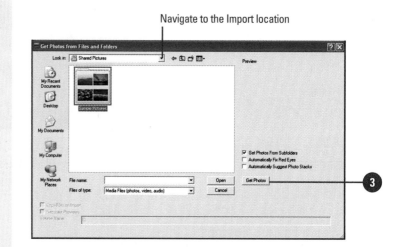

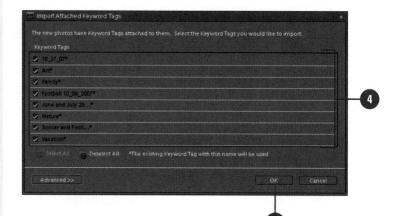

Import Tags Attached to Photos Using Advanced Options

1. In the Organizer, click the **File** menu, and then point to **Get Photos and Videos**.

2. Click any of the commands on the submenu to get files.

3. Select the options you want, and then click the button to start the import process, such as Get Photos.

   If an imported photo included one or more tags, the Import Attached Keyword Tags dialog box appears.

4. Click **Advanced**.

5. Select the check box next to the tag names you want to import.

   The tags not selected are removed from the photos during the import process.

6. To rename a tag, click the button under **Import as New Keyword Tag Named**, type a name, and then press Enter.

7. To map a tag to an existing tag, click the button under **Use an Existing Keyword Tag**, and then select a tag.

8. To clear your changes and return to the Import Attached Keyword Tags dialog box, click **Reset to Basic**.

9. Click **OK**.

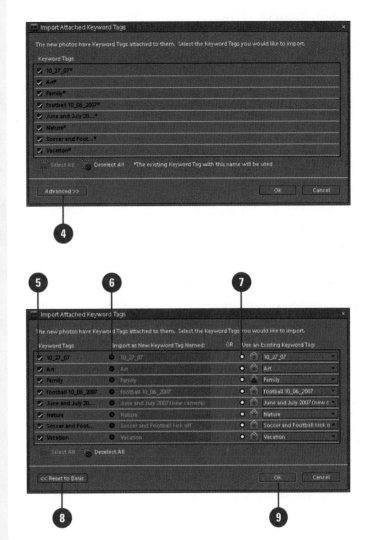

Getting Photos from Files and Folders

Before you import photos and videos into the Organizer, it's important to set file import preferences to specify the options you want for the import process. When you get photos from your computer, the files are not copied or moved. The Organizer creates links to them and adds them to the catalog. If you have photo files on your computer that are not already included in the catalog and don't appear in the Organizer, you can use the Get Photos from Files and Folders dialog box to navigate to the folder location with the files you want and then add them, or you can drag them directly from an Explorer window to the Organizer window.

Import Photos from Files and Folders

1. In the Organizer, click the **File** menu, and then point to **Get Photos and Videos**.

2. Click **From Files and Folders**.

3. Navigate to the folder location with the files you want to import into the Organizer.

4. Select the folder or the specific photo files you want to import.

5. If you want to get photo files from subfolders, select the **Get Photos From Subfolders** check box.

6. Click **Get Photos**.

    TIMESAVER *Drag the photos from an Explorer window into the Organizer. Depending on the number of photos and the speed of the computer, you might need to wait for the operation to complete.*

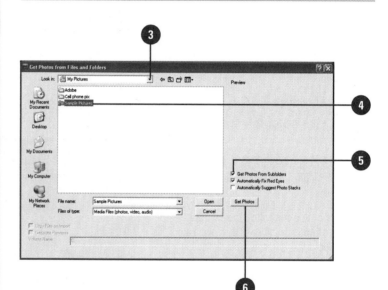

Add Photos from Specific Folders

1 In the Organizer, click the **Display** button on the Shortcuts bar, and then click **Folder Location**.

2 In the folder hierarchy panel, display the folder with the files you want to import.

3 Right-click the folder, and then click **Add Unmanaged Files to Catalog**.

4 Click **OK**.

When files are imported, the folder's icon changes from an Unmanaged Folder icon to a Managed Folder icon.

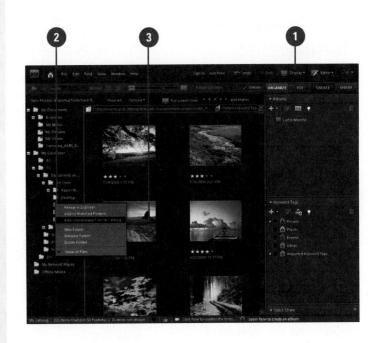

Getting Photos by Searching

Instead of manually looking for photos and other media files to import into the Organizer, you can have Photoshop Elements search your computer and then automatically import them. You can select options to exclude system and program folders, which typically don't contain photos, and exclude small files, which typically are not large enough to be photos. These options help speed up the search. As you import files into the Organizer, you can have Photoshop Elements automatically fix red eye on any photos that need it.

Search for Photos on Your Computer

1. In the Organizer, click the **File** menu, and then point to **Get Photos and Videos**.

2. Click **By Searching**.

3. Click the **Look In** list arrow, and then select the location where you want to perform the search.

4. Select the **Exclude System and Program Folders** check box to exclude folders from the search that typically don't contain photos.

5. Select the **Exclude Files Smaller Than xxx KB** check box to exclude small files that typically are not large enough to be photos.

    You can specify the size you want in kilobytes.

6. Click **Search**.

7. Select the folders with the photos you want to import. Press Ctrl to select more than one folder.

8. Select the **Automatically Fix Red Eyes** check box to automatically correct red eyes for photos that need it when you import the files.

9. Click **Import Folders**.

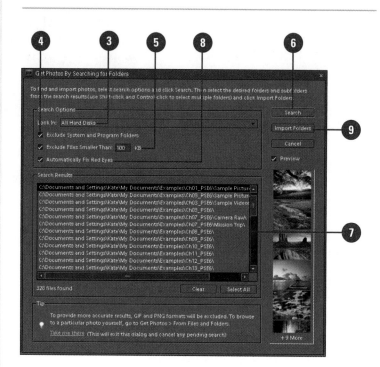

Getting Photos from a CD or DVD

When you get photos from a CD, DVD, or other external device, such as a scanner, digital camera, card reader, or mobile phone, Photoshop Elements first copies the photos to a folder on your computer, and then creates a link to the file. When you get photos from a CD or DVD, you can choose to make full- or low-resolution copies of the files. Full-resolution copies are best for editing, while low-resolution are best for previewing photos and saving disk space.

Import Photos from a CD or DVD

1 In the Organizer, click the **File** menu, and then point to **Get Photos and Videos**.

2 Click **From Files and Folders**.

3 Navigate to the CD or DVD drive with the files you want to import into the Organizer.

4 Select the photos you want to import into the Organizer. Press Ctrl to select more than one photo file.

5 Click the **Copy Files on Import** option to make full-resolution copies of the photos, or click the **Generate Previews** option to make low-resolution copies of the photos.

6 If you're keeping a master photo offline, type a volume name for the CD or DVD and label the disc to make it easier to find and download the master when needed.

7 Select the **Automatically Suggest Photo Stacks** check box to group visually similar photos together into stacks upon your approval.

8 Select the **Automatically Fix Red Eyes** check box to automatically correct red eyes for photos that need it when you import the files.

9 Click **Get Photos**.

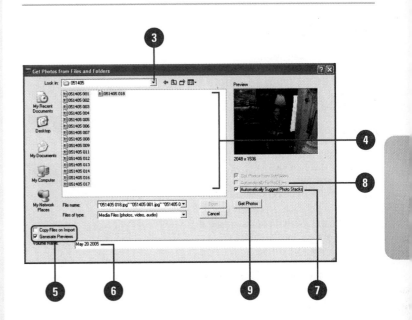

Getting Photos from a Camera or Card Reader

If you have a digital camera attached to your computer with a cable, you can copy photos directly from the camera to a folder on your hard disk and then import them into the Organizer. Many digital cameras store images on a memory card, which you can remove from your camera and insert into a card reader attached or built-in to your computer. The card works like a removable drive. You can copy photos from the card to a folder on your hard disk and then import them into the Organizer. When you download photos from a camera, card reader, or mobile phone, Photoshop Elements uses the Adobe Photo Downloader (APD) dialog box. You can set options to automatically use the APD upon device connection in Camera or Card Reader preferences.

Import Photos from a Camera or Card Reader

① Connect your camera or insert the memory card into your card reader already attached to your computer.

If the Adobe Photo Downloader dialog box appears, skip to Step 3. The dialog box automatically appears when an option is set in Camera or Card Reader preferences.

TROUBLE? *When you attach the camera or card reader to you computer, you may be asked to install software device drivers.*

② In the Organizer, click the **File** menu, point to **Get Photos and Videos**, and then click **From Camera or Card Reader**.

③ Click **Browse**, and then specify the folder location where you want to import the photos.

④ Navigate to the location with the image files you want to import, and then click **OK**.

⑤ Click the **Create Subfolder(s)** list arrow, and then select a format or **Custom Name** to create subfolder names.

Standard dialog box

6 Click the **Rename Files** list arrow, and then select a format or **Custom Name** to rename the files.

7 If necessary, type the filename and starting number for renaming filenames with sequential numbers at the end.

8 Select the **Preserve Current Filename in XMP** to use the current filename as the filename stored in the photo's metadata.

9 Click the **Delete Options** list arrow, and then select the option you want for deleting photos.

10 Select the **Automatic Download** check box to import photos from the connected device the next time you use it with the settings you've selected as the defaults.

11 Click **Advanced Dialog** to expand the dialog box, select individual photos you want to import, and select the advanced options you want for tags and metadata.

12 Click **Get Photos**.

If the photos contain metadata, the Import Attached Tags dialog box appears, where you can specify the options you want.

See Also

See "Setting Camera or Card Reader Preferences" on page 32 for information on setting options to import photos.

Advanced dialog box

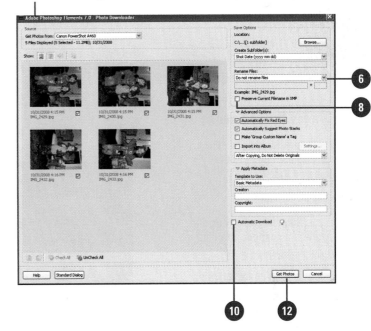

Getting Photos from a Scanner

If you have a scanner attached to your computer with a cable, you can scan photos directly from the scanner to a folder on your hard disk and then import them into the Organizer. When you get photos from a scanner, you need to follow the scanning instructions provided by the scanner's manufacturer to complete each photo scan. As you import files into the Organizer, you can have Photoshop Elements automatically fix red eye on any photos that need it.

Import Photos from a Scanner

1. In the Organizer, click the **File** menu, and then point to **Get Photos and Videos**.

2. Click **From Scanner**.

3. Click the **Scanner** list arrow, and then select a scanner attached to your computer or network.

4. To select a location for scanner files, click **Browse**, select a folder, and then click **OK**.

5. Click the **Save As** list arrow, and then select the file type in which to save scanner files and then set a related quality level, if available.

   The higher the quality level, the higher the file size.

6. Select the **Automatically Fix Red Eyes** check box to automatically correct red eyes for photos that need it when you import the files.

7. Click **OK**.

8. Select the scanning options you want from the ones available from your scanner, and then scan your photo.

See Also

See "Setting Scanner Preferences" on page 34 for information on setting default options to import photos.

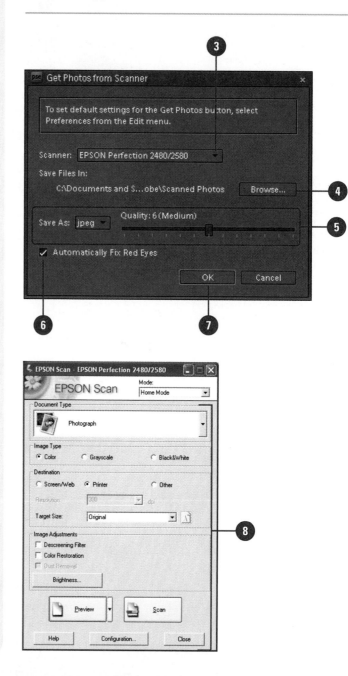

Getting Photos from a Mobile Phone

If you have a Nokia phone, Photoshop Elements recognizes the phone when you connect it to your computer with a cable and can import the photos directly from the phone. Instead of using this task, you should use the instructions for *Getting Photos from a Camera or Card Reader*. For all other mobile phones, you can use the From Files and Folders command shown in this task. You start by sending the photos to your computer from your phone. Then you import them using the same steps you would use to import any photos stored on your computer's hard drive.

Import Photos from a Mobile Phone

1. In the Organizer, click the **File** menu, and then point to **Get Photos and Videos**.

2. Click **From Files and Folders**.

3. Navigate to the folder location (such as Cell Phone pix) from which you want to import the photos.

4. Select the folder or the specific photo files you want to import.

5. Select the **Automatically Fix Red Eyes** check box to automatically correct red eyes for photos that need it when you import the files.

6. Click **Get Photos**.

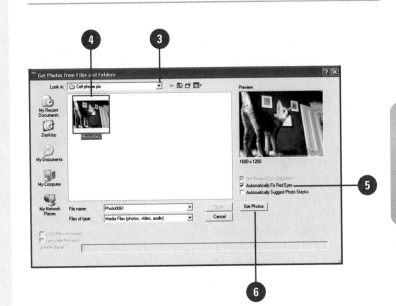

See Also

See "Getting Photos from a Camera or Card Reader" on page 50 for information on getting photos from a Nokia phone.

Getting Photos from a Video in the Editor

If you have a digital video in a file format that Photoshop Elements can recognize, such as ASF, AVI, MPEG, M1V, and WMV, you can open it in the Editor, play the video in the Frame From Video dialog box and then capture frames as individual photo files. The individual photo files are saved with the name of the video file and a number. For example, videoname01, videoname02, videoname03, etc. In addition to Photoshop Elements, you also need to install the latest version of standard video software, such as QuickTime or Windows Media Player, which you can get for free online at *www.apple.com* and *www.microsoft.com*.

Capture Frames from a Digital Video in the Editor

1. In the Editor, click the **File** menu, and then point to **Import**.

2. Click **Frame From Video**.

3. Click **Browse**.

4. Navigate to the location with the video file you want to import, select the file, and then click **Open**.

5. Click the **Play** button to start the video, and then pause the video where you want to capture the frame.

6. To capture a frame as the video runs, click the **Grab Frame** button or press the spacebar.

7. Use the forward and backward arrows to display the next screen you want to capture.

8. When you're finished, click **Done**.

9. Click the **File** menu, and then click **Save** to save each screen capture file to a folder.

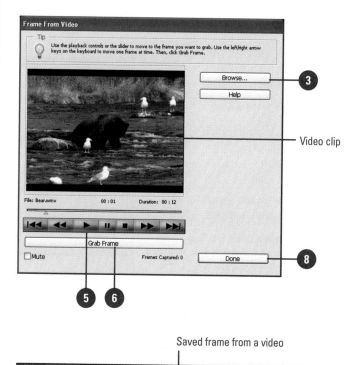

Video clip

Saved frame from a video

Adding Photos to the Organizer from the Editor

If you open or import a file in the Editor that is not currently included in the catalog, you can add the photo to the Organizer while you save the file in the Editor. All you need to do is select the Include in the Organizer check box in the Save As dialog box while you save the photo. The next time you open the Organizer, the saved photos appear in the catalog for use in the Organizer.

Add Photos to the Organizer from the Editor

1. In the Editor, open or import the photo file you want to add to the Organizer.

2. Click the **File** menu, and then click **Save As**.

3. Select the **Include in the Organizer** check box.

4. Select the **Save in Version Set with Original** check box to save the current version with the original version.

5. Navigate to the folder location where you want to save the photo.

6. Click **Save**.

7. If prompted, click **OK** to save the current version with the original version in a version set.

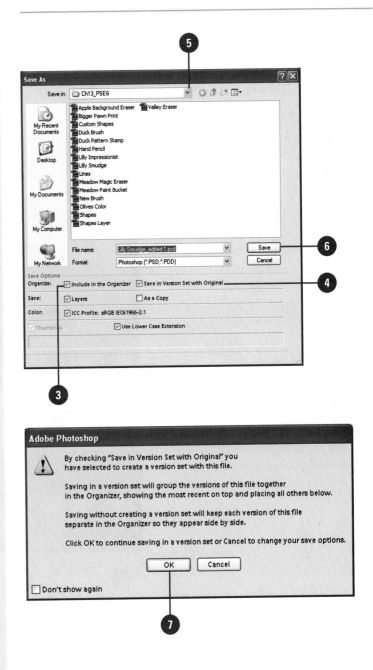

Creating and Opening a Catalog

You can create a new catalog or open an existing one by using the Catalog Manager. Typically, users create a single catalog for all the media files on their computer when you start Photoshop Elements for the first time. However, you can create more than one for different purposes, such as one catalog for work-related photos and media files, and another one for personal use. When you create a new catalog, you can create one that is accessible by all users on your computer or just the current user logged on. If you have more than one catalog on your computer, you can switch between them at any time. When you open the Organizer, the last opened catalog appears.

Create a New Catalog

1. In the Organizer, click the **File** menu, and then click **Catalog**.

   TIMESAVER *Press Ctrl+Shift +C to open the Catalog Manager dialog box.*

2. Select one of the catalog options:

   ◆ **Catalogs Accessible by All Users.** Creates a catalog for all users.

   ◆ **Catalogs Accessible by the Current User.** Creates a catalog for only the current user.

   ◆ **Custom Location.** Creates a catalog in the specified location.

3. Click **New**.

4. Type a name for the new catalog.

5. Select the **Import free music into this catalog** check box to include free music.

6. Click **OK**.

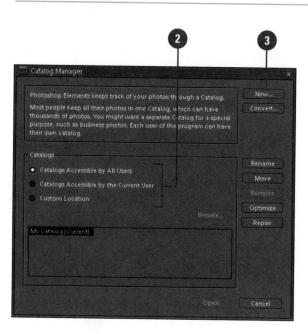

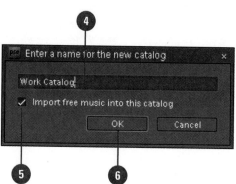

Open a Catalog

1. In the Organizer, click the **File** menu, and then click **Catalog**.

2. Select one of the catalog options to display the catalog you want to open:

   - **Catalogs Accessible by All Users.** Displays catalogs for all users.

   - **Catalogs Accessible by the Current User.** Displays catalogs for only the current user.

   - **Custom Location.** Displays catalogs in the specified location.

3. Select the catalog you want to open from the list.

4. Click **Open**.

Did You Know?

You can convert a catalog to another type. Click the File menu, click Catalog, click Convert, select a catalog to convert, and then click Convert. If a catalog is not available, click Find More Catalogs to select a catalog folder location. When you're finished, click Done.

② ③ ④

Catalog Manager

Photoshop Elements keeps track of your photos through a Catalog.

Most people keep all their photos in one Catalog, which can have thousands of photos. You might want a separate Catalog for a special purpose, such as business photos. Each user of the program can have their own catalog.

New...
Convert...

Catalogs
○ Catalogs Accessible by All Users
○ Catalogs Accessible by the Current User
○ Custom Location
Browse...

Rename
Move
Remove
Optimize
Repair

My Catalog
Work Catalog [Current]

Open   Cancel

Managing Catalogs

The Catalog Manager makes it easy to work with the different catalogs you may have on your computer. In the Catalog Manager, catalogs are organized in different ways: accessible by all users, accessible by the current user, and custom location. When you select one of these options, the catalogs in that category appear below in the list. After you select a catalog, you can use the buttons in the Catalog Manager to rename, move, remove, optimize (re-builds data for efficiency), and repair (corrects structure errors) it for better use.

Manage Catalogs

① In the Organizer, click the **File** menu, and then click **Catalog**.

② Select one of the catalog options:

◆ **Catalogs Accessible by All Users.** Displays catalogs for all users.

◆ **Catalogs Accessible by the Current User.** Displays catalogs for only the current user.

◆ **Custom Location.** Displays catalogs in the specified location.

③ Select one of the catalog options:

◆ Rename. Click **Rename**, type a name, and then click **OK**.

◆ Move. Click **Move**, select a catalog option to switch to, and then click **OK**.

◆ Remove. Click **Remove**, and then click **Yes** to confirm.

◆ Optimize. Click **Optimize** to optimize the catalog, and then click **OK** upon completion.

◆ Repair. Click **Repair** to repair the catalog. If no problems, click **OK** or **Repair Anyway**.

◆ Convert. Click **Convert** to convert catalogs with previous versions of Photoshop Elements.

④ Click **Cancel**.

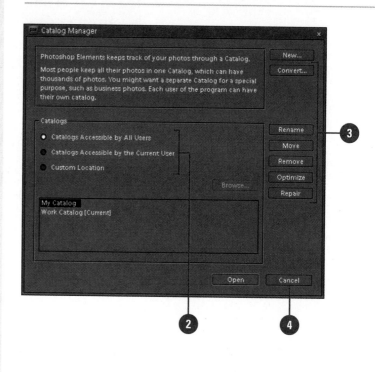

For Your Information

Upgrading Catalogs to Photoshop Elements 6

When you start Photoshop Elements 6 for the first time, it may not automatically open the catalog from an earlier version of Photoshop Elements or Photoshop Album. If this happens, click Convert in the Catalog Manager dialog box, select the Show Previous Converted Catalogs check box to show converted or backed up catalogs from earlier versions, select your catalog, such as My Catalog (use the Find More Catalogs button if needed), click Convert, click Done, select the catalog, and then click OK. Photoshop Elements 6 lets you view and edit the following: PSE 5.0 (all creations), PSE 4.0 (slide shows only), PSE 3.0 (no creations), or Photoshop Albums (no creations). If your catalog doesn't convert correctly, try renaming it first.

Moving Files in a Catalog

Because the photos and other media files in the Organizer are links to the actual files, if you move the files on your computer, the Organizer will lose the link location and need to reconnect to it. Instead of moving files in an Explorer window, you should move files in the Organizer using the Move command on the File menu. The Move command updates the links in the catalog, so links are not lost.

Move Files in a Catalog

1. In the Organizer, select one or more files you want to move.

2. Click the **File** menu, and then click **Move**.

   TIMESAVER *Press Ctrl+Shift +V to move files in a catalog.*

3. Click **Browse**.

4. Navigate to the new location for the files, select the folder, and then click **OK**.

5. If you want to remove files from the catalog, select them, and then click the **Remove** button.

6. If you want to add files from the catalog, click the **Add** button, use the Add Photos dialog box to select the photos you want, click **Add Selected Photos**, and then click **Done**.

7. Click **OK**.

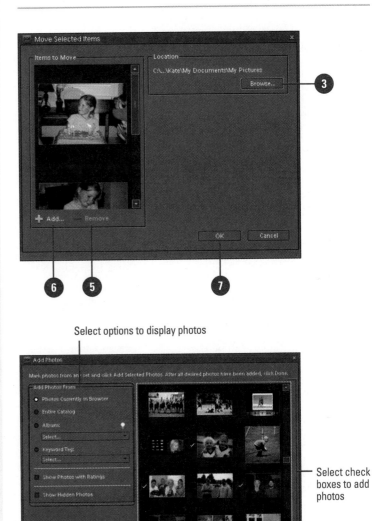

Select options to display photos

Select check boxes to add photos

Click to add selected photos

Deleting Files from a Catalog

If you no longer use or want to have a file in the catalog, you can delete it. You have the choice to delete the file from the catalog and leave the original file on your computer, or delete them both. When you delete the original file, it's permanently removed from your computer, which you cannot undo.

Delete Files from a Catalog

1. In the Organizer, select one or more files in the Photo Browser or one file in Date view you want to remove.

2. Click the **Edit** menu, and then click **Delete from Catalog** or **Delete Selected Items from Catalog**.

3. If you want to delete the files from your computer, select the **Also delete selected item(s) from the hard disk** check box.

4. Click **OK**.

5. If prompted to delete projects, click **Yes** or **No**.

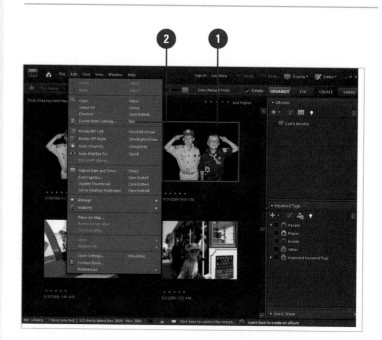

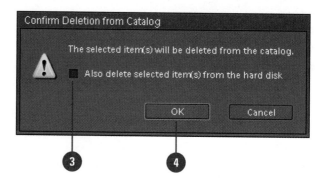

Did You Know?

You can rename a file in the catalog.
Select a file in the Photo Browser, click the File menu, click Rename, type a name, and then click OK.

You can also rename a batch of files, which renames all the files with the same text and adds a number at the end in successive order. To rename a batch of files, select the files you want to rename in the Photo Browser, click the File menu, click Rename, type a name for the common base, and then click OK.

Backing Up a Catalog

After you have worked with photos and media files in the Organizer for a while, it's important to back up the catalog, so you don't lose any information if you have problems with your computer. You can back up the currently opened catalog to a CD, DVD, or hard drive location. Photoshop Elements uses a wizard to make it easy to perform a backup.

Back Up a Catalog

1. In the Organizer, open the catalog you want to back up.

   ◆ If prompted, click Reconnect to locate missing or moved files.

2. Click the **File** menu, and then click **Backup Catalog to CD, DVD or Hard Drive**.

   TIMESAVER *Press Ctrl+B to back up a catalog.*

3. On first use, click the **Full Backup** option. If you have already performed a full backup, click the **Incremental Backup** option.

4. Click **Next**.

5. Select a destination drive.

6. Specify any of the following options that apply to the selected destination:

   ◆ **Name.** Specify a backup name.

   ◆ **Write Speed.** Select a speed to write a CD or DVD.

   ◆ **Backup Path.** Click Browse to select a location.

   ◆ **Previous Backup File.** Click Browse to select a file.

7. Click **Done** to perform the backup.

8. Click **OK** upon completion.

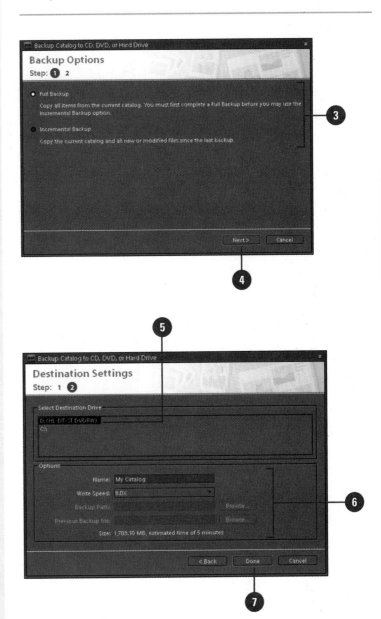

Restoring a Catalog Backup

After you have backed up a catalog, you can restore it at any time. Before you can restore a catalog backup, you need to select the backup file with the .tly extension you want to restore from the location where you stored it. You can restore a catalog backup in the original location to replace the current one or in a new location.

Restore a Catalog Backup

1. In the Organizer, open the catalog you want to backup.

2. Click the **File** menu, and then click **Restore Catalog from CD, DVD or Hard Drive**.

3. Select the location with the backup catalog you want to restore:

   ◆ **CD/DVD.** Click the **CD/DVD** option, click the **Select Drive** list arrow, and then select a CD or DVD drive.

   ◆ **Hard drive.** Click the **Hard drive/Other Volume** option, click **Browse**, navigate to the folder with the catalog backup, select the catalog backup file (with the .tly extension), and then click **Open**.

4. Select the location where you want to restore the backup catalog:

   ◆ **Original Location.** Click to restore the catalog backup to the original location replacing the current catalog.

   ◆ **New Location.** Click to specify a new location to restore the catalog backup. Click **Browse** to select a folder. Select the **Restore Original Folder Structure** check box.

5. Click **Restore**.

6. Click **OK** upon completion.

Catalog backup file

Viewing Photos in the Organizer

4

Introduction

The Organizer in Photoshop Elements makes it easy to view, find, edit, and manage your photos and other media files. When you open the Organizer, the Photo Browser view appears by default. The Photo Browser is the main display view in the Organizer. It shows thumbnails—a mini-preview—of all the photos in a catalog. You can display several different types of media files, including photos, videos, audios, projects, and PDFs. For videos, the first frame appears in the Photo Browser, which you can double-click to view it in a built-in media player. You can change the view in the Photo Browser to display any combination of media types you want. If you only need to work with photos, you can change the view to hide all the other media file types except photos.

If you need a larger view of your photos, you can use the Full Screen and Side by Side views, which allow you to view your photos in a full screen view without windows, menus, and palettes. In both of these views, a Control bar appears at the top of the screen, which allows you to access common display and editing commands. Side by Side view splits the screen in half and displays a photo on each side, which you can use to browse through photos on one side in order to compare them with the photo on the other side.

In the Organizer, you can also view and find photos by date using Date view. Date view allows you to browse through and locate photos by using a calendar, which you can also use to keep track of recurring events, such as birthdays and holidays, and even add notes. The Organizer also includes a Map view provided by Yahoo! Maps, where you can arrange photos by geographic location. It's an electronic version of a map on the wall with pictures attached with push pins.

Viewing Photos in the Photo Browser

The Photo Browser is a display view in the Organizer that shows thumbnails of all the photos in a catalog. A thumbnail is a miniature preview of a photo that is small and displays quickly for easy management. When you open the Organizer, the Photo Browser appears by default. In the Photo Browser, you can use the Display button on the Shortcuts bar to change the display view between three different options: Thumbnail View (default), Import Batch, and Folder Location. Each of the views displays a thumbnail with ratings and the date and time below it. Thumbnail view displays thumbnails by newest or oldest first; Import Batch displays thumbnails sorted by their location; and Folder Location displays thumbnails by selecting folders in a file hierarchy, similar to the Folders list in Microsoft Windows. In any of the views you can change the size of the thumbnails and show or hide information details about the photos.

View Photos in the Photo Browser

1. In the Organizer from Date view, click the **Display** button, and then click **Photo Browser**.

   TIMESAVER *In Date view, click the Return To Photo Browser button.*

   In most cases, you'll already be in Photo Browser view.

2. Click the **Display** button on the Shortcuts bar, and then click one of the following views:

   ◆ **Thumbnail View.** Displays a miniature preview of all photos in the Organizer.

   ◆ **Import Batch.** Displays thumbnails by the imported location.

   ◆ **Folder Location.** Displays a split pane with a file hierarchy in the left pane and a thumbnails view in the right pane.

3. To switch to Date view, click the **Display** button, and then click **Date View**.

Views

Change the View in the Photo Browser

1. In the Organizer, click the **Display** button, and then click **Photo Browser**, if necessary.

   In most cases, you'll already be in Photo Browser view.

2. Click the **Display** button on the Shortcuts bar, and then click **Thumbnails View, Import Batch,** or **Folder Location**.

3. To hide thumbnail ratings, date, time, and any other information below the thumbnail, deselect the **Details** check box on the Navigation bar.

4. To change the size of the thumbnails, use the following options on the Navigation bar:

   ◆ **Small Thumbnail Size.** Click the button to display thumbnails in the smallest size.

   ◆ **Slider.** Drag the slider to display thumbnails in the size you want.

   ◆ **Single Photo View.** Click the button to display the selected photo in the view.

   TIMESAVER *Press Ctrl+Shift+S to display the selected image in Single Photo View.*

Single Photo view

Did You Know?

You can show or hide file names, grid lines, and borders. In the Organizer, click the View menu, and then click Show File Names, Show Grid Lines, or Show Borders around Thumbnails. The file names appear below thumbnails along with other details.

Viewing Photos by Folder Location

Folder Location view splits the Photo Browser into two panels: a folder hierarchy on the left and a thumbnail view on the right. The folder hierarchy in the left panel displays a tree structure of all the folders on your computer (by default), where you can select the folder contents you want to view in thumbnail view in the right panel. The folder hierarchy is similar to the Folders list in Microsoft Windows. If you don't want to display all the folder on your computer, you can show only the ones you want. In Folder Location view, you can manage folders, add unmanaged files to your catalog, tag files with their folder name, and add or remove folders from Watched Folder list. Files in the catalog are called **managed files**, while files not part of the catalog are called **unmanaged files**.

View Photos by Folder Location

1. In the Organizer, click the **Display** button, and then click **Photo Browser**, if necessary.

2. Click the **Display** button on the Shortcuts bar, and then click **Folder Location**.

3. Use any of the following options to manage photos in Folder Location view:

   ◆ **Expand or Collapse Folders.** Click the plus (+) and minus (-) icons to expand or collapse a folder.

   ◆ **Display Files in Selected Folder.** Right-click in the folder hierarchy, and then deselect **Show All Files**. Click a folder to display the file contents in the right panel.

   ◆ **Display All Managed Files.** Right-click in the folder hierarchy, and then select **Show All Files**.

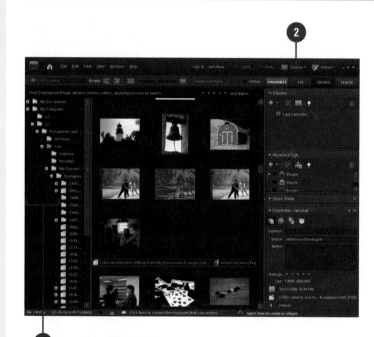

Expand or collapse folders

Did You Know?

You can resize the folder hierarchy area. Click the border between the Photo Browser and the folder hierarchy area and drag to resize.

- **Move Files.** Click a folder to display the file you want to move, and then drag it to the folder to which you want to move it in the folder hierarchy.

- **Add or Remove from Watched Folder list.** Right-click a folder in the folder hierarchy, and then click **Add To Watched Folders** or **Remove From Watched Folders**.

- **Add Files to Catalog.** Right-click a folder in the folder hierarchy, and then click **Add Unmanaged Files To Catalog**.

- **Rename Folder.** Right-click a folder in the folder hierarchy, click **Rename Folder**, and then type a name.

- **Delete Folder.** Right-click a folder in the folder hierarchy, click **Delete Folder**.

- **Create Folder.** Right-click a folder in the folder hierarchy where you want to insert a new folder, click **New Folder**, and then type a name.

- **Tag Files.** Click the **Instant Keyword Tag** button to tag each item in a folder with the name of the folder as a tag.

See Also

See "Setting Folder View Preferences" on page 30 for information on changing the default Folder Location view.

Instant Keyword Tag

3 Commands to display and work with files and folders

Viewing Specific Files in the Photo Browser

In the Photo Browser, you can display several different types of media files, including photos, videos, audio files, projects, and PDFs. You can change the view to display any combination of media types you want. If you only need to work with photos, you can change the view to hide all the other media file types except photos. The number of files in the Organizer can become large, so any way to reduce the clutter is a bonus. If you want to create your own set of files to view, you can mark the ones you don't want, and then hide them.

View Photos in the Photo Browser

1. In the Organizer, click the **Display** button, and then click **Photo Browser**, if necessary.

2. Click the **View** menu, point to **Media Types**, and then select the media type you want to show or hide.

   ◆ **Photos.** Displays photos files.

   TIMESAVER *Press Ctrl+1.*

   ◆ **Video.** Displays videos files.

   TIMESAVER *Press Ctrl+2.*

   ◆ **Audio.** Displays audio files.

   TIMESAVER *Press Ctrl+3.*

   ◆ **Projects.** Display project files.

   TIMESAVER *Press Ctrl+4.*

   ◆ **PDF.** Displays PDF (Portable Document Format) files.

   TIMESAVER *Press Ctrl+5.*

Mark Photos as Hidden or Visible

1 In the Organizer, select the photos you want to mark as hidden or visible.

2 Click the **Edit** menu, point to **Visibility**, and then click one of the following:

◆ **Mark As Hidden.** Hides photos by marking them.

TIMESAVER *Press Alt+F2 to mark files as hidden.*

◆ **Mark As Visible.** Removes the hidden mark from photos.

3 Click the **Edit** menu, point to **Visibility**, and then click **Show All Files** or **Show Only Hidden Files** to show or hide the photos marked as hidden.

TIMESAVER *Click the View menu, and then click Hidden Files.*

Did You Know?

You can sort photos in the Photo Browser. In the Organizer, click the Photo Browser Arrangement list arrow on the Navigation bar, and then click Date (Newest First) or Date (Oldest First).

Photos marked as hidden

Viewing Video Clips in the Photo Browser

If you have imported videos into the Organizer, the first frame of a video clip appears in the Photo Browser along with a Filmstrip icon. Photoshop Elements comes with a built-in Media Player that you can use to play a video. All you need to you need to do is double-click the first frame of the video clip in the Photo Browser to open the Media Player and start the video clip. The Media Player includes all the standard controls to play, stop, and control the video playback.

View Video Clips in the Photo Browser

1. In the Organizer (in Photo Browser view), double-click the video clip you want to open the Media Player.

2. To start the video clip, click the **Play** button.

3. To view the video clip frame by frame, drag the **Current Position** slider.

4. To adjust the volume, drag the **Volume** slider.

5. To stop the video clip, click the **Stop** button.

6. When you're finished, click the **Close** button.

Video clip

Selecting Photos in the Photo Browser

Before you can work with photos in the Photo Browser, you need to select them. You can select one or more photos in the Photo Browser depending on what you want to do. If you want to edit a single photo, then select an individual photo. If you want to create a photo collage, then select more than one. You can select multiple photos that are adjacent (next to each other), or nonadjacent (not next to each other). When you're done working with one or more selected photos, you can make another selection or use the Deselect command on the Edit menu to deselect the originally selected photos.

Select and Deselect Photos in the Photo Browser

1. In the Organizer (in Photo Browser view), use any of the following methods:

    ◆ **One Item.** Click the thumbnail.

    ◆ **Multiple Adjacent Items.** Hold down the Shift key, and then click the first and last thumbnail.

    ◆ **Multiple Nonadjacent Items.** Hold down the Ctrl key, and then click the thumbnails.

    TIMESAVER *Press Ctrl+A to select all items.*

    A selected photo thumbnail is highlighted with a blue outline.

2. To deselect items, click another item or click the **Edit** menu, and then click **Deselect**.

    TIMESAVER *Press Ctrl+Shift +A to deselect all items.*

Selected item

Viewing Photos in Full Screen View

Full Screen view allows you to view your photos in a full screen slide show view without windows, menus, and palettes. When you move the mouse, a Control bar appears at the top of the screen, which allows you to access common display and editing commands. When you switch to Full Screen view, the Full Screen View Options dialog box appears, asking you to specify the options—such as Page Duration and Repeat Slide Show—you want to use. If you don't want to see this dialog box the next time you use Full Screen view, you can change the options in the dialog box.

View Photos in Full Screen View

1. In the Organizer (in Photo Browser view), click the **Display** button, and then click **View Photos in Full Screen**.

   TIMESAVER *Press F11 to switch to Full Screen view.*

2. If the Full Screen View Options dialog box appears, click **Cancel**.

3. Move the mouse to display the Control bar.

4. Click the **Play** button on the Control bar to start the slide show.

5. When you're finished, click the **Exit** button on the Control bar.

   TIMESAVER *Press Esc to exit Full Screen view.*

See Also

See "Using the Control Bar" on page 75 for information on using the buttons on the Control bar.

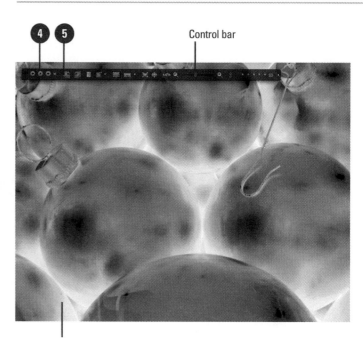

Control bar

Full Screen view

Set Options in the Full Screen View Options Dialog Box

1. In the Organizer (in Photo Browser view), click the **Display** button, and then click **View Photos in Full Screen**.

2. Select the Full Screen view options you want to use:

   ◆ **Background Music.** Specify the audio to play in the slide show.

   ◆ **Play Audio Captions.** Select to play available audio captions.

   ◆ **Page Duration.** Specify the display time for each slide.

   ◆ **Include Captions.** Select to include available captions.

   ◆ **Allow Photos to Resize.** Select to resize photos.

   ◆ **Allow Videos to Resize.** Select to resize videos.

   ◆ **Show Filmstrip.** Select to display all of the selected images in a strip of thumbnails.

   ◆ **Fade Between Photos.** Select to add fade transitions.

   ◆ **Start Playing Automatically.** Select to start the slide show in Full Screen automatically.

   ◆ **Repeat Slide Show.** Select to loop the slide show.

3. To not show the Full Screen Options dialog box, deselect the **Show this dialog before viewing photos in full screen** check box.

4. Click **OK**.

5. When you're finished, move the mouse to display the Control bar, and then click the **Exit** button.

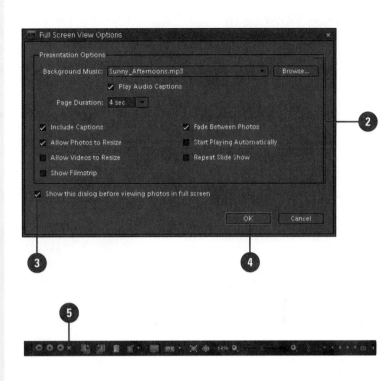

Viewing Photos in Side by Side View

Side by Side view allows you to view and compare your photos in a full screen view without windows, menus, and palettes. Side by Side view splits the screen in half and displays a photo on each side. You can select a side and then browse through photos in order to compare them with the one on the other side. When you move the mouse, a control bar appears at the top of the screen, which allows you to access common display and editing commands for the selected side. If you prefer to view photos from the top and bottom, you can use the Side by Side button on the Control bar to switch the display view.

View Photos in Side by Side View

1. In the Organizer (in Photo Browser view), click the **Display** button, and then click **Compare Photos Side by Side**.

   TIMESAVER *Press F12 to switch to Compare Photos Side by Side view.*

2. In Side by Side view, click the side you want to use, either left or right (default).

   The left side is labeled 1 and the right side is labeled 2 after you click it.

3. Move the mouse to display the Control bar.

4. Click the **Previous** or **Next** buttons on the Control bar to display photos from the Organizer.

   You can compare the photos on the two sides.

5. To change the view from Side by Side to Above and Below, click the **Side by Side View** button arrow on the Control bar, and then click **Above and Below**.

6. When you're finished, click the **Exit** button on the Control bar.

   TIMESAVER *Press Esc to exit Full Screen view.*

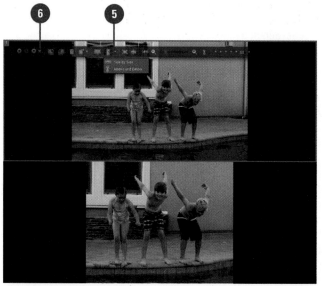

Using the Control Bar

The Control bar appears in Full Screen and Side by Side views when you move the mouse. The Control bar provides access to common navigation, viewing, and editing commands.

The left side of the Control bar displays navigation controls and the right side displays viewing and editing controls. You can click the Show/Hide Only Navigation Controls button on the right side of the Control bar to show or hide the viewing and editing controls.

The navigation controls on the Control bar include the following:

- **Previous.** Displays the previous photo in the Organizer. (Press Left Arrow)

- **Play/Pause.** Plays or pauses the slide show. (Press Spacebar)

- **Next.** Displays the next photo in the Organizer. (Press Right Arrow)

- **Exit.** Exits the view. (Press Esc)

The viewing and editing controls on the Control bar include the following:

- **Rotate 90° Left or Right.** Rotates the select photo 90° left or right. (Press Ctrl+Left Arrow or Ctrl+Right Arrow)

- **Delete.** Deletes the selected photo. (Press Del)

- **Action Menu.** Displays a menu with commands to fix photos, and change properties.

- **Full Screen View.** Displays photos in Full Screen view. (Press F11)

- **Side by Side View.** Displays photos in Side by Side view and changes the display view. (Press F12)

- **Fit in Window.** Displays photos to fit your screen. (Press Ctrl+O)

- **Actual Pixels.** Displays photos in actual size. (Press Ctrl+Alt+O).

- **Zoom In or Zoom Out.** Displays photos in different percentage view.

- **Sync Panning and Zooming.** Displays the photos on both sides in Side by Side view in the same percentage view.

- **Set Rating.** Sets the rating for the selected photo, which is used for searching and file management.

- **Hide.** Sets the selected photo to be hidden in the Photo Browser.

Navigation controls

Viewing and editing controls

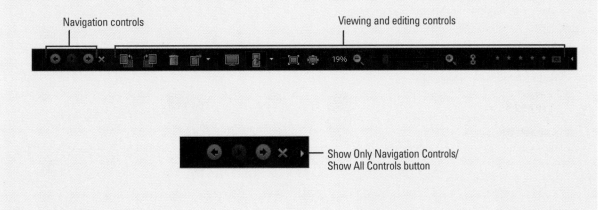

Show Only Navigation Controls/
Show All Controls button

Viewing and Finding Photos in Date View

In the Organizer, you can view and find photos by date using Date view. Date view allows you to browse through and locate photos by using a calendar. You can find photos from a certain day, month, or year. Since Date view is based on a calendar, you can keep track of recurring events, such as birthdays and holidays, and even add notes and other important information.

View and Find Photos in Date View

1 In the Organizer, click the **Display** button, and then click **Date View**.

2 Click the **Year**, **Month**, or **Day** button to select a calendar view.

3 Select the day in which you want to view photos:

◆ **Month View.** Click the **Previous** or **Next** buttons, and then click a day to view photos in the right panel or double-click a day to switch to Day view.

TIMESAVER *Hold down the Previous and Next button to navigate fast.*

◆ **Year View.** Click a day to view photos in the right panel or double-click a day to switch to Day view.

◆ **Day View.** Click the **Previous Item** or **Next Item** to navigate multiple photos on the same day. Click the **Play** button to view them as a slide show.

You can also click the Full Screen View button to view the multiple photos in a slide show view.

4 If you can't find a photo, click the **Unknown Date** icon to view any photos without a date.

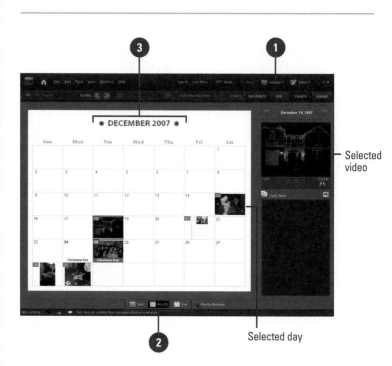

Selected video

Selected day

Add a Note or Caption in Date View

① In the Organizer, click the **Display** button, and then click **Date View**.

② Select the day in which you want to add a note or caption.

③ To add a note, type the note text in the Daily Note box.

- ◆ **Note.** Type the note text in the Daily Note box.

- ◆ **Caption.** Click the **Day** button, and then type text in the Caption box.

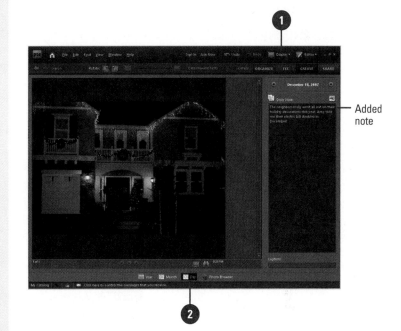

Added note

Add an Event in Date View

① In the Organizer, click the **Display** button, and then click **Date View**.

② Click the **Event** icon, or right-click the day you want, and then click **Add Event**.

③ Type a name for the event.

④ Use the list arrows to specify the event's date, if necessary.

⑤ Select or deselect the **Repeating Event** check box. If you selected it, click an option for the recurring interval.

⑥ Click **OK**.

See Also

See "Setting Date View Preferences" on page 35 for information on using Date view.

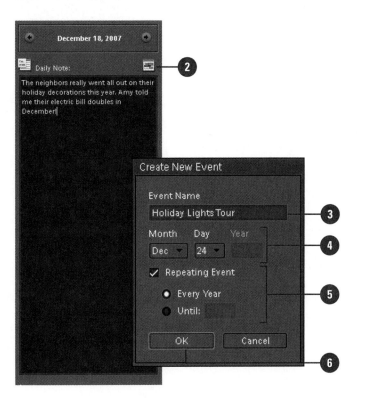

Viewing Photos in Map View

The Organizer also includes a Map view (provided by Yahoo! Maps), which allows you to arrange photos by geographic location. It's an electronic version of a map on the wall with pictures attached with push pins. In Map view, you can pin photos to point on the map. Photos pinned in Map view appear with a red pin. If multiple photos appears in the same location, a three-pin cluster appears in Map view. After you place photos on the map, you can move them around and share your completed result on the web or from a CD/DVD.

Add Photos to Map View

1. In the Organizer, click the **Display** button, and then click **Show Map**.

2. If the Map Your Photos with Yahoo! Maps dialog box appears, read the message, select or deselect the **Don't Show Again** check box, and then click **OK**.

   Map view appears in a palette on the left side of the Organizer workspace.

3. To add photos to Map view, use any of the following methods:

   ◆ **Drag and Drop.** In Map view, navigate to the spot on the map, and then drag a photo to the map where you want it.

   ◆ **Place.** Right-click a photo, click **Place on Map**, enter an address, click **Find**, select the address you want, and then click **OK**.

4. When you're finished, click the **Close** button in the Map palette.

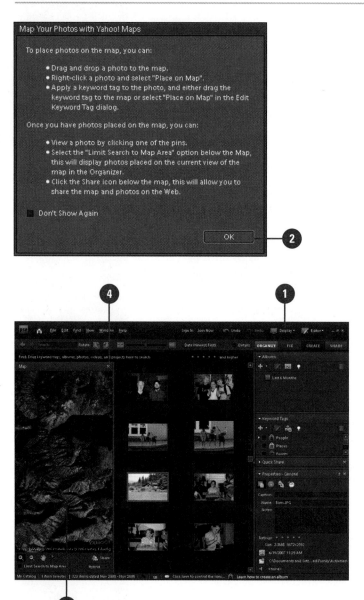

3 Drag photo here

Work with Photos in Map View

1. In the Organizer, click the **Display** button, and then click **Show Map**.

2. If the Map Your Photos with Yahoo! Maps dialog box appears, read the message, select or deselect the **Don't Show Again** check box, and then click **OK**.

   Map view appears in a palette on the left side of the Organizer workspace.

3. Place the photos you want on the map.

   ◆ Zoom. Click the **Zoom In** or **Zoom Out** buttons to change the view percentage.

   ◆ Map Position. Click the **Hand Tool** button, and then drag the map to change the position.

   ◆ Display Photo. Click the **Hand Tool** button, and then click the pin with the photo you want to display. Click the **Close** button to exit the photo.

   ◆ Move Pins. Click the **Move** button, and then drag a pin to another location.

   ◆ Delete Pins. Right-click a pin, and then click **Remove From Map**.

   ◆ Share Maps. Click the **Share** button to share your map on the web or on a CD.

   ◆ Limit Search. Select the **Limit Search to Map Area** check box to view all the photos related to the pins visible on the map.

Display photo in Map view

Finding Photos in the Organizer

5

Introduction

In the Organizer, you can find photos in several different ways. You can use the Keyword Tags palette, Find bar, Search box on the Organizer's toolbar, Find menu, Timeline, and the star rating filter.

Many of the search methods rely on keyword tags. A keyword tag is an information label that a program or you create and attach to photos to make them easier to locate. You can create your own custom tags with information important to you and attach multiple tags to the same photo for improved organization using the Keyword Tags palette. When you create a new keyword tag, you can place it under any category or sub-category for added organization. If you have attached a keyword to a photo and then later decide you no longer want it, you can remove the keyword tag from the photo.

The Find bar is useful for quick and easy searches. You can perform a search for photos by simply dragging keyword tags and other items onto the bar. Likewise, you can type a word or phrase into the Search box to quickly search for related photos. The Find menu, on the other hand, is more effective for detailed searches for specific attributes related with a photo. The Find menu provides almost every conceivable way to search for photos and other media files in the Photo Browser. For example, you can find photos by metadata details using multiple search criteria.

In the Photo Browser, the Timeline organizes all your photos in a chronological order along a timeline. The Timeline is separated into months and years, and displays a bar to indicate the number of photos in the specified time, where you can click to view the photos you want. In the Organizer, you can rate your photos based on your own rating scale from 1 to 5 stars. After your have rated your photos and other media files, you can use the star rating filter on the Find bar to quickly find the images and files you want.

What You'll Do

Use the Keyword Tags Palette

Create a Keyword Tag

Work with Categories or Sub-Categories

Find Faces for Keyword Tagging

Attach Keyword Tags to Photos

Attach Keyword Tags Using Folder Names

Remove Keyword Tags from Photos

Search for Photos by Keyword Tags

Search for Photos Using the Find Bar

Find Photos Using the Find Menu

Find Photos by Metadata Details

Find Photos by Searching for Text

Find Photos Using the Timeline

Find Photos with Star Ratings

Using the Keyword Tags Palette

A **keyword tag** is an information label that a program or you create and attach to photos to make them easier to locate. You can create your own custom keyword tags with information important to you and attach multiple keyword tags to the same photo for improved organization. For example, you can create a custom keyword tag called *Whale* and attach it to every photo that includes a whale. You can create and manage keyword tags using the Keyword Tags palette. The Keyword Tags palette, available in the Task pane, includes four default categories: People, Places, Events, and Other. You can create, modify, and reorder categories and sub-categories for better organization and management. You can also create, edit, delete, and move keyword tags.

Use the Keyword Tags Palette

1. In the Organizer (in Photo Browser view), display the Keyword Tags palette in the Task pane.

2. Use the following methods to work with the Keyword Tags palette:

   ◆ **Expand/Collapse.** Click the triangle next to the category or subcategory to expand or collapse the keyword tags within it.

   ◆ **Move/Reorder.** Drag a keyword tag, category, or sub-category from one position to another. A horizontal line appears to indicate the new position.

   TROUBLE? *If you cannot move a keyword tag, go to Keyword Tags and Album preferences and click the Manual option for Categories, Sub-Categories, and Keyword Tags.*

Keyword tag

Move/Reorder

Expand/Collapse

See Also

See "Setting Keyword Tags and Albums Preferences" on page 36 for information on setting preference options.

Creating a Keyword Tag

In the Keyword Tags palette, you can quickly and easily create, edit, and delete keyword tags. When you create a new keyword tag, you can place it under any category or subcategory in the Keyword Tags palette, which you can always change and modify later. When you create a new keyword tag, the tag appears with a question mark icon, which changes when the keyword tag is applied to a photo or other media file.

Create a Keyword Tag

1. In the Organizer (in Photo Browser view), display the Keyword Tags palette in the Task pane.

2. Click the **New** button in the Keyword Tags palette, and then click **New Keyword Tag**.

   TIMESAVER *Press Ctrl+N to create a new keyword tag.*

3. Click the **Category** list arrow, select a category or subcategory.

   Subcategories are indented in the list.

4. Type the name for the keyword tag.

5. To associate the tag with a place on a map, click **Place on Map**, type an address, and then click **Find**.

6. To include a note, type the information you want about the keyword tag.

7. Click **OK**.

Did You Know?

You can edit a keyword tag. Select the keyword tag in the Keyword Tags palette, click the Edit button, change the options you want, and then click OK.

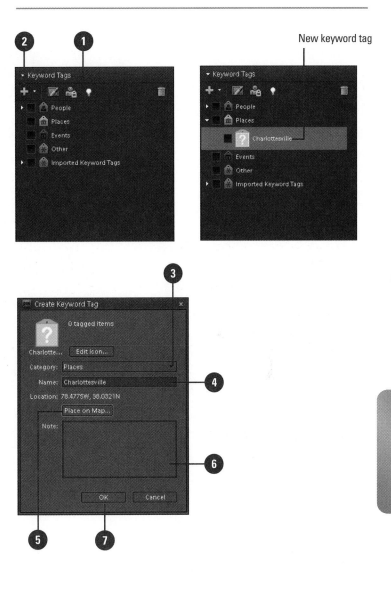

New keyword tag

Working with Categories or Sub-Categories

Categories and sub-categories make it easier to manage and work with keyword tags. When you create a new keyword tag, you can place it under any category or sub-category in the Keyword Tags palette. As photos and projects change, you can change category and sub-category names and locations, or delete ones you no longer use. You can make all of these changes in the Keyword Tags palette.

Create a Keyword Tag Category or Sub-Category

① In the Organizer (in Photo Browser view), display the Keyword Tags palette in the Task pane.

② Click the **New** button in the Keyword Tags palette, and then click **New Category**.

③ Click **Choose Color**, select a color using the Color Picker, and then click **OK**.

④ Type a category name.

⑤ Click a category icon.

⑥ Click **OK**.

Did You Know?

You can delete a category or sub-category. Before you delete a category or sub-category, remember that this also deletes all the keyword tags within it. Display the Keyword Tags palette in the Task pane, select the category or sub-category you want to delete, click the Delete button in the Keyword Tags palette, and then click OK.

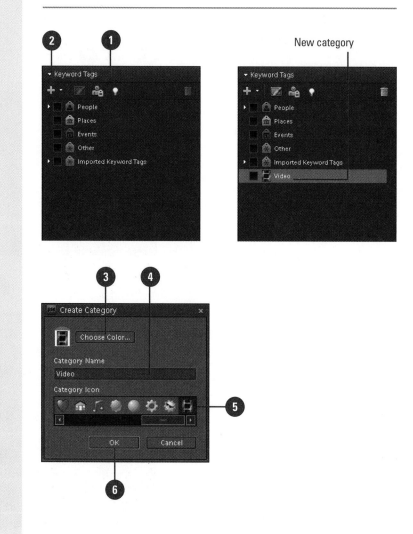

Create a Keyword Tag Sub-Category

1. In the Organizer (in Photo Browser view), open the Keyword Tags palette in the Task pane.

2. Click the **New** button in the Keyword Tags palette, and then click **New Sub-Category**.

3. Type a sub-category name.

4. Click the **Parent Category or Sub-Category** list arrow, and then select the category or sub-category where you want to place the new sub-category.

5. Click **OK**.

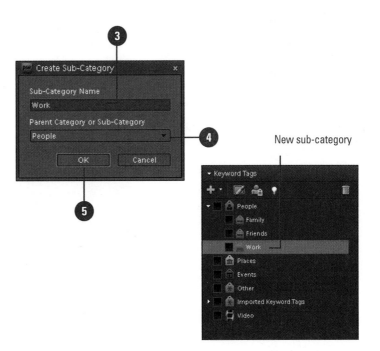

New sub-category

Edit a Category or Sub-Category

1. In the Organizer (in Photo Browser view), open the Keyword Tags palette in the Task pane.

2. Select the category or sub-category you want to edit.

3. Click the **Edit** button in the Keyword Tags palette.

4. Make the changes you want.

5. Click **OK**.

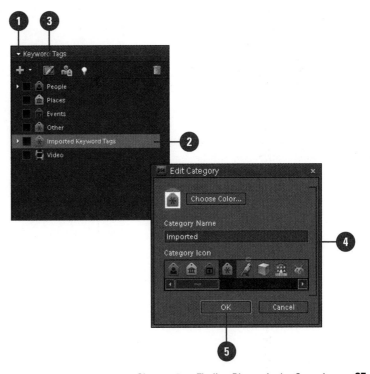

Finding Faces for Keyword Tagging

The Keyword Tags palette includes the option to automatically find faces for keyword tags. The Find Faces for Tagging button in the Keyword Tags palette displays faces in photos that you can use to apply existing keyword tags, or create and apply new tags. When you apply a tag to a face, Photoshop Elements removes that face from the dialog box to reduce clutter and confusion.

Find Faces for Keyword Tagging

① In the Organizer (in Photo Browser view), display the Keyword Tags palette in the Task pane.

② Click the **Find Faces for Tagging** button in the Keyword Tags palette, and then click **Yes** to confirm and click **OK** to skip photos, if necessary.

◆ To get better results from the faces search, press Ctrl as you click the **Find Faces for Tagging** button. However, the search time is longer.

③ Work with faces using any of the following options:

◆ Apply a Tag to a Face. Drag the tag onto the face or drag the face onto the tag. You can tag multiple selected photos at once.

◆ View Entire Photo. Select the face and view the thumbnail.

◆ Remove a Face. Select the face, and then click **Don't tag selected Items**.

④ Use the Keyword Tags palette in the dialog box to create, edit, and organize keywords.

⑤ Click **Done**.

Attaching Keyword Tags to Photos

After you have created a keyword tag, you can attach it to one or more photos. You can attach multiple tags to the same photo or set of photos. You attach keyword tags to photos by either dragging one or more selected photos from the Photo Browser onto the selected tags in the Keyword Tags palette, or dragging selected tags in the Keyword Tags palette onto any of the selected photos in the Photo Browser.

Attach Keyword Tags to Photos

1 In the Organizer (in Photo Browser view), display the Keyword Tags palette in the Task pane.

2 Select the photos you want to attach keyword tags.

3 Use either of the following methods:

◆ Select one or more tags and then drag them from the Keyword Tags palette onto the selected photos.

◆ Select one or more tags and then drag the photos onto the tags in the Keyword Tags palette.

Did You Know?

You can export and import keyword tags. Display the Keyword Tags palette, click the New button in the Keyword Tags palette, click Save Keyword Tags to File, click an export option, click OK, type a name, specify a folder location, and then click Save to export the file as an XML (Extensible Markup Language) file. You can use the From File command on the New button menu to import the keyword tags from an exported file.

Attaching Keyword Tags Using Folder Names

In Folder Location view, you can quickly attach keyword tags to all the managed files (photos included in the catalog) in a folder using the name of the folder as the keyword tag. If you have your photos organized into folders with descriptive names, this can be a very quick and easy way to attach keyword tags to photos. In Folder Location view, photos are organized and displayed by folder with a path location and name at the top along with an Instant Keyword Tag button. The Instant Keyword Tag button attaches the folder name as a keyword tag to all the photos in a selected folder. If you don't want to attached a keyword tag to a photo, you need to remove it from the folder, or remove the keyword tag later.

Create and Attach Keyword Tags Using Folder Names

1 In the Organizer (in Photo Browser view), click the **Display** button, and then click **Folder Location**.

2 In the folder hierarchy, select the folder containing the photos you want to tag, if necessary.

3 Click the **Instant Keyword Tag** button.

4 Click the **Category** list arrow, and then select a category or sub-category.

Sub-categories are indented in the list.

5 Change the name for the keyword tag, if desired.

6 To include a note, type the text you want about the keyword tag.

7 Click **OK**.

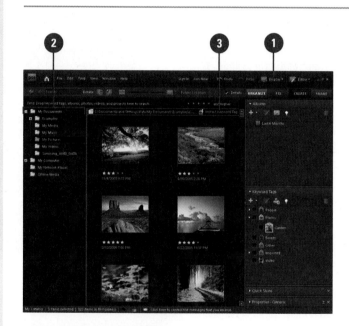

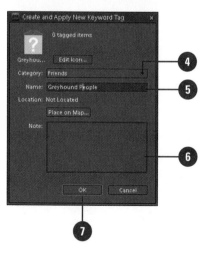

Did You Know?

You can change a keyword tag's icon. Select the keyword tag in the Keyword Tags palette, click the Edit button, click Edit Icon, click the arrows, Find, or Import to display the photo you want to use, resize and move the cropping marquee on the photo, click OK, and then click OK.

Removing Keyword Tags from Photos

If you have attached a keyword to a photo and then later decide you no longer want it, you can remove the keyword tag from the photo. The Photo Browser uses two different ways to remove keyword tags from a single photo. You can right-click the photo thumbnail, or right-click a keyword tag icon under a photo, depending on your current view, and then select a remove keyword tag command.

Remove a Keyword Tag from a Photo

① In the Organizer (in Photo Browser view), display the Keyword Tags palette in the Task pane.

② Use any of the following methods to remove a keyword tag from photos:

◆ **Photo in Thumbnail view.** Right-click the photo, point to **Remove Keyword Tag**, and then click **<tag name>**.

◆ **Photo in larger view.** Right-click a keyword tag icon under the photo, and then click **Remove <tag name> Keyword Tag**.

◆ **Multiple Photos in any view.** Select the photos, right-click one of them, point to **Remove Keyword Tag from Selected Items**, and then click **<tag name>**.

Right-click a keyword tag ②   ①

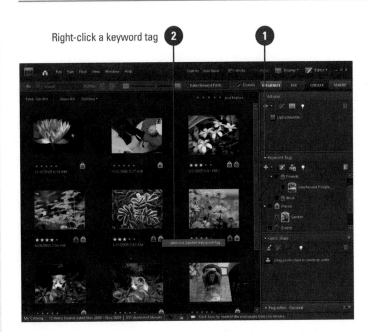

Did You Know?

You can change keyword tags to sub-category or vice versa. Right-click a keyword tag in the Keyword Tags palette, and then click Change <name> keyword tag to a sub-category, or right-click a sub-category in the Keyword Tags palette, and then click Change <name> sub-category to a keyword tag.

Searching for Photos by Keyword Tags

After you have taken the time to attach keyword tags to your photos, you can use the power of the Keyword Tags palette to quickly locate the photos you want to view or edit. Searching for photos with attached keyword tags is quick and easy. All you need to do is double-click the keyword tag or click the boxes next to each of the tags that you want to display. If you want to create a more detailed search, you can use the Find bar. When you search by keyword tags, the results are displayed in views of best matches (all criteria matches), close matches (one or more, but not all criteria matches), and no matches. You can switch between these views by using the Options menu on the Find bar.

Search for Photos by Keyword Tags

① In the Organizer (in Photo Browser view), display the Keyword Tags palette in the Task pane.

② Use any of the following methods:

◆ Double-click a keyword.

◆ Click the box next to one or more tags.

◆ Drag one or more tags from the Keyword Tags palette to the Find bar.

③ To change the views in the search results, click the **Options** button, and then click the view you want:

◆ **Show/Hide Best Match Results.** Click to toggle between showing and hiding the best match results where all the criteria matches.

◆ **Show/Hide Results That Do Not Match.** Click to toggle between showing and hiding results that do not match.

Keyword tag
search results

Searching for Photos Using the Find Bar

The Find bar allows you to quickly search for photos by dragging keyword tags and other items onto the bar. The Find bar appears below the Navigation bar in the Photo Browser with the text *Find: Drag keyword tags, albums, photos, videos, and projects here to search*. After you drag an item to the Find bar to perform a search, you can refine the search by dragging other items to the Find bar. The Find bar expands to show the search tag, available options, and the result below in the Photo Browser.

Search for Photos Using the Find Bar

1. In the Organizer (in Photo Browser view), open the Keyword Tags palette.

2. Drag a tag onto the Find bar.

   The Find bar expands to show the tag and search results appear in the Photo Browser.

3. To refine the search, drag another tag onto the Find bar.

4. To start a new search, right-click a tag, category, or sub-category, and then click **New Search Using <tag, category, or subcategory name>**.

5. To close the Find bar, click **Show All**.

Did You Know?

You can exclude photos from a search. In the Keyword Tags palette, right-click the tag of the photos you want to exclude from the search, click Exclude Photos with <tag, catalog, or subcategory name> from Search Results. To undo the exclude command from a tag, click the Exclude icon next to the tag in the Keyword Tags palette.

2 Drag a tag here

Finding Photos Using the Find Menu

The Find menu provides almost every conceivable way to search for photos and other media files in the Photo Browser. For example, you can find photos by caption or note, filename, all version sets, all stacks, history, media type, details (metadata), items with unknown date or time, visual similarity, untagged items, and items not in any albums. The Find menu is not the best for quick searches. It's most effective for detailed searches for specific attributes related with a photo.

Find Photos Using the Find Menu

1. In the Organizer, display the Photo Browser.

2. Use the Find menu to use the find option you want:

   ◆ **Untagged Photos.** Click the **Find** menu, and then click **Untagged Items**.

   ◆ **Captions or Notes.** Click the **Find** menu, click **By Caption or Note**, type a search word or phrase, select an option to match the only the beginning or any part of any word, and then click **OK**.

   ◆ **Filename.** Click the **Find** menu, click **By Filename**, type a filename, and then click **OK**.

   ◆ **All Version Sets.** Click the **Find** menu, and then click **All Version Sets**. To expand a version set, right-click it, point to **Version Set**, and then click **Expand Items in Version Set**.

   ◆ **Visual Similarity.** Select one to four photos, click the **Find** menu, and then click **By Visual Similarity With Selected Photo(s)**.

Find	
Set Date Range...	Ctrl+Alt+F
Clear Date Range	Ctrl+Shift+F
By Caption or Note...	Ctrl+Shift+J
By Filename...	Ctrl+Shift+K
All Version Sets	Ctrl+Alt+V
All Stacks	Ctrl+Alt+Shift+S
By History	▶
By Media Type	▶
By Details (Metadata)...	
Items with Unknown Date or Time	Ctrl+Shift+X
By Visual Similarity with Selected Photo(s)	
Untagged Items	Ctrl+Shift+Q
Items not in any Album	
Find Faces for Tagging...	

By Media Type submenu	
Photos	Alt+1
Video	Alt+2
Audio	Alt+3
Projects	Alt+4
PDF	Alt+5
Items with Audio Captions	Alt+6

- **Photos Used in Projects.** Click the **Find** menu, point to **By History**, and then **Used in Projects**. Select one or more items, and then click **OK**.

- **Imported On.** Click the **Find** menu, point to **By History**, and then click **Imported on**. Select one or more items, and then click **OK**.

- **E-mailed To.** Click the **Find** menu, point to **By History**, and then click **E-mailed to**. Select one or more items, and then click **OK**.

- **Exported On.** Click the **Find** menu, point to **By History**, and then click **Exported on**. Select one or more items, and then click **OK**.

- **Order or Shared Online.** Click the **Find** menu, point to **By History**, and then click **Ordered Online** or **Shared Online**. Select one or more items, and then click **OK**.

- **By Media Type.** Click the **Find** menu, point to **By Media Type**, and then select one of the following media types: **Photos**, **Video**, **Audio**, **Projects**, **PDF**, or **Items with Audio Captions**.

- **Unknown Dates or Times.** Click the **Find** menu, and then click **Items with Unknown Date or Time**.

Search by media type: video

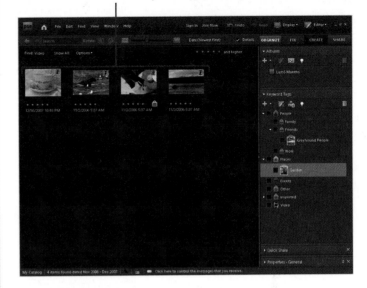

Finding Photos by Metadata Details

When you take a photo with your digital camera, the image file includes additional information besides the photo, know as **metadata**. The metadata for a photo typically includes the date and time, shutter speed and aperture, and camera model. In addition to the default metadata, you can add your own custom metadata and keyword tags to an image file too. Finding photos by metadata is useful when you want to search for several different details. The Find by Details (Metadata) dialog box allows you to search for multiple attributes with specific criteria. After you perform a search, you can use the Modify Search Criteria command on the More Options menu (on the Find bar) to make adjustments.

Find Photos by Metadata Details

1. In the Organizer, display the Photo Browser.

2. Click the **Find** menu, and then click **By Details (Metadata)**.

3. Click the Search for files which matches options you want, either **Any one of the following search criteria[OR]** or **All of the following search criteria[AND]**.

4. Click the first pop-up menu, and then select a metadata type.

5. Click the second pop-up menu, and then select a range for the search, such as Is, or Contains.

6. Click the third pop-up menu, and then type or choose the metadata name or value you want to find.

7. To include another set of metadata search criteria, click the plus sign (+) to the right of the third pop-up, and then specify new values for the two or three pop-up menus (repeat Steps 4 thru 6).

8. To remove a set of metadata search criteria, click the minus sign (-) to the right of the third pop-up.

9. Click **Search**.

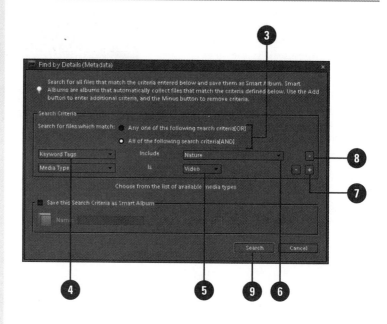

Modify Search Criteria

① In the Organizer, display the Photo Browser.

② Perform a search by details (metadata) using the Find menu or any other search method.

③ In the search results, click the **Options** menu on the Find bar, and then click **Modify Search Criteria**.

④ To add a set of metadata search criteria, click the plus sign (+) to the right of the third pop-up, and then specify new values for the two or three pop-up menus.

⑤ To remove a set of metadata search criteria, click the minus sign (-) to the right of the third pop-up.

⑥ Click **Search**.

Did You Know?

You can write keyword tag information into your files. In the Photo Browser, select one or more files, click the File menu, click Write Keyword Tag And Properties Info To Photos, and then click Yes. This manually writes tag information into the IPTC Keyword section in the header of the file.

Finding Photos by Searching for Text

You can type words in the Search box (**New!**) under the menu bar to find files with matching text. The matching text can occur in images' author, captions, dates, date formats, filenames, keyword tags, metadata, notes, album names, album groups, camera information, camera make, camera models, folders, or formats. You can also use Boolean operators (such as "AND") to search for various combinations of multiple search terms.

Find Photos Using the Search Box

1 In the Organizer, display the Photo Browser.

2 Click the **Search** box, enter the text for which you want to search, and then press Enter.

3 To refine your search, add any of the following Boolean search operators:

◆ Type **AND** between two terms to require search results to contain both terms.

◆ Type **OR** between two terms to allow search results that contain either one.

◆ Type **NOT** before a search term to exclude search results that contain it.

See Also

If you want to restrict your search to specific types of data (for example, search only filenames), use a metadata search instead of the Search box. See "Finding Photos by Metadata Details" on page 94 for more information.

Finding Photos Using the Timeline

In the Photo Browser, the Timeline organizes all your photos in a chronological order along a timeline. The Timeline is separated into months and years, and displays a bar to indicate the number of photos in the specified time. When you want to view the photos within a time range, simply point to the Time to view a tool tip showing the range, and then click a point or drag to select a range of time. You can also search for keyword tags to refine a search and then use the Timeline to find photos within a specific time period.

View and Find Photos Using the Timeline

1 In the Organizer (in Photo Browser view), click the **Window** menu, and then click **Timeline**.

TIMESAVER *Press Ctrl+L to show and hide the Timeline.*

2 Click the **Display** button on the Shortcuts bar, and then click **Thumbnails View**, **Import Batch**, or **Folder Location**.

3 Navigate the Timeline using any of the following methods:

◆ Use the arrows at the ends of the Timeline to display a section of the Timeline.

◆ Click a bar, or drag the date marker to view photos in the range.

◆ Drag the end-point markers to view a range.

4 To set a date range, click the **Find** menu, and then click **Set Date Range**, type a start and end date, and then click **OK**.

◆ To reset the date range, click the **Find** menu, and then click **Clear Date Range**.

5 To hide the Timeline, click the **Window** menu, and then click **Timeline**.

Finding Photos with Star Ratings

Rating are a part of everyday living. We rate almost everything. From restaurants to movies, everyone has a rating. It's a 1-star, a 5-star, or something in between. In the Organizer, you can rate your photos based on your own rating scale from 1 to 5 stars. After your have rated your photos and other media files, you can use the star rating filter on the Find bar to quickly find the images and files you want. If you want to find files with ratings higher or lower than the selected star rating, you can use the Ranking menu next to the star rating filter to select the options you want.

Find Photos with Star Ratings

1. In the Organizer, display the Photo Browser.

2. Click one of the stars in the star rating filter on the Find bar.

3. Click the Ranking menu next to the star rating filter, and then select one of the options.

   ◆ **and higher.** Find items in the selected star rating and higher.

   ◆ **and lower.** Finds items in the selected star rating and lower.

   ◆ **Only.** Finds only items in the selected star rating.

Working with Photos in the Organizer

Introduction

Albums in Photoshop Elements are similar to the photo albums you have at home. Albums allow you to store and organize photos into groups. In addition to creating individual albums, you can also create a group of albums. You can add a photo to one or more albums and arrange photos in any order you want. Instead of adding photos to an album one or more at a time, you can create a smart album, which is an album set with search criteria. After you set the search criteria, any photo in the catalog that meets the criteria automatically appears in the smart album. You create and work with albums, album groups, and smart albums in the Albums palette on the Task pane.

The tools on the Fix tab make it easy to correct common photo problems, such as poor exposure in contrast, color balance, or color saturation. The tools include Auto Smart Fix, Auto Color, Auto Levels, Auto Contrast, Auto Sharpen, Auto Red Eye Fix, and Crop. The word *Auto* in front of most of the commands indicates that Photoshop Elements does all the work. All you need to do is select the photos you want to change and then click the button on the Fix tab you want to use. It's as easy as that.

A stack is a group of photos with visually similar properties. A stack is useful for keeping similar variations of the same photo together in one place. A version set is a type of stack that contains one original photo and its edited versions. When you edit a photo in the Organizer, Photoshop Elements automatically creates a copy of the edited photo and saves it in a version set with the original. This keeps the original intact, yet still makes the changes you want. When you edit a photo in the Editor using Full Edit or Quick Fix, you need to manually save your changes to create a version set.

What You'll Do

Use the Albums Palette

Create an Album and Album Group

Add Photos to an Album

Create and Edit a Smart Album

Work with Albums and Album Groups

Fix Photos Using Auto Smart Fix

Correct Color in Photos with Auto Color

Correct Exposures with Auto Levels

Improve Contrast with Auto Contrast

Sharpen Photos with Auto Sharpen

Remove Red Eye with Auto Red Eye Fix

Crop Photos

Rotate Photos

Stack and Unstack Photos

Work with Stacks

Work with Version Sets

Change the Date and Time of Files

Using the Albums Palette

Albums in Photoshop Elements are similar to the photo albums you have at home. Albums allow you to organize photos into groups. You can add a photo to one or more albums and arrange albums in any order you want. To help with organization, you can create album groups. Each photo in an album has a number in the upper-left corner, indicating its order in an album. You create, edit, remove, and organize photos within albums in the Albums palette in the Task pane.

Use the Albums Palette

① In the Organizer (in Photo Browser view), display the **Albums** palette in the Task pane.

② Use the following methods to work with the Albums palette:

- ◆ **Expand/Collapse.** Click the triangle next to the category or subcategory to expand or collapse the albums within it.

- ◆ **Create, Delete, and Edit.** Use the **New**, **Delete**, and **Edit** buttons in the Albums palette to create, delete, and edit albums, and album groups.

- ◆ **Show/Hide.** Click an album; a show icon (binoculars) appears next to it.

- ◆ **Move/Reorder.** Drag an album from one position to another. A horizontal line appears to indicate the new position.

TROUBLE? *If you cannot move a keyword tag, click the Manual option for Categories, Sub-Categories, and Keyword Tags in Keyword Tags and Album preferences.*

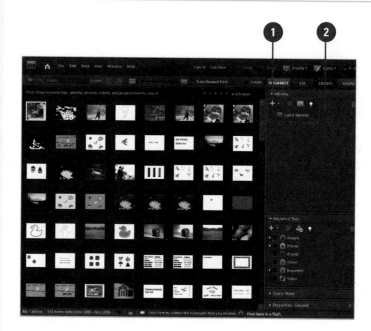

See Also

See "Setting Keyword Tags and Albums Preferences" on page 36 for information on setting preference options.

Creating an Album

In the Albums palette, you can quickly and easily create, edit, and delete albums. When you create a new album, you can place it into any group, which you can always change and modify later. When you create a new album, the icon in the Albums palette appears with a questions mark icon until you add photos to the album. The first photo you add to the album is the one used as the icon.

Create an Album

1. In the Organizer (in Photo Browser view), display the **Albums** palette in the Task pane.

2. Click the **New** button in the Albums palette, and then click **New Album**.

3. Click the **Group** list arrow, and then select a group in which you want to store the album.

4. Type the name for the album.

5. To include a note, type the information you want about the album.

6. Click **Done**.

7. To add a photo to an album, use either of the following methods:

   ◆ Drag the photo from the Photo Browser into the album in the Albums palette.

   ◆ Drag the album from the Albums palette onto the photo in the Photo Browser.

Did You Know?

You can edit an album. Select the album in the Albums palette, click the Edit button, change the options you want, and then click OK.

Creating an Album Group

In addition to creating individual new albums, you can also create a group of new albums. Album groups are useful for organizing albums by subject or content. For example, you might create an album group for *Kids Activities*, and create individual albums within the group for each of the kids activities, such as *Soccer*, *Dance*, or *Band*.

Create an Album Group

1. In the Organizer (in Photo Browser view), display the **Albums** palette in the Task pane.

2. Click the **New** button in the Albums palette, and then click **New Album Group**.

3. Type the name for the album group.

4. To nest the album group within another group, click the **Parent Album Group** list arrow, and then select a group you want.

5. Click **OK**.

6. To add an album to an album group, drag the album into the album group in the Albums palette.

Did You Know?

You can edit an album group. Select the album group in the Albums palette, click the Edit button, change the options you want, and then click OK.

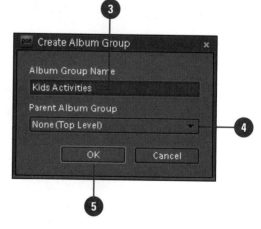

Adding Photos to an Album

After you create an album or album group, you can add one or more photos to it. You can add one or more photos to an individual album or add a photo to multiple albums. You add photos to albums by either dragging one or more selected photos from the Photo Browser onto the selected album or albums in the Albums palette, or dragging selected albums in the Albums palette onto any of the selected photos in the Photo Browser.

Add Photos to an Album or Album Group

① In the Organizer (in Photo Browser view), display the **Albums** palette in the Task pane.

② Select the photos you want to add to an album or album group.

③ Use either of the following methods:

◆ Drag the selected photos from the Photo Browser into the album in the Albums palette.

◆ Drag the selected albums from the Albums palette onto the photos in the Photo Browser.

Did You Know?

You can remove a photo from an album. Right-click a photo, point to Remove (Selected Items from Album), and then click <album name>.

You can locate missing files in your catalog. Select one or more icons for files that have been moved or renamed. Click the File menu, point to Reconnect, and then click Missing File or All Missing Files. If an exact match for a file isn't found, click Browse to manually find files or click Cancel to stop.

Creating and Editing a Smart Album

A **smart album** is an album set with search criteria. After you set the search criteria, any photo in the catalog that meets the criteria automatically appears in the smart album. As you add photos to the catalog, the smart album automatically checks the search criteria to determine whether it matches. You don't have to do anything. A smart album automatically keeps itself up to date. The criteria you set for a smart album can include more than one criterion to make the smart album more customized. You create and edit smart albums using buttons in the Albums palette.

Create a Smart Album

1. In the Organizer (in Photo Browser view), display the **Albums** palette in the Task pane.

2. Click the **New** button in the Albums palette, and then click **New Smart Album**.

3. Type the name for the album group.

4. Click the Search for files which matches options you want, either **Any one of the following search criteria[OR]** or **All of the following search criteria[AND]**.

5. Click the first pop-up menu, and then select a metadata type.

6. Click the second pop-up menu, and then select a range for the search, such as Is, or Contains.

7. Click the third pop-up menu, and then type or choose the metadata name or value you want to find.

8. To include another set of metadata search criteria, click the plus sign (+) to the right of the third pop-up, and then specify new values for the two or three pop-up menus (repeat Steps 5 thru 7).

9. To remove a set of metadata search criteria, click the minus sign (-) to the right of the third pop-up.

10. Click **OK**.

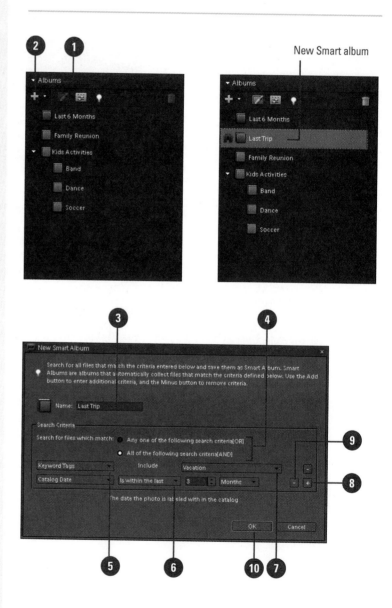

New Smart album

Edit a Smart Album

① In the Organizer (in Photo Browser view), display the **Albums** palette in the Task pane.

② Select the smart album you want to edit in the Albums palette.

③ Click the **Options** menu on the Find bar, and then click **Modify Search Criteria**.

④ To add a set of metadata search criteria, click the plus sign (+) to the right of the third pop-up, and then specify new values for the two or three pop-up menus.

⑤ To remove a set of metadata search criteria, click the minus sign (-) to the right of the third pop-up.

⑥ Click **Search**.

Did You Know?

You can edit the name of a smart album. Select the smart album in the Albums palette, click the Edit button, change the name, and then click OK.

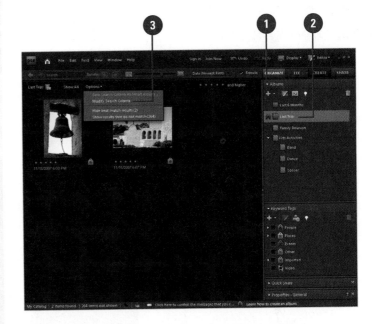

Working with Albums and Album Groups

After you create an album or album group, you can display photos, sort photos, and change the order of photos. You can open an album or album group by selecting it in the Albums palette. The photos in the album appear in the Photo Browser, where you can sort them by date from newest to oldest or oldest to newest, or change the order of the photos by dragging photos to a new location.

Display Photos in an Album

1 In the Organizer (in Photo Browser view), display the **Albums** palette in the Task pane.

2 Click the triangle next to a group to expand or collapse it.

3 Click an album in the Albums palette.

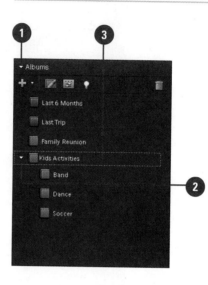

Sort Photos in an Album

1 In the Organizer (in Photo Browser view), display the **Albums** palette in the Task pane.

2 Click the triangle next to a group to expand or collapse it.

3 Select an album in the Albums palette.

4 Click the **Photo Browser Arrangement** menu, and then click **Date (Newest First)** or **Date (Date (Oldest First)**.

Change the Order of Photos in an Album

1 In the Organizer (in Photo Browser view), display the **Albums** palette in the Task pane.

2 Click the triangle next to a group to expand or collapse it.

3 Click an album in the Albums palette.

4 Click the **Photo Browser Arrangement** menu, and then click **Album Order**.

5 Select one or more photos, and then drag the selection to the left or right of a photo in the album.

5 Photo moved here

Did You Know?

You can delete an album or album group. Select the album or album group you want to remove in the Albums palette, and then click the Delete button in the Albums palette.

You can merge albums. Select the albums you want to merge in the Albums palette, right-click the selected albums, click Merge Albums, select the album into which you want to merge the selected albums, and then click OK.

You can export and import an album structure. You can share the album structure used to store photos with others. Display the Albums palette, click the New button in the Albums palette, click Save Albums To File, click an export option, click OK, type a name, specify a folder location, and then click Save to export the file as an XML (Extensible Markup Language) file. You can use the From File command on the New button menu to import the album structure from an exported file.

Fixing Photos Using Auto Smart Fix

The tools on the Fix tab make it easy to correct common photo problems, such as poor exposure or contrast, color balance, and color saturation. Many of the tools correct specific photo problems, such as contrast or sharpness, except the Auto Smart Fix tool. The Auto Smart Fix tool analyzes photos and corrects the overall exposure of the image. Before Auto Smart Fix corrects a photo, it makes a copy of the original and makes the adjustment to the copy, and saves it in a version set, so you can keep the original intact as well as make the changes you want.

Make Adjustments Using Auto Smart Fix

1. In the Organizer (in Photo Browser view), click the **Fix** tab.

2. Select one or more photos in the Photo Browser you want to fix.

3. Click **Auto Smart Fix** on the Fix tab.

   Auto Smart Fix creates copies of the selected photos, making adjustments to the copies, and saving the copies to a version set of the photos.

4. Click the arrow to the right of the fixed photo to display/hide the original photo and the altered one.

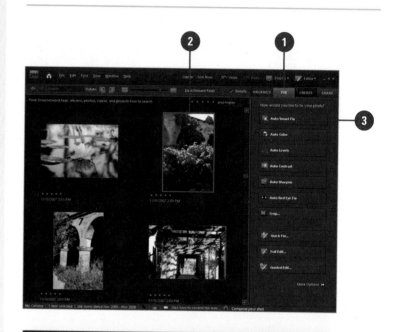

Original photo   Modified photo

Correcting Color in Photos with Auto Color

Auto Color is one of the tools on the Fix tab in the Organizer. Auto Color analyzes photos and corrects common problems in color balance. For example, if you have a greenish or bluish tint in one of your pictures due to incorrect lighting or camera settings, you can use the Auto Color button to fix it. Before Auto Color corrects a photo, it makes a copy of the original and makes the adjustment to the copy, and saves it in a version set, so you can keep the original intact as well as make the changes you want.

Correct Color in Photos with Auto Color

1. In the Organizer (in Photo Browser view), click the **Fix** tab.

2. Select one or more photos in the Photo Browser you want to fix.

3. Click **Auto Color** on the Fix tab.

   Auto Color creates copies of the selected photos, making adjustments to the copies, and saving the copies to the version sets of the photos.

4. Click the arrow to the right of the fixed photo to display/hide the original photo and the altered one.

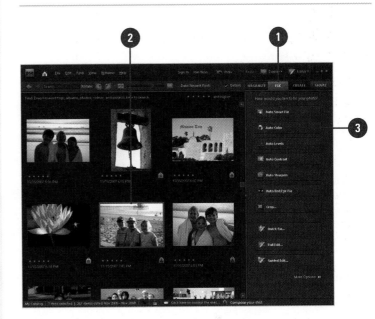

Correcting Exposures with Auto Levels

Auto Levels is one of the tools on the Fix tab in the Organizer. Auto Levels analyzes photos and corrects common problems in lightness, known as **luminance**. For example, if you have a photo that lacks detail due to under- or over-exposure, you can use the Auto Levels button to fix it. Before Auto Levels corrects a photo, it makes a copy of the original and makes the adjustment to the copy, and saves it in a version set, so you can keep the original intact as well as make the changes you want.

Correct Photo Exposures with Auto Levels

① In the Organizer (in Photo Browser view), click the **Fix** tab.

② Select one or more photos in the Photo Browser you want to fix.

③ Click **Auto Levels** on the Fix tab.

Auto Levels creates copies of the selected photos, making adjustments to the copies, and saving the copies to the version sets of the photos.

④ Click the arrow to the right of the fixed photo to display/hide the original photo and the altered one.

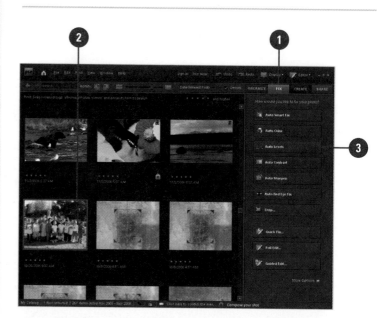

Improving Contrast with Auto Contrast

Auto Contrast is one of the tools on the Fix tab in the Organizer. Auto Contrast analyzes photos and corrects common problems in contrast, which is the difference in brightness between light and dark areas of an image. For example, if you have a photo that lacks a distinction between bright and dark areas, you can use the Auto Contrast button to fix it. Before Auto Contrast corrects a photo, it makes a copy of the original and makes the adjustment to the copy, and saves it in a version set, so you can keep the original intact as well as make the changes you want.

Improve Contrast with Auto Contrast

1. In the Organizer (in Photo Browser view), click the **Fix** tab.

2. Select one or more photos in the Photo Browser you want to fix.

3. Click **Auto Contrast** on the Fix tab.

   Auto Contrast creates copies of the selected photos, making adjustments to the copies, and saving the copies to the version sets of the photos.

4. Click the arrow to the right of the fixed photo to display/hide the original photo and the altered one.

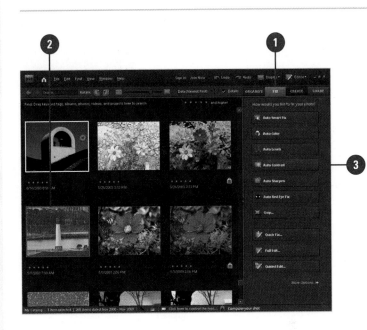

Sharpening Photos with Auto Sharpen

Auto Sharpen is one of the tools on the Fix tab in the Organizer. Auto Sharpen analyzes photos and corrects common focus problems. For example, if you have a photo that is blurry and out of focus, you can use the Auto Sharpen button to fix it. Before Auto Sharpen corrects a photo, it makes a copy of the original and makes the adjustment to the copy, and saves it in a version set, so you can keep the original intact as well as make the changes you want.

Sharpen Photo with Auto Sharpen

1. In the Organizer (in Photo Browser view), click the **Fix** tab.

2. Select one or more photos in the Photo Browser you want to fix.

3. Click **Auto Sharpen** on the Fix tab.

   Auto Sharpen creates copies of the selected photos, making adjustments to the copies, and saving the copies to the version sets of the photos.

4. Click the arrow to the right of the fixed photo to display/hide the original photo and the altered one.

Removing Red Eye with Auto Red Eye Fix

Have you ever taken the perfect photo and then noticed one or more of the people in the photo have red eyes? Now you don't have to retake the photo. You can use the Auto Red Eye Fix button on the Fix tab to quickly correct the problem. Auto Red Eye Fix finds red pupils in a photo, and changes them to a natural black. Before Auto Red Eye Fix corrects a photo, it makes a copy of the original and makes the adjustment to the copy, and saves it in a version set, so you can keep the original intact as well as make the changes you want.

Remove Red Eye with Auto Red Eye Fix

1. In the Organizer (in Photo Browser view), click the **Fix** tab.

2. Select one or more photos in the Photo Browser you want to fix.

3. Click **Auto Red Eye Fix** on the Fix tab.

   Auto Red Eye Fix creates copies of the selected photos, making adjustments to the copies, and saving the copies to the version sets of the photos.

4. Click the arrow to the right of the fixed photo to display/hide the original photo and the altered one.

Did You Know?

You can fix red eye several different ways. In addition to the Auto Red Eye Fix button on the Fix tab in the Organizer, you can also use the Red Eye tool on the toolbox, and the Auto Red Eye Fix on the Enhance menu and Full Edit tab in the Editor.

See Also

See "Working with the Red Eye Tool" on page 279 for information on using the Red Eye tool on the toolbox.

Red eye

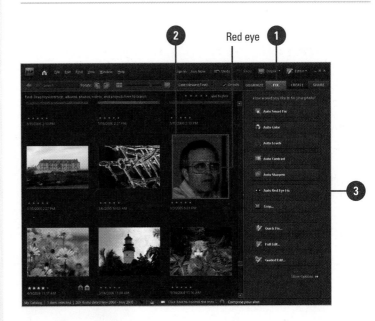

Red eye fixed

Cropping Photos

You can crop a photo to isolate just one portion of the picture. For example, if you have a photo of two people standing side-by-side, and you want a separate image of each person, you can crop each person to create two images. The Crop button on the Fix tab opens the Crop Photo dialog box, where you can resize the cropping box, select an aspect ratio (the ratio of an image's width to its height), and view the photo before the change, after the change, or both. When you crop a photo, Photoshop Elements makes a copy of the original before it makes the adjustment to the copy, and saves it in a version set. This keeps the original intact, yet still makes the changes you want.

Crop Photos

1. In the Organizer (in Photo Browser view), click the **Fix** tab.

2. Select the photo in the Photo Browser you want to crop.

3. Click **Crop** on the Fix tab.

   The Crop Photo dialog box appears.

4. Use the View buttons at the bottom to display the photo the way you want.

5. Resize the cropping box on the photo to the size you want.

6. To constrain the photo to a certain ratio, click the **Aspect Ratio** list arrow, and then select the ratio size you want. For a custom ratio, set your own width and height.

7. Click the **Commit** button (green check mark) under the cropping box or the **Apply** button to accept the cropping size.

   ◆ To cancel the crop, click the **Cancel** button (red circle with a line through it) under the cropping box.

8. To change the photo view before the change, after the change, or both, click the **View** list arrow, and then select the view you want.

9. Click **OK**.

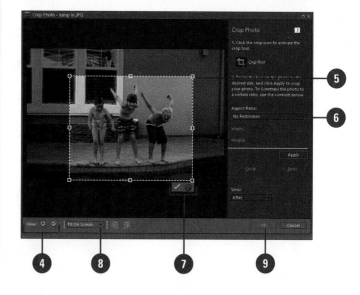

Rotating Photos

If you scanned a photo on the incorrect side, you can change its orientation by rotating it. Rotating turns an object 90 degrees to the right or left. You can rotate any photo in the Photo Browser by using the Rotate Left or Rotate Right button on the Navigation bar. When you rotate a photo, Photoshop Elements makes a copy of the original before it makes the adjustment to the copy, and saves it in a version set. This keeps the original intact, yet still makes the changes you want.

Rotate Photos 90 Degrees Left or Right

1. In the Organizer (in Photo Browser view), display the photos you want to rotate.

2. Select one or more photos in the Photo Browser you want to rotate.

3. Use either of the following methods:

   ◆ **Counter clockwise 90 Degrees.** Click the **Rotate Left** button on the Navigation bar.

   ◆ **Clockwise 90 Degrees.** Click the **Rotate Right** button on the Navigation bar.

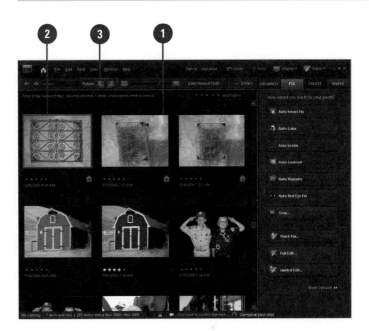

Stacking and Unstacking Photos

A stack is a group of photos with visually similar properties. A stack is useful for keeping similar variations of the same photo together in one place, which also reduces clutter in the Photo Browser. Instead of looking for each version of a photo, you can easily access all of them in one place. The newest photo you place in a stack appears at the top of the stack. If you have taken a series of photos of a scene, object, or person in rapid succession, you can have Photoshop Elements stack the visually similar photos automatically.

Stack or Unstack Photos

1 In the Organizer (in Photo Browser view), select the photos you want to include in the stack or the stack you want to unstack.

2 Use the following method to stack or unstack photos:

◆ **Stack.** Right-click the photo you want on top of the stack, point to **Stack,** and then click **Stacked Selected Photos.**

TIMESAVER *Press Ctrl+Alt+S to stack selected photos.*

◆ **Unstack.** Right-click the stack you want to unstack, point to **Stack,** and then click **Unstack Photos.**

3 Click the arrow to the right of the fixed photo to display/hide the original photo and the altered one.

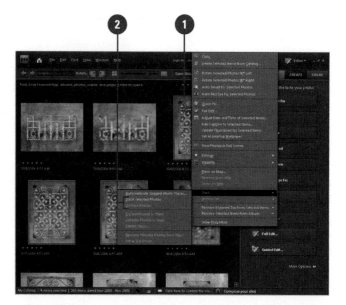

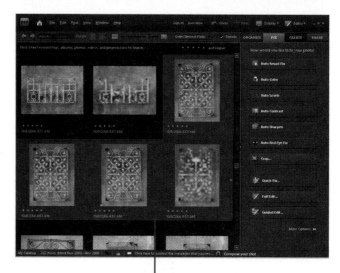

3 Stacked photos

Stack Visually Similar Photos Automatically

1 In the Organizer (in Photo Browser view), select a group of photos or an entire catalog.

2 Click the **Edit** menu, point to **Stack**, and then click **Automatically Suggest Photo Stacks**.

TIMESAVER *Press Ctrl+Alt+K to automatically suggest photo stacks.*

3 Look at the suggested stacks to determine whether you want to create a stack. Use any of the following to change the arrangement:

◆ **Remove Selected.** Select one or more photos, and then click **Remove Selected Photos**.

◆ **Show Removed.** Select the **Show Removed Photos** check box to display removed photos.

◆ **Return Removed.** Drag the photo from the Removed Photos panel back to the suggested stack.

◆ **Move Photo.** Drag the photo from one stack to the other.

◆ **Revert Back.** Click **Reset**.

4 Click **Stack All Groups**.

Entire catalog selected

Working with Stacks

If you have taken a series of photos of a scene, object, or person in rapid succession, you can have Photoshop Element stack the visually similar photos automatically or you can do it yourself. Stacking similar photos keeps them all together in one place for easy access. You can quickly expand a stack to view all the photos within it or collapse it to save viewing space in the Photo Browser. When you expand a stack, you can also remove photos from it. Removing photos from a stack removes them from the stack, but keeps them in your catalog, while deleting photos from a stack, deletes them from your catalog, but not from your computer.

View All Photos in a Stack

1. In the Organizer (in Photo Browser view), display the stacks you want to view.

2. Use either of the following to expand or collapse the photos in a stack:

   ◆ **Expand Stack.** Click the triangle next to the stack thumbnail or right-click a stack, point to **Stack**, and then click **Expand Photos in Stack**.

   TIMESAVER *Click the View menu, and then click Expand All Stacks.*

   ◆ **Collapse Stack.** Click the triangle next to the stack thumbnail or right-click a stack, point to **Stack**, and then click **Collapse Photos in Stack**.

   TIMESAVER *Click the View menu, and then click Collapse All Stacks.*

Stack

Did You Know?

You can specify the top photo in a stack. Expand the stack you want to change, right-click the photo you want as the top, point to Stack, and then click Set As Top Photo.

Remove Photos from a Stack

1. In the Organizer (in Photo Browser view), display the stacks you want to change.

2. Click the triangle next to the stack thumbnail or right-click a stack, point to **Stack**, and then click **Expand Photos in Stack**.

3. Select the photos you want to remove from the stack.

4. Right-click the photos, point to **Stack**, and then click **Remove Selected Photos from Stack**.

Did You Know?

You can delete photos from a stack. Expand the stack you want to change, select the photos you want to delete, and then press the Delete key. To delete all photos in a stack, select a collapsed stack, and then press the Delete key. To delete all photos in a stack except the top one, select the collapsed stack, click the Edit menu, point to Stack, and then click Flatten Stack.

You can edit photos in a stack. Expand the stack you want to change, select the photo you want to edit, click the Editor button, and then click Go To Quick Fix or Go To Full Edit. If you have Adobe Photoshop installed, you can also click Edit With Photoshop.

Working with Version Sets

A version set is a type of stack that contains one original photo and its edited versions. When you edit a photo in the Organizer, Photoshop Elements automatically creates a copy of the edited photo and a version set. If you edit a photo in the Editor using Full Edit or Quick Fix, you need to manually save your changes to create a version set. If you edit a photo that's already in a stack, the photo and edited copy are put in a version set that is nested in the original stack. Removing photos from a version set removes them from the stack, but keeps them in your catalog, while deleting photos from a version set deletes them from your catalog, but not from your computer.

View All Photos in a Version Set

1. In the Organizer (in Photo Browser view), display the version set you want to view.

2. Use either of the following to expand or collapse the photos in a version set:

   ◆ **Expand Version Set.** Click the **Expand** button next to the version set thumbnail or click the **Edit** menu, point to **Version Set**, and then click **Expand Items in Version Set**.

   ◆ **Collapse Version Set.** Click the **Collapse** button next to the version set thumbnail or click the **Edit** menu, point to **Version Set**, and then click **Collapse Items in Version Set**.

Version set

Did You Know?

You can revert back to the original version of a photo. Select the version set, click the Edit menu, point to Version Set, and then click Revert To Original.

You can find all version sets. Click the Find menu, and then click All Version Sets.

Remove Photos from a Version Set

1. In the Organizer (in Photo Browser view), display the version set you want to change.

2. Click the **Expand** button next to the version set thumbnail or click the **Edit** menu, point to **Version Set**, and then click **Expand Items in Version Set**.

3. Select the photos you want to remove from the version set.

4. Click the **Edit** menu, point to **Version Set**, and then click **Remove Item(s) from Version Set**.

Did You Know?

You can delete photos from a version set. Expand the version set you want to change, select the photos you want to delete, and then press the Delete key. To delete all photos in a version set, select the version set, click the Edit menu, click Delete From Catalog, and then select the Delete All Photos In Version Set option.

You can manually save a version set. Edit a file in the Editor, click the File menu, click Save As, select the Save In Version Set With Original check box, specify a name for the file, and then click Save.

You can edit photos in a version set. Expand the version set you want to change, select the photo you want to edit, click the Editor button, and then click Go To Quick Fix or Go To Full Edit. If you have Adobe Photoshop installed, you can also click Edit With Photoshop.

Changing the Date and Time of Files

If the clock on your camera is incorrect and you don't realize it until after you take a lot of pictures, don't worry. You can change the date and time of the photos or other media files in the Photo Browser. The Organizer allows you to manually change the date and time to whatever you want, the Modified Date of a file, the oldest photo in the selection, or ahead or back by a specified number of hours.

Change the Date and Time of Files

1. In the Organizer (in Photo Browser view), select the files you want to change.

2. Click the **Edit** menu, and then click **Adjust Date and Time**.

3. Select the following option you want:

   ◆ **Change to a Specified Date and Time.** Allows you to manually change the date and time.

   ◆ **Change to Match File's Date and Time.** Changes the time to the Modified Date of the file.

   ◆ **Shift to New Starting Date and Time.** Allows you to adjust the date and time in relation to the oldest photo in the selection (not shown).

   ◆ **Shift by Set Number of Hours (Time Zone Adjust).** Allows you to adjust the time ahead or back by a specified number of hours.

4. Click **OK**.

5. As requested, specify the options and information you want, and then click **OK**.

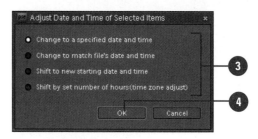

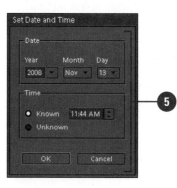

Working with Photos in the Editor

Introduction

Working in the Editor allows you to create, edit, and work with photos, media files, and specialty projects. If you are familiar with Adobe Photoshop CS4, working in the Editor in Photoshop Elements should be seamless, and if you've used earlier versions of Photoshop, catching up won't take long.

You can create as many new files as you need for your current project. However, creating a new file requires more thought than creating a new word processing file. You need to make decisions about resolution and color mode. If you're not sure how to decide, you can use the Preset menu, which takes the guesswork out of creating compatible, photo, web, mobile device, film and video files in Photoshop Elements.

Photoshop Elements lets you open image files created in different formats, such as TIFF, JPG, GIF, EPS, and PNG, as well as open Adobe Photoshop files in the PSD or PDD formats. If you have taken photos on a digital camera, you can open the camera raw image files and retain all the information about how the photo was taken. In addition to opening image files, you can also open PDF (Portable Document Format) files in Photoshop Elements.

When you finish working on a Photoshop Elements file, you need to save it before you close it or exit Photoshop Elements. Photoshop Elements lets you save image files in different formats, such as PSD (default, single page), PSE (default, multi-page), TIFF, JPG, GIF, EPS, and PNG, as well as use compress schemes (lossy and lossless) to reduce file sizes. Before you save a file, you have the ability to save more than just color information. You can save copyright, camera, and even image category information. If you make a lot of editing changes to a file after you have saved it and then decide that you no longer want to keep the changes, you can use the Revert command to revert back to the last saved version.

What You'll Do

Create a New File

Select Color Modes and Resolution

Create a New File Using Presets

Open a File

Open a PDF File

Insert Images in a File

Open Raw Files from a Digital Camera

Work with Open Files

Process Multiple Files

Change Image Size and Resolution

Use Full Edit and Quick Fix

Use Guided Edit

Attach Information to a File

Save a File

Revert to the Last Saved Version

Understand File Formats

Understand File Compression

Close a File

Creating a New File

Creating a new file requires more thought than creating a new word processing file. For example, there are resolution and color mode considerations to make. You can create as many new files as you need for your current project. However, since opening more than one file takes more processing power, it's probably best to work on one new file at a time. Once a new file is created, you have access to all of Photoshop Elements' design and manipulation tools to create anything your imagination can see.

Create a New File

1. In the Editor, click the **File** menu, point to **New**, and then click **Blank File**.

2. Type a name for the file.

    IMPORTANT *Typing a name does not save the file. You still need to save your file after you create it.*

3. Click the **Preset** list arrow, and then select a preset option, or choose your own options to create a custom file.

    ◆ **Width and Height.** Select from various measurements, such as points, centimeters, and inches.

    ◆ **Resolution.** Select a resolution, such as 72 pixels/inch (ppi) for online use and 300 ppi for print.

    ◆ **Color Mode.** Select a color mode, such as RGB for color and Grayscale for noncolor.

    ◆ **Background Contents.** Select a background color or a transparent background.

4. Click **OK**.

Selecting Color Modes and Resolution

Selecting a Color Mode

A **color mode**, also known as **color space**, determines how Photoshop Elements displays and prints an image. You choose a different color mode (based on models used in publishing) for different tasks. You can choose a color mode while you create a new file or change a color mode for an existing file. The common color modes include:

Bitmap. Best for printing black-and-white drawing images. This mode uses only two color values (black and white).

Grayscale. Best for printing black-and-white and duotone images. This mode uses a maximum of 256 shades of gray.

Indexed Color. Best for online and multimedia color images. This mode uses a pixel value as an index to a palette of 256 or fewer colors.

RGB (Red, Green, and Blue) Color. Best for online and multimedia color images. RGB are the primary colors on video monitors.

For more information on color, see Chapter 11, "Adjusting and Correcting Color."

Selecting Image Resolution

Photoshop Elements works primarily with raster documents. **Raster** documents are images composed of pixels. A **pixel** is a unit of information that holds the color and detail information of the image. Thinking of a Photoshop Elements image as a brick wall, with the individual bricks in the wall representing the individual pixels in the image, is an excellent way to envision a file. Files opened in Photoshop Elements have a specific resolution. The **resolution** of the image, along with its width and height, represents how many pixels the image contains. Since

pixels (the bricks in a wall) represent information, the more pixels a file contains, the more information Photoshop Elements has to manipulate or enhance the image.

A typical 17-inch monitor displays pixels at a resolution of 1024x768. You can figure out how many pixels are present on a monitor at 1024x768 by multiplying 1024 x 768, which equals to 786,432 pixels on the screen. The resolution is equal to how many pixels fit into each monitor inch, which is known as **ppi** (pixels per inch). A typical monitor displays pixels at 72ppi.

To determine the size of an image in inches, we divide the pixels by the ppi. For example, for an image 1024 pixels wide, 1024 / 72 = 14.2 inches. To determine the pixels present in an image, you multiple the size by the ppi. For example, for a 3 inch image, 3 x 72 = 216. As the image resolution drops, so does the output quality of the image. **Pixelization** occurs when the resolution is so low that the edges of the pixel begin to appear. The higher the resolution (more pixels), the sharper the image. However, the higher the resolution, the larger the file size. To optimize the use of a file, you need to use the correct resolution for a specific task. Use 72ppi for web pages, CD-ROMs, and Multimedia; use 150ppi for an inkjet printer; use 200ppi for photo printers; and use 300ppi for commercial printing.

When working with images, it's always a good idea to start with a larger image size. You can reduce the size of the image (subtract pixels) without losing any appreciable quality. If you need to enlarge an image, you run the risk of losing image quality. When you enlarge an image, the number of pixels doesn't increase as the image does, so the pixels become larger which means a rougher image.

Creating a New File Using Presets

When you create files for specific purposes, such as a mobile device, web, film, or video, you know the importance of creating files that will perfectly match the requirements of output to the screen. The preset file sizes available in the Preset menu let you create images at a size and pixel aspect ratio that compensate for scaling when you incorporate them into the output you want. When you work with the Preset menu, the guesswork of creating compatible, photo, web, scrapbooking (**New!**), mobile device, film, and video documents in Photoshop Elements is a thing of the past.

Create a New File Using Presets

1. In the Editor, click the **File** menu, point to **New**, and then click **Blank File**.

2. Click the **Preset** list arrow, and then select from the available presets:
   - Clipboard
   - Default Photoshop Elements Size
   - U.S. or International Paper
   - Photo
   - Scrapbooking (**New!**)
   - Web
   - Mobile & Devices
   - Film & Video
   - Custom

3. Click the **Size** list arrow, and then select the preset you want. The options vary.
   - **Photo.** For example, Landscape 4 x 6.
   - **Scrapbooking.** For example, 12 in x 12 in.
   - **Web.** For example, 640 x480.
   - **Mobile & Devices.** For example, 176 x 208.
   - **Film & Video.** For example, HDTV 1080p/29.97.

4. Adjust the options, such as Width, Height, Resolution, Color Mode, and Background Contents.

5. Click **OK**.

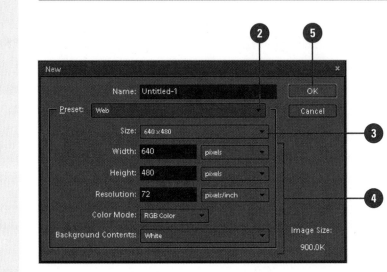

Opening a File

Photoshop Elements lets you open Photoshop document files in the default PSD or PDD formats as well as open image files created in different formats, such as TIFF, JPG, GIF, EPS, and PNG. If you want to simply open a Photoshop document or image file, the Open dialog box is the most efficient way. However, if you need to manage, organize, or process files, the Process Multiple Files command is the way to go. You open an existing Photoshop Elements file or image file the same way you open files in other programs.

Open a Document or Image File

1. In the Editor, click the **File** menu, and then click **Open** to display all file types in the file list of the Open dialog box.

   TIMESAVER *Point to the Open Recently Edited File command on the File menu to quickly open a recent file.*

2. Click the **Files of type** list arrow, and then select a format.

3. Click the **Look in** list arrow, and then select the location where the image you want to open is stored.

4. Click the image file you want to open.

   TIMESAVER *Press and hold the Shift key to select multiple files to open in the Open dialog box.*

5. Click **Open**.

6. In some cases, such as an EPS file, set format-specific options, and then click **OK**.

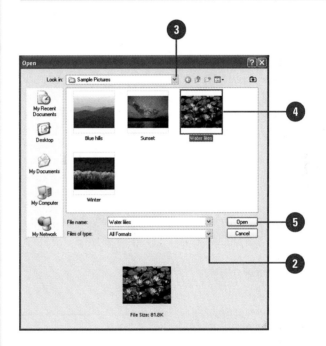

See Also

See "Understanding File Formats" on page 147 for information on the different file formats.

See "Setting File Associations" on page 480 for information on which file types to open in Photoshop Elements.

For Your Information

Opening a File as Another Format

The Open As command on the File menu allows you to open a file in Photoshop Elements as another format, which can help you open a file whose format Windows doesn't know. Click the File menu, click Open As, select the file you want to open, display all files, select the desired format from the Format list arrow, and then click Open. If the file does not open, then the chosen format may not match the file's true format, or the file may be damaged.

Opening a PDF File

In addition to opening image files, you can also open PDF (Portable Document Format) files in Photoshop Elements. A PDF file is a common file format you can create using Adobe Acrobat software. After you open a PDF file, the Import PDF dialog box opens where you can preview the pages and images in a multipage format, and then decide what you want to open in the Editor. You can import full pages or individual images from a PDF file.

Open a PDF File

1. In the Editor, click the **File** menu, and then click **Open**.

2. Click the **Files of type** list arrow, and then click **Photoshop PDF**.

3. Click the **Look in** list arrow, and then select the location where the file you want to open is stored.

4. Click the PDF file you want to open.

5. Click **Open**.

6. To import images, click the **Images** option, and then select the images you want to open.

7. To import entire pages, click the **Pages** option.

8. If you selected the Pages option, select any of the following options:

   - Select the pages you want to open, and then click **OK**.

   - Under Page options, use the existing name or type a new one.

   - Click the **Mode** list arrow, and then select a color mode.

   - Select a resolution.

9. Select the **Suppress Warnings** check box to hide any error messages during the import process.

10. Click **OK**.

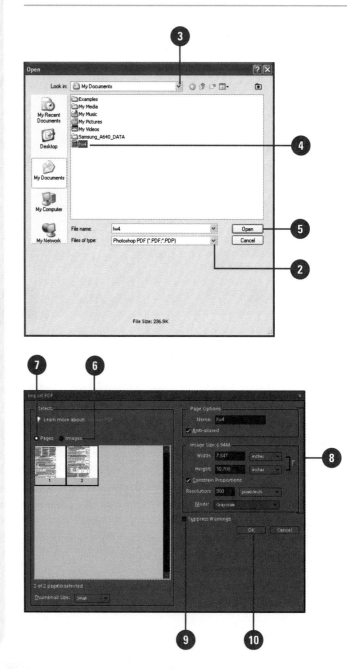

Inserting Images in a File

You can use the Place command to insert artwork into an open document. To increase your control of the new image information, Photoshop Elements places the new image into a separate layer. You can place files in PDF, Adobe Illustrator, and EPS formats. When you first place a vector-based image into Photoshop Elements, you have the ability to modify the width, height, and rotation as a pure vector image. However, since Photoshop Elements is primarily a raster program, when you finalize your changes, Photoshop Elements rasterizes the file information (converts the vector into pixels). Which means you cannot edit the placed documents as you would a vector shape or path.

Insert an Image in a File Using the Place Command

1. In the Editor, open the document in which you want to place another file.

2. Click the **File** menu, and then click **Place**.

3. Select the document you want to place into the active document.

4. Click **Place**.

   Photoshop Elements places the image in a new layer, directly above the active layer, and then encloses it within a free-transform bounding box.

5. Control the shape by manipulating the corner and side nodes of the freeform bounding box.

6. Press Enter to rasterize the image at the resolution of the active document.

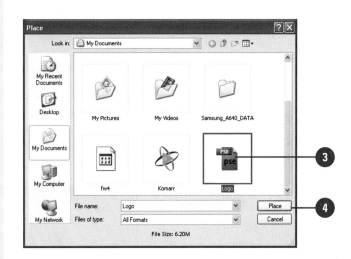

Freeform bounding box

Did You Know?

You can scan images into a file. With the scanner hardware and software connected and installed (including the Twain plug-in), click the File menu, point to Import, click Twain, set scan settings, and then click Scan.

Opening Raw Files from a Digital Camera

Camera raw image file formats are created by most mid to high-end digital cameras and contain all the information about how the image was taken. The raw format turns off all camera adjustments, and simply saves the image information to the digital film. When you open a raw image file, Photoshop Elements opens the Camera Raw, which allows you to adjust the image details. Camera Raw now supports more camera formats and can automatically apply default conversion settings when you use raw images in a photo project (**New!**). If you're not sure what to do, you can click Auto to have Camera Raw do it or drag color sliders to adjust options manually. You can adjust color tones, reduce noise, correct for lens defects, and retouch—with the Heal, Clone and Red Eye tools—images. To adjust color tones, you can change exposure, highlights recovery, fill light, blacks, brightness, contrast and saturation—with Vibrance and Saturation. Raw images are larger; however, the increase in file size is actually more information that can be used by the Camera Raw to adjust the image. In addition raw images can be converted into 16-bit, which provides more control over adjustments, such as tonal and color correction. Once processed, raw images can be saved in the DNG (Digital Negative), TIFF, PSD, PSB, or JPEG formats. You can use the Process Multiple Files command to automate the processing of camera raw files.

Open a Camera Raw File

1. In the Editor, click the **File** menu, and then click **Open**.

2. Click the **Files of type** list arrow, and then click **Camera Raw**.

3. Select a single camera raw image file, or Ctrl+click to select more than one file.

4. Click **Open**.

   Photoshop Elements opens the image into the Camera Raw dialog box, displaying the Basic tab.

5. Click the **Basic** or **Detail** button.

6. To automatically make tonal adjustments, click **Auto** on the Basic tab, and then make any other manual adjustments.

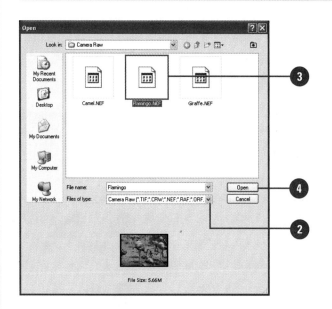

7 Use the following tools to modify the image:

- ◆ Use the **Zoom**, **Hand**, **Rotate**, **Crop**, and **Straighten** tools to change the size, orientation, and position of the image.

- ◆ Use the **White Balance** tools to set the image white balance or the **Color Sample** tool to sample a color from the image.

- ◆ Use the **Retouch** (Heal or Clone) or **Red Eye** tools to fix the image.

8 Select from the available image view options:

- ◆ **Image Preview.** Displays the active image.

- ◆ **Zoom Level.** Changes the view of the active image.

- ◆ **Histogram.** Displays information on the colors and brightness levels in the active image.

9 Select the list arrows to change the (color) Space, (bit) Depth, Size, and Resolution of the image.

10 Click **Save Image(s)** to specify a folder destination, file name, and format for the processed images.

11 Select the images you want to synchronize (apply the same settings to) in the Filmstrip (if desired, click Select All), and then click **Synchronize**.

12 Click the **Camera Raw Menu** button to **Load**, **Save**, or **Delete** a specific set of Raw settings.

13 When you're done, click **Done** to process the file, but not open it, or click **Open Image(s)** to process and open it in Photoshop Elements. Hold Alt to use **Open Copy** or **Reset**.

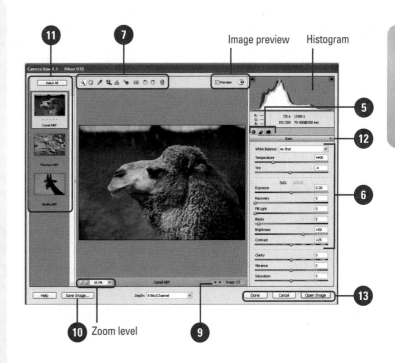

Image preview   Histogram

Zoom level

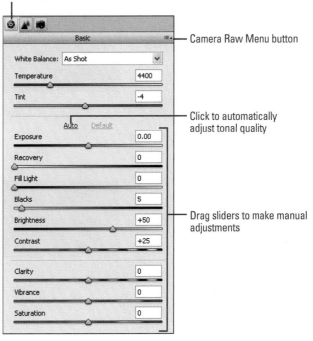

Basic button

Camera Raw Menu button

Click to automatically adjust tonal quality

Drag sliders to make manual adjustments

Working with Open Files

When you open a file—an individual photo or a multiple-page project—in the Editor, a thumbnail of the image appears in the Project Bin. An individual photo appears as a thumbnail, while a multiple-page project appears as a multi-page slide thumbnail, which includes an expand/collapse arrow to the right to show or hide individual pages. The Project Bin is useful for working with open files in the Editor. However, it's especially useful for switching between multiple open photos.

Use the Project Bin to Work with Open Files

1. In the Editor, open the files you want to use.

2. To change which files appear in the Project Bin, click the **Show** list arrow in the Project Bin, and then click **Show Open Files** or **Show Files from Organizer**.

3. Use any of the following options:

   ◆ **Open Photo.** Drag a file from any location on your computer into the Project Bin, or click the **File** menu, and then click **Open**.

   ◆ **Display Open Photo.** Double-click the thumbnail in the Project Bin.

   ◆ **Expand/Collapse Project.** Click the Expand/Collapse arrow next to the project thumbnail in the Project Bin.

   ◆ **Reorder Photos.** Drag thumbnails in the Project Bin.

   ◆ **Close Photo.** Right-click the thumbnail in the Project Bin, and then click **Close**.

   ◆ **Hide Photo.** Right-click the thumbnail in the Project Bin, and then click **Minimize**. Double-click its thumbnail to show it again.

   ◆ **View Photo Info.** Right-click the thumbnail in the Project Bin, and then click **File Info**.

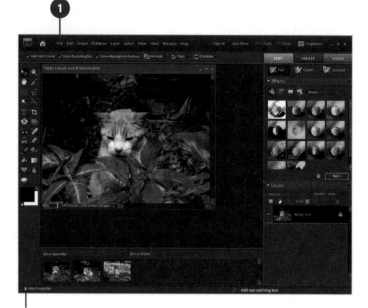

Expand/collapse Project Bin

- **Duplicate Photo.** Right-click the thumbnail in the Project Bin, and then click **Duplicate**.

- **Rotate Photo.** Right-click the thumbnail in the Project Bin, and then click **Rotate 90° Left** or **Rotate 90° Right**.

- **Show Filenames.** Right-click the thumbnail in the Project Bin, and then click **Show Filenames**.

- **Open/Close Project Bin.** Click the **Window** menu, and then click **Project Bin**.

- **Show/Hide Project Bin.** Click the **Project Bin** button.

④ To take other actions, click the **Bin Actions** list arrow in the Project Bin, and then select any of the following commands:

- **Create.** Opens the Create tab.

- **Share.** Opens the Share tab.

- **Print Bin Files.** Prints Project Bin files.

- **Save Bin as an Album.** Saves Project Bin files as an album.

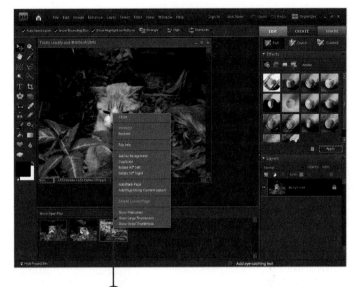

③ Right-click thumbnail to display commands

Did You Know?

You can automatically show or hide the Project Bin. Click the Edit menu, point to Preferences, click General, select the Project Bin Auto-hide check box, and then click OK. You can also right-click in the Project Bin, and then click Auto-hide. The Project Bin opens automatically when you move your cursor to the bottom of the screen and stays closed the rest of the time.

Processing Multiple Files

There is nothing more exciting than working on a new creative process, and watch as your designs come to life. Conversely, there is nothing more tiresome than having to apply that new creative concept to 50 other images. For example, you just spent three hours coming up with a procedure to color correct a photograph, and the process took two filters, and three adjustments. The photo looks great; however, you now have 50 other images with the exact problem. The solution is to batch process the images. Batch file processing lets you apply an action to an entire folder of images, and all you have to do is click a button. Now, what could be simpler than that?

Process Multiple Files

1. In th Editor, click the **File** menu, and then click **Process Multiple Files**.

2. Click the **Process Files** list arrow, and then select from the available options:

   ◆ **Folder.** Processes files in the specified folder. Click **Browse** to select the folder.

   ◆ **Import.** Processes image files from a digital camera or scanner.

   ◆ **Opened Files.** Processes all open files.

3. Select the **Include All Subfolders** check box to process files in subfolders of the selected folder.

4. Select the **Same as Source** check box to use the source location as the destination location, or click **Browse**, select a folder destination location, and then click **OK**.

5. To rename multiple files, select the **Rename Files** check box, and then select from the following options:

   ◆ **Name.** Click the first list menu, and then select a file naming option. Click the second list menu, and then select a file naming option that appends to the first option.

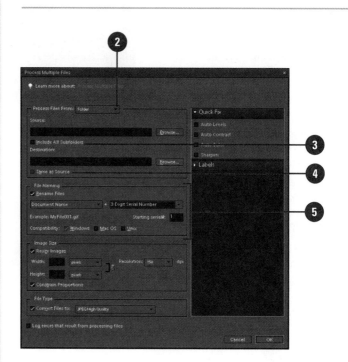

- ◆ **Starting Serial#.** Specify the starting number if the appended file naming option numbers files consecutively.

- ◆ **Compatibility.** Select the check box next to the operating system (Windows, Mac OS, or Unix) with which you want the filenames to be compatible.

6 To resize multiple image files, select the **Resize Images** check box, and then select from the following options:

- ◆ **Width and Height.** Select a measurement type (pixels, inches, cm, mm, or percent), and then enter a width and height.

- ◆ **Resolution.** Select a resolution, such as 72 pixels/inch (ppi) for online use and 300 ppi for print.

- ◆ **Constrain Proportions.** Select to constrain the width and height proportions to the same percentage.

7 To convert files to another format, select the **Convert Files to** check box, and then select a file format from the list arrow.

8 To automatically apply quick fixes to photos, select the check boxes in the Quick Fix area next to the fixes you want: Auto Levels, Auto Contrast, Auto Color, or Sharpen.

9 To attach a label to image files in the form of a caption or watermark, select a label option from the Labels menu in the Labels palette, enter the text, and then customize the text using the available options.

10 Select the **Log errors that result from processing files** check box to record errors in a file without stopping the process.

11 Click **OK**.

Changing Image Size and Resolution

You can modify the size and resolution of a file after opening. However, be aware that changing the size and/or the resolution of an image forces Photoshop Elements to add or subtract pixels from the image in a process called **interpolation**. For example, when you change the resolution of an image from 72 ppi (pixels per inch) to 144 ppi, Photoshop Elements must add more pixels. Conversely, if you reduce the resolution, Photoshop Elements must remove pixels. The image interpolation method determines how Photoshop Elements completes this process. You can use the Nearest Neighbor method for the fastest way, but it produces the poorest visual image. Or, you can use the Bicubic Sharper method which takes the longest to perform, but produces the best visual results. In addition to changing the image size and resolution, you can also change the canvas size to add space on one or all sides, where you can add text or shape, or resize an image to fit the space.

Change Image Size

1. In the Editor, open the image you want to change.

2. Click the **Image** menu, point to **Resize**, and then click **Image Size**.

3. Select the **Resample Image** check box.

4. Click the **Resample Image** list arrow, and then select an option:

   ◆ **Nearest Neighbor.** Best for quick results with low quality.

   ◆ **Bilinear.** Best for line art.

   ◆ **Bicubic.** Best for most purposes with high quality (default).

   ◆ **Bicubic Smoother.** Best for enlarging an image.

   ◆ **Bicubic Sharper.** Best for reducing an image.

5. To maintain image proportions, select the **Constrain Proportions** check box.

6. Enter the desired sizes in the image size boxes.

   If you choose to constrain proportions in step 5, when you change a size, the other boxes will adjust automatically.

7. Click **OK**.

Icon indicates constrained proportions

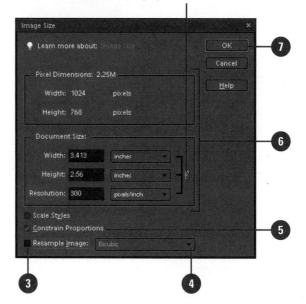

Change Image Resolution

1. In the Editor, open the image you want to change.

2. Click the **Image** menu, point to **Resize**, and then click **Image Size**.

3. Clear the **Resample Image** check box.

4. Enter a resolution, which automatically adjusts the Height and Width fields.

5. Click **OK**.

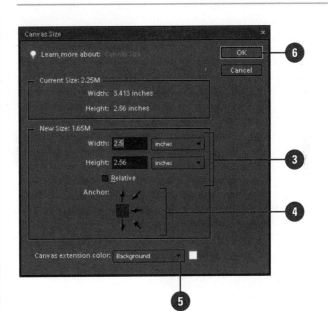

Change Canvas Size

1. In the Editor, open the image you want to change.

2. Click the **Image** menu, point to **Resize**, and then click **Canvas Size**.

3. Specify the canvas size you want:

   ◆ **Manual.** Specify a width and height with the units of measurement you want.

   ◆ **Relative.** Select the **Relative** check box to increase or decrease the canvas size by a specific amount. Specify a width and height amount (positive or negative).

4. Click an anchor square to indicate where to position the existing image on the new canvas.

5. Click the **Canvas extension color** list arrow, and then select a color: **Foreground**, **Background**, **White**, **Black**, **Gray**, or **Other**.

6. Click **OK**.

Using Full Edit and Quick Fix

The Full and Quick buttons on the Edit tab allow you to perform basic and advanced edits on your photos. Quick Fix allows you to make general fixes using Smart Fix and Red Eye Fix as well as make lighting, color, and sharpening adjustments. Many of the quick fixes can be done with an Auto button and are also available on the Enhance menu, so you don't need to be a professional. Photoshop Elements does all the work for you. If you want to make more advanced edits or add special effects to an image, Full Edit provides all the tools, commands, and palettes you need, including the TouchUp palette (**New!**) with the tools Red Eye Removal, Whiten Teeth, Make Dull Skies Blue, or Black and White - High Contrast.

Use Full Edit

1. In the Editor, open the file you want to change.

2. Click the **Edit** tab.

3. Click the **Full** button on the Edit tab.

4. Click the **Window** menu, and then click the palettes you want to display.

   The Effects and Layers palettes appear by default.

5. Display the **Effects** palette, click the **All** button, select the effect you want, and then click **Apply**.

   ◆ To limit the display of effects, click the Filters, Layers Styles, or Photo Effects button.

6. Display the **Layers** palette, and then use the layer options you want.

See Also

See Chapter 14, "Working with Layer Styles and Photo Effects," on page 323 for information on using layer styles and photo effects.

See Chapter 10, "Working with Layers," on page 201 for information on using layers.

Use Quick Fix

① In the Editor, open the file you want to change.

② Click the **Edit** tab.

③ Click the Edit tab's **Quick** button.

④ Display the **General Fixes** palette, and then use the options you want:

◆ **Smart Fix.** Click the **Auto** button or drag the slider to manually fix the image.

◆ **Red Eye Fix.** Click the **Auto** button to correct red eye.

⑤ Display the **Lighting** palette, and then use the options you want:

◆ **Levels.** Click the **Auto** button to correct color levels.

◆ **Contrast.** Click the **Auto** button to adjust contrast levels.

◆ **Lighten Shadows, Darken Highlights, or Midtone Contrast.** Drag the sliders to adjust the levels.

⑥ Display the **Color** palette, and then click the **Auto** button or drag the sliders to manually change colors.

⑦ Display the **Sharpen** palette, and then click the **Auto** button or drag the slider to sharpen the image.

⑧ Display the **TouchUp** palette (**New!**), and then click the **Red Eye Removal Tool**, the **Whiten Teeth** tool, the **Make Dull Skies Blue** tool, or the **Black and White - High Contrast** tool. Paint in the image to apply the effect.

⑨ To display before and after views, click the View list arrow, and then click **After Only**, **Before Only**, **Before & After - Horizontal**, or **Before & After - Vertical**.

⑩ To reset the options to the original settings, click **Reset**.

Using Guided Edit

The Guided button on the Edit tab makes it easy to perform basic photo editing, lighting and exposure fixes, color correction, photo touch-ups and blending, and artistic effects. The photo editing options allow you to crop, rotate, straighten, and sharpen photos. If you need to fix a photo, you can touch up scratches, blemishes or tear marks as well as enhance colors, remove a color cast, and correct skin tone. If you want to create the perfect photo from a series, you can use Photomerge Faces, Group Shot, or Scene Cleaner (**New!**) to blend two photos together.

Use Guided Edit

1. In the Editor, open the file you want to change.

2. Click the **Edit** tab.

3. Click the **Guided** button.

4. Click the Guided option you want:

   ◆ **Crop Photo.** Click the **Crop Box Size** list arrow, select an option, and then resize the box.

   ◆ **Rotate and/or Straighten Photo.** Click the **Maintain Image Size** or **Maintain Canvas Size** option. Click the **Rotate 90 Left** or **Rotate 90 Right** button or click the **Straighten** button and draw a line on the image to rotate it to the angle of the line.

   ◆ **Sharpen Photo.** Click the **Auto** button or drag the slider to manually apply the sharpening.

   ◆ **Lighten or Darken.** Click the **Auto** button, or drag the sliders to lighten shadows, darken highlights, and adjust contrast.

   ◆ **Brightness and Contrast.** Click the **Auto** button, or drag sliders to manually change brightness and contrast.

   ◆ **Adjust Levels (New!).** Click the **Create Levels Adjustment Layer** button and drag sliders to adjust the image's tonal values.

   ◆ **Enhance Colors.** Click the **Auto** button, or drag sliders to adjust hue, saturation, and lightness.

- ◆ **Remove a Color Cast.** Click the **Color Cast Eyedropper** tool, and then click on part of the image that you want to be pure gray, white, or black.

- ◆ **Correct Skin Tone.** Click the **Skin Tone Eyedropper Tool**, and then click on a person's skin. To make changes, drag sliders for **Tan**, **Blush**, and **Ambient Light**.

- ◆ **Touch Up Scratches, Blemishes or Tear Marks.** Click the **Spot Healing Brush** button and click the flaw to remove it.

  Click the **Healing Brush** button and Alt+click in a good image area and drag over the flaw.

- ◆ **Guide for Editing a Photo (New!).** Use to apply editing steps in recommended order.

- ◆ **Fix Keystone Distortion.** Use to fix lens distortion and image perspective problems.

- ◆ **Group Shot.** Use to combine people in multiple photos to create the perfect group photo.

- ◆ **Faces.** Use to combine facial features from multiple photos to create the perfect portrait.

- ◆ **Scene Cleaner (New!).** Use to remove objects from pictures.

- ◆ **Action Player (New!).** Use to play Photoshop Actions.

- ◆ **Line Drawing, Old-Fashioned Photo, or Saturated Slide Film Effect.** Follow the steps to apply artistic effects to your photo.

5 To see before and after versions, click the button to toggle **After Only**, **Before & After - Horizontal**, or **Before & After - Vertical** views.

6 To reset the settings, click **Reset**.

7 Click **Done** to apply the changes or click **Cancel** to ignore them.

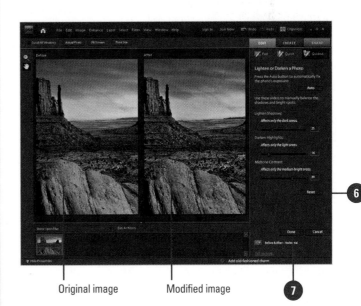

Original image   Modified image

Attaching Information to a File

Before you save a file, you have the ability to save more than just color information. You can save copyright, camera, and even image category information. This data is saved with the file as metadata in the XMP format (Extensible Metadata Platform), and can be accessed by any application that reads XMP data. In addition, if the image is a photograph, you can save data on the type of image, where it was shot, the camera used, even information on shutter speed and F-Stop. That information will not only protect your intellectual property, but will supply you with vital statistics on exactly how you created that one-of-a-kind image.

Attach Information to a File

1. In the Editor, open the file you want to change.

2. Click the **File** menu, and then click **File Info**.

3. Click **Description**, and then enter information concerning the author and any copyright information.

4. Click **Camera Data 1 and 2**, and then enter information about the camera that took the image.

   If the picture was taken with a digital camera that records Metadata, much of this information will already be filled out.

5 Click **Advanced** to view high-end information on the active document, such as EXIF, and PDF document properties.

6 Click **OK**.

Did You Know?

You can add metadata to files saved in the psd, pdf, eps, png, gif, jpg, and tif formats. The information is embedded in the file using XMP (eXtensible Metadata Platform). This allows metadata to be exchanged between Adobe applications and across operating systems.

You can view metadata in the Organizer. Click the Metadata button at the top of the Properties palette.

You can use the XMP Software Development Kit to customize the creation, processing, and interchange of metadata. You can also use the XMP kit to add fields to the File Info dialog box. For information on XMP and the XMP SDK, check the Adobe Partner Connection at www.adobe.com/cfusion/partnerportal/.

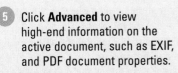

Mission02.JPG

Description
Camera Data 1
Camera Data 2
Advanced

Advanced

TIFF Properties (tiff, http://ns.adobe.com/tiff/1.0/)
XMP Core Properties (xmp, http://ns.adobe.com/xap/1.0/)
EXIF Properties (exif, http://ns.adobe.com/exif/1.0/)
XMP Media Management Properties (xmpMM, http://ns.adobe.com/xap/1.0/mm/)
Dublin Core Properties (dc, http://purl.org/dc/elements/1.1/)
Adobe Photoshop Properties (photoshop, http://ns.adobe.com/photoshop/1.0/)
    photoshop:ColorMode: 3
    photoshop:ICCProfile: sRGB IEC61966-2.1
    photoshop:History
PDF Properties (pdf, http://ns.adobe.com/pdf/1.3/)
http://ns.adobe.com/png/1.0/

Powered By
xmp

Save...   Delete

OK   Cancel

Saving a File

When you finish working on your Photoshop Elements image, you need to save it as a document or image file before you close it or exit Photoshop Elements. A document file (in the Photoshop format) contains one or more layers, which can contain images, text, shapes, and adjustments. Before you save a file, there are questions that you must ask yourself first, like *How will the image be output?* Each output device, whether monitor or paper, requires a specific format, and it's best to know this information at the beginning of the creation process. Knowing the final output of an image helps you create the design with the output in mind. In Photoshop Elements, you can save files in the Photoshop (PSD) document format (the default) or one of the other image formats, which includes JPEG, GIF, or PNG. When you save a file in an image format, multiple layers in a document are flatten into one.

Save a Document or Image File

1. In the Editor, click the **File** menu, and then click **Save**.

2. Enter a name for the file in the File Name box.

3. Click the **Format** list arrow, and then select a format. (default: Photoshop (PSD, PDD))

4. Click the **Save in** list arrow, and then choose where to store the image.

5. Select from the available Save options:

   ◆ **Include in the Organizer.** Makes the file available in the Organizer.

   ◆ **Save in Version Set with Original.** Saves a copy of the edited file with the original in a version set.

   ◆ **As A Copy.** Saves a copy of the file while keeping the current file on your desktop.

   ◆ **Layers.** Maintains all layers in the image. If this option is cleared or unavailable, all visible layers are flattened or merged (depending on the selected format).

6 Select from the available Color options:

◆ **ICC Profile.** Embeds proof profile information in an untagged document. If the document is tagged, the profile is embedded by default.

7 Select from other available options:

◆ **Thumbnail.** Saves thumbnail data for the file.

To use this option, you need to open the Saving Files preferences in the Editor. Click the **Image Previews** list arrow, and then select the **Ask When Saving** option.

◆ **Use Lower Case Extension.** Makes the file extension lowercase.

8 Click **Save**, and then click **OK**, if necessary, to maximize the compatibility of the saved file.

See Also

See "Understanding File Formats" on page 147 for information on the different file formats.

For Your Information

Understanding the Save Commands

When you use the Save command on the File menu to save an existing document, Photoshop Elements performs the save without opening a dialog box. That means the original document file has been replaced with the current state of the image. To preserve the original document, use the Save As command on the File menu, and then give the document file a new name. For example, a file originally named landscape.psd could be saved as landscape_1.psd. Every hour, stop, select Save As, and create another version of the file (landscape_2.psd, landscape_3.psd). That way you have an historical record of the progress made on the document, and if you ever need to go back in time, you have the image files necessary to make the trip easy.

Reverting to the Last Saved Version

If you make a lot of editing changes to a file after you have saved it and then decide that you no longer want to keep the changes, you can use the Revert command on the Edit menu to revert back to the last saved version. The Revert action is also added as a history state in the Undo History palette, so you can undo it if you want. Every time you save your document, Photoshop Elements marks this point as the latest saved version used by the Revert command.

Revert to the Last Saved Version

1. In the Editor, click the **File** menu, and then click **Save**, if necessary.

   This saves the document with the changes you want to keep.

2. Edit the photo in Full Edit or Quick Fix with the changes you want.

3. Click the **Edit** menu, and then click **Revert**.

See Also

See "Undoing and Redoing Actions with the Undo History Palette" on page 168 for information on using the Undo History palette.

Understanding File Formats

File Formats	
Format	**Usage**
Photoshop	Uses a PSD (Photoshop, default for a single page) or PDD format, which saves layers, notes, editable text, adjustment layers, layer styles, and color profiles.
BMP	Uses a BMP (Bitmap), RLE, or DIB (Device Independent Bitmap) format.
Camera Raw	Uses a TIF, CRW, NEF, RAF, ORF, MRW, DCR, MOS, RAW, PEF, SRF, DNG, X3F, CR2, ERF, SR2 format, which is taken from a digital camera.
CompuServe GIF	Uses a GIF (Graphic Interchange Format) format, which is used for clipart and text for the web. A format for images on the web that only use 256 colors. GIF's compress images by selectively disregarding color and repeating simple patterns. It supports transparency and animation.
Photo Project	Uses the PSE format (default for multiple pages) to save Photoshop Elements projects.
Photoshop EPS	Uses a EPS (Encapsulated PostScript Format) format, which saves vector information (i.e. paths).
EPS TIFF	Uses the EPS (Encapsulated PostScript Format) format.
Filmstrip	Uses the FLM format.
JPEG	Uses a JPG, JPEG, or JPE (Joint Photographers Expert Group) format. A compression method used to reduce the size of image files primarily for the web.
JPEG 2000	Uses a JPF, JPX, JP2, J2C, J2K, or JPC (Joint Photographers Expert Group) format for compatibility.
Generic EPS	Uses a AI3 (Adobe Illustrator), AI4, AI5, AI6, AI7, AI8, PS, EPS, AI, EPSF, or EPSP format.
PCX	Uses a PCX (PC Paintbrush bitmap) format, which is used primarily in PC formats.
Photoshop PDF	Uses a PDF (Portable Document File) format, which creates a file that can be read by anyone who has a PDF reader program (such as Adobe).
Photoshop RAW	Uses a RAW format that is used for saving and transferring files between programs and computer platforms.
PICT File	Uses a PICT or PICT Resource format that is used for the Macintosh operating system.
Pixar	Uses the Pixar format for images that are high-end animation, and 3-D rendering programs.
PNG	Uses the PNG (Portable Network Graphic) format. This is used for saving images onto the web that supports up to 16 million colors and 256 levels of transparency.
Scitex CT	Uses the SCT (Continuous Tone) format in high-end Scitex image-rendering computers.
Targa	Uses a TGA, VDA, ICB or VST format for high-end image editing on the Windows platform.
TIFF	Uses a TIFF or TIF (Tagged Image File) format. This can be opened by most image- editing or layout program. A common format for printing and saving flat images without losing quality.
Wireless Bitmap	Uses WBM and WBMP format.

Understanding File Compression

Compression is Photoshop Elements' way of reducing the size of a document file. Kind of like the ultimate weight-loss program... just click a button, and the file is half its original size. Photoshop Elements employs two types of compression schemes: lossy and lossless. **Lossy** compression reduces the size of the file by removing color information... information that can never be restored to the saved document. Lossy compression schemes can achieve file reductions of 80 percent or greater.

The **lossless** method reduces file size by using compression algorithms that reduce the size of a file without removing image information. Lossy methods are used primarily for images displayed in browsers, or web images. The relatively slow speed of the Internet forces web designers, to employ

lossy compression methods to reduce images down to their smallest values. Lossless methods are used when the reduction of a file's size is important, but not so much that you would consider removing information. For example, reducing the size of a group of high-quality TIFF images, so they fit on a rewritable CD. Lossless compression methods can reduce files sizes up to 50 percent, or even a bit more.

Both methods compress files based on the actual image information. For example, images that contain a lot of solid color information would compress quite well using the GIF (Graphics Interchange) or PNG8 formats; where an image with a lot of soft blending colors, such as a photograph, would be best compressed using the JPEG (Joint Photographic Experts Group) format.

Lossy

Lossless

Format Type, Compression Type, and Output Uses

Format	Compression	Uses
JPEG	Lossy	**Web/Slide Presentations.** PDFs, photographs, and images that contain lots of colors that softly blend together.
GIF	Lossless	**Web.** Clip art, text, and any images that contain solid colors and images with hard edges.
PNG-8	Lossless	**Web.** Clip art, text, and any images that contain solid colors and images with hard edges.
PNG-24	Lossless	**Web/Slide Presentations/PDF/Print.** Photographs and images that contain lots of colors that softly blend together. Because the PNG-24 format is lossless, it can not compress images as small as the JPEG format. Therefore, the JPEG format is still the format of choice for compressing images for the web.
RLE	Lossless	**Images.** Images that have been reduced using run-length encoding. Black-and-white or cartoon-style graphics that contain transparent portions.
CCITT	Lossless	**Images.** Images, such as faxes, that contain only black and white.
ZIP	Lossless	**Used on all image types for Image Storage and Transfer.** The Zip compression application lets you compress images without affecting image quality.
LZW	Lossless	**Used primarily on TIF images for Image Storage and Transfer.** The LZW compression scheme lets you com press images without affecting image quality. To open an LZW image, the opening application must have the proper LZW decompression code.

Closing a File

To conserve your computer's resources, close any Photoshop Elements files you are not working on. You can close open files one at a time, or you can use one command to close all open files without closing the program. Either way, if you try to close a file without saving your final changes, a dialog box appears, prompting you to do so.

Close a File

1. In the Editor, click the **Close** button in the active window.

   TIMESAVER *Press Ctrl+W to close the active document.*

2. If necessary, click **Yes** to save your changes.

Did You Know?

You can close all files in one step. In the Editor, click the File menu, and then click Close All. If necessary, click Yes to save your changes for each document. You can also press Alt+Ctrl+W to close all documents.

Click to close

1

Navigating and Using the Editor

Introduction

When you go on a road-trip vacation, you need two things to make the trip a success—good navigational aids (maps), and an understanding of how to measure distances between two points on a road map (1 inch equals 100 miles). When you are working in the Editor, one of the keys to making the journey a success is to understand the navigational and measurement aids available. Photoshop Elements' navigation and measurement systems are more that just information; they represent control of the photo and control of the creative process.

Photoshop Elements lets you choose a measurement system to fit a specific project. For example, if you're working on images destined for the web or a monitor, you'll be using pixels as a measurement system. Conversely, if you're outputting to paper, or possibly a 4-color press, you'll likely choose inches or picas. Selecting between different measurement systems does not impact the quality of the final photo; only how you measure distance. Trust me on this one; understanding how to measure distance helps to make the journey an enjoyable experience.

Having problems squinting at the small details of a photo? Using the Zoom tool is a great way to gain control over a document. Zooming into a section of a document makes touching up the fine details just that much easier. In addition, the Info palette gives you up-to-date information on the exact position of the cursor inside the document, as well as detailed color information that can be indispensable in color-correcting a photo.

Making changes to a photo is all part of the processing of creating the results you want. If you don't like a change, you can use the Undo History palette to restore the photo. Think of the Undo History palette as having a magical mistake correction tool, which never wears out.

Changing the View Size with the Navigator Palette

The Navigator palette in the Editor gives you an overall view of the photo and the ability to navigate through the document or change the zoom size. Viewing images at different sizes gives you the ability to focus on small elements of the design, without impacting the overall quality of the photo. Once small areas of a photo are enlarged, it's easier for you to make minute changes. Zoom size determines the visible size of a photo, as seen in the document window. Zooming in (enlarging the photo) gives you a handy magnifying glass that lets you work on and manipulate fine details, and then you can zoom out (reducing the photo) to view how the changes impact the entire photo. The Navigator palette contains a thumbnail view of the photo, and under the thumbnail are easy-to-use controls that let you adjust the zoom of the photo. In addition, changes made in the Navigator palette are immediately viewable in the active document window (what you see is what you get).

Change the View Size with the Navigator Palette

1. In the Editor, display the **Navigator** palette.

2. Use one of the following methods to change the view size:

   ◆ Drag the triangular slider to the right to increase the zoom or to the left to decrease the zoom.

   ◆ Click the small and large mountain icons, located to the left and right of the triangular slider, to decrease or increase the zoom.

   ◆ Enter a value from .33 to 1600 percent into the Zoom box.

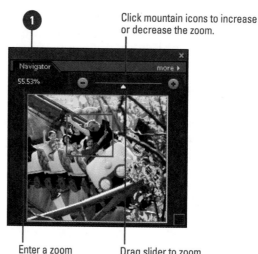

Click mountain icons to increase or decrease the zoom.

Enter a zoom value

Drag slider to zoom

Did You Know?

There are additional ways to zoom in using the Navigator palette. In the View box, hold down the Ctrl key, and then drag to resize the active document.

You can constrain the view box to drag horizontally or vertically. Hold down the Shift key, and then drag the view box horizontally or vertically.

For Your Information

Navigator Palette Shortcut

You can control the view of the document through a great shortcut. In the Editor, simply click once in the Zoom input box on the Navigator palette, and then use the Up/Down arrow keys to increase or decrease the zoom value of the document 1 percentage point at a time. Not fast enough for you? Then hold down the Shift key, and use the Up or Down arrow keys to change the zoom size 10 percentage points at a time. Press the Enter key to see your changes reflected in the active document window.

Changing the View Area with the Navigator Palette

Zoomed images are typically larger than the size of the document window. When this happens, Photoshop Elements adds navigational scroll bars to the bottom and the right of the document window. However, using awkward scroll bars is not the only way to change the viewable area of the photo; the Navigator palette gives you a visual approach to changing the view area of the photo. The view box in the Navigator palette represents the visible boundaries of the active document window, which is the viewable area of the photo.

Change the View Area with the Navigator Palette

① In the Editor, display the **Navigator** palette.

② Drag the view box in the thumbnail of the active photo.

③ Click within the thumbnail.

The position of the view box changes, which also changes the viewable area of the photo in the document window.

Did You Know?

You can show the Navigator palette. If the Navigator palette is not visible, click the Window menu, and then click Navigator.

You can change the zoom size of a photo using the Navigator thumbnail. Hold down the Ctrl key, and then drag in the thumbnail. When you release your mouse, the selected area expands. It's just like using the Zoom tool, except you're dragging in the Navigator's thumbnail. Conversely, if you drag a second time (this time using a larger rectangle), the photo zooms out.

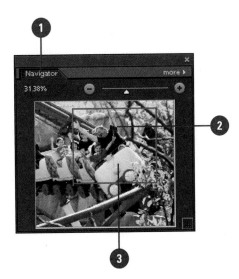

Document window view

Changing the Color of the Navigator Palette View Box

The view box defines the viewable area of the photo—the default color of the view box is red. It's important for the color of the view box to stand out against the photo. However, some documents contain images that are the same color as the view box, making the view box difficult to identify. By changing the color of your view box to work with your photo, you can make sure your view box stands out against the photo. This may seem like a small thing to do, but it significantly cuts down on my frustration level, when I'm attempting to identify the view box.

Change the View Box Color

1. In the Editor, display the **Navigator** palette.

2. Click the **More Options** button, and then click **Palette Options**.

3. Click the **Color** list arrow, and then click a pre-defined color, or click **Custom** to select a color from the Color Picker dialog box.

4. Click **OK**.

View box

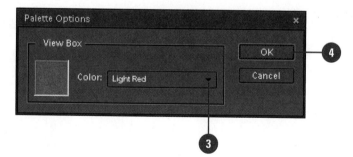

Changing the View

Changing the view allows you to look at a photo up close or far away. You can change the view by using the View menu, the Zoom tools on the toolbox, and the Navigation palette. The View menu allows you to zoom in and out, fit the photo to the screen, and display the photo at the actual size. The Zoom In and Zoom Out commands let you view an photo at different magnifications. The Fit on Screen command displays the photo to fit on the screen, while the Actual Pixels command displays the photo at 100%.

Change the View

1. In the Editor, click the **View** menu, and then click any of the following commands:

   ◆ **Zoom In.** Displays the photo with an increase view percentage.

   TIMESAVER *Press Ctrl+=* *(equal sign).*

   ◆ **Zoom Out.** Displays the photo with a decreased view percentage.

   TIMESAVER *Press Ctrl+-* *(minus sign)*

   ◆ **Fit on Screen.** Displays the photo to fit on the screen in the document window.

   TIMESAVER *Press Ctrl+0* *(zero).*

   ◆ **Actual Pixels.** Displays the photo at 100% in the document window.

   TIMESAVER *Press Alt+Ctrl+0* *(zero).*

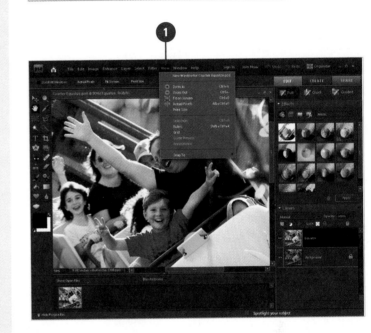

Changing the View with the Zoom Tool

Working with the Zoom tool gives you one more way to control exactly what you see in Photoshop Elements. Just like the Navigator palette, the Zoom tool does not change the active photo, it only lets you view the photo at different magnifications. The Zoom tool is located at the top of the toolbox, and resembles a magnifying glass. The maximum magnification of a document is 1600 percent, and the minimum magnification is less than 1 percent of the original photo size. Increasing the magnification of a photo gives you control over what you see and gives you control over how you work. Large documents are difficult to work with and difficult to view. Many documents, when viewed at 100 percent, are larger than the maximized size of the document window. When this happens, viewing the entire photo requires reducing the zoom.

Zoom In the View of an Image

1. In the Editor, select the **Zoom** tool on the toolbox.

2. Use one of the following methods:

   ◆ **Click on the document.**

   The photo increases in magnification centered on where you clicked.

   ◆ **Drag to define an area with the Zoom tool.**

   The photo increases in magnification based on the boundaries of the area you dragged.

2 — Click and drag method

— Zoom in

Zoom Out the View of an Image

① In the Editor, select the **Zoom** tool on the toolbox.

② Hold down the Alt key, and then click on the screen to reduce the zoom of the active document.

The zoom reduction centers on where you click on the active document.

IMPORTANT *Since images viewed in Photoshop Elements are composed of pixels (like bricks in a wall), the only way to really see what the printed results of your artwork will look like is to view the photo (even if it is too big for the screen) at 100 percent.*

Did You Know?

You can zoom in or out using shortcut keys regardless of what tool you're currently using. To zoom in, press Ctrl+Spacebar and click or drag to define an area. To zoom out, press Ctrl+Space-bar+Alt and click or drag to define an area.

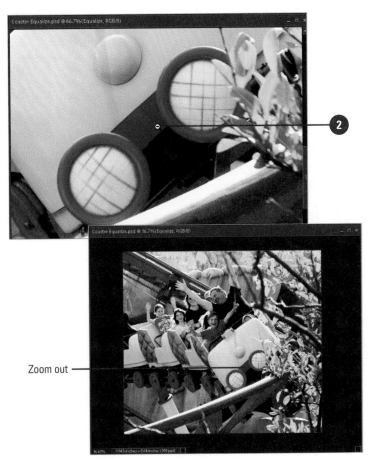

Zoom out

Increasing or Decreasing Magnification

Since changing the zoom size of a photo is fundamental to the creative process, Photoshop Elements gives you several ways to accomplish zooming. An additional way to zoom is using the options on the Options bar. To access the Zoom tool options, you must have the Zoom tool selected. Photoshop Elements gives you two handy zoom preset values. To automatically zoom the document to 100 percent, double-click the Zoom tool. To automatically fit the photo to the monitor, double-click the Hand tool.

Increase the Magnification of an Image

1. In the Editor, click the **Zoom In** or **Zoom Out** buttons on the Options bar, and then click in the document window to increase or decrease the zoom.

2. Select the **Resize Windows To Fit** check box on the Options bar to resize image windows to match the size of their contents.

3. Click **1:1** (Actual Pixels), **Fit Screen**, or **Print Size** on the Options bar to quickly zoom the screen to a preset size.

   TIMESAVER *It's possible to change the zoom of a document without ever leaving the keyboard. Hold the Ctrl key, and then press the plus "+", or minus "-" keys. The plus key increases the zoom size, and the minus key decreases the zoom size.*

Did You Know?

You can zoom in on more than one document. If you have more than one open document, click Zoom All Windows on the Options bar.

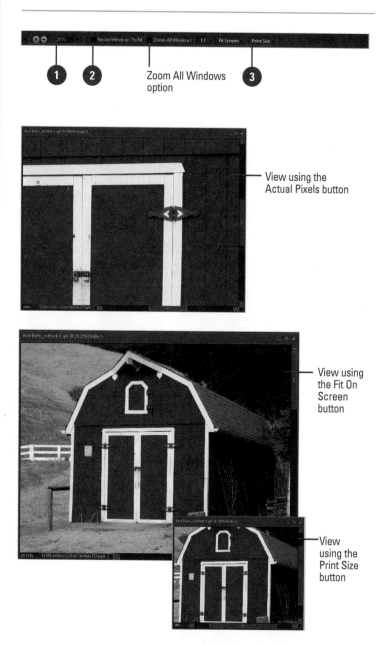

Zoom All Windows option

View using the Actual Pixels button

View using the Fit On Screen button

View using the Print Size button

158

Moving Images in the Document Window

One of those little used, but handy tools to have is Photoshop Elements' Hand tool. The Hand tool (called so because it resembles an open hand) lets you quickly move the active photo within the document window without ever using the scroll bars. For example, you've zoomed the photo beyond the size that fits within the document window and you need to change the visible portion of the document. It's a simple operation, but a handy one to know.

Move an Image in the Document Window

① In the Editor, select the **Hand** tool on the toolbox.

② Drag in the active document to move the photo.

Did You Know?

You can quickly access the Hand tool whenever you need it. Hold down the Spacebar to temporarily change to the Hand tool. Drag in the active document to the desired position, and then release the Spacebar. You're instantly returned to the last-used tool. It's important to note that you cannot use the spacebar to access the Hand tool if you are currently using the Type tool.

Working with One Image in Multiple Windows

There are times when you're working on a photo in Photoshop Elements, and you need to see two separate views of the photo. For example, you're working on retouching a photo and you need a zoomed in view to do fine detail work. At the same time, you want to see a normal view to get an idea of how the retouching is affecting the normal-sized photo. Being able to view one photo at two different views is a valuable tool. The Image submenu on the Window menu provides options to help you work with multiple windows. The Match Zoom and Match Location commands allow you to match the zoom and location in multiple windows. You can also use the Cascade and Tile commands to display windows across the Photoshop Elements window.

Create Two Views of One Image

1. In the Editor, open an image.

2. Click the **View** menu, and then click **New Window for <document name>**.

   A copy of the active document is created in a new document window.

3. Select the **Zoom** tool on the toolbox, and then increase the zoom of the new document to the desired level.

4. Select an editing or painting tool, and then begin working on the new photo in the zoomed window.

   The effects of your work instantly display in the normal document window.

5. When you're done with the new window, click the **Close** button.

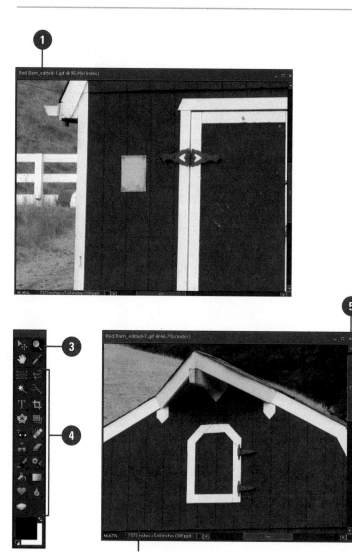

New window with zoomed document

Arrange and Match Multiple Windows

1. In the Editor, open one or more documents.

2. Click the **Window** menu, point to **Images**, and then click **Match Zoom** or **Match Location**.

3. Select the **Zoom** tool or **Hand** tool on the toolbox.

4. Hold down the Shift key, and click in or drag an area.

   The other images are zoomed to the same percentage or location you clicked.

Did You Know?

You can prevent the zoomed window from expanding. With the Zoom tool selected, move into the Options bar and deselect Resize Windows To Fit.

Moving Layers Between Two Open Documents

Photoshop Elements has a lot of tricks up its electronic sleeves, and one of the handiest is the ability to move layers between open documents. For example, you have a photo of a landscape and sky, but you don't like the sky, so you erase it. You then open another document with a sky that suits the design of your document. It's a simple matter to move the layer containing the sky into any other open document.

Move Layers Between Documents

① In the Editor, open two or more documents.

② Click on the document containing the layer you want to move to make it the active document.

③ Select the **Move** tool on the toolbox.

④ Drag the layer you want to move from the open document window into the second document.

IMPORTANT *If the document you're moving a layer into contains more than one layer, Photoshop Elements places the layer you're moving directly above the active layer in the second document. If that puts the layer in the wrong stacking order, drag it up and down in the Layers palette until it's correctly positioned.*

Drag layer

Did You Know?

You can also drag a layer thumbnail onto a document. In the Editor, drag the layer thumbnail from the Layers palette into the document window of the second document.

From the Experts Corner

Removing the Excess

If you're dragging a layer from a document that contains more pixels than the receiving document, the areas of the photo outside the viewable area of the document are still there, taking up file space. To delete them, first position the photo exactly where you want, click the Select menu, and then click Select All. Select the Image menu, and then click Crop. That's it. All the photo information outside the viewable window is removed.

Working with the Info Palette

Photoshop Elements' Info palette gives you a wealth of data on the current document's color space, as well as information on the x/y position of your mouse cursor within the active document window. In addition, when you're using one of the drawing or measuring tools, the Info palette gives you up-to-date information on the size of the object you're creating. Photoshop works with black, white, shades of gray, and every color in between.

Create a Specific Size Object

1. In the Editor, display the **Info** palette.

2. Select a drawing tool on the toolbox.

3. Drag in the document window to create a shape.

4. Release the mouse when the Info palette displays the correct dimensions.

   IMPORTANT *The bottom of the Info palette displays the current size of the working document.*

See Also

See Chapter 13, "Using the Paint, Shape Drawing, and Eraser Tools" on page 291 for information on using drawing tools.

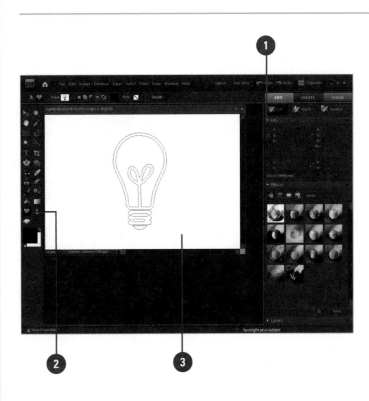

Changing How the Info Palette Measures Color

Knowledge of the colors used in a document is important, but so is a thorough understanding of the color mode of the document. Different documents require different color modes. For example, images displayed on a monitor use the RGB (red, green, blue) color mode, and images sent to a 4-color press use CMYK (cyan, magenta, yellow, black). Not only does the Info palette measure color, it also measures color in specific color modes.

Change How the Info Palette Measures Color

1. In the Editor, display the **Info** palette.

2. Click the **More Options** button, and then click **Palette Options**.

3. Click the **Mode** list arrows for First Color and Second Color Readout, and then select from the available options.

4. Click **OK**.

   The Info palette now measures color based on your selections.

Did You Know?

The Info palette now allows you display information such as: Document Size, Efficiency, Scratch Sizes, and more. At the bottom of the Info Palette Options dialog, you can select from the available options. The Info palette can even display whether the photo is using 8, 16, or 32 bit color channels.

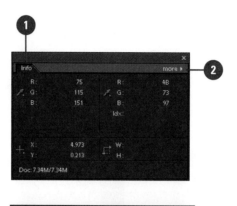

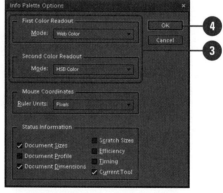

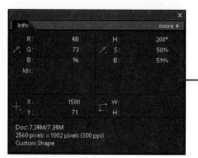

The Info palette after changes to the color options have been made.

Working with Rulers

Carpenters know that precise measurements are essential to making things fit, so they have a rule: Measure Twice, Cut Once. In keeping with the idea that precise measurements are essential, Photoshop Elements gives you several measuring methods; among them are the rulers. Rulers are located on the top and left sides of the active document window, and serve several purposes. They let you measure the width and height of the active photo, they let you place guides on the screen to control placement of other photo elements, and they create markers that follow your cursor as you move. As you can see, rulers serve a very important role. Ruler guides help you correctly align photo design elements.

Show and Hide Rulers

1 In the Editor, click the **View** menu, and then click **Rulers**.

> **TIMESAVER** *Press Shift+Ctrl+R to turn the ruler on and off.*

A check mark appears next to the Rulers option when the rulers are shown. The rulers appear along the vertical and horizontal edge of the document window.

NOTE *The rulers appear with the measurement system selected in the Units and Rulers preferences.*

> **TIMESAVER** *Right-click either ruler, and then select a measurement option from the menu.*

2 To hide the rulers, click the **View** menu, and then click **Rulers** again.

> **TIMESAVER** *Double-click a ruler to display the Units & Rulers Preference dialog box.*

Horizontal ruler **1**

Vertical ruler

See Also

See "Setting Units & Rulers Preferences" on page 488 for more information on setting Units and Rulers preferences.

For Your Information

Changing the Rulers' Zero Origin

The upper-left corner of the image is set to the zero mark on both rulers by default. If you want to change it to another starting point, you can change the rulers' origin. Position the pointer over the upper-left corner of the rulers in the document window, and drag diagonally down onto the image. As you drag, a set of cross hairs appears, indicating the new origin on the rulers. To reset the ruler origin to its default position, double-click the upper-left corner of the rulers.

Examining the Undo History Palette

In the Editor, the Undo History palette helps you streamline the way you work in Photoshop Elements. As you work in Photoshop Elements, the Undo History palette is tracking all your actions for the entire document. With the Undo History palette, you can undo or redo actions to correct mistakes.

The Undo History palette doesn't replace the Undo and Redo commands on the Edit menu, it simply tracks every action you perform in Photoshop Elements. When you undo or redo one or more commands, the Undo History palette displays the results; the Undo/Redo slider moves according to the commands you select.

You can open the Undo History palette using the Window menu like any of the other palettes in Photoshop Elements. Each action you take in the active document during a work session (since you created or opened the document) appears on a separate line in the Undo History palette. The first action you perform in a work session appears at the top of the list and the last action appears at the bottom. Unlike other palettes in Photoshop Elements, the Undo History palette includes a slider on the left side you can use to undo/redo actions; the Undo/Redo slider initially points to the last action you performed. The More button (shown with the text *More* or double arrows, depending on whether the palette is docked or undocked) displays commands, such as Clear Undo History, specific to the Undo History palette.

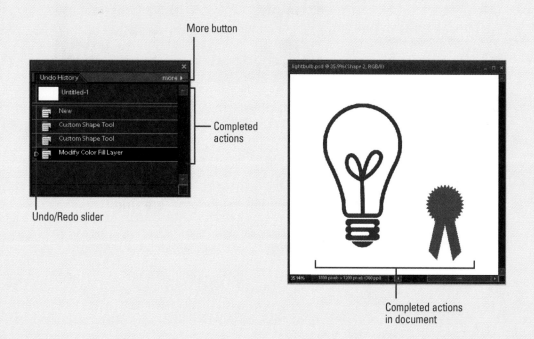

More button

Completed actions

Undo/Redo slider

Completed actions in document

Using the Undo History Palette

You can use the Window menu to open/display the Undo History palette like any of the other palettes in Photoshop Elements. Each action you take in the active document during a work session appears on a separate line in the Undo History palette. Actions you take in other Photoshop Elements documents don't appear in other Undo History palette lists. If you no longer need the actions in the Undo History palette, you can delete an individual action or the entire list. When you close a document, Photoshop Elements clears the Undo History palette.

Use the Undo History Palette

◆ **Open or Close Undo History Palette.** In the Editor, click the **Window** menu, and then click **Undo History**.

◆ **Delete an Item in the Undo History Palette.** In the Editor, display the Undo History palette, select the item you want to remove, click the **More** button, and then click **Delete**.

◆ **Delete All Items in the Undo History Palette.** In the Editor, display the Undo History palette, click the **More** button, and then click **Clear Undo History**.

Close button

Undo History	more ▶

Untitled-1

New

Custom Shape Tool

Custom Shape Tool

Modify Color Fill Layer

Undoing and Redoing with the Undo History Palette

You can undo or redo a single action or series of actions quickly with the Undo History palette. The Undo History palette contains the Undo/Redo slider which you can drag up to undo (restore previous actions) a series of actions, or drag down to redo (restore actions you've undone) a series of actions. You can also undo and redo previous actions one at a time using the Undo and Redo commands on the Edit menu or Shortcuts bar. When you use these commands, the actions in the Undo History palette change based on the command results. The Undo History palette and the Undo command can undo actions up to a maximum number (from 2 to 1000) set in the Performance tab of the Preferences dialog box.

Undo Actions with the Undo History Palette

1. In the Editor, display the **Undo History** palette.

2. Click the action name or drag the **Undo/Redo** slider up until the slider points to the last action you want to keep.

   Photoshop Elements undos and grays out each selected action, starting from the bottom.

3. When you're done, close the Undo History palette.

Did You Know?

You can undo actions using the Undo command. Click the Edit menu, and then click Undo, or press Ctrl+Z.

See Also

See "Examining the Undo History Palette" on page 166 for information on different elements in the Undo History palette.

Drawn shape removed with undo.

Redo Actions with the Undo History Palette

1 In the Editor, display the **Undo History** palette.

2 Click the action name or drag the **Undo/Redo** slider down until the slider points to the last action you want to redo.

Photoshop Elements redoes and removes the gray highlighting for each selected action.

3 When you're done, close the Undo History palette.

Did You Know?

You can redo actions using the Redo command. Click the Edit menu, and then click Redo, or press Ctrl+Y.

You can change the number of undo levels for the Undo command. In the Editor, click the Edit menu, click Preferences, click the Performance tab, enter a number (from 2 to 1000) in the Undo Level box, and then click OK.

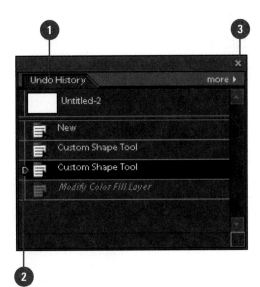

For Your Information

Performing Multiple Undos

The History palette represents the ability to perform multiple undo commands as many as you choose for your History States. However, when you press Ctrl+Z you only move back and forth between the last command, just like a normal undo. To perform multiple undo commands press Ctrl+Shift+Z to move forward through all your History steps, or press Alt+Shift+Z to move backwards through the available History steps.

Clearing Memory and the Undo History Palette

As you work with photos, the contents of the Clipboard and the Undo History palette can start to take up a lot of memory (RAM), which can start to slow down your computer. If you have 1 GB of RAM or more, this shouldn't be a problem. However, if you have 512 MG or less, it could be a problem. To avoid memory problems, you can clear Clipboard contents and the entire Undo History palette. When you close a document, Photoshop Elements clears the Undo History palette, while the Clipboard remains the same until you clear its contents.

Clear Memory and the Undo History Palette

◆ **Clear Clipboard Memory.** In the Editor, click the **Edit** menu, point to **Clear**, and then click **Clipboard Contents**.

◆ **Clear Undo History Palette Memory.** In the Editor, click the **Edit** menu, point to **Clear**, and then click **Undo History**.

> **TIMESAVER** *In the Editor, click the Undo History palette More button, and then click Clear Undo History to clear Undo History palette memory.*

◆ **Clear Clipboard and Undo History Palette Memory.** In the Editor, click the **Edit** menu, point to **Clear**, and then click **All**.

Clear Clipboard contents or Undo History

Using the Status Bar

To work efficiently in Photoshop Elements you need information about the active document. Details about the document's size, resolution, color mode, and current size all help in the design and preparation of the final photo. Photoshop Elements displays current information about the active document on the Status bar, located at the bottom of the document window.

Use the Status Bar

1 In the Editor, click the **black triangle** near the Status bar info box, and then select from the following options:

- **Document Sizes.** The left number indicates the flattened size of the photo file, and the right number indicates the size of the open file, based on layers and options.

- **Document Profile.** Displays information on the color profile assigned to the document.

- **Document Dimensions.** Represents the width and height of the photo.

- **Scratch Sizes.** The left number indicates the scratch disk space required by Photoshop Elements, and the right number indicates the available scratch disk space.

- **Efficiency.** Displays a percentage that represents Photoshop Elements' efficiency based on available RAM and scratch disk space.

- **Timing.** Records the amount of time required to perform the last command or adjustment.

- **Current Tool.** Displays the current tool.

Click black triangle here

Working with Guides

Use Guides from a Photoshop File

1. In the Editor, open a Photoshop file with guides.

2. Drag one or more objects to a guide to align them.

3. To have the object snap to a guide line, click the **View** menu, point to **Snap To**, and then click **Guide**.

   As you drag close to a guide line, the object snaps to the guide line.

   ◆ A check mark appears next to the Guide option when the Snap To feature is enabled, while no check mark appears when the option is disabled.

A guide is a vertical or horizontal line that appears in a document window you can use to align objects. The grid is useful in designing a layout that is proportional and balanced. If you have a Photoshop file with guides present, you can view and use them in Photoshop Elements. Unfortunately, you can't add or move them in Photoshop Elements. You can also use the Snap To option with the guide to enable objects to snap to a guide line when they get close it.

Viewing Notes

Notes can be found everywhere—you see them stuck to the side of refrigerators, bulletin boards, and even covering your computer monitor. Notes serve a purpose to remind you of important duties and events. If you work in Photoshop, the ability to save notes can help you remember an important part of the design, or they can instruct another designer to the how's and why's of your document. If you have a Photoshop file with notes, you can view and delete them in Photoshop Elements. Unfortunately, you can't add them.

View a Note from a Photoshop File

1. In the Editor, open a Photoshop file with a note.

2. Click the **View** menu, and then click **Annotations**.

3. Double-click a note icon to see its contents.

4. Read the text for your note.

   TIMESAVER *Double-click the note icon to open and close a note. You can also right-click a note icon to access a shortcut menu with note commands.*

5. Click the **Close** button.

6. Click on the active document to create a new blank note.

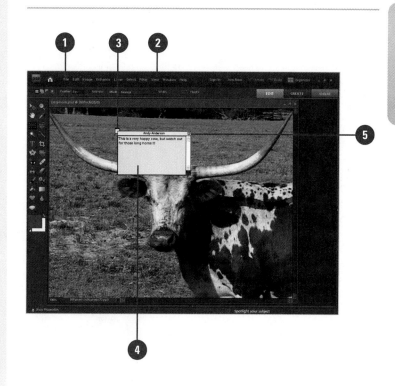

Working with Notes

Action	Keystrokes
Collapse a note	Click the Close button in the upper right-hand corner of the note.
Reopen a note	Double-click on the Note icon.
Delete a note	Select the note icon, and then press Delete.

Listen to an Audio Annotation

In addition to text notes, Photoshop lets you create audio notes. To create an audio note, your computer needs to have the ability to record sound. The good news is that most computers sold today, especially laptops, have the ability to record sound. Besides being an excellent way to communicate information, audio annotations give a sense of emotion or urgency, which sometimes can't be communicated using the written word. If you have a Photoshop file with audio annotations, you can view and delete them in Photoshop Elements. Unfortunately, you can't create them. Audio notes require that the receiving computer has an audio output, and while this might seem quite common with today's technology, you might want to include a text note along with the audio note.

Listen to an Audio Annotation from a Photoshop File

1. In the Editor, open a Photoshop file with an audio annotation.

2. Click the **View** menu, and then click **Annotations**.

3. Double-click the **Audio Annotation** button to play the new message.

   IMPORTANT *Notes and Audio Annotations are not contained on a specific layer; they are part of the Photoshop document and therefore visible in the document window at all times.*

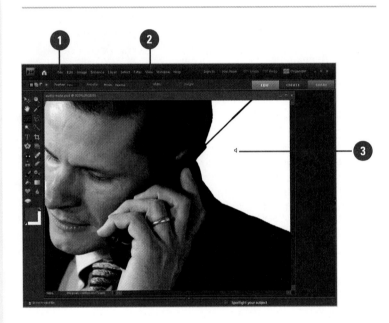

Did You Know?

You can delete an audio annotation. Click on the speaker symbol, and then press the Backspace key.

Mastering the Art of Selection

Introduction

Mastering the Editor in Photoshop Elements requires skill in many diverse areas. While modifying an image's color, enhancing an old photograph, removing dust and scratches, may require different skills, they have one common thread—selection. Without selection, Photoshop Elements gives you total access to the active document. If you choose to paint a black stroke, select the Paint Brush tool, the color black, and begin painting. Photoshop Elements will let you apply black paint to any portion of the image. Selection is your way to instruct Photoshop Elements what portions of the active document you want to change.

The Marquee tools are considered Photoshop Elements' "good old" selection tools. In fact they've been a part of Photoshop Elements since the early days. Where the Marquee tools let you select areas of an image in a structured way (squares, circles, lines), the Lasso tools add a bit of freeform selection to the mix. Lasso tools require a certain amount of hand/eye coordination. For example, you can use the Lasso tool to create a customized selection area around just about any object in a document, be it an animal, vegetable, or mineral. It just requires a good eye, a steady hand, and a really big mouse pad (I hate it when I run out of mouse pad).

Selection lets you influence a specific area of the image, for example, changing the color of a car from red to blue. This is where selection really shows its strength. When you select an area of a document, the selection becomes the work area-filters, adjustments, and brushes will only work within the selection boundary. Since selection is such an important aspect of controlling what happens in a document, Photoshop Elements gives you many ways to create your desired selection. Mastering the art of selection gives you control over not just what you do, but where you do it.

What You'll Do

Use the Rectangular Marquee Tool

Use the Elliptical Marquee Tool

Use the Lasso Marquee Tool

Use the Magnetic Lasso Tool

Use the Polygonal Lasso Tool

Use the Quick Selection Tool

Use the Magic Wand Tool

Use the Selection Brush Tool

Use the Magic Extractor

Refine a Selection Edge

Modify and Change an Existing Selection

Add, Subtract, and Crop a Selection

Save Selections

Load and Delete Saved Selections

Copy and Paste Selections

Move Selections

Using the Rectangular Marquee Tool

The Rectangular Marquee tool lets you create rectangular and square selection marquees. The Rectangular Marquee tool is excellent for a quick crop, or selecting and moving blocks of image information. Select the Rectangular Marquee tool on the toolbox from the available Marquee options, and then drag the tool using the mouse (or drawing tablet) to control your movements. To further control a selection, hold down the Shift key to produce a perfect square, and hold down the Alt key to create a selection marquee from center out. Releasing the mouse instructs the Rectangular Marquee tool to create the selection.

Use the Rectangular Marquee Tool

1. In the Editor, select the **Rectangular Marquee** tool on the toolbox.

2. Use the selection options on the Options bar to create a new selection, or add to, subtract from, or intersect with an existing selection.

3. Enter a numerical value (0 to 250) in the Feather box to create a feathered selection edge.

4. Click the **Style** list arrow, and then select from the available styles:

   ◆ **Normal.** Lets you create freeform rectangular, or square marquee selections.

   ◆ **Fixed Aspect Ratio.** Lets you create selections using a specific ratio, such as a 2 to 1 ratio. Enter the Fixed Aspect Ratio values in the Width and Height boxes.

   ◆ **Fixed Size.** Lets you create selections based on an absolute size such as 30 pixels by 90 pixels. Enter the Fixed Size values in the Width and Height boxes.

5. Drag the selection area you want.

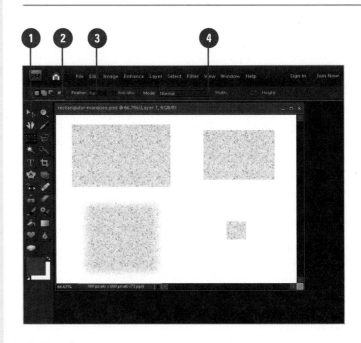

Using the Elliptical Marquee Tool

The Elliptical Marquee tool lets you create oval or circular selection marquees. When used with the Layer Mask option, and a couple of creative filters, you can create some awesome vignettes. Select the Elliptical Marquee tool on the toolbox from the available Marquee options, move into the document, and then drag the tool using the mouse to control your movements. To further control a selection, hold down the Shift key to produce a perfect circle, and hold down the Alt key to create a selection marquee from center out. Releasing the mouse instructs the Elliptical Marquee tool to create the selection.

Use the Elliptical Marquee Tool

1. In the Editor, select the **Elliptical Marquee** tool on the toolbox.

2. Use the selection options on the Options bar to create a new selection, or add, subtract, or intersect an existing selection.

3. Enter a numerical value (0 to 250) in the Feather option to create a feathered selection edge.

4. Select the **Anti-alias** check box to create a softer selection.

5. Click the **Style** list arrow, and then select from the available styles:

   - **Normal.** Lets you create freeform elliptical, or circular marquee selections.

   - **Fixed Aspect Ratio.** Lets you create selections using a specific ratio, such as a 1 to 1 ratio (perfect circle). Enter the Fixed Aspect Ratio values in the Width and Height boxes.

   - **Fixed Size.** Lets you create selections based on an absolute size, such as 100 pixels by 200 pixels (oval). Enter the Fixed Size values in the Width and Height boxes.

6. Drag the selection area you want.

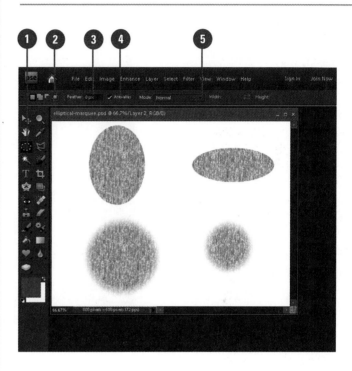

Using the Lasso Marquee Tool

The Lasso Marquee is a freeform tool that requires a bit of hand-to-eye coordination. Select the Lasso tool on the toolbox from the available Lasso options, move into the active document, and then drag the tool, using the mouse (or drawing tablet) to control your movements. Hold down the Alt key, and then drag to draw straight-line segments (called the Polygonal Lasso tool). Releasing the mouse instructs the Lasso tool to close the selection shape. That's all there is to it. I did mention that it requires good hand-to-eye coordination, didn't I? When you use this tool, don't drink too much coffee, and have a really big mouse pad.

Use the Lasso Marquee Tool

1. In the Editor, select the **Lasso** tool on the toolbox.

2. Use the selection options on the Options bar to create a new selection, or add, subtract or intersect an existing selection.

3. Enter a numerical value (0 to 250) in the Feather box to create a feathered selection edge.

4. Select the **Anti-alias** check box to create a softer selection (useful with intensely rounded or curved selections).

5. Drag the selection area you want.

   ◆ Drag to the beginning point to complete the selection.

   ◆ Release the mouse during the drag to have Photoshop Elements complete the selection to the beginning point.

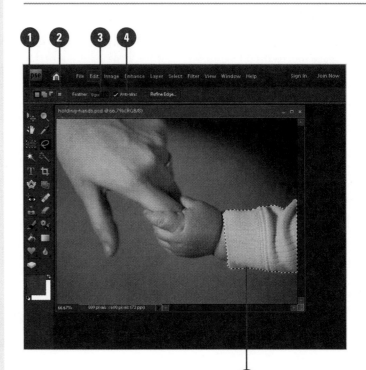

Did You Know?

You can deselect a selection. Click outside the selection, press Ctrl+D, or click the Select menu, and then click Deselect.

Use the Lasso Marquee Tool with the Polygonal Lasso Tool

1. In the Editor, select the **Lasso** tool on the toolbox.

2. Use the selection options on the Options bar to create a new selection, or add, subtract or intersect an existing selection.

3. Enter a numerical value (0 to 250) in the Feather box to create a feathered selection edge.

4. Select the **Anti-alias** check box to create a softer selection (useful with intensely rounded or curved selections).

5. Drag the selection area you want.

6. Hold down the Alt key, and the release the mouse.

7. Continue to hold down the Alt key, move to a different area of the window, and then click to draw a straight line between the two points.

8. Complete the selection using either of the following methods:

   ◆ Drag and release the mouse to the beginning point to complete the selection.

   ◆ Release the mouse to have Photoshop Elements complete the selection to the beginning point.

See Also

See "Using the Polygonal Lasso Tool" on page 182 for information on using the polygonal selection tool.

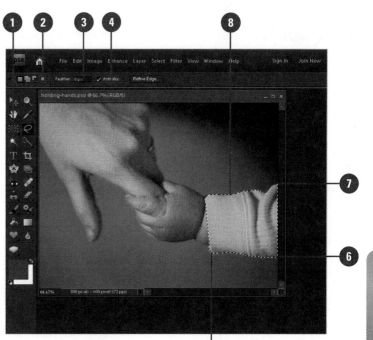

Using the Magnetic Lasso Tool

The Magnetic Lasso creates a selection by following along the edge of a visible object. For example, it will follow around the edge of a building that contrasts against a bright blue sky. In reality there are no edges in a photographic document, so the tool follows along the shifts of brightness created when one image interacts with another. Select the Magnetic Lasso tool on the toolbox from the available Lasso options. Click on the visible edge of an image, and then move (don't drag) abound the object. The Magnetic Lasso will follow the visible edge of the object; occasionally adding anchor points to the line as you move. Double-clicking the mouse instructs the Magnetic Lasso tool to close the selection shape.

Use the Magnetic Lasso Tool

1. In the Editor, select the **Magnetic Lasso** tool on the toolbox.

2. Use the selection options on the Options bar to create a new selection, or add, subtract or intersect an existing selection.

3. Enter a numerical value (0 to 250) in the Feather box to create a feathered selection edge.

4. Select the **Anti-alias** check box to create a softer selection (useful with intensely rounded or curved selections).

5. Enter a Width value (0 to 256) to instruct the Magnetic Lasso tool how many pixels to consider for the edge.

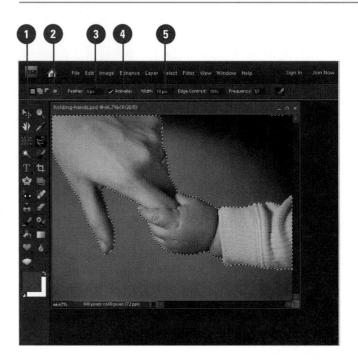

6. Enter an Edge Contrast value (0 to 100) to instruct the Magnetic Lasso how much of a shift in the brightness values to use in determining the edge.

7. Enter a Frequency value (0 to 100) to instruct the Magnetic Lasso where points are added to the selection line.

8. Click once to create an anchor point, and then move the pointer along the edge you want to trace.

9. If the border doesn't snap to the desired edge, click once to add a anchor point manually. Continue to trace the edge, and add anchor points as needed.

10. Double-click or click the starting point to complete the selection.

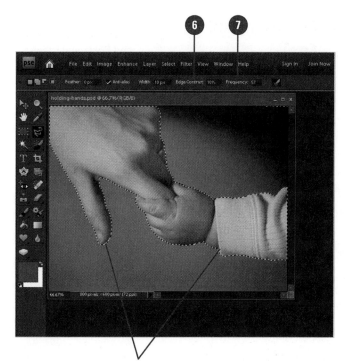

Magnetic Lasso selection

Did You Know?

You can remove anchor points. When you're using the Magnetic Lasso tool and you want to reverse the selection, simply back track the mouse all the way back to the last anchor point. To move even farther backwards, press the Backspace key to remove the last anchor.

You can temporally use the Magnetic Lasso tool as a freeform Lasso tool. Hold down the Alt key, and then drag to draw. Release the mouse to return to the Magnetic Lasso tool.

Using the Polygonal Lasso Tool

The Polygonal Lasso creates straight-line selections. Perfect for creating a selection around a windowpane, or the roofline of a house. Select the Polygonal Lasso tool on the toolbox from the available Lasso options, and click to create a point; then move and click to create straight lines between the two points. Keep clicking and moving your mouse until the desired selection shape appears. Double-clicking the mouse instructs the Polygonal Lasso tool to close the selection shape.

Use the Polygonal Lasso Tool

1. In the Editor, select the **Polygonal Lasso** tool on the toolbox.

2. Use the selection options on the Options bar to create a new selection, or add, subtract or intersect an existing selection.

3. Enter a numerical value (0 to 250) in the Feather box to create a feathered selection edge.

4. Select the **Anti-alias** check box to create a softer selection (useful with intensely rounded or curved selections).

5. Click to create anchor points, and then double-click or click the starting point to complete the selection.

Did You Know?

You can temporally use the Polygonal Lasso tool as a freeform Lasso tool. Hold down the Alt key, and then drag to draw. Release the mouse to return to the Polygonal Lasso tool.

Using the Quick Selection Tool

The Quick Selection tool makes it easier to select the areas of an image you want. Simply paint a loose selection using an adjustable round brush tip to select the area you want. As you paint with the Quick Selection tool, the selection expands outward and automatically finds and follows defined edges in the image. You can also enable the Auto-Enhance option to reduce roughness and blockiness in the selection edge.

Use the Quick Selection Tool

1. In the Editor, select the **Quick Selection** tool on the toolbox.

2. Use the selection options on the Options bar to create a new selection, or add or subtract an existing selection.

3. Click the **Brush** list arrow, and then select the brush options you want: Diameter, Hardness, Spacing, and Size.

4. Select the **All Layers** check box to create a selection based on all layers, not just the currently selected one.

5. Select the **Auto-Enhance** check box to reduce roughness and blockiness in the selection edge.

6. Paint the selection you want.

   TIMESAVER *Press the right bracket (]) or left bracket ([) to increase or decrease size of the Quick Selection tool brush tip.*

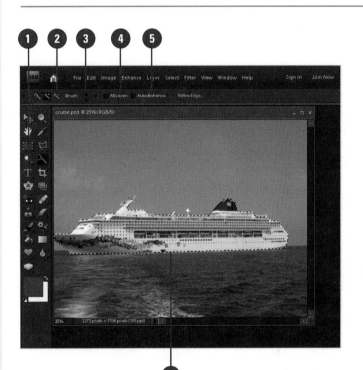

Using the Magic Wand Tool

The Magic Wand tool (so named since it appears like a magic wand) is unique in the fact that you do not drag and select with this tool, you simply click. The Magic Wand tool creates a selection based on the shift in brightness range within an image. If there is a definable shift in the brightness of the pixels, it can be a very powerful tool for the selection of odd shaped areas. For example, a bright colored sunflower contrasted with a bright blue sky would be a snap for the Magic Wand tool. To use the Magic Wand, click on the Magic Wand Tool button on the toolbox. Sometimes it's easier to select what you don't want. In this example, the blue sky was selected and removed. However, you might have wanted to select the sunflower, and move it into another image. If that's the case, it was still easier to select the sky using the Magic Wand, clicking the Select menu, and then clicking Inverse to reverse the selection.

Use the Magic Wand Tool

1. In the Editor, select the **Magic Wand** tool on the toolbox.

2. Use the selection options on the Options bar to create a new selection, or add, subtract or intersect an existing selection.

3. Enter a Tolerance value (0 to 255). The higher the value the more information the Magic Wand tool selects.

4. Select the **Anti-alias** check box to create a softer selection (useful with intensely rounded or curved selections).

5. Select the **Contiguous** check box to select adjacent pixels within the active document.

6. Select the **All Layers** check box to sample image information from all layers.

7. Click an area to make a selection.

Using the Selection Brush Tool

With the Selection Brush tool, you can paint over an area to select it or paint over an area you don't want to select. The Selection Brush tool uses two modes: Selection and Mask. Selection mode allows you to paint over areas to make a selection, while Mask mode allows you to paint over areas you don't want to make a selection. You can make a rough selection using another selection tool, and then add to the selection using the Selection Brush tool in Selection mode, or subtract from it using the Mask mode.

Use the Selection Brush Tool

1. In the Editor, select the **Selection Brush** tool on the toolbox.

2. Click the **Add to Selection** or **Subtract from Selection** button on the Options bar.

3. Select any of the following options on the Options bar:

   ◆ **Preset Brushes.** Click the **Brush Presets** list arrow, click the **Brushes** list arrow, select a brush type, and then select the brush you want.

   ◆ **Brush Size.** Click the **Brush Size** list arrow, and then select the brush size you want.

4. Click the **Mode** list arrow, and then click **Selection** (to add to the selection) or **Mask** (to subtract from the selection).

   If you select Mask mode, specify an Overlay Opacity, and an Overlay Color.

5. Click the **Hardness** list arrow, and then drag the slide to specify a percentage.

6. Draw in your photo to select or deselect areas.

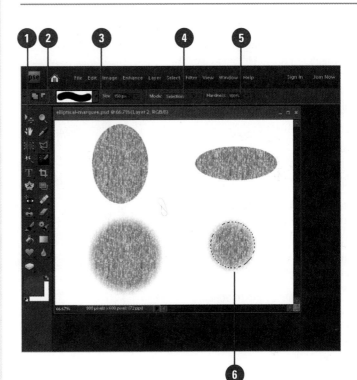

Using the Magic Extractor

The Magic Extractor makes it easy to select people or objects, so you can use them in other photos on different backgrounds. For example, you can remove yourself from an individual photo and then place it on a group photo. You can save the extracted image as a file, so you can use it in other photos. The Magic Extractor makes selections based on the foreground and background areas of a photo. You make selections by placing colored marks in the areas you want to select. After you mark the areas, only the foreground area appears in the photo in the Editor.

Use the Magic Extractor

1. In the Editor, click the **Oval** or **Rectangular** tool on the toolbox, and then make an initial selection if you want to limit what takes place in the Magic Extractor.

2. Click the **Image** menu, and then click **Magic Selector**.

   The Magic Extractor dialog box appears.

3. Select the **Foreground Brush** tool, if necessary.

4. Click multiple times or draw lines to mark the area you want to extract.

   ◆ To help mark your selection, use the **Zoom** tool or **Hand** tool to magnify and navigate the photo.

   ◆ To use a different brush color or size, select a size from the **Brush Size** list arrow, or click the **Foreground** or **Background Color** box, click a color, and then click **OK**.

5. Select the **Background Brush** tool.

6. Click multiple times or draw lines to mark the area you don't want to include in the selection.

   With objects with varied colors and textures, drag across all the colors and textures to create the best selection.

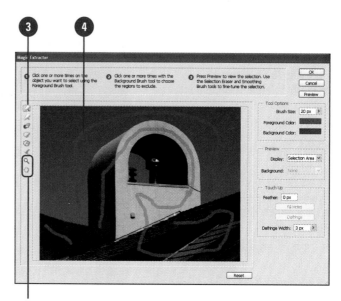

Zoom and Hand tool

7 To view the current selection, click **Preview**.

◆ **Display.** Click to display the preview with the selection area or original photo.

◆ **Background.** Click to select a different background.

8 Use any of the following options to fine-tune the selection:

◆ **Add or Subtract from Selection.** Select the **Foreground Brush** tool or **Background Brush** tool, and then draw more marks.

◆ **Erase Foreground or Background Marks.** Select the **Point Eraser** tool, and then click or drag over marks.

◆ **Add to Selection.** Select the **Add to Selection** tool, and then click or drag over areas.

◆ **Subtract from Selection.** Select the **Subtract from Selection** tool, and then click or drag over areas.

◆ **Smooth Edges.** Select the **Smoothing Brush** tool, and then drag over areas.

◆ **Soften Selection Edges.** Specify a higher value in the Feather box.

◆ **Fill Holes.** Click **Fill Holes** to fill remaining holes in the main selection.

◆ **Remove Fringe Colors.** Click **Defringe** to remove fringe colors left between the foreground and background. Specify the amount of defringe.

9 To reset everything to start over, click **Reset**.

10 Click **OK** to extract the selected area or click **Cancel** to dismiss the changes.

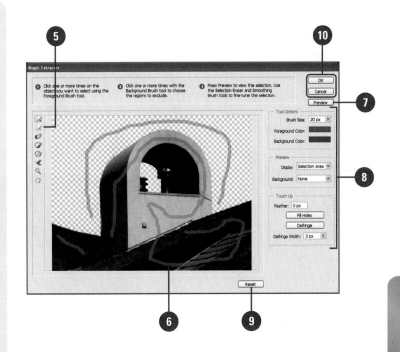

Refining a Selection Edge

After you make the initial selection, you can use the Refine Edge dialog to fine-tune the selection to your exact specifications. The Refine Edge feature allows you to adjust the selection using the following options: Smooth, Feather, and Contract/Expand. You can also change the view mode to preview the selection against different backgrounds.

Use the Refine Edge Tool

1. In the Editor, use one of the selection tools to make a selection.

2. Click **Refine Edge** on the Options bar, or click the **Select** menu, and then click **Refine Edge**.

3. Select the **Preview** check box to preview changes.

4. Drag the sliders to adjust the selection.

   ◆ **Smooth.** Smooths out the rough edges of the selection (from 0 to 100).

   ◆ **Feather.** Creates a soft edge around the selection boundary (from 0 to 250 pixels).

   ◆ **Contract/Expand.** Decreases or increases the selection edge.

5. To change the view modes, click a Selection View icon.

   A description appears below the view mode. Click the **Description** button, if necessary.

   ◆ Double-click the Quick Mask view to change the color mask.

6. Use the **Zoom** or **Hand** tools to change the view size or position.

7. Click **OK**.

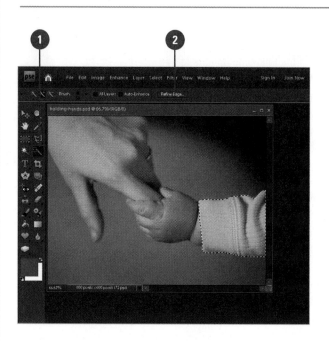

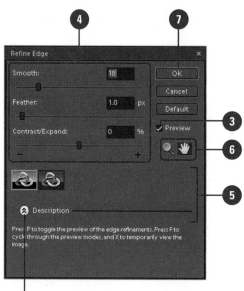

Description button

Modifying an Existing Selection

Selections can be as simple as dragging a circle or square with one of the marquee tools to a more complicated freeform selection. Whatever the case, Photoshop Elements allows you to enhance any selection with its useful modification tools. After creating a selection, you can modify it with the various options that Photoshop Elements offers in order to make complex selections easier to use. With selection being an important part of the process, practice is the key to success.

Modify an Existing Selection

① With a selection in the Editor, click the **Select** menu, and then select an option:

◆ **All.** Selects all pixels within the active document.

◆ **Deselect or Reselect.** Clears the current selection or recreates the last selection.

◆ **Reselect or Inverse.** Lets you select or reverse the previous selection.

◆ **All Layers.** Lets you select all the layers in the Layers palette (excluding the Background).

◆ **Deselect Layers.** Deselects all layers in the Layers palette.

◆ **Similar Layers.** Selects similar layers such as: all type layers, or all shape layers.

◆ **Feather.** Creates a visually softer selection edge.

◆ **Modify.** Lets you create a selection encompassing only the edges of the current selection, expand the selection, contract it, or smooth its edges.

◆ **Grow.** Lets you increase a selection by adding pixels.

◆ **Similar.** Lets you increase a selection by adding non-contiguous pixels.

◆ **Load, Save, and Delete Selection.** Lets you load, save or delete a previously saved selection.

Selection

Available selection options

Changing an Existing Selection

You can use several commands to change an existing selection to meet your exact needs. You can use the Expand and Contract commands to increase or decrease the size of an existing section. The Border command adds a new selection border around an existing selection. The new soft-edged, anti-aliased selection border appears based on the thickness you specify in pixels. The border selection consists of only the pixels between the two selection borders. The Smooth command finds and removes stray pixels within a color range, while the Similar command find and includes similar colors in a selection.

Expand or Contract a Selection

1. In the Editor, create a selection using any of the selection tools.

2. Click the **Select** menu, point to **Modify**, and then click **Expand** or **Contract**.

3. Enter a pixel value between 1 and 100.

4. Click **OK**.

   Any portion of the selection border that touches the edge is unchanged.

Frame a Selection with a New Selection Border

1. In the Editor, create a selection using any of the selection tools.

2. Click the **Select** menu, point to **Modify**, and then click **Border**.

3. Enter a pixel value between 1 and 200.

4. Click **OK**.

Expand selection

Contract selection

Remove Pixels from a Color Selection

 1 In the Editor, create a selection using any of the selection tools.

2 Click the **Select** menu, point to **Modify**, and then click **Smooth**.

3 Enter a pixel value for Sample Radius between 1 and 100.

4 Click **OK**.

Add Similar Color to a Selection

1 In the Editor, create a selection using any of the selection tools.

2 Click the **Select** menu, and then click **Similar**.

The selection includes pixels throughout the photos (not just adjacent ones) within the tolerance range specified in the Options bar. A higher tolerance value adds a broader range of colors.

◆ To include only adjacent pixels within the tolerance range, click the **Select** menu, and then click **Grow**.

3 To increase the selection, use the Similar or Grow commands again.

Adding, Subtracting, and Cropping a Selection

To say that Photoshop Elements will help you make selections easy would be an understatement. Not only can you modify selections in any number of ways, Photoshop Elements gives you the option to change your mind by adding and subtracting to an existing selection or even using the selection tools to crop the image. Since most selections are not perfect the first time around, knowing how to modify a selection marquee gives you the control you need to make perfect selections. Adding and subtracting to an image is accomplished by simple keyboard shortcuts, or items on the Options bar. Either way you can create complex selections with ease.

Add to an Existing Selection

1 In the Editor, create a selection using any of the selection tools.

2 Add to the selection by holding down the Shift key, and then use a selection tool to add to the existing selection (the selected areas do not need to be contiguous).

3 Release the mouse and the Shift key to complete the addition.

Two separate selections

Subtract from an Existing Selection

1 In the Editor, create a selection using any of the selection tools.

2 Subtract from the selection by holding down the Alt key.

3 Create a selection that intersects with the existing selection.

4 Release the mouse and the Shift key to complete the subtraction.

Crop an Image

 1 In the Editor, create a selection using any of the selection tools.

The selection area does not have to be a rectangle.

2 Click the **Image** menu, and then click **Crop** to crop the image.

Did You Know?

Cropping an image brings focus. Cropping a document brings focus to the information contained within the image. For example, if you take a photograph of someone standing in front of a building. Is the focus the building or the person? If the focus is the person, then crop out the building. Cropping eliminates distractions, which would otherwise take away from the message of the image. A picture may be worth a thousand words; however, sometimes a picture can say too much.

Image cropped

For Your Information

Cropping an Image with a User-Defined Shape

You can crop an image using a user-defined shape, such as a heart. Open the image you want to crop. Select the Custom Shape tool from the toolbox. Choose the desired raster shape on the Options Bar. Create a new layer directly above the image layer, and use the Custom Shape tool to draw the cropping shape. Select the Move tool and place the shape directly over the area of the image you want to crop. In the Layers palette, drag the shape layer directly under the image layer. The shape disappears, but that's fine. Move your cursor into the Layers palette (cursor changes to a hand with an extended finger) until the tip of the finger is touching the line separating the image layer from the shape layer. Hold down the Alt key (cursor changes to a double-circle), and then click. You created a clipping group, and your image is cropped into the shape. If you don't like the position of the crop, select the shape layer, and use the Move tool. To make the crop permanent, hide all layers except the shape and image layers, click the Options button on the Layers palette, and then click Merge Visible or Merge Clipping Group.

Saving Selections

Photoshop Elements' primary method of creating selections is through the use of tools on the toolbox, such as the Marquee, Lasso, and Magic Wand, and while they create impressive and complex selections, Photoshop Elements has other ways to capture and save that tricky selection. You can save a selection and then load it at a later time to work on a photo. If you have already saved a selection and want to modify it, you can save an existing selection with an added, subtracted, or intersected sections.

Save a New Selection

1 In the Editor, open the photo you want to change.

2 Make the selection you want to save.

3 Click the **Select** menu, and then click **Save Selection**.

4 Click the **Selection** list arrow, and then click **New**.

5 Type a name for the selection.

6 Click the **New Selection** option.

7 Click **OK**.

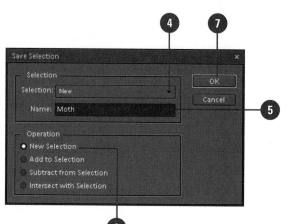

Modify a Saved Selection

1. In the Editor, open the photo you want to change.

2. Make the selection you want to save.

3. Click the **Select** menu, and then click **Save Selection**.

4. Click the **Selection** list arrow, and then click the selection you want to modify.

5. Select the Operation option you want:

   ◆ **Replace Selection.** Replaces the saved selection with current selection.

   ◆ **Add to Selection.** Adds the current selection to the saved selection.

   ◆ **Subtract from Selection.** Subtracts the current selection from the saved selection.

   ◆ **Intersect with Selection.** Replaces the saved selection with the intersection between the current selection and the saved selection.

6. Click **OK**.

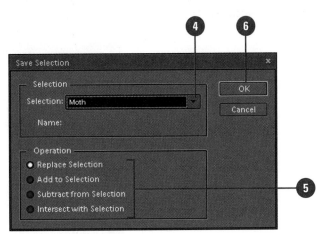

Loading and Deleting Saved Selections

After you save a selection, you can load it at a later time to work on a photo. If you have already saved a selection and want to modify it with a new selection, you can load the saved selection and then add, subtract, or intersect a new section. After you're done with a saved selection, you can delete it.

Load a Saved Selection

1. In the Editor, click the **Select** menu, and then click **Load Selection**.

2. Click the **Selection** list arrow, and then select the saved selection you want to load.

3. Select the **Invert** check box to invert the loaded selection.

4. Click **OK**.

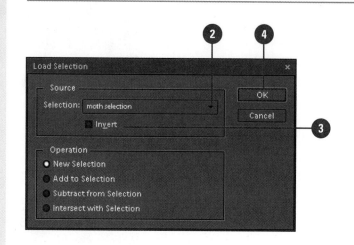

Loaded selection

Delete a Saved Selection

1. In the Editor, click the **Select** menu, and then click **Delete Selection**.

2. Select the saved selection you want to remove.

3. Click **OK**.

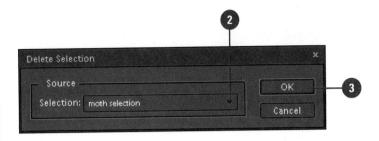

Modify a New Selection with a Saved Selection

1. In the Editor, open the photo with the saved selection you want to change.

2. Make the selection you want to save.

3. Click the **Select** menu, and then click **Load Selection**.

4. Click the **Selection** list arrow, and then click the selection you want to modify.

5. Select the Operation option you want:

   ◆ **Replace Selection.** Replaces the saved selection with the current selection.

   ◆ **Add to Selection.** Adds the current selection to the saved selection.

   ◆ **Subtract from Selection.** Subtracts the current selection from the saved selection.

   ◆ **Intersect with Selection.** Replaces the saved selection with the intersection between the current selection and the saved selection.

6. Click **OK**.

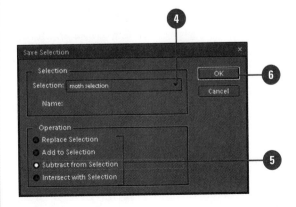

Copying and Pasting Selections

After you make a selection, you can use the Move tool and Copy and Paste commands to copy of all or a part of a photo in other photos. You can use the Move tool to quickly create a copy of a selection while you move it. In addition, you can use the Copy and Copy Merged commands to copy a selection or all layers of a selection to the Clipboard. After you copy a selection, you can use the Paste or Paste into Selection commands to place the copied selection where you want it. When you exit Photoshop Elements, anything you have stored in the Clipboard is erased unless you select the Export Clipboard check box in General Preferences for the Editor.

Copy a Selection with the Move Tool

1 In the Editor, create a selection using any of the selection tools.

2 Click the **Move** tool on the toolbox.

3 Press the Alt key, point inside the selection border, and then drag the selection to a new location.

◆ **Offset Copies.** To offset a copy by 1 pixel, hold down the Alt key and then press an arrow key. To offset a copy by 10 pixels, hold down the Alt+Shift keys and then press an arrow key.

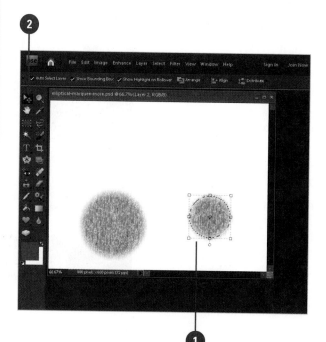

Offset copy

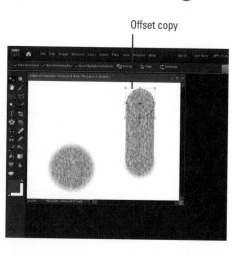

Copy and Paste a Selection with Menu Commands

1. In the Editor, create a selection using any of the selection tools.

2. Click the **Edit** menu, and then click one of the following commands:

   - **Copy.** Copies the selection to the Clipboard.

   - **Copy Merge.** Copies all layers in the selected area to the Clipboard.

   TIMESAVER *Press Shift+Ctrl+C to copy merge.*

3. To paste the contents of the Clipboard to a photo, display the photo, click the **Edit** menu, and then click **Paste**.

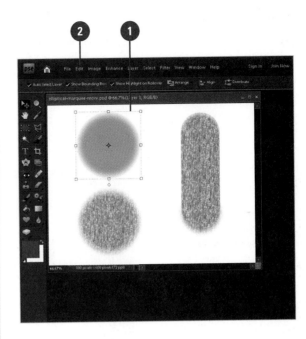

Paste a Selection into Another

1. In the Editor, create a selection using any of the selection tools.

2. Click the **Edit** menu, and then click **Copy**.

3. Create a selection in the photo in which you want to paste the copied selection.

4. Click the **Edit** menu, and then click **Paste into Selection**.

   TIMESAVER *Press Shift+Ctrl+V to paste into selection.*

5. Click the **Move** tool on the toolbox, point inside the selection border, and then drag the selection to a new location.

6. When you're done, deselect the pasted selection to accept the change.

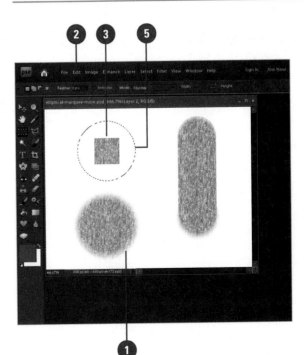

Moving Selections

The Move tool allows you to cut out a selection from one photo and place it in another area of the photo or an entirely different photo. You can simply drag a selection using the Move tool to complete the operation, or you can use additional options on the Options bar. These options include Auto Select Layer, Show Bounding Box, Show Highlight on Rollover, and the Arrange, Align, and Distribute menus.

Move a Selection

1. In the Editor, create a selection using any of the selection tools.

2. Click the **Move** tool on the toolbox.

3. Select the **Auto Select Layer** check box to automatically select the topmost layer where you point instead of the selected layer.

4. Select the **Show Bounding Box** check box to display the bound box around the selected item.

5. Select the **Show Highlight on Rollover** check box to highlight individual layers as the mouse hovers over the image.

6. Select any of the following options on the Options bar:

   ◆ **Arrange Menu.** Select a command to move the selected layer in a different stacking order.

   ◆ **Align Menu.** Select a command to align one or more layers left, center, right, top, middle or bottom.

   ◆ **Distribute Menu.** Select a command to space multiple layers apart to the left, center, right, top, middle, or bottom.

7. Point inside the selection border, and then drag the selection to a new location.

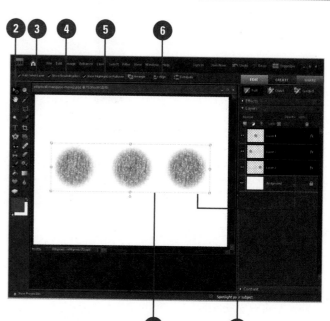

Layers selected

Working with Layers

Introduction

To be successful with Photoshop Elements, the single most important item you will need is control. You need control over color, control over the elements of the design, even control over what order design elements appear. If control is what you crave, then layers, more than any other single Photoshop Elements feature, help you gain control. Layers give you the ability to separate individual elements of your design, and then let you control how those elements appear. You can think of layers as transparency sheets one on top of the other. You can blend the elements of two or more layers, and even create layers to adjust and control contrast, brightness, and color balance. Layers are the digital designers canvas, and they are just as real as a stretched canvas is to a natural media designer. The strokes you apply to a real canvas, using a brush, appear as strokes in a layer when you use any of the painting tools. The natural artist uses oils, and watercolors; the Photoshop Elements artist uses electronic inks.

In Photoshop Elements, multiple layers are how you control the information within a document. There are times when you will create several layers, each with a piece of the document design. The multiple layers give you the ability to adjust and move each element. Eventually, during the course of the design, the multiple layers are no longer necessary. You don't want to link them together, or even place them within a folder; you'll want to combine them into a single unit. Once again, Photoshop Elements comes to the rescue by giving you several options for combining layers without flattening the entire document.

Understanding the Layers Palette

With the Layers palette, you can control elements of a design by assigning separate layers to each individual object. In addition, layer effects control the application of everything from drop shadows to gradient overlays, and adjustment layers let you control color overlays and image corrections. To access the Layers palette, select the Layers palette or, if the Layers palette is not visible, click the Windows menu, and then click Layers.

Blending Modes. Select this option to change how two or more layers interact or "blend" together.

Opacity. Select a value from 0 to 100 percent to change the opacity of the active layer.

Create New Layer. Click this button to create a new layer in the active document.

Create New Fill Or Adjustment Layer. Click this button, and then select from the available fill or adjustment layers.

Delete Layer. Click this button to delete the active layer.

Link Layers. Hold down the Shift key and click to select two or more layers, and then click this button to link the layers.

Lock options. Click the Lock Transparent Pixels or Lock All button.

Layers Options. Click this button to access a menu of layer specific commands.

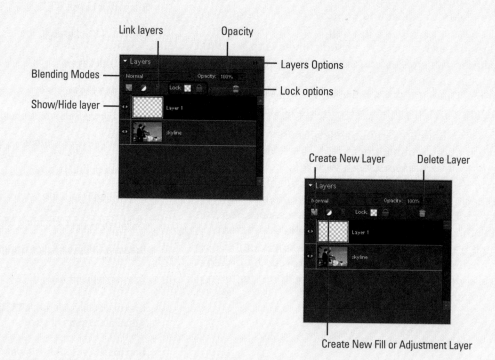

Link layers   Opacity

Blending Modes

Layers Options

Lock options

Show/Hide layer

Create New Layer   Delete Layer

Create New Fill or Adjustment Layer

Defining Layer Designations and Attributes

Not only does Photoshop Elements give you the ability to generate layers, it gives you the ability to generate layers with different designations. The designation of a layer determines the type of information the layer contains. For example, type layers hold editable text, and a mask layer holds image masks. The ability to control the designation of a layer helps to organize the different elements that typically make up an image.

Background. The Background is a unique type of layer element (technically, it's not called the Background layer; just the Background). Backgrounds are always positioned at the bottom of the layer stack and they cannot be moved. In addition, the Background does not support transparency.

Layer. Clicking the Create New Layer button creates layers. New layers are always inserted directly above the active layer. Traditional layers support all of the Editor's drawing and shape tools, opacity and fill and blending mode options, but do not support type. Traditional layers can be moved up and down in the layer stack by dragging.

Fill. Fill layers contain color gradients, solid colors, or patterns. To create a fill layer, click the Create New Fill Or Adjustment Layer button, and then select the fill type you want.

Type. Type layers control vector text. To create a type layer, select one of Editor's Type tools, click in the active document and begin typing. Photoshop Elements automatically creates the type layer directly above the active layer in the Layers palette.

Mask. Masks create transparent areas in the visible image. Use masks to remove elements of an image without physically erasing them.

Shape. Shape layers control vector data by the use of a vector mask. You can create a shape layer in one of several ways: Select the Pen tool from the toolbox, click the Shape Layer button (located on the Options bar, and then begin drawing, or select any of the Editor's Shape tools using the Shape layer option.

Adjustment. Adjustment layers let you control everything from contrast to color. To create an Adjustment layer, click the Create New Fill or Adjustment Layer button on the Layers palette, and then select from the available options. The adjustment layer is placed directly above the active layer, and controls the information in all the underlying layers.

Creating a New Layer

Layers give you control over the design elements of your document, so Photoshop Elements makes sure you have plenty of them. You have the ability to create up to 8,000 layers. While that may be more layers than you would ever use in one single document, it guarantees that you have the creative options to carry your designs to any level you desire. To create a new layer, you must first have an open document. A new image has a single layer. If you have more than one document open, make sure the active image is the one to which you want to add a layer. You can quickly add a layer using a menu or button or add a layer and select options using a dialog box. You can select options to name the layer, designate it as a clipping group, or even change its color blending mode and opacity.

Add Layers to an Active Document

① In the Editor, open a document and display the **Layers** palette.

② Click the **Create New Layer** button.

The new layer is inserted directly above the active layer with default name and settings, which is Normal mode with 100% opacity.

③ To rename the new layer, double-click the layer name in the Layers palette, type a name, and then click **OK**.

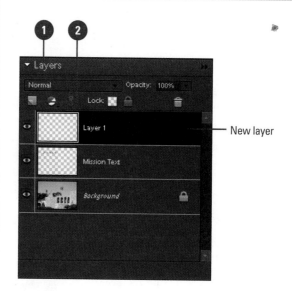

New layer

Did You Know?

You can move a layer in the stacking order. Press the Ctrl key, and then use the Left/Right Bracket keys ([ ]). The Left Bracket key moves the layer down and the Right Bracket key moves the layer up.

Add Layers and Select Options

1. In the Editor, open a document and display the **Layers** palette.

2. Click the **More Options** button, and then click **New Layer**.

   TIMESAVER *Hold down the Alt key, and then click the Create New Layer button to open the New Layer dialog box.*

3. Select the layer options you want:

   - **Name.** Enter the name of the layer into the Name box.

   - **Group With Previous Layer.** Select the check box to group the new layer with the previous layer in the Layers palette.

   - **Color.** This option lets you color-code your layers. Click the Color list arrow, and then select from the available colors.

   - **Mode.** Click the Mode list arrow, and then select from the available blending modes.

   - **Opacity.** This option controls the visibility of the new layer. Select a value from 0 to 100 percent.

4. Click **OK**.

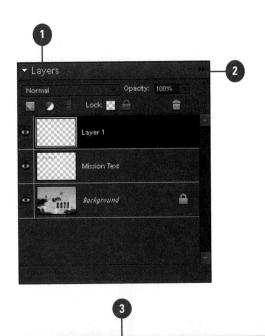

Did You Know?

You can control to what layers an adjustment is applied. To confine the effects of an adjustment layer to the layer immediately below, hold down the Alt key, and then click on the visible line separating the adjustment layer from the next lower layer.

For Your Information

Selecting Layer Options

When you create a new layer, the size of the file does not increase. It's only when you begin painting, or adding information to the layer that the size of the document will begin to grow. For example, creating a blank layer in a document with a file size of 10 MB does nothing to increase the size of the file. However, opening a 10 MB file, and creating a copy of the original document layer, will create a file size of 20 MB. Layers are great creative tools, but you only want to use them when you need them. Remember, performance is directly related to the size of the active document file, and the bigger the file size, the slower Photoshop Elements performs.

Selecting Layers

Photoshop Elements lets you select multiple layers either in the Layers palette, or directly in the document window, using the Move tool. Say, for example, you want to quickly move two or more layers but you don't want to spend the time linking and then unlinking them; you could quickly select the layers, and then perform the move. Or, perhaps you want to delete several layers and you don't want to delete them one at a time. The ability to select multiple layers gives you the ability to exert more control over Photoshop Elements, and that control quickly changes into creative energy. A single selected layer is called the active layer.

Select Layers

1 In the Editor, open a multiple layered document and display the **Layers** palette.

2 Select multiple layers in the Layers palette using the following options:

◆ **Contiguous Layers.** Click on the first layer, and then Shift+click the last layer to select first, last, and all layers in-between.

◆ **Non-Contiguous Layers.** Click on a layer, hold down the Ctrl key, and then click on another layer.

3 Select layers in the document window using the following options:

◆ **Single and Multiple Layers.** Select the **Move** tool, select the **Auto Select Layer** check box in the Options bar, and then click on an object in the document window. The layer holding that object is selected. To add or subtract layers from the selection, Shift+click (or drag).

TIMESAVER *Select the Move tool, hold down the Ctrl key, and then click on an object. Hold down the Shift+Ctrl, and click on another object to add that object's layer to the selection.*

4 To deselect all layers, click the **Select** menu, and then click **Deselect Layers**.

Contiguous Multiple Layers selected

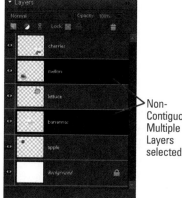

Non-Contiguous Multiple Layers selected

Creating a Selection from a Layer

Traditional layers are basically similar to sheets of transparent acetate or clear plastic. Once created they support all painting tools, as well as shape and gradient tools. While traditional layers may start out as transparent pieces of plastic, they don't remain that way for long. In fact, a layer can, over time, be a complicated mix of non-transparent (the image), and transparent areas. It's also possible you might want to make a selection out of that complicated image. Photoshop Elements knows this and gives you an easy way to convert the shape of an image on a layer into a selection.

Create a Selection from a Layer

1. In the Editor, open a document and display the **Layers** palette.

2. Hold down the Ctrl key, and then click on the image thumbnail of the layer you want converted into a selection. Be sure you click on the image thumbnail, not the layer name like previous versions.

   The visible portions of the image on the layer are converted into a selection.

   IMPORTANT *Since Photoshop Elements creates the selection based on the image information, there must be transparent and non-transparent areas within the image or the command selects the entire layer as if you had clicked the Select menu, and then clicked All.*

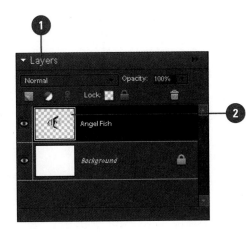

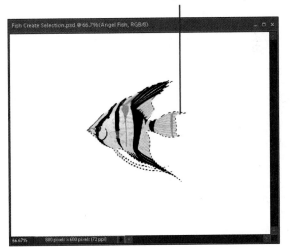

Selection based on the visible portions of the layer.

Creating a Layer from a Selection

On the previous page, you learned how to create a selection based on the image information within a layer. In addition to creating a selection from a layer, Photoshop Elements gives you the ability to instantly create a layer from a selection. Creating layers from selections opens up all kinds of opportunities for generating special effects. For example, selecting an object from one layer, and then making a layer with that selection, or making a selection of a portion of a image, creating the layer, and applying a layer style to the copy. The possibilities are endless, and the fun is exploring those possibilities.

Create a Layer from a Selection

① In the Editor, open a document and display the **Layers** palette.

② Click on the layer containing the information you want to convert into a layer.

③ Select an area of an image using any of the selection tools.

④ Click the **Layer** menu, point to **New**, and then click **Layer Via Copy** or **Layer Via Cut**.

> **TIMESAVER** *Press Ctrl+J to copy or press Shift+Ctrl+J to cut a layer.*

Photoshop Elements converts the selected area into a new layer.

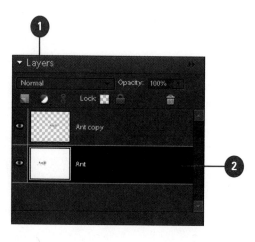

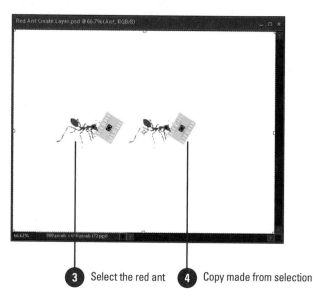

③ Select the red ant   ④ Copy made from selection

Did You Know?

You can make a copy of all elements within a layer. Select the layer in the Layers palette, and then click Ctrl+J. Since there are no selections, Photoshop Elements creates a copy of the entire layer.

You can make copies of layer objects without selecting them. To make a copy of a layer that contains an object, select the layer in the Layers palette, select the Move tool, hold down the Alt key, and then click and drag (in the document window).

Simplifying a Layer

If you have a type layer, shape layer, gradient layer, solid color layer, pattern fill layer, frame layer, a smart object, or a layer group (from a Photoshop document), you can convert it into a normal image layer. You need to simplify these layers before you can apply filters to them or edit them with the Painting tools. When you simplify a layer, you can no longer use the type and shape editing options.

Convert a Layer to an Image Layer

1. In the Editor, open a document and display the **Layers** palette.

2. Select the layer you want to convert to an image layer.

3. Use one of the following options depending on the layer type:

   ◆ **Shape Layer.** If you selected a shape layer, click **Simplify** on the Options bar.

   ◆ **Type, Shape, Fill Layer.** If you selected a type, shape, or fill layer, click the **Layer** menu, and then click **Simplify Layer**.

   ◆ **Photoshop Layer Group.** If you selected a layer group from a Photoshop document, click the **Layer** menu, and then click **Simplify Layer**.

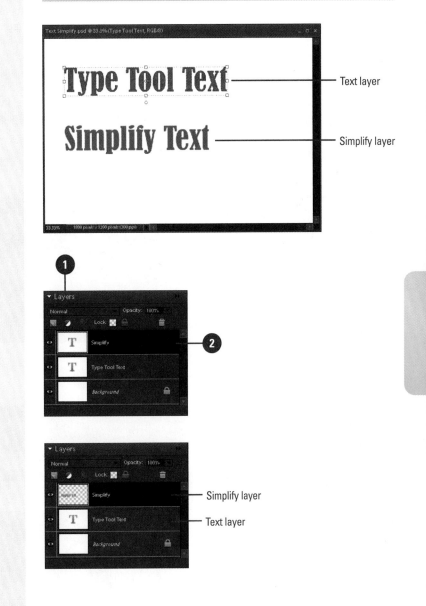

Text layer

Simplify layer

Simplify layer

Text layer

Converting a Background into a Layer

The Background serves a unique function. Since some layout programs do not support Photoshop Elements' multiple layers and transparency, in a process called **flattening**, a final image must sometimes be converted into a Background. When an image is flattened, all of the documents layers are compressed into a single element in the Layers palette designated as the Background. That means no more layers, no more transparency, and no more control. Backgrounds are a necessary evil because Photoshop Elements does not stand alone, and it's sometimes necessary to move images from Photoshop Elements into other applications. However, there are times you start with an image that's on a Background and you want to apply transparency, blending modes, or other adjustments that cannot be applied to a Background, or move it to another position. In those cases you will need to convert the Background into a traditional layer. The Background layer must remain at the bottom of the Layers palette.

Convert a Background

1. In the Editor, open a document and display the **Layers** palette.

2. Double-click the Background layer in the Layers palette to open the New Layer dialog box.

   ◆ You can also click the **Layer** menu, point to **New**, and then click **Layer from Background**.

3. Rename the layer in the Name box (leave the other options at their default values).

4. Click **OK**.

   The Background is converted into a traditional layer.

Did You Know?

You can make a layer the Background layer. If the image already has a Background layer, you cannot create one from another layer. In the Editor, open a document, select a layer in the Layers palette, click the Layer menu, point to New, and then click Background From Layer.

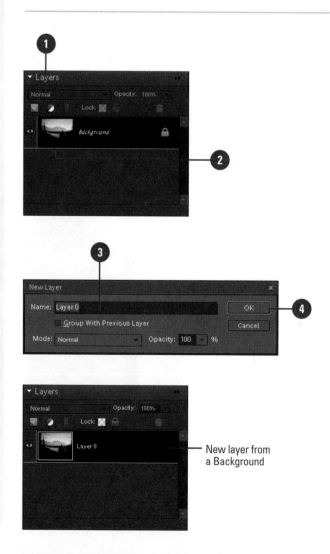

New layer from a Background

Convert a Multi-Layered Document into a Background

1. In the Editor, open a document and display the **Layers** palette.

2. Click the **More Options** button, and then click **Flatten Image**.

   The multi-layer document is compressed into a single-layer Background.

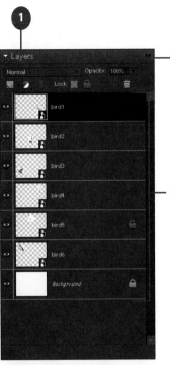

6 separate layers plus the Background

Multiple layers compressed into a single Background layer

Did You Know?

You can create a composite image of a multi-layered document without flattening the image. Create and select a new layer, and then hold down the Alt key. Now, go to the Layers palette, click the Layers Options button, and then click Merge Visible. The Editor creates a composite of all the visible layers in the new layer. You now have the control and flexibility of a multiple-layered document, along with a separate composite layer, and control gives you the confidence to be more creative.

See Also

See "Using Merge Layer Options" on page 216 for more information on how to merge two or more layers without flattening all the layers.

Working with Layers Using the Layers Palette

When you work on multi-layered documents, it's important to understand the ways Photoshop Elements gives you to control image information. For example, working on a document that contains 20 layers is a difficult proposition. Fortunately, Photoshop Elements gives you control over the document, everything from layer names to locking pixel information is available in Photoshop Elements' bag of image-control tricks. When linking two layers together, you can move or resize the layers at the same time, thus saving valuable time. Let's explore some of the ways you can control image information on the Layers palette.

Work with Layers Using the Layers Palette

1 In the Editor, open a document, display the **Layers** palette, and then use one of the following options:

- ◆ Create Layers. To create a normal image layer, click the **New Layer** button.

  To create a fill or adjustment layer, click the **Create Adjustment Layer** button, and then select the fill (first three) or adjustment (after first three) layer option you want.

- ◆ Select Layers. To select a layer, click the layer's thumbnail or name. To select more than one layer, Ctrl-click each layer.

- ◆ Name/Rename Layers. To name a layer, double-click on the current layer name, type a new name, and then press Enter.

- ◆ Show/Hide Layers. To temporarily hide or show a layer (make its contents invisible or visible in the document window), click the **Eye** icon, located in the Show/Hide box.

  To display just one layer, Alt-click the **Eye** icon for the layer. Alt-click in the **Eye** icon again to show all layers.

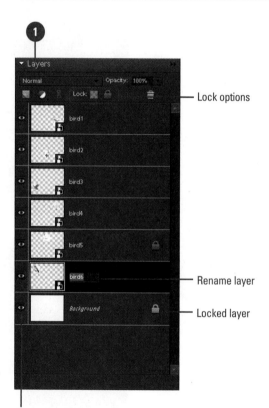

Lock options

Rename layer

Locked layer

Show/Hide layer

◆ **Link/Unlink Layers.** To link two or more layers, hold the Shift key and click the layers you want to link, and then click the **Link Layers** button. The link icon indicates the layers are linked. Linking lets you move or resize the layers as a unit.

To unlink layers, select a linked layer, and then click the **Link Layers** button.

◆ **Lock/Unlock Layers.** Click the **Lock All** button in the Layers palette to lock all layer properties. Click the button again to unlock it.

Click the **Lock Transparency** button in the Layers palette to lock the transparent areas of the layer. Click the button again to unlock it.

◆ **Change Layer Order.** To change the position of a layer in the stack, drag the layer up or down. A dark line appears as a visual cue to indicate the new layer location.

◆ **Move Layer Content.** Select the layer with the content you want to move, select the **Move** tool on the toolbox, and then drag within the image to move the content position.

◆ **Change Layer Thumbnails.** Click the **More Options** button, click **Palette Options**, select the size and contents options you want, and then click **OK**.

Create layer

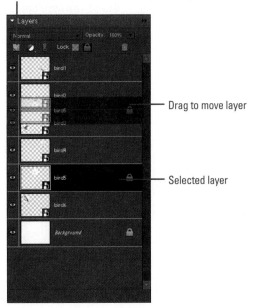

Drag to move layer

Selected layer

More options

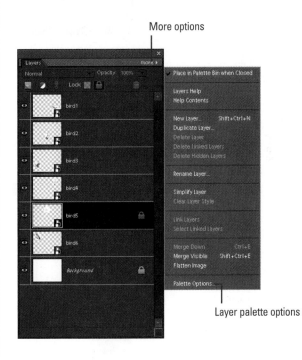

Layer palette options

Stacking and Moving Layers

Layers are like stacked transparencies with images and other content. You can change the stacking order of the stacked layers to display the content you want. You can change the stacking order by simply dragging layers in the Layers palette or using commands on the Arrange submenu on the Layers menu. The Background layer must remain at the bottom of the Layers palette. To move it, you need to convert it to a normal image layer. If the content on a layer is blocked by the content on another layer, you can move the content on a layer.

Change Layer Stacking Order

1. In the Editor, open a document and display the **Layers** palette.

2. Select one or more layers you want to move.

3. Drag the layers up or down the Layers palette to a new location.

   ◆ You can also click the **Layer** menu, point to **Arrange**, and then click **Bring to Front**, **Bring Forward**, **Send Backward**, or **Send to Back**.

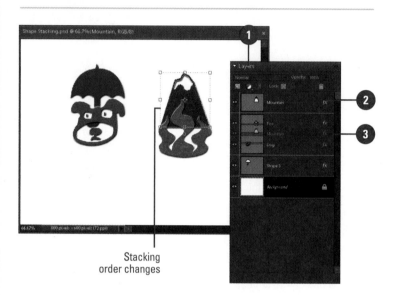

Stacking order changes

Move the Content in a Layer

1. In the Editor, open a document and display the **Layers** palette.

2. Select one or more layers you want to move.

3. Select the **Move** tool on the toolbox.

4. Drag within the image to move the content in the selected layers. To constraint your movement up, down, left, right, or to a 45-degree diagonal, hold down the Shift key.

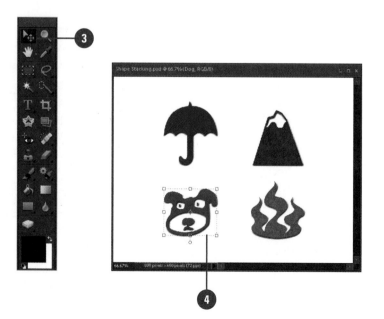

Moving Layers Between Documents

Photoshop Elements documents typically contain multiple layers. One web survey concluded that the designer creates documents with an average of 14 layers. Controlling layers is an important aspect of design, because the more control you maintain, the more organized you are, and the better your designs will be. But what about controlling layers across multiple documents? For example, you're working on a design, and you need access to some additional image information. The only problem is that the additional information is located in another Photoshop Elements document. Photoshop Elements gives you the ability to move layers between open documents.

Move Layers Between Documents

1. In the Editor, open multiple documents and display the **Layers** palette.

2. To have more than one document in view, click the **Window** menu, point to **Image**, and then click **Tile** or **Cascade**.

3. Click on the document containing the layer you want to move.

4. Drag the layer from the Layers palette into the window of the receiving document.

    Photoshop Elements creates a new layer with a copy of the image information from the other document.

Drag clouds layer here

Did You Know?

You can control the position of the moved layer. Hold down the Shift key while dragging the layer into the other document. Photoshop Elements aligns the new layer to the center of the receiving document.

You can move selected portions of a layer. Select the area you want to move, click the Move tool, and then drag the selected area directly from the document window into the window of the receiving document.

Clouds layer

New layer from donor document

Using Merge Layer Options

The Merge Down option lets you merge one selected layer into the layer directly below. Merged layers take on the characteristics of the layer they are being merged into. For example, when you merge a layer into a layer that uses the Darken blending mode, the two merged layers will still use Darken, or if you merge a layer into the Background, the merged layer becomes a part of the Background. The Merge Visible option gives you the ability with one click to merge all of the layers that have the Show option enabled (Eye icon shown).

Merge Down

1. In the Editor, open a document and display the **Layers** palette.

2. Select one or more layers you want to merge.

3. Click the **More Options** button, and then click **Merge Down** (for single selection) or **Merge Layers** (for multiple selection).

   The selected layers merge into the next layer down (single selection) or the uppermost layer (multiple selection).

   TIMESAVER *Press Ctrl+E to merge layers down.*

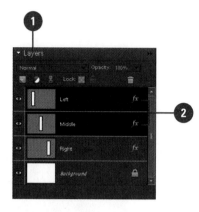
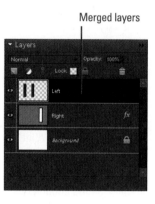

Merged layers

Merge Visible

1. In the Editor, open a document and display the **Layers** palette.

2. Click the **Show** option for all layers you want to merge.

3. Click the **More Options** button, and then click **Merge Visible**.

   TIMESAVER *Press Shift+Ctrl+E to merge visible.*

   All layers with the Show option enabled are merged together.

   TIMESAVER *Press Alt, click the Layer menu, and then click Merge Visible to merge all visible layers into a new layer.*

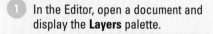
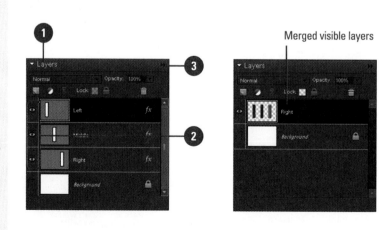

Merged visible layers

Linking and Unlinking Layers

If you're currently looking at the Layers palette, and wondered where the linking button is, don't worry; it's not missing, it's just been moved. Linking multiple layers is a snap. Simply select one or more layers, and then click the Link Layers button at the top of the Layers palette. You can link two or more layers or groups. Unlike selected multiple layers, linked layers retain their relationship (stay together) until you unlink them, which allows you to move or resize the layers as a unit.

Link Layers

① In the Editor, open a multiple layered document and display the **Layers** palette.

② Select two or more layers.

③ Click the **Link Layers** button.

The selected layers are now linked. A link icon appears next to the linked layers.

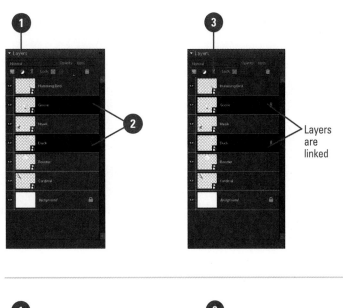

Layers are linked

Unlink Layers

① In the Editor, open a multiple layered document that contains links and display the **Layers** palette.

② Select a layer that contains the link icon.

TIMESAVER *To unlink several linked layers, select them before continuing.*

③ Click the **Link Layers** button.

TIMESAVER *To temporarily disable link, Shift+click the link icon for the linked layer. A red X appears. Shift+click the link icon again to enable it the link.*

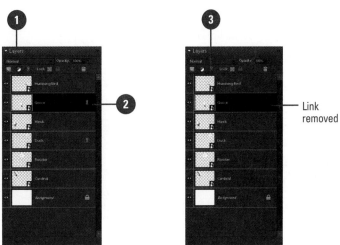

Link removed

Deleting Layers

Photoshop Elements lets you add layers to a document (up to 8,000), and it lets you delete layers. Remember that once you've deleted a layer, saved, and closed the document, there is no way to recover the deleted layer. However, while the document is open, there is always the chance of recovering the deleted layer through the History palette.

Delete Layers

① In the Editor, open a document, display the **Layers** palette, and then select the layer you want to delete.

② Hold down the Alt key, and then click the **Delete Layer** button.

◆ If you don't hold down the Alt key, click **OK** in the con-firmation dialog box.

◆ To drag delete, click the layer you want to delete, and then drag it to the **Delete Layer** button.

The select layer has been removed from the Layers palette.

Delete Linked Layers

① In the Editor, open a document, display the **Layers** palette, and then select one of the linked layers you want to delete.

② Hold down the Alt key, and then click the **Delete Layer** button.

Photoshop Elements deletes all the linked layers.

Selected layers are removed from the Layers palette.

Did You Know?

You can delete hidden layers from the Layers palette. Click the More Options button, and then click Delete Hidden Layers.

Duplicating a Layer

There are times when you will need a copy of a layer. Duplicating a layer is a simple process which creates a pixel-to-pixel copy of the selected layer. Once the copied layer is created, it becomes a separate image within the document. You can then begin to make any additions to the new layer. Duplicating a layer gives you the ability to control each layer separately and to create any desired effect.

Duplicate a Layer

1 In the Editor, open a document and display the **Layers** palette.

2 Select the layer you want to duplicate.

3 Click the **More Options** button, and then click **Duplicate Layer**.

4 Enter a name for the new layer.

5 To place the layer in another open document, click the **Document** list arrow, and then select a document.

6 Click **OK**.

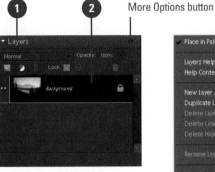

More Options button

Did You Know?

You can duplicate a layer with the Create New Layer button. Drag the layer over the Create New Layer button and Photoshop Elements creates an exact copy of the layer and appends the word "copy" at the end of the original layer name.

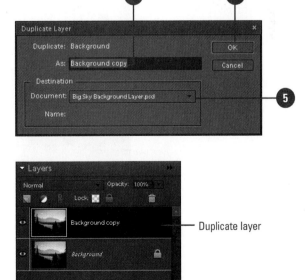

Duplicate layer

Working with Layer Blending Modes

Layer Blending Modes are one of the most creative areas in the Layers palette. With blending modes you can instruct Photoshop Elements to mix the image information between two or more layers. For example, the Multiply blending mode instructs Photoshop Elements to mix the image information of two or more layers together. Blending modes give you control over images up and over that what you would expect to find in the real world.

Mix Layer Information with Blending Modes

1. In the Editor, open a multiple layered document and display the **Layers** palette.

2. Select a layer.

   Since blending modes work downward, select the layer directly above the layer you want to blend.

3. Click the **Blending Mode** list arrow, and then select a blending mode.

   Photoshop Elements uses the selected blending mode to visually blend the image on the active layer with the layers below it.

4. Click the **Opacity** list arrow, and then drag the slider to lower the opacity of the layer.

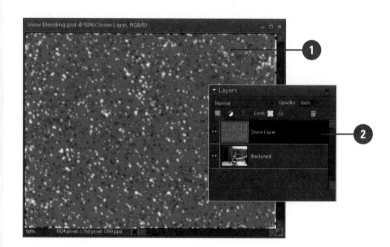

The snow layer blended with the backyard layer

Did You Know?

You can control the number of layers a blending mode is applied. Hold down the Alt key, and then click on the visible line separating the adjustment layer from the next lower layer.

Creating a Clipping Layer Group

A clipping group is a group of layers with a mask. A mask creates a transparent area in the visible image. Use masks to remove elements of an image without physically erasing them. The bottommost layer, known as the base layer, defines the visible area of the group, or mask, while the layers above it, known as the overlay layers, show through the base layer. For example, you can have a shape as the base layer and a photo as the overlay layer. The photo appears within the shape's outline. In the Layers palette, the name of the base layer in the group is underlined, while the thumbnails for the overlay layers are indented and displayed with a clipping group icon (a left down arrow). You can group only successive layers, one on top of the other.

Group and Ungroup Layers in a Clipping Group

1. In the Editor, open a document and display the **Layers** palette.

2. Select the top layer of a pair of layers you want to group.

3. Click the **Layer** menu, and then click **Group with Previous**.

   TIMESAVER *Press Ctrl+G to create a clipping layer group.*

   Photoshop Elements creates a clipping layer group.

4. To remove layers from a clipping group, select the layer you want to remove (except the base layer), and then drag it below the base layer or drag it between two ungrouped layers.

   TIMESAVER *Press Alt, and then click the line separating two grouped layers.*

5. To ungroup layers in a clipping group, select the base layer in the clipping group or the layer immediately above the base layer, click the **Layer** menu, and then click **Ungroup**.

   TIMESAVER *Press Shift+Ctrl +G to ungroup layers in a clipping layer group.*

Using Adjustment and Fill Layers

If you want to visually control an Photoshop Elements document, then adjustment layers are the ultimate tool. The purpose of an adjustment layer is to visually illustrate how a specific adjustment, such as Hue & Saturation, is applied to the image. Since the adjustment is contained within a separate layer, the original image never changes. This gives you the ability to experiment with different settings, and since adjustment layers are saved with the document, you can save and return at a later time to make further adjustments.

Another advantage of adjustment layers is size. Adjustment layers do not increase the size of a Photoshop Elements document. Most layers are composed of pixels, so adding traditional layers to a document increases the size of the file. Since adjustment layers are simply a set of mathematical information, they do not increase the size of the file.

Photoshop Elements has two ways to apply adjustments to an image. The first is going through the Enhance menu, and choosing Adjust commands, however, when you apply the adjustment it's permanent. The other is using an adjustment layer—the very definition of control over time. When working with adjustment layers, you can modify, merge, or even create a temporary composite image, all while your original image stays intact. With all of their advantages, you may never perform adjustments using the Image menu again.

In addition to letting you apply adjustments to an image without changing the original data, adjustment layers, because they are separate layers, give you the ability to apply standard layer controls, such as blending modes, opacity, and fill. Adjustment layers come with their own built-in masks, which allow you to control how and where the adjustment is applied to the image.

Click to create Fill or
Adjustment layers

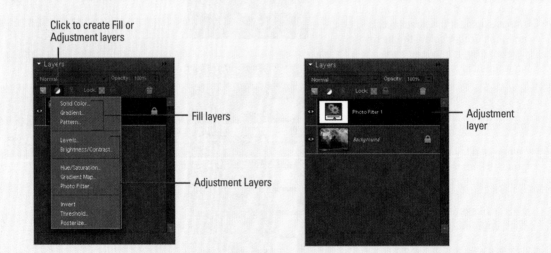

Fill layers

Adjustment Layers

Adjustment layer

Creating an Adjustment Layer

Adjustment layers are applied within the Layers palette. By default, all layers beneath the adjustment layer are affected by the adjustment. In addition, adjustment layers will work on any type of layer, including the Background. You can have as many adjustment layers as needed. For example, you might create a Levels adjustment layer to control the contrast of an image, and add a Curves adjustment layer to correct image color. When you create an adjustment layer, a white box representing the adjustment for that layer appears along with a name based on the layer type, such as Gradient Map 1, in the Layers palette. The new adjustment layer affects all the layers below it in the Layers palette, so you may want to move it to another position, depending on your needs.

Create an Adjustment Layer

1. In the Editor, open a document and display the **Layers** palette.

2. Select the layer you want to adjust.

3. Click the **Create New Fill or Adjustment Layer** button, and then select from the available adjustment options:

   ◆ **Levels.** Corrects tonal values in the image.

   ◆ **Brightness/Contrast.** Lightens or darkens the image.

   ◆ **Hue/Saturation.** Adjusts color in the image.

   ◆ **Gradient Map.** Maps pixels to the color in the selected gradient in the image.

   ◆ **Photo Filter.** Adjusts the color balance and temperature in the image.

   ◆ **Invert.** Creates a negative of the image.

   ◆ **Threshold.** Creates a black and white image.

   ◆ **Posterize.** Creates a flat appearance (decrease brightness) in the image.

4. If a dialog box opens, make changes to the adjustment, and then click **OK**.

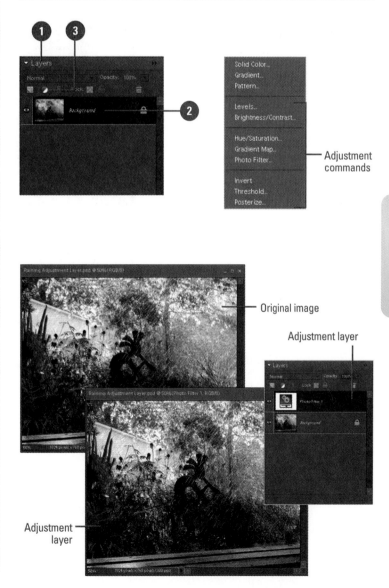

Adjustment commands

Original image

Adjustment layer

Adjustment layer

Creating a Fill Layer

Fill layers let you fill a layer with a solid color, gradient, or pattern. When you create a fill layer, a white box representing the fill for that layer appears along with a name based on the layer type, such as Color Fill 1, in the Layers palette. Also, fill layers do not affect the layers below them. If you want to paint on a fill layer, you need to convert, or simplify, it to a traditional layer.

Create a Fill Layer

1. In the Editor, open a document and display the **Layers** palette.

2. Select the layer you want to adjust.

3. Click the **Create New Fill or Adjustment Layer** button, and then select from the available adjustment options:

   ◆ **Solid Color.** Creates a layer with a solid color.

   ◆ **Gradient.** Creates a layer with a gradient.

   ◆ **Pattern.** Creates a layer with a pattern.

4. In the dialog box that opens, make changes to the fill style, and then click **OK**.

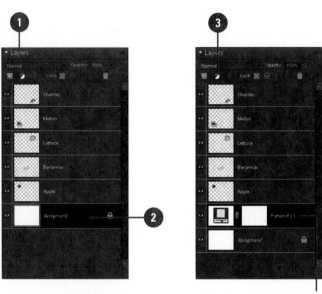

Fill pattern layer

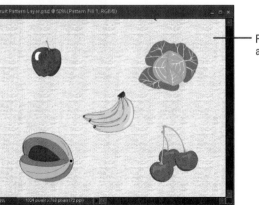

Fill pattern applied

Changing Fill or Adjustment Layer Content

If an adjustment layer doesn't quite suit your artistic needs, you can change it. Instead of deleting an adjustment or fill layer and creating a new one, you can use the Change Layer Content command to select another file or adjustment layer and then specify the options you want. Since adjustment and fill layers keep settings isolated in a separate layer, you can experiment with different settings until the image is exactly what you want. The beauty of adjustment and fill layers is in the control they offer to the Photoshop Elements user.

Change Fill or Adjustment Layer Content

1. In the Editor, open a document and display the **Layers** palette.

2. Select the fill or adjustment layer you want to change.

3. Click the **Layer** menu, point to **Change Layer Content**, and then select the fill or adjustment layer option you want.

   The dialog box for that specific adjustment reopens. Options for each adjustment dialog box vary.

4. Make the changes you want for the specific adjustment.

5. Click **OK**.

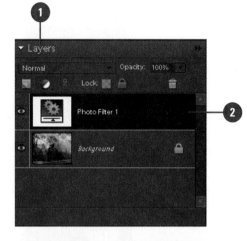

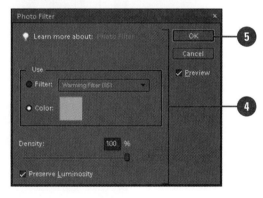

Modifying a Fill or Adjustment Layer

When you modify a traditional layer, any changes made to the image are permanent, as soon as you click OK. But that's not true of adjustment or fill layers. Adjustment and fill layers keep the changes isolated in a separate layer, and this allows you to modify the adjustment or fill minutes, or even days later. With this type of creative control at your fingertips, you can experiment with different settings until the image is exactly what you want.

Modify a Fill or Adjustment Layer

1. In the Editor, open a document and display the **Layers** palette.

2. Double-click on the thumbnail of the Fill or Adjustment layer you want to modify.

   ◆ You can also select the layer, click the **Layer** menu, and then click **Layer Content Options**.

   The dialog box for that specific adjustment reopens. Options for each adjustment dialog box vary.

3. Make the changes you want for the specific adjustment.

4. Click **OK**.

Did You Know?

You can move adjustment layers up and down in the layer stack. Since each adjustment layer interacts with other adjustment layers, changing the order of the layers creates a totally different image

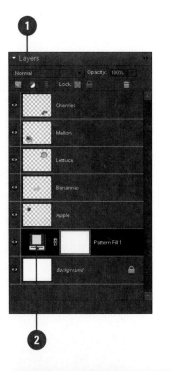

Deleting a Fill or Adjustment Layer

When you delete a fill or adjustment layer you are simply deleting the adjustment, not the image. Adjustment layers do not contain image data; they only manipulate the information contained within the image layer. Deleting an adjustment layer is as easy as deleting any other layer type. The effect is the same; the function of the layer is removed from the document. For example, if you delete a Curves adjustment layer, the effects are removed and the image returns to its original state. When you delete an adjustment layer, the change to the image induced by the adjustment layer is removed, and the image returns to normal.

Delete a Fill or Adjustment Layer

1. In the Editor, open a document and display the **Layers** palette.

2. Select the fill or adjustment layer you want to delete.

3. Hold down the Alt key, and then click the **Delete Layer** button.

   ◆ If you don't hold down the Alt key, click **OK** in the confirmation dialog box.

   ◆ To drag delete, click the layer you want to delete, and then drag it to the **Delete** Layer button.

Did You Know?

You can convert an adjustment layer into a permanent adjustment. Select the adjustment layer in the Layers palette, and then press Ctrl+E to merge the adjustment layer with the layer below it.

The adjustment layer is removed from the document.

Using Blending Modes with Fill or Adjustment Layers

Adjustment layers perform two functions—they adjust the image and they give you control. Since an adjustment is held in a separate layer, you have the advantage of isolating the adjustment, and all the options that apply to a normal a layer. Combine that with an adjustment layers ability to manipulate pixel information and you have a very powerful image-editing tool. Blending Modes change how two or more layers interact. For example, the multiply blending mode instructs Photoshop Elements to mix the pixels of two or more layers, thus creating an entirely new image from the mix. With that in mind, the five modes that produce the most stunning results are Multiply, Screen, Hard Mix, Difference, and Exclusion. The opacity of an adjustment layer controls the intensity of the selected adjustment. You can reduce the opacity of the Hue & Saturation adjustment to 50 percent, and it would reduce its effect on the image. Since each adjustment layer has its own opacity settings, multiple adjustment layers can be fine-tuned to create the desired impact on the image.

Use Blending Modes with Fill and Adjustment Layers

1. In the Editor, open a document and display the **Layers** palette.

2. Click the layer you want to adjust.

3. Click the **Blending Mode** list arrow, and then select from the available options.

   The results of the blend are visible in the document window.

Blending Mode applied

Control Through Opacity

1. In the Editor, open a document and display the **Layers** palette.

2. Click the layer you want to adjust.

3. Click the **Opacity** list arrow, and then drag the slider to change the opacity of the layer.

   The results of the change appear in the document window.

   TIMESAVER *Click inside the Opacity box, and then use the Up and Down arrow keys to increase or decrease the opacity 1 percentage point at a time. Hold the Shift key, and then use the Up and Down Arrow keys to increase or decrease the opacity 10 percentage points at a time. You can also select the percentage in the box and enter a value.*

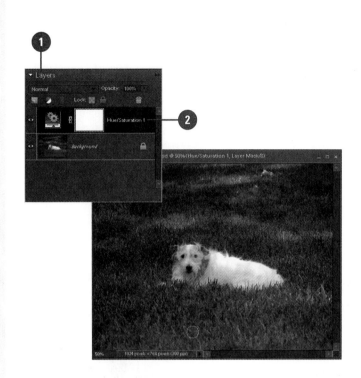

The effect of lowering the opacity of the layer by 50% mutes the adjustment layer.

Merging Fill or Adjustment Layers

Photoshop Elements lets you create as many adjustment layers as needed. For example, you might create a Levels adjustment layer to balance image contrast, Curves to correct color, and a Photo Filter, to create an overall warming effect to the image. Each adjustment layer works with the other adjustment layers to produce the final image. It's not unusual to have three, four, or even five adjustment layers controlling a single image. At some point in the design, you might decide to save space by merging some or all of the adjustment layers. However, when you merge the adjustment layers, the image looses the effect produced by the adjustments. The reason lies in how Photoshop Elements works with adjustment layers. Each adjustment layer controls one part of the adjustment. The layers themselves do not hold an image; they hold mathematical data on how to change an image. Each adjustment layer holds data relating to a specific adjustment, such as Curves or Levels. A single adjustment layer cannot hold more than one set of adjustments. That's why you have multiple adjustment layers. Merging two or more adjustment layers together forces Photoshop Elements to discard all of the adjustment data and the merged adjustment layers turn into a traditional simplified layer. To solve the problem, try merging the adjustment and the image layers into a single layer.

Merge Fill or Adjustments Layers

1. In the Editor, open a document containing an image layer, and two or more adjustment layers.

2. Display the **Layers** palette.

3. Click the **More Options** button, and then select from the following merge options:

   ◆ **Merge Layers.** Merges only the layers selected in the Layers palette into a single layer.

   ◆ **Merge Down.** Merges the selected layer and the one below it.

   ◆ **Merge Visible.** Merges only the layers that are visible, leaving the hidden layers untouched.

   ◆ **Flatten Image.** Merges all layers into a flattened background. If you have one or more layers hidden, a warning dialog box asks if you want to discard the hidden layers.

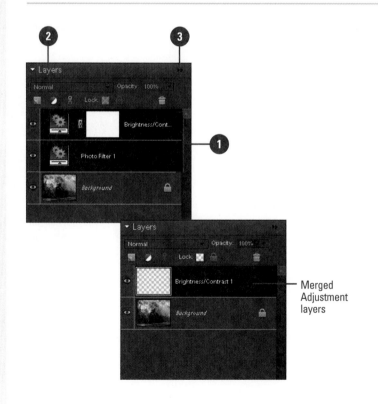

Merged Adjustment layers

Creating a Temporary Composite Image

When you merge adjustment layers into the image, you wind up with a single layer, which contains all of the adjustments. By merging the adjustment layers, you do lose control over the individual adjustment layers. It's basically a trade off of smaller file sizes, fewer layers to contend with, but less control over the image. Let's say you want the best of both worlds—a single layer that contains the image, all of the adjustments, and the original image with separate adjustment layers. It's possible, all you have to do is create a composite layer.

Create a Temporary Composite Image

① In the Editor, open a document that contains an image, and two or more visible adjustment layers.

② Display the **Layers** palette, create a new layer at the top of the layer stack, and then select it.

③ Hold down the Alt key, click the **More Options** button, and then click **Merge Visible**.

Photoshop Elements combines all of the visible layers into the new layer; while leaving the original layers untouched.

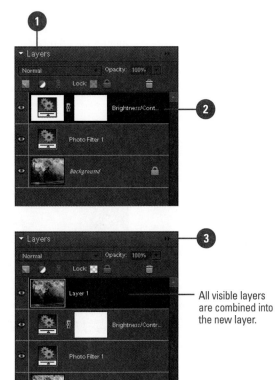

All visible layers are combined into the new layer.

Did You Know?

You can use the composite layer option on any multiple layered PSD document. Once you've created the composite layer, you can perform other adjustments without impacting the original images, or even drag and move the composite into another PSD document.

You can use the link option to control the composite image. In the Editor, create a new layer, and then link the layers you want included in the composite. Follow the steps for creating a composite, except click Merge Linked.

Using Masks with Adjustment Layers

When you create an adjustment layer, the effects of the adjustment are applied to the entire image. For example, if you use the Curves adjustment, the entire image receives the effects of the adjustment. It's true you can modify the adjustment with the use of layer blending modes, and opacity settings but, the effects are applied equally to the entire image. The problem is that many times you don't want the adjustment applied to the entire image. For example, color correcting a portion of the image, or lightening the shadows of an image without applying the same lightening adjustment to the highlights. Photoshop Elements handles this problem with the use of masks. When you create an adjustment layer, Photoshop Elements creates a mask with the image. The mask controls how the adjustment is applied to the image, and you control the effect by painting in the mask with black, white, or a shade of gray. When you paint the mask with black, it masks the adjustment, painting with white fully applies the adjustment. If you paint with 50 percent gray, then 50 percent of the adjustment is applied to the image.

Paint on an Adjustment Mask

1 In the Editor, open a document and display the **Layers** palette.

2 Click the layer mask thumbnail in which you want to paint a mask.

3 Select a **Paintbrush** tool.

4 Select a brush size on the Options bar.

5 Set the **Foreground Color** box on the toolbox to black as the painting color.

6 Paint the areas of the image in the document window you want to mask. The adjustment layer must be selected.

The areas painted black mask the adjustment, and return the image to normal.

7 To restore the masked areas, switch to white and drag across the image in the areas previously painted black.

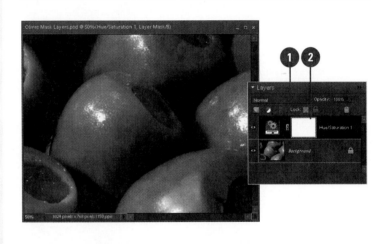

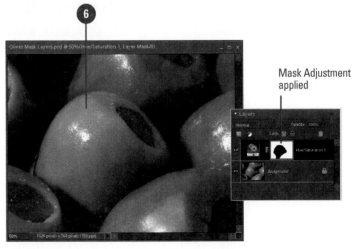

Mask Adjustment applied

Creating Masks with Selections

You can create an instant mask using traditional selection techniques. Before creating the adjustment layer, select the area of the image you want the adjustment applied. Use any of the Selection tools for this purpose. When you create the adjustment layer, Photoshop Elements converts the selection into a mask, and only the selected areas of the image receive the adjustment.

Create Masks with Selections

1 In the Editor, open a document, and then use any of the Selection tools to create a selection around the area of the image you want the adjustment applied.

2 Display the **Layers** palette.

3 Click the **Create New Fill or Adjustment Layer** button, and then select from the available adjustments.

Photoshop Elements creates a mask based on your selection with the selected areas receiving the adjustment and the non-selected areas masked.

Did You Know?

You can use any of the filters on an adjustment layer mask.
For example, you could use the Gaussian Blur filter to soften the edge between adjustment and mask. Experiment with different filters for different creative effects.

Mask adjustment applied

Setting Layers Palette Options

Photoshop Elements doesn't have a lot of options for controlling the palette; in fact, there is only one—changing the size of the thumbnail. Thumbnail size options come in three sizes, or you can select to have no thumbnail shown. When you change the size of the thumbnail, you're instructing Photoshop Elements to spend more, or less processing time on the display of the image. The larger the thumbnail, the easier it is to see, but the longer it takes for Photoshop Elements to draw the images in the Layers palette. If you're experiencing performance issues with Photoshop Elements, and you're using a large thumbnail, you might consider downsizing the thumbnail image.

Set Layers Palette Options

1. In the Editor, open a document and display the **Layers** palette.

2. Click the **More Options** button, and then click **Palette Options**.

3. Click a thumbnail size or the **None** option.

4. Click the **Layer Bounds** or **Entire Document** option.

5. Select the **Use Default Masks On Adjustments** check box to automatically insert a mask when creating a new Adjustment layer.

6. Click **OK**.

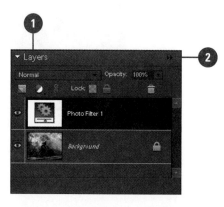

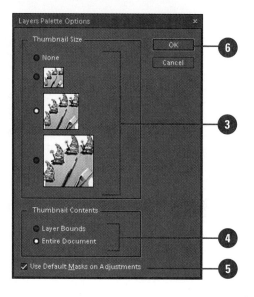

Adjusting and Correcting Color

Introduction

In the world of design, color is one of the most important elements. When you're creating a brochure, advertisement, or banner using Photoshop Elements, good use of color attracts the attention of the viewer. It also helps draw the elements of your design into one cohesive unit. Color is a strong motivator and is used in all aspects of our daily life.

Since color is so important to design, Photoshop Elements lets you use industry-standard color sets, or you can create and save your own customized color palettes. You can also color correct a photograph by removing the color entirely or selectively remove colors from portions of the image. In addition, Photoshop Elements gives you ways to select areas based on color, and then fill those areas with any color you choose.

Not only is it important to understand how color is used, it's also important to understand how Photoshop Elements manages color information. Channels are where color information is stored. The number of channels in an image is based on its **color mode**, or color model, such as RGB (Red, Green, Blue). A firm understanding of channels and color modes, and their function in Photoshop Elements will go a long way in helping you control and manage color.

When adjusting your image, you can use various commands—Auto Contrast and Color, Curves, Color Balance, and Brightness/Contrast, Saturate and Desaturate, just to name a few. You can also use the Match and Selective Color adjustments to further fine-tune your image. Photoshop Elements also provides a photo filters adjustment, as well as a shadow and highlight adjustment to correct those over or underexposed images. With all of the commands and adjustments available, the real dilemma will be where do you begin?

Working with Color Modes and Depth

Color modes define the colors represented in the active document. Although you can change the color mode of a document, it is best to select the correct color mode at the start of the project. Photoshop Elements' color modes are Bitmap, Grayscale, Indexed Color, and RGB (Red, Green, and Blue). See "Selecting Color Modes and Resolution" on page 125 for information on best use for each color mode. The number of channels in an image depends on its color mode. For example, CMYK image contains at least four channels, one for each color.

Color modes determine the number of colors, the number of channels, and the file size of an image. For example, a RGB image has at least three channels (like a printing plate), one for each red, green, and blue color information. Color modes not only define the working color space of the active document, they also represent the color space of the output document. It's the document output (print, press, or monitor), which ultimately determines the document color mode. Color modes do not just determine what colors the eye sees; they represent how the colors are mixed, and that's very important because different output devices use different color mixes.

Therefore, when selecting a color mode, know the file format of the document, and where it will be used. An image taken with a digital camera, and then opened in Photoshop Elements would most likely be in the RGB color mode. An image displayed on a monitor would be RGB, or possibly Indexed Color. If you were creating a Photoshop Elements document from scratch, the color mode chosen would represent the eventual output of the document, such as a web page, inkjet printer, or a 4-color press.

Switching Between Color Modes

Unfortunately, images do not always arrive in the correct format. For example, you take several photographs with your digital (RGB) camera, but the images are being printed on a 4-color (CMYK) press, or you want to colorize a grayscale image. Changing color modes is a snap, but changing the color mode of an image isn't the problem. The problem is what happens to the digital color information when you change color modes. Some of the color information is changed or lost. See topics in this chapter for specific steps to switch between color modes.

Working with Color Depth

It's all about the numbers, and that's a fact. The number of colors available for displaying or printing each pixel in an image is called **color depth**—also known as pixel depth or bit depth. A higher bit depth means more available colors and more accurate color representation in an image. A bit depth setting of 2-bit displays 4 colors; 4-bit displays 16 colors; 8-bit displays 256 colors; 16-bit displays 32,768 colors; and 24-bit and 32-bit, both of which display 16.7 million colors. Normal digital images have 8-bits of data per channel. For example, an RGB image with 8-bit channels is capable of producing 16.7 million colors (a 24-bit RGB image: 8 bits x 3 channels) possible colors per pixel. While that may seem like a lot of color information, when it comes to color correction and adjustment, it isn't. You can change an image's bits to 8 bits by displaying the image, clicking the Image menu, pointing to Mode, and then clicking 8 Bits/Channels.

Understanding the RGB Color Mode

The RGB color mode is probably the most widely used of all the color modes. RGB generates color using three 8-bit channels: 1 red, 1 green, and 1 blue. Since each channel is capable of generating 256 steps of color; mathematically that translates into 16,777,216 possible colors per image pixel. The RGB color mode (sometimes referred to as Additive RGB) is the color space of computer monitors, televisions, and any electronic display. This also includes PDAs (Personal Digital Assistants), and cellular phones. RGB is considered a device-dependent color mode. Device-dependent means that the colors in images created in the RGB color mode will appear different on various devices. In the world of computer monitors and the web, what you see is very seldom what someone else sees; however, understanding how Photoshop Elements manages color information goes a long way to gaining consistency over color.

Convert an Image to RGB Color

1. In the Editor, open an image.

2. Click the **Image** menu, point to **Mode**, and then click **RGB Color**.

   Photoshop Elements converts the image into the RGB color mode.

Convert to RGB

Understanding the Grayscale Color Mode

The grayscale color mode utilizes an 8-bit pixel (8 on/off light switches) to generate 1 black, 1 white, and 254 shades of gray. Although scanning and working on old black and white images might seem the obvious reason for using the grayscale color mode; the speed and power of Photoshop Elements, combined with faster computer systems, has prompted most photo restorers to switch to the RGB color space because of its greater versatility, and its ability to generate millions of colors (or shades of gray). Yet despite the move to RGB, the grayscale color mode is still used extensively on black and white images, where file size is a consideration (grayscale images are 2/3^{rds} smaller than RGB), and where output to rag style papers, such as newsprint, lack the ability to produce the detailed information available with RGB.

Convert an Image to Grayscale

1 In the Editor, open an image.

2 Click the **Image** menu, point to **Mode**, and then click **Grayscale**.

The image is automatically converted into the grayscale color mode.

3 If prompted, click **Merge** to merge multiple layers into one or **Don't Merge** to maintain individual layers.

4 Click **OK** to discard color information.

Did You Know?

You can colorize a grayscale image. In the Editor, convert the image into the RGB mode, create a new layer above the image layer, and then select a color, brush, and brush size on the Options bar. The trick is to change the blending mode of the brush on the Options bar to Color. Then, as you paint on the image, the selected color will replace the original grays. When you paint, the color is applied and controlled in the new layer, and you have the additional option of using layer opacity to control the intensity of the effect.

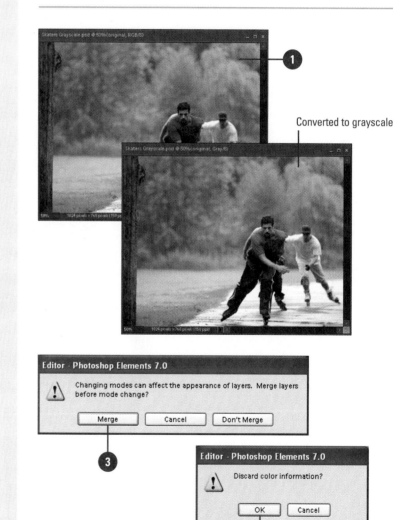

Converted to grayscale

Understanding the Bitmap Color Mode

Bitmap images consist of two colors: black and white. Bitmap images are sometimes referred to as 1-bit images. Think of a bitmap as a light switch with two positions, on and off. Each pixel in a bitmap image is either on or off, black or white. Because they are only 1-bit, the file size of a bitmap image is typically very small. Bitmap images have limited use, but are employed for black and white ink drawings, line art, sketches, and for creating halftone screens.

Convert an Image to Bitmap

1 In the Editor, open an image.

2 Click the **Image** menu, point to **Mode**, and then click **Bitmap**.

3 If prompted, click **OK** to convert the image to grayscale before it can be converted to a bitmap.

4 Enter a value for Output Resolution.

5 Click the **Use** list arrow, and then select from the available options:

◆ **50% Threshold.** Converts pixels with gray values above the middle gray level (128) to white and below to black. The result is a high-contrast, black-and-white image.

◆ **Pattern Dither.** Converts an image by organizing the gray levels into geometric patterns of black and white dots.

◆ **Diffusion Dither.** Converts pixels with gray values above the middle gray level (128) to white and below to black using an error-diffusion process. The result is a grainy, film like texture.

6 Click **OK**.

50% Threshold

Diffusion Dither

Understanding the Indexed Color Mode

The indexed color mode gives you two advantages. You can create images as small as grayscale (8-bit pixels), and you get color instead of shades of gray. Its small file size, and its ability to generate color make it a winning color mode for images displayed on web pages, as well as graphics used in computer-generated presentations. Its one drawback is the number of colors generated, indexed images generate a maximum of 256 colors (the same as the steps of gray in a grayscale image). The good news is you get to choose the colors. When you convert an image into the indexed color mode, Photoshop Elements creates a color lookup table (CLUT) to store the image's color information. When a color in the image cannot be found in the lookup table, Photoshop Elements substitutes the closest available color.

Convert an Image to Indexed Color

1. In the Editor, open an image.

2. Click the **Image** menu, point to **Mode**, and then click **Indexed Color**.

3. Select from the following Indexed Color Mode options:

   ◆ **Palette.** Click the list arrow to choose from the available color palettes, or click Custom and create your own palette.

   ◆ **Colors.** Select the number of colors for the lookup table (9 to 256).

   ◆ **Forced.** Force the lookup table to hold specific colors. Black And White adds a pure black and a pure white to the color table; Primaries adds red, green, blue, cyan, magenta, yellow, black, and white; Web adds the 216 web-safe colors; and Custom allows you to specify your own colors.

   ◆ **Transparency.** Select the check box to preserve transparent areas of the image (if there are no transparent areas, this option is disabled).

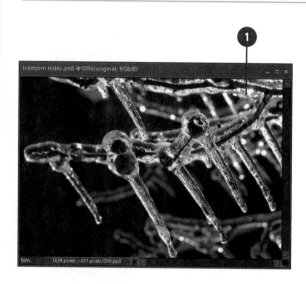

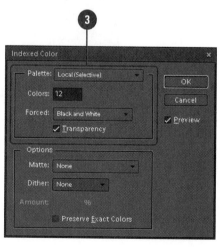

④ Select from the following options:

◆ **Matte.** Click the list arrow to fill transparent areas of the original image with a specific color.

◆ **Dither.** Click the list arrow, and then select a pixel-mixing (dither) scheme. Dithering helps transitional areas of the image (shadows, light to dark) appear more natural.

◆ **Amount.** If the Dither option is selected, the Amount instructs Photoshop Elements how much color information to use in the dithering process (0 to 100).

◆ **Preserve Exact Colors.** Select the check box to hold exact color measurements in the lookup table.

⑤ Click **OK**.

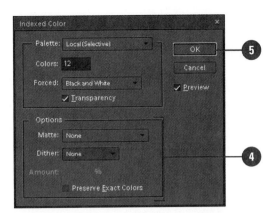

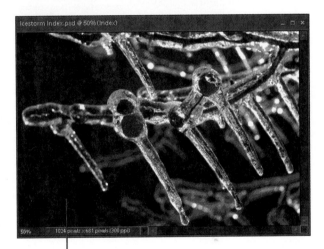

Indexed color image

Did You Know?

You can adjust the color lookup table (CLUT) of an indexed image. In the Editor, click the Image menu, point to Mode, and then click Color Table. Click the Table list arrow, select Custom, and then click on one of the colors in the table. Photoshop Elements opens a color picker dialog box, and lets you change the selected image color.

You can use a predefined indexed color table. In the Editor, click the Image menu, point to Mode, and then click Color Table. Click the Table list arrow, select a color table (Black Body, Grayscale, Spectrum, and System—Mac OS or Windows), and then click OK.

Using the Color Swatches Palette

Photoshop Elements not only lets you select virtually any colors you desire, it also lets you store those colors for future use. For example, you create a color scheme for a recurring brochure and you want a way to save those colors, or you're working on an Internet graphic and you need a web-safe color palette. Whatever your color needs, Photoshop Elements stands ready to meet them. The Color Swatches palette gives you access to 7 different color palettes and options that lets you create your own custom color palettes. The Color Swatches palette lets you select virtually any color you need.

Choose a Color Swatch in the Color Swatches Palette

1. In the Editor, display the **Color Swatches** palette.

2. Click the **Swatches** list arrow, and then select from the following color palettes:

   - **Default.** Displays a color palette of RGB and pure colors.

   - **Mac OS.** Displays a color palette designed for the Mac; uses hexadecimal values.

   - **Photo Filter Colors.** Displays a color palette of warming and cooling filtered colors.

   - **Web Hues.** Displays a color palette of hues for use on the web (Mac OS or Windows); uses hexadecimal values.

   - **Web Safe Colors.** Displays a color palette of 216 colors for use on the web (Mac OS or Windows); uses hexadecimal values.

   - **Web Spectrum.** Displays a color palette for use on the web (Mac OS or Windows); uses hexadecimal values.

   - **Windows.** Displays a color palette designed for Windows; uses hexadecimal values.

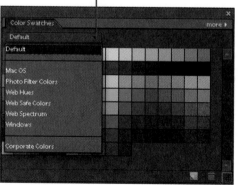

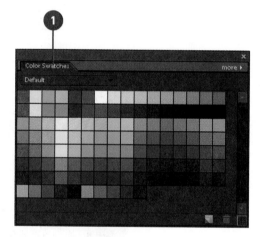

Choose Colors on the Color Swatches Palette

1 In the Editor, display the **Color Swatches** palette.

2 Click the **Swatches** list arrow, and then select the color swatch you want.

3 Select a color, and then change any of the following:

◆ **Foreground.** Change the color by clicking on any color in the Swatches palette.

◆ **Background.** Change the color by holding down the Ctrl key, and then clicking on any color in the Swatches palette.

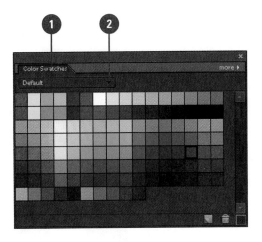

Change the Color Swatches Palette Display

1 In the Editor, display the **Color Swatches** palette.

2 Click the **More Options** button, and then select from the following color palettes:

◆ **Small Thumbnail.** Displays small color squares (default).

◆ **Large Thumbnail.** Displays large color squares.

◆ **Small List.** Displays small color squares with a color name in a list.

◆ **Large List.** Displays large color squares with a color name in a list.

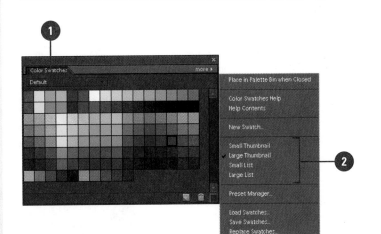

Creating Custom Color Swatches

Photoshop Elements not only lets you select virtually any colors you desire, it also lets you store those colors for future use. In addition to letting you select any color you need, the Color Swatches palette lets you add colors to a color swatch and save it as a custom color swatch that you can load and reuse later on this or any other computer.

Add Colors to the Color Swatches Palette

① In the Editor, set the foreground color in the toolbox to the color you want to add.

② Display the **Color Swatches** palette.

③ Click the **Swatches** list arrow, and then select the swatch you want to use.

④ Move the cursor below the last swatch color until it resembles a paint bucket; resize the palette, if necessary.

> **TIMESAVER** Click the New Swatch button at the bottom of the palette to add the color with the name Swatch 1.

⑤ Click once, name the color, and then click **OK**.

Did You Know?

You can delete a color from a Color Swatches palette. In the Editor, display the Color Swatches palette, click the Swatches list arrow, select the color swatch with the color you want to delete, hold down the Alt key, and then click the color you want to delete, or drag it to the Trash button.

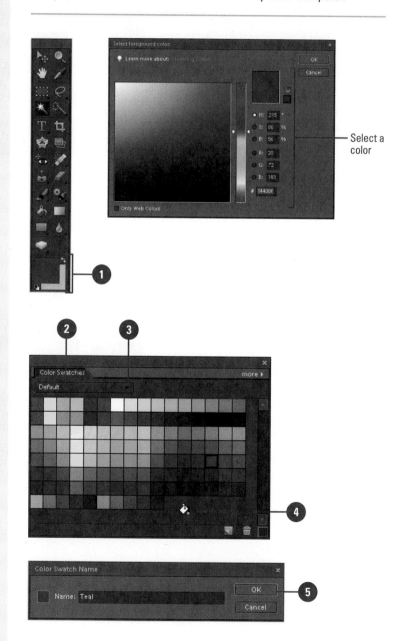

Select a color

Save a Customized Color Swatches Palette

1. In the Editor, display the **Color Swatches** palette.

2. Create a customized swatch palette by adding and/or deleting colors from an existing palette.

3. Click the **More Options** button, and then click **Save Swatches**.

4. Enter a name for the set (with the .ACO extension) in the File name box.

   The default folder location appears, displaying Adobe/Photoshop Elements 7.0/Presets/Color Swatches.

   When you store a color swatch palette in the default folder, it appears in the Swatches menu.

5. Click **Save**.

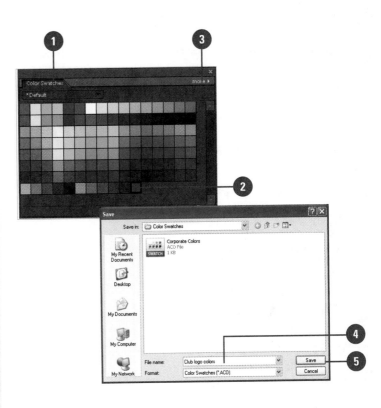

Load a Customized Color Swatches Palette

1. In the Editor, display the **Color Swatches** palette.

2. Click the **More Options** button, and then click **Load Swatches**.

   The default folder location appears, displaying Adobe/Photoshop Elements 7.0/Presets/Color Swatches.

3. Select the swatch palette file (.ACO) you want to load from the Color Swatches folder.

4. Click **Load**.

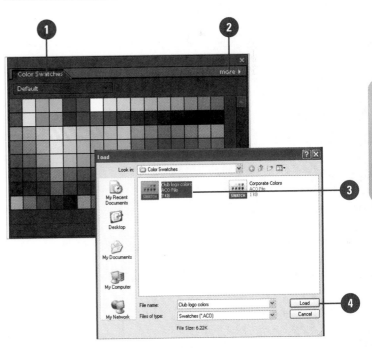

Working with Strokes and Fills

Photoshop Elements gives you many choices when it comes time to add or modify the colors of a document—paint brushes, airbrushes, and drawing tools, just to name a few. Two little used but powerful tools are the Stroke Selection and Fill Layer Commands, which work with selection tools. For example, you may want to create a unique stoke around an object, or fill a specific area of a document with a color or pattern. If that's the case, then the Stroke Selection and Fill Layer commands are the best and quickest ways to perform those operations.

Create a Stroke

① In the Editor, create a selection using any of the selection tools, or really get fancy and make a selection from one of the Shape drawing tools.

TIMESAVER *To further control the process, perform the stroke (or fill) operations on a new layer.*

② Click the **Edit** menu, and then click **Stroke (Outline) Selection**.

③ Enter a Width value (1 to 250) for the stroke.

④ Click the **Color** box, and then select a color (the color box defaults to the foreground color).

⑤ Select a location option (Inside, Center, or Outside) for the stroke of the selection marquee.

⑥ Click the **Mode** list arrow, and then select a blending mode.

⑦ Enter an Opacity percentage value (0 to 100) for the stroke.

⑧ Select the **Preserve Transparency** check box to protect any transparent image areas (if there are no transparent areas, this option is disabled).

⑨ Click **OK**.

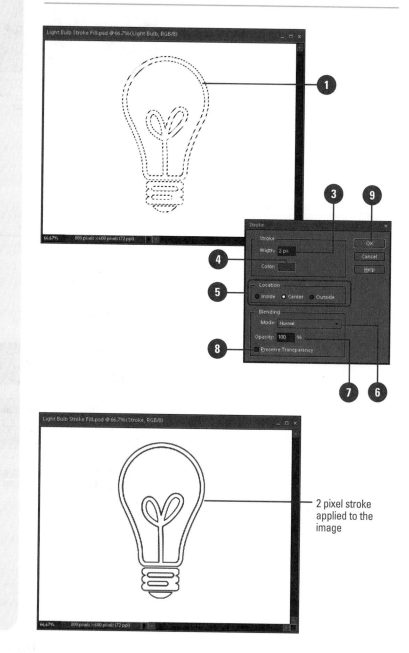

2 pixel stroke applied to the image

Create a Fill

① In the Editor, create a selection using any of the selection tools.

② Click the **Edit** menu, and then click **Fill Selection**.

③ Click the **Use** list arrow, and then select a fill option:

 ◆ Foreground Color

 ◆ Background Color

 ◆ Color

 ◆ Pattern

 ◆ Black

 ◆ 50% Gray

 ◆ White

④ Click the **Mode** list arrow, and then select a blending mode.

⑤ Enter an Opacity value (0 to 100) for the stroke.

⑥ Select the **Preserve Transparency** check box to protect any transparent image areas (if there are no transparent areas, this option is disabled).

⑦ Click **OK**.

Did You Know?

You can use the Fill Selection command for more than filling an area with a solid color or unique pattern. For example, selecting a sepia color, and changing the Fill Blending mode to Color, tints the selected area with sepia, creating an old-style, sepia-toned image. Experiment with the Fill blending modes to create unique image effects.

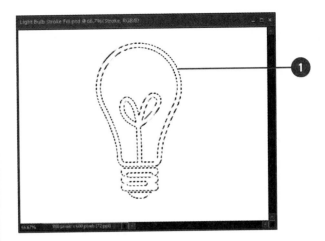

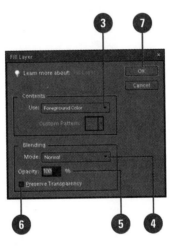

Fill applied to the image

Using Automatic Lighting and Color Commands

The automatic lighting and color commands make it easy to correct lighting and color problems in your photos. The Auto commands receive their adjustment cues from information within the active image, including any erroneous color information. For example, if the image contains a large border (typically white), the Auto commands will factor that information into the correction of the image. It's best to correct any dust, and scratch problems, and crop out any borders before applying the Auto Contrast and Color commands.

Use Automatic Lighting and Color Commands

1. In the Editor, open an image.

   ◆ To adjust a specific area, select it with one of the selection tools.

2. Click the **Enhance** menu, and then select one of the following Auto commands:

   ◆ Auto Smart Fix. Corrects overall color balance of an image.

   ◆ Auto Levels. Adjusts the overall contrast of an image and may affect its color. This maps the lightest and darkest pixels in each color channel to black and white.

   ◆ Auto Contrast. Adjusts the the overall contrast of an image without affecting color. This maps the lightest and darkest pixels to black and white.

   ◆ Auto Color Correction. Adjusts the contrast and color of an image. This neutralizes the midtones and sets the white and black points using set values.

   ◆ Auto Sharpen. Adjusts the sharpness of an image.

   ◆ Auto Red Eye Fix. Detects and removes red eyes in an image.

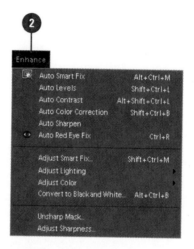

Original image

Auto Smart Fix applied

Working with the Histogram Palette

The Histogram palette gives you many options for viewing tonal and color information about the active image. The Histogram's default display is the tonal range of the entire image. However, you can use any of the selection tools, select a portion of the active document, and display a histogram for that portion of the image. The tonal range and color values for an image are vitally important to generating great graphics, and the Histogram palette is a great resource for instant up-to-date information. You can view information about a specific pixel or range using the Histogram palette. To view information about a range of values, drag in the histogram to highlight the range.

Work with the Histogram Palette

1. In the Editor, display the **Histogram** palette.

   ◆ Click the **Window** menu, and then click **Histogram**.

2. Click the **Channel** list arrow, and then select the color channels you want to view:

   ◆ **RGB.** Displays the tonal range for all Red, Green, and Blue colors.

   ◆ **Red, Green, or Blue.** Displays the tonal range for either Red, Green, or Blue.

   ◆ **Luminosity.** Displays the tonal range for luminosity (lightness).

   ◆ **Colors.** Displays the tonal range for all colors (in color).

3. Click the **Source** list arrow, and then select an image source: **Entire Image**, **Selected Layer**, or **Adjustment Composite**.

4. To view information about a range of values, drag in the histogram to highlight the range.

5. To refresh the image cache (rescans the image), click the **Uncached Refresh** button.

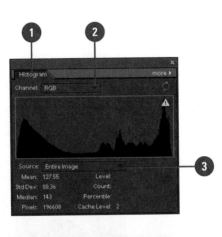

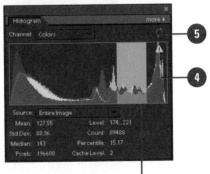

Color tonal range

Controlling Tonal Range with Levels

Through interactive feedback using a histogram, the Levels adjustment gives you live information about the tonal values in the active image. It's an excellent tool to perform overall tonal adjustments, and some color correction. Auto Levels is considered a quick fix color adjustment which, in some cases, works just as well as manually correcting color. However, with all the problems that exist in the average photo, it's always best to manually adjust an image. The Levels adjustment lets you adjust the tonal range of an image by giving you three sliders—shadows, midtones, and highlights. Dragging the sliders precisely adjusts the tonal ranges of an image. In addition, the Output sliders lets you adjust the ink percentages used for the output to print. By adjusting the output ink levels, you avoid the overly black images that sometimes accompany printing images using high dot-gain papers.

Control Tonal Range with Levels

1. In the Editor, open a document in which you want to change the tonal range.

2. Click the **Enhance** menu, point to **Adjust Lighting**, and then click **Levels**.

   TIMESAVER *Press Ctrl+L to adjust lighting color levels.*

3. Select the **Preview** check box to view the adjustments directly in the active document window.

4. Click the **Channel** list arrow to select whether to work on the entire image, or just one of the images default color channels (useful for color correction).

5. Drag the **Shadow** input slider to the right to adjust the balance of black in the image.

6. Drag the **Midtone** input slider left or right to lighten or darken the midtones of the image.

7. Drag the **Highlight** input slider to the left to adjust the balance of white in the image.

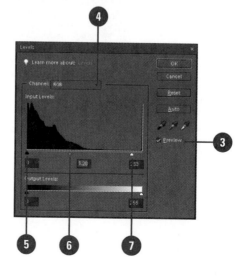

⑧ Drag the **Black** and **White Output Levels** sliders left and right to adjust the percentage of ink used in printing the image.

⑨ Use the eyedropper tools to select black, white, and midtone points directly within the active image.

⑩ Click **OK**.

Photoshop Elements uses the Levels adjustment layer to apply the tonal changes to the image.

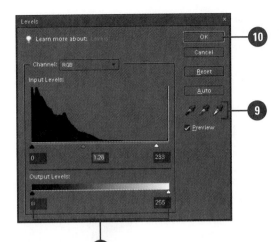

Tonal changes applied

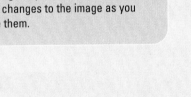

Did You Know?

You can apply the same Levels adjustments using an adjustment layer. In the Editor, display the Layers palette, select the layer you want to change, click the Create Fill Or Adjustment Layer button, and then click Levels. Make your adjustments using the Levels options, and then click OK.

You can view the Levels histogram anytime. In the Editor, click the Window menu, and then click Histogram. Photoshop Elements opens a Histogram palette that lets you view tonal changes to the image as you make them.

Using the Shadows/Highlights Adjustment

The Shadows/Highlights adjustment lets you quickly correct the problems associated with the over and under-exposed areas of an image such as deep shadows or bright highlights. In addition, the Shadows/Highlights adjustment makes quick work out of images that have really dark shadows or overexposed areas by adjusting the problem areas without changing the middle range of the image.

Use the Shadows/Highlights Adjustment

1. In the Editor, open an image.

2. Click the **Enhance** menu, point to **Adjust Lighting**, and then click **Shadows/Highlights**.

3. Select the **Preview** check box to view changes to the active image.

4. Drag the **Lighten Shadows** slider right or left to adjust the shadow areas of the active image.

5. Drag the **Darken Highlights** slider left or right to adjust the highlight areas of the active image.

6. Drag the **Midtone Contrast** slider left or right to decrease or increase the contrast in the midtone areas of the image.

7. Click **OK**.

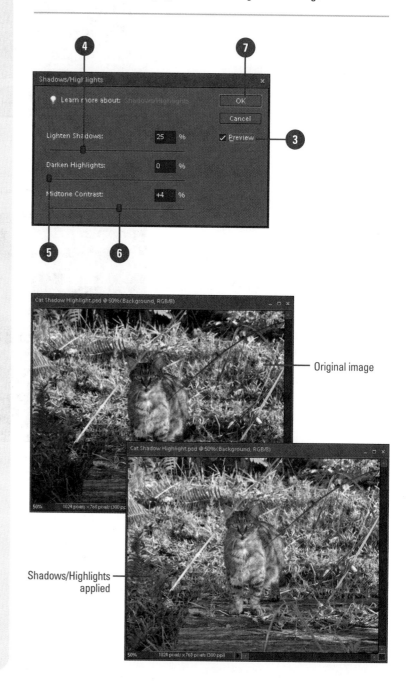

Original image

Shadows/Highlights applied

Using the Brightness/Contrast Adjustment

The Brightness/Contrast adjustment changes an image by an overall lightning or darkening of the image pixels. While good for special effects, its linear way of changing an image's brightness and contrast does not lend itself to photo restoration. Curves and Levels are much better for this type of work. The Brightness/Contrast adjustment performs linear adjustment to an image. For example, moving the brightness slider to the right will increase the brightness values of all the pixels in the image equally. Since photographs are not linear in nature, the Brightness/Contrast adjustment is not recommended for use on images. For images, use the Levels, and Curves (non-linear) adjustments, and use Brightness/Contrast for clip art, text, and non-photographic images.

Use the Brightness/Contrast Adjustment

1 In the Editor, open an image.

2 Click the **Enhance** menu, point to **Adjust Lighting**, and then click **Brightness/Contrast**.

3 Select the **Preview** check box to view changes to the active image.

4 Drag the **Brightness** slider left to decrease the brightness values or right to increase the values of the colors in the active image.

5 Drag the **Contrast** slider to the left to decrease the color steps or left to increase the steps in the image.

6 Click **OK**.

Did You Know?

You can use selection to control the Brightness/Contrast adjustment.
In the Editor, use any of the selection tools to isolate a portion of the image before using the Brightness/Contrast adjustment, and then only the selected areas will be adjusted.

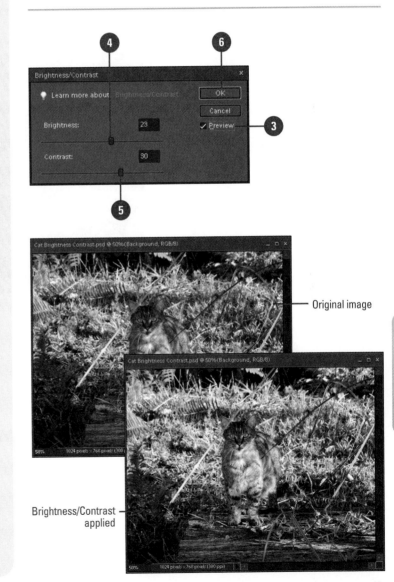

Original image

Brightness/Contrast applied

Using the Color Curves Adjustment

The Color Curves adjustment lets you adjust tonal ranges in the image without changing image exposure. Curves is an excellent adjustment for lightening the dark shadows of an image to bring out detail, or for creating special effects like solarization. During the adjustment process you can control how individual settings (Highlights, Brightness, Contrast, and Shadows) are converted. If you're not sure how or where to start, you can select a preset style designed for a specific use. The styles include Backlight, Darken Highlights, Default, Increase Contrast, Increase Midtones, Lighten Shadows, and Solarize. A before and after preview appears in the Adjust Color Curve dialog box, where you can compare the results to the original image.

Use the Color Curves Adjustment

1. In the Editor, open an image.

2. Click the **Enhance** menu, point to **Adjust Color**, and then click **Adjust Color Curves**.

3. Select a style for the color curve you want.

   Each style provides a preset amount of highlights, brightness, contrast, and shadows.

4. Drag the **Adjust Highlights**, **Adjust Brightness**, **Adjust Contrast**, and **Adjust Shadows** sliders to the level you want for your image.

5. To reset the options back to the original settings, click **Reset**.

6. Click **OK**.

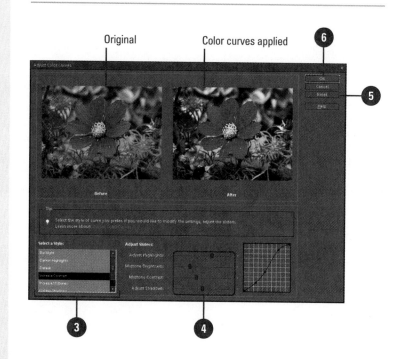

Original   Color curves applied

Using the Hue/ Saturation Adjustment

The Hue/Saturation adjustment gives you separate control over an image's hue, saturation, and lightness, and its Colorize option lets you apply a color cast to an image that's similar to a duotone effect. The Remove Color command removes all the color from an image, which preserves the Hue and Lightness values of the pixels, and changes the Saturation value to zero (desaturate). The result is a grayscale image.

Use the Hue/Saturation Adjustment

1. In the Editor, open an image.

2. Click the **Enhance** menu, point to **Adjust Color**, and then click **Adjust Hue/Saturation**.

   TIMESAVER *Press Ctrl+U to adjust Hue/Saturation levels.*

3. Select the **Preview** check box to see how your image looks.

4. Drag the **Hue**, **Saturation**, and **Lightness** sliders to the level you want for your image.

5. Click the **Edit** list arrow, select a color, and then drag the sliders to adjust the values for that range of colors.

6. Select the **Colorize** check box to color tint the image with the current foreground color.

7. Click **OK**.

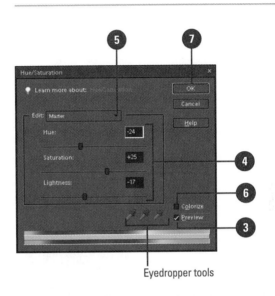

Eyedropper tools

Original image

Hue/Saturation applied

Did You Know?

You can saturate or desaturate selected areas of an image using the Sponge tool. In the Editor, click the Sponge tool, select Saturate or Desaturate on the Options bar, and then drag to slowly remove color from the image.

Using the Replace Color Adjustment

The Replace Color command lets you create a selection, based on image color, and replace that color selection with any other color. The Replace Color adjustment accomplishes this by giving you access to the three items that control color: Hue, Saturation, and Lightness. Hue gives you the ability to change the image's physical color, Saturation controls the amount of color, and Lightness determines how bright the color is, based on its Hue and Saturation.

Use the Replace Color Adjustment

① In the Editor, open a color document.

② Click the **Enhance** menu, point to **Adjust Color**, and then click **Replace Color**.

③ Select the **Preview** check box to view the changes in the active document.

④ Click on the active document using the Selection eyedroppers to select, add, or subtract colors.

⑤ Click the **Color** box to select a specific color for the selection.

⑥ Drag the **Fuzziness** slider to increase or decrease the number of similar colors that are included in the selection.

⑦ Click the **Selection** or **Image** option to toggle between a view of the selection mask and the active image (white areas of the mask represent selection).

⑧ Drag the **Hue**, **Saturation**, and **Lightness** sliders to change the selected areas.

⑨ Click **OK**.

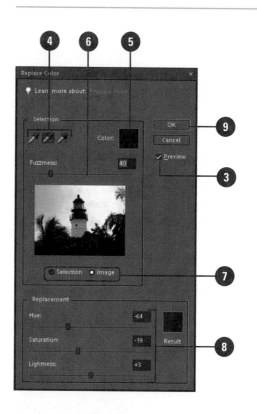

Replace Color applied

Using the Color Variations Adjustment

The Color Variations adjustment gives you a look at how working with analogous and complementary colors impacts the color in a document. For example, if an image has an overall green cast, it needs additional magenta. Understanding how colors interact and work to produce different colors helps you decide the correct course of action to take, and the Variations adjustment is an excellent teacher.

Use the Color Variations Adjustment

1. In the Editor, open a document.

2. Click the **Enhance** menu, point to **Adjust Color**, and then click **Color Variations**.

   The Original and Current Pick are displayed in the upper-left portions of the Variations dialog box.

3. To restore the image, click **Before** any time during the adjustment process.

4. Click the **Shadows**, **Midtones**, **Highlights**, or **Saturation** options to apply a color shift.

5. Drag the **Amount** slider to determine how much change occurs with each adjustment.

6. Click the color thumbnails surrounding the image to add specific colors to the After image.

7. Click **Lighten** or **Darken** to change the brightness of the After image.

8. Click **OK**.

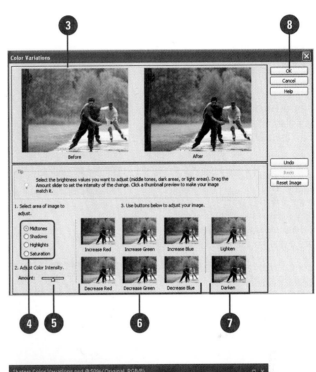

Color Variation applied

Using the Remove Color Cast Adjustment

A color cast is an incorrect color shift in a photo. Typically, you notice a color cast in the form of too much yellow in a photo. The Remove Color Cast command changes the overall mixture of colors to remove color casts from a photo. All you need to do to use the Remove Color Cast command is click the area with the color cast that should be white, black, or neutral gray. Photoshop Elements changes the image based on where you click to remove the color cast.

Use the Remove Color Cast Adjustment

① In the Editor, open a color document.

② Click the **Enhance** menu, point to **Adjust Color**, and then click **Remove Color Cast**.

③ Select the **Preview** check box to view the changes in the active document.

④ Click the area with the color cast that should be white, black, or neutral gray.

The image changes based on where you click to remove the color cast.

⑤ To reset the options back to the original settings, click **Reset**.

⑥ Click **OK**.

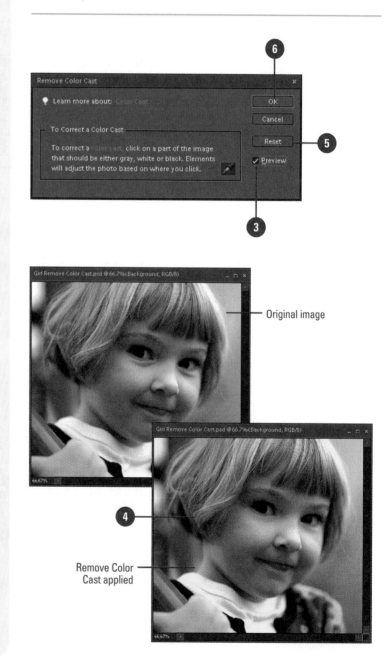

Original image

Remove Color Cast applied

Did You Know?

You can remove all color from an image to display grayscale shades. In the Editor, display the Layers palette, select the layer you want to change, click the Enhance menu, point to Adjust Color, and then click Remove Color. The image's color mode remains the same.

258

Adjusting Color for Skin Tone

The Adjust Color for Skin Tone command lets you subtly adjust the overall color in a photo to adjust the color for skin tone. You can automatically adjust skin tones and other colors in the photo or manually adjust the brown (Tan) and red (Blush) colors using sliders to achieve the results you want. You can adjust the overall color of skin tones using the Temperature slider.

Adjust Color for Skin Tone

1. In the Editor, open a color document.

2. Click the **Enhance** menu, point to **Adjust Color**, and then click **Adjust Color for Skin Tone**.

3. Select the **Preview** check box to view the changes in the active document.

4. Click the area of skin you want to correct.

5. Drag any of the following sliders to fine-tune the skin tone:

   - **Tan.** Increase or decreases the level of brown in skin tones.

   - **Blush.** Increases or decreases the level of red in skin tones.

   - **Temperature.** Changes the overall color of skin tones

6. To reset the options back to the original settings, click **Reset**.

7. Click **OK**.

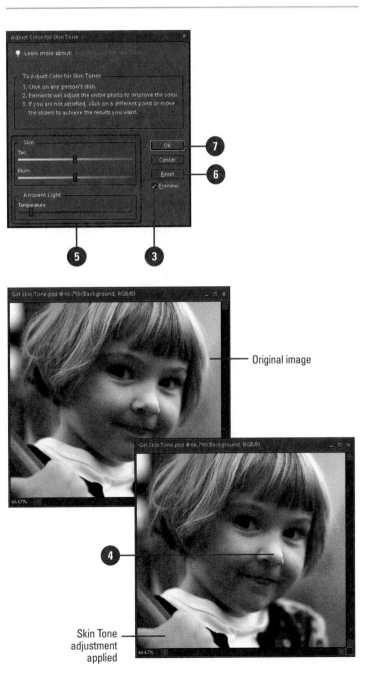

Original image

Skin Tone adjustment applied

Using the Gradient Map Adjustment

The Gradient Map adjustment replaces the tonal values of the image with the colors supplied by a gradient. It's a great tool for generating special color effects. In addition, the Gradient Map adjusts the active image's colors to the colors of the selected gradient; taking the shadows of the image and mapping them to one endpoint of the gradient, and the highlights to the other point.

Use the Gradient Map Adjustment

1. In the Editor, open an image.

2. Click the **Filter** menu, point to **Adjustments**, and then click **Gradient Map**.

3. Select the **Preview** check box to view changes to the active image.

4. Click the **Gradient Used For Grayscale Mapping** list arrow to adjust the gradient.

5. Select or clear the **Dither** or **Reverse** check boxes for the Gradient Options.

6. Click **OK**.

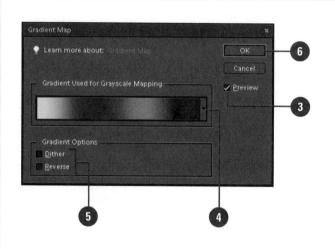

Gradient Map applied

Using the Photo Filter Adjustment

The Photo Filter adjustment lets you apply a specific filter or color to an image. Applying the Photo Filter adjustment to an image is similar to placing a colored filter in front of a camera lens. Photographers use filters to help correct color problems associated with unique lighting conditions—early morning sunlight or indoor florescent lighting—you can use Photo Filter adjustments to get the same results.

Use the Photo Filter Adjustment

1. In the Editor, open an image.

2. Click the **Filter** menu, point to **Adjustments**, and then click **Photo Filter**.

3. Select the **Preview** check box to view changes to the active image.

4. Click the **Filter** option, click the **Filter** list arrow, and then select from the available color filter options.

5. Click the **Color** option to choose your own color.

6. Drag the **Density** slider left or right to adjust the intensity of the filter effect on the active image.

   The higher the value, the greater the effect.

7. Select the **Preserve Luminosity** check box to preserve the color of the image highlights.

8. Click **OK**.

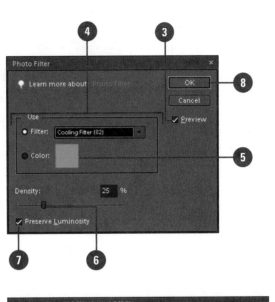

Original image

Photo Filter applied

Using the Invert and Equalize Commands

The Invert command reverses the colors and tonal values to their opposite values; in effect creating a negative. The Equalize command exaggerates the contrast between similar color values. It's useful in finding stray pixels in a seemingly solid color area, or for a special color effect.

Use the Invert Command

1. In the Editor, open an image.

2. Click the **Filter** menu, point to **Adjustments**, and then click **Invert**.

   TIMESAVER *Press Ctrl+I to use the Invert command.*

   The brightness values of each image channel are reversed, creating a negative color or grayscale image.

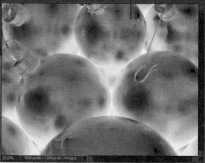
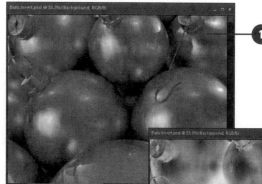

Invert adjustment applied to the image

Use the Equalize Command

1. In the Editor, open an image.

2. Click the **Filter** menu, point to **Adjustments**, and then click **Equalize**.

   The brightness values of the image pixels are distributed in a way that more accurately represents the entire range of brightness levels from white to black.

Equalize adjustment applied to the image

Using the Threshold and Posterize Adjustments

The Threshold adjustment splits an image into black and white, based on the original brightness levels of the pixels. It's useful for locating the darkest and lightest pixels in an image, or for creating some great looking black and white special effects. The Posterize adjustment creates a simpler image by reducing the number of colors. It's useful for creating an image with a clip art look, or for reducing the number of colors in preparation for the web.

Use the Threshold Adjustment

1 In the Editor, open an image.

2 Click the **Filter** menu, point to **Adjustments**, and then click **Threshold**.

3 Select the **Preview** check box to view changes to the active image.

4 Drag the **Threshold** slider to the right or left to change the point in which black and white are defined.

For example, setting the threshold slider to a value of 75 creates an image where all pixels with a brightness value of 75 or less are black, and all pixels with a value of 76 or higher are white.

5 Click **OK**.

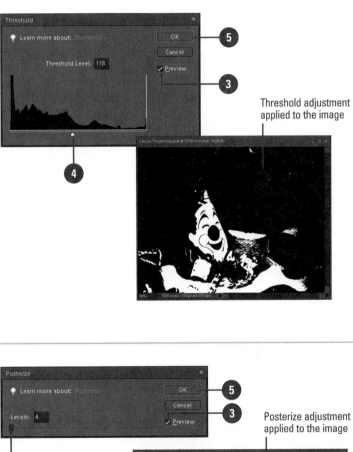

Threshold adjustment applied to the image

Use the Posterize Adjustment

1 In the Editor, open an image.

2 Click the **Filter** menu, point to **Adjustments**, and then click **Posterize**.

3 Select the **Preview** check box to view changes to the active image.

4 Drag the slider to select a Levels value (2 to 255) to define the number of colors used.

Lower values produce less colors, and more visual contrast.

5 Click **OK**.

Posterize adjustment applied to the image

Using the Black and White Adjustment

The Convert to Black and White adjustment allows you to convert a color image to grayscale. During the adjustment process you can control how individual colors (Reds, Greens, and Blues) are converted. You can also adjust the color contrast. If you're not sure how or where to start, you can select a preset style designed for a specific use. The styles include Newspaper, Portraits, Scenic Landscape, and Urban/Snapshots. A before and after preview appears in the Convert to Black and White dialog box, where you can compare the results to the original image.

Convert an Image to Black and White

1 In the Editor, open an image.

2 Click the **Enhance** menu, and then click **Convert to Black and White**.

> **TIMESAVER** *Press Alt+Ctrl+B to convert an image to black and white.*

3 Select a style for the black and white conversion.

Each style provides a preset amount of the red, green, and blue color channels.

4 Drag the **Red, Green, Blue**, and **Contrast** sliders to the level you want for your image.

5 To undo/redo the previous adjustment, click **Undo** or **Redo**.

6 To reset the options to the original settings, click **Reset**.

7 Click **OK**.

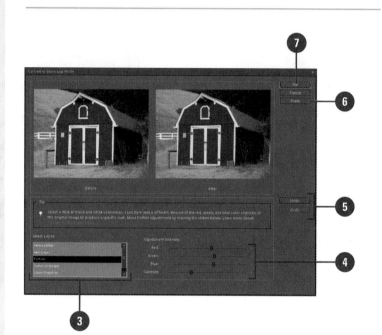

Using Transformation and Retouching Tools

12

Introduction

Once a selection is made in the Editor, the next step is to get to work. The Transform commands let you move, modify, or resize the area enclosed within the selection area. Transform gives you several options, such as Skew, Distort, and Perspective, which you can use to modify an existing selection, while Scale allows you to resize a photo, layer, selection, or shape. If you have scanned a photo that is not straight, you can use several commands to straighten, crop, rotate, and flip the photo the way you want. You can even use the Divide Scanned Photos command to automatically divide and straighten each photo into a separate file. With the Cookie Cutter tool, you can crop a photo into a shape, just like a cookie cutter cuts dough into a shape.

One of Photoshop Elements' most powerful features is its ability to retouch a photographic image. If a photo is out-of-focus, you can use the Adjust Sharpness or Unsharp Mask filter, or Sharpen tool. If you want to reduce detail in a photo to highlight another area, the Blur tool allows you to manually soften hard edges or areas. The Correct Camera Distortion filter fixes flaws when shooting images that appear distorted. If you need to fix a specific area of a photo, you can use several different tools. You can use the Dodge and Burn tools to lighten or darken specific areas of a photo, the Sponge tool to bring out or mute color, the Clone Stamp tool to sample a part of a photo to apply it (fix) to another area, and the Healing Brush and Spot Healing Brush tools to correct small imperfections, making them disappear into the surrounding image. An additional touch up tool is the Red Eye tool, which not only gives the digital restorer an excellent tool for removing pesky red eye, it also removes the green and white reflections in pets' eyes. Finally, the Smart Brush tool (**New!**) enables you to touch up photos in dozens of ways, from brightening eyes and teeth to applying lipstick or a sepia tone, by just painting in the effect you want.

What You'll Do

Use Free Transform and Transform

Use 3D Transform

Resize an Image to Scale

Use the Cookie Cutter Tool

Use Straighten and Crop

Use Rotate and Flip

Correct Camera Distortion

Use the Adjust Sharpness Filter

Use the Sharpen Tool

Use the Unsharp Mask Filter

Use the Blur Tool

Use the Clone Stamp Tool

Use the Dodge and Burn Tools

Use the Sponge Tool

Use the Healing Brush Tool

Work with the Spot Healing Brush

Work with the Red Eye Tool

Retouch with the Smart Brush

Work with the Detail Smart Brush

Using Free Transform and Transform

Once a selection is made, the next step is to get to work. Selections are not just to control color correction, or image enhancement. It's possible you may need to use some of the Transform commands. The transform commands let you move, modify, or resize the area enclosed within the selection area. Unlike the Free Transform command, Transform gives you several options, such as Skew, Distort, and Perspective, which you can use to modify an existing selection. The selection area is visually defined by a bounding box with nodes, or anchor points, in the four corners and the center of each axis.

Use the Free Transform Command

1. In the Editor, open an image.

2. Select an area of an image using any of the selection tools.

3. Click the **Image** menu, point to **Transform**, and then click **Free Transform**.

   TIMESAVER *Press Ctrl+T to use the Free Transform command.*

4. Move to any of the four corners, and then drag to expand or contract the size of the selection.

   ◆ If needed, drag the slider to reduce/display the selection to drag the resize or rotate handles.

   Move outside the bounding box selection until your cursor resembles a bent arrow, and then drag to rotate the selection.

   Drag the horizontal or vertical center nodes to expand the image.

5. Press Enter, or double-click inside the bounding box to apply the transformation, or click the **Commit** (green check mark) or **Cancel** (red circle with a line through it) button under the bounding box.

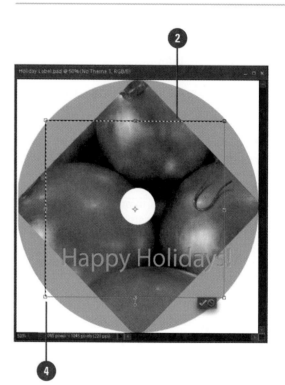

Use the Transform Command

1. In the Editor, open an image.

2. Select an area of an image using any of the selection tools.

3. Click the **Image** menu, point to **Transform**, and then select an option:

   - **Skew.** Lets you select a node and drag it in vertical or horizontal direction without affecting the other nodes.

   - **Distort.** Lets you select a node and drag it in any direction desired without affecting the other nodes.

   - **Perspective.** Lets you change the perspective of a selection.

4. Select any settings you want on the Options bar and modify the transformed image.

   - If needed, drag the slider to reduce/display the selection so that you can see the resize or rotate handles.

5. Click the **Commit** (green check mark) or **Cancel** (red circle with a line through it) button under the bounding box.

4 Perspective

Did You Know?

You can create proportional transform boundaries. Holding down the Shift key while dragging a corner handle maintains the proportions of the image.

You can use the Free Transform command to create distorted images. Hold down the Ctrl key while dragging a corner handle to create a distorted selection.

Using 3D Transform

The 3D Transform filter allows you to take a 2D object and view it as a 3D object. You can transform a 2D object into a 3D cube, sphere, or cylinder and then modify it in 3D using wireframes. You can change a 3D cube into a box, a 3D sphere into a can, or a 3D cylinder into a bottle. In addition, you can use the Zoom and Hand tools to change your preview of the image.

Use the 3D Transform Filter

1. In the Editor, open an image.

2. Select the photo, layer, or selection you want to transform.

3. Click the **Filter** menu, point to **Render**, and then click **3D Transform**.

4. Click **Options**.

5. Select from the following options:

   ◆ **Resolution.** Sets the quality of the rendered image: Low, Medium, or High.

   ◆ **Anti-aliasing.** Sets the level of anti-aliasing smoothing to apply: None, Low, Medium, or High.

   ◆ **Display Background.** Select to displays the original image outside of the wireframe in the preview and the rendered image.

6. Click **OK**.

7. Create a 3D wireframe by dragging one of the following tools over the image area:

   ◆ **Cube Tool.** Maps the image to a cubic surface, such as a cabinet.

   ◆ **Sphere Tool.** Maps the image to a spherical surface, such as a ball.

   ◆ **Cylinder Tool.** Maps the image to a cylindrical surface, such as a can.

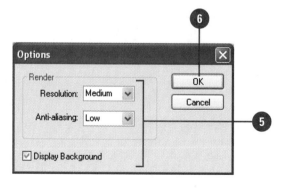

8 To move or reshape the wireframe, use any of the following:

- **Move Frame.** Select the **Selection** tool, and then drag a frame edge.

- **Move Anchor.** Select the **Direct Selection** tool, and then drag an anchor point.

- **Add Anchor.** Select the **Add Anchor Point** tool, and then click the right side of the frame.

- **Convert Anchor.** Select the **Convert Anchor Point** tool, and then click the point (smooth to corner, or corner to smooth).

- **Delete Anchor.** Select the **Delete Anchor Point** tool, and then click the point.

9 To move or rotate the object within the wireframe, use any of the following:

- **Move Object.** Select the **Pan Camera** tool, and then drag the object.

- **Rotate Object.** Select the **Trackball** tool, and then drag the object.

10 Enter a value between 1 and 130 in the Field of View box to make the wireframe fit the image better.

11 Enter a value between 0 and 99 in the Dolly Camera box to adjust the position of the camera closer or further from the image.

12 Click **OK**.

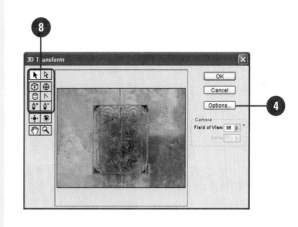

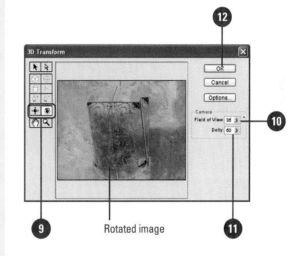

Rotated image

3D Transform applied

Resizing an Image to Scale

You can use the Scale command in Photoshop Elements to resize a photo, layer, selection, or shape. You can use options available on the Options bar to help you draw the bounding box to the size you want. If the bounding box is still not right, you can move and resize it to get the exact results you want.

Use the Scale Commands

1 In the Editor, open an image.

2 Select the photo, layer, selection, or shape you want to scale.

3 Click the **Image** menu, point to **Resize**, and then click **Scale**.

4 Use any of the following options to scale the selected item:

◆ **Height and Width.** Drag a resize handle to the height and width you want.

◆ **Percentage.** Specify a height and width percentage in the Options bar.

◆ **Relative Proportions.** Select the **Constrain Proportions** check box in the Options bar, and then drag a resize handle to the height and width you want.

If you deselect this check box, you can also hold down the Shift key as you drag to constrain proportions.

5 Click the **Commit** (green check mark) or **Cancel** (red circle with a line through it) button under the bounding box.

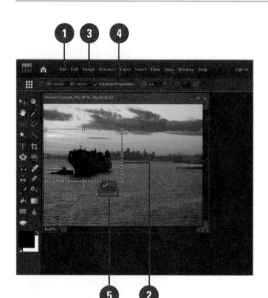

Scale applied

Using the Cookie Cutter Tool

The Cookie Cutter tool allows you to crop a photo into a shape, just like a cookie cutter cuts dough into a shape. After you select a shape in the Options bar, you can drag the shape within the photo to specify the area you want to crop. You can use Shape Options to help you draw the shape the way you want. If the shape is still not right, you can move and resize the shape to get the exact results you want.

Use the Cookie Cutter Tool

1. In the Editor, open an image.

2. Select the **Cookie Cutter** tool on the toolbox.

3. Click the **Shapes** list arrow on the Options bar to view the shapes library.

   ◆ Click the triangle on the right side of the library to select other libraries.

4. Double-click the shape you want.

5. Click the **Shape Options** list arrow on the Options bar, and then select the option you want:

   ◆ **Unconstrained.** Draws a shape to any size.

   ◆ **Defined Proportions.** Draws a shape in proportion (height and width) to the original cookie cutter shape.

   ◆ **Defined Size.** Crops the photo to the exact size of the original shape.

   ◆ **Fixed Size.** Specify an exact size of the shape.

   ◆ **From Center.** Select to draw from center.

6. Enter a Feather value to soften the edges of the shape.

7. Drag within the image to create the shape size.

8. Click the **Commit** (green check mark) or **Cancel** (red circle with a line through it) button under the bounding box.

Using Straighten and Crop

If you have scanned photo that is not straight, you can use several commands to straighten and crop the photo the way you want. If you have several photos on a scanned page with clear separation between them, you can use the Divide Scanned Photo command to automatically divide and straighten each photo into a separate file. If you have an individual photo, you can straighten it or crop a portion to isolate just one part of the image. When you crop a photo and then enlarge the area you cropped, you lose photo detail. You can use the Straighten Image or Straighten and Crop Image commands to automatically perform these operations, or use the Crop tool on the toolbox or the Crop command to crop a photo by hand.

Use the Divide Scanned Photos Command

1 In the Editor, open the file with the scanned photos you want to change.

The photos in the file must have a clear separation between them.

2 Click the **Image** menu, and then click **Divide Scanned Photo**.

Photoshop Elements automatically divides and straightens each image in a separate file.

Did You Know?

You can also use the Straighten tool on the toolbox. Select the Straighten tool on the toolbox, click the Canvas Options list arrow on the Options bar, and then select an option: Grow Or Shrink Canvas To Fit, Crop To Remove Background, or Crop To Original Size. Select or deselect the Rotate All Layers check box on the Options bar, and then drag a selection box around the area you want to straighten.

Divided scanned photo

Use the Straighten and Crop Commands

1. In the Editor, open an image.

2. If you want to work with a portion of the image, select an area using any of the selection tools.

3. Click the **Image** menu, point to **Rotate**, and then select the command you want:

   - **Straighten and Crop Image.** Straightens and crops the current image.

   - **Straighten Image.** Straightens the current image.

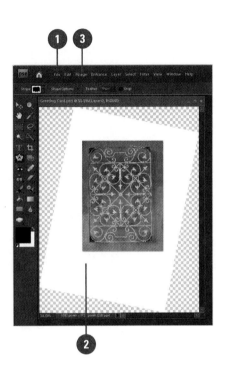

Use the Crop Tool

1. In the Editor, open an image.

2. Click the **Crop** tool on the toolbox, and then drag a selection.

   TIMESAVER *Click the Image menu, and then click Crop.*

3. Drag a cropping handle to resize the bounding box to the area you want to use. The area outside of the bounding box is cropped out.

4. Click the **Commit** (green check mark) or **Cancel** (red circle with a line through it) button under the bounding box.

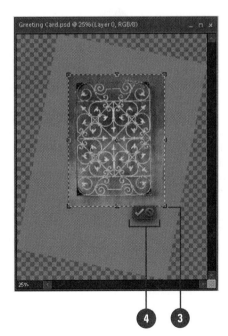

Using Rotate and Flip

After you open a photo, you can change its orientation by rotating or flipping it. This is useful when you want to change the orientation of an object or image, such as changing the direction of an arrow. You can rotate or flip an entire photo, a selection or a layer. Rotating turns an item 90 degrees to the right or left or 180 degrees; flipping turns an item 180 degrees horizontally or vertically. For a more freeform rotation, which you cannot achieve in 90 or 180 degree increments, use the Free Rotate Selection command and then drag a handle on the bounding box.

Use the Rotate Commands

1 In the Editor, open an image.

2 Deselect a selection to rotate the entire photo, make a selection to rotate that selection, or select a layer to rotate that layer.

3 Click the **Image** menu, point to **Rotate**, and then select the command you want:

- ◆ **90° Left, 90° Right, or 180°.** Rotates the entire image 90 degrees left or right, or 180 degrees.

- ◆ **Custom.** Rotates the entire image to a specified angle right or left.

- ◆ **Free Rotate Selection/Layer.** Rotates the selection or active layer to a specified angle right or left.

- ◆ **Selection 90° Left, Selection 90° Right, or Selection 180°.** Rotates the selection in a photo 90 degrees left or right, or 180 degrees.

- ◆ **Layer 90° Left, Layer 90° Right, or Layer 180°.** Rotates the selected layer within a photo 90 degrees left or right, or 180 degrees.

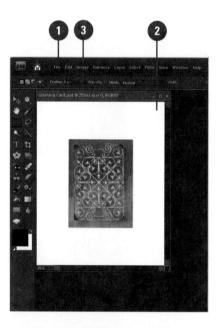

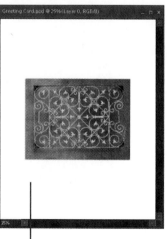

Rotation applied

Use the Flip Commands

① In the Editor, open an image.

② Deselect a selection to flip the entire photo, make a selection to flip that selection, or select a layer to flip that layer.

③ Click the **Image** menu, point to **Rotate**, and then select an option:

- ◆ **Flip Horizontal or Flip Vertical.** Flips the entire image.

- ◆ **Flip Selection Horizontal or Flip Selection Vertical.** Flips the selected area.

- ◆ **Flip Layer Horizontal or Flip Layer Vertical.** Flips the active layer or layers.

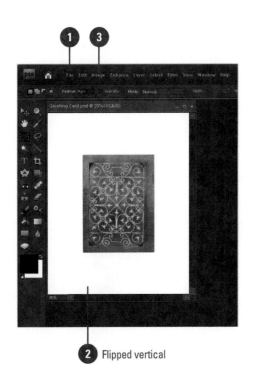

② Flipped vertical

Correcting Camera Distortion

The Correct Camera Distortion filter fixes flaws when shooting images, such as barrel and pincushion distortion, and vignetting. **Barrel** distortion causes straight lines to bow out toward the edges of the image. On the other hand, **Pincushion** distortion has the opposite effect (straight lines bend inward). **Vignetting** is a defect where edges of an image are darker than the center. In addition, you can use the Correct Camera Distortion filter to rotate an image or fix perspective caused by tilting the camera. Although some of these corrections can be made with the Transform commands, the image grid makes adjustments easier.

Use the Lens Correction Filter

1. In the Editor, open an image.

2. Click the **Filter** menu, and then click **Correct Camera Distortion**.

   ◆ If prompted, click **OK** to simplify a layer.

3. Select the **Preview** check box to view the changes to the image.

4. Select from the following tools:

   ◆ **Hand Tool.** Select the tool, and then click and drag to move the image within the view window.

   ◆ **Zoom Tool.** Select the tool, and then click in the view window to zoom in, or Alt+click to zoom out.

5. Drag the **Remove Distortion** slider left or right to precisely remove pincushion or barrel distortion.

6. Select from the following Vignette options:

   ◆ **Amount.** Drag left or right to lighten or darken the edges of the image.

   ◆ **Midpoint.** Drag left or right to select the midpoint for the vignette correction.

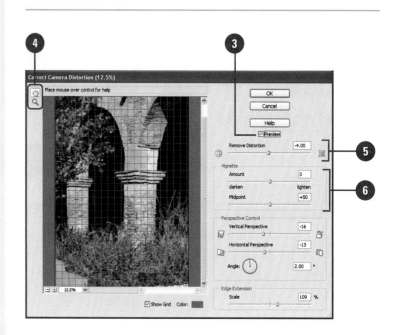

7 Select from the following Transform options:

◆ **Vertical Perspective.** Drag left or right to change the image's vertical perspective.

◆ **Horizontal Perspective.** Drag left or right to change the image's horizontal perspective.

◆ **Angle.** Drag the angle option to rotate the image clockwise, or counter clockwise.

◆ **Scale.** Drag left or right to change the scale (size) of the image.

8 Select the **Show Grid** check box to view or hide the visible grid.

9 Click the **Color** box to change the color of the grid.

10 Click **OK**.

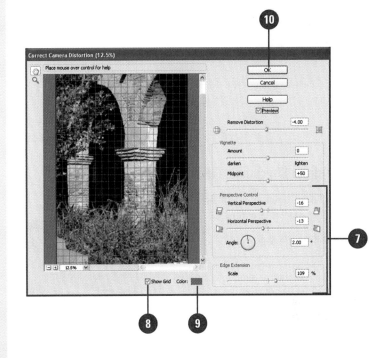

Using the Adjust Sharpness Filter

The Adjust Sharpness filter attempts to sharpen the pixels of an out-of-focus image in much the same way as Unsharp Mask. The major difference is the ability of Adjust Sharpness to remove previously applied Gaussian, Lens, and Motion Blur filters. For example, you've applied a Lens blur to an image, but later decide to reduce the effect. The problem is that Unsharp Mask will attempt to sharpen what it assumes to be an out-of-focus image. If you want Photoshop Elements to automatically sharpen an image, you can use the Auto Sharpen command on the Enhance menu or the Quick Fix tab.

Use the Adjust Sharpness Filter

1. In the Editor, open an image and display the **Layers** palette.

2. Select the layer you want to sharpen.

3. Click the **Enhance** menu, and then click **Adjust Sharpness**.

4. Select the **Preview** check box to view the results.

5. Select from the following Sharpen settings:

   ◆ **Amount.** Drag the slider to determine the amount of sharpness applied to the image.

   ◆ **Radius.** Drag the slider to determine the width of the sharpening effect.

   ◆ **Remove.** Click the list arrow, and then select what type of blur effect you are removing from the image.

   ◆ **Angle.** Enter the angle of the Motion Blur filter to remove.

   ◆ **More Refined.** Select for a more accurate (slower) sharpening effect.

6. Click **OK**.

Using the Sharpen Tool

The Sharpen tool allows you to manually sharpen the pixels of an out-of-focus image. With the Sharpen tool, you can select the areas of the image you want to sharpen. It's best to make small sharpening adjustments with the Strength option, so you can see the changes as they take place and prevent oversharpening (a grainy look). If you want to use additional sharpening controls, you can use the Adjust Sharpness command on the Enhance menu. On the other hand, if you want Photoshop Elements to automatically sharpen an image, you can use the Auto Sharpen command on the Enhance menu or the Quick Fix tab.

Use the Sharpen Tool

① In the Editor, open an image.

② Select the **Sharpen** tool on the toolbox.

③ Select from the following Sharpen options on the Options bar:

  ◆ **Brushes menu.** Click the **Brushes** list arrow on the Options bar next to the brush sample, select a Brushes category, and then select the brush you want.

  ◆ **Size.** Click the **Size** list arrow on the Options bar, and then select the size you want in pixels.

  ◆ **Mode.** Click the **Mode** list arrow, and then select the blend mode you want.

  ◆ **Strength.** Click the **Strength** list arrow on the Options bar, and then select a sharpening percentage.

  ◆ **All Layers.** Select the check box to sharpen all visible layers. Deselect the check box to sharpen only the active layer.

④ Drag over the part of the image you want to sharpen.

Sharpen applied

Using the Unsharp Mask Filter

The Unsharp Mask filter creates a visually sharper image by locating pixels that differ in value from surrounding pixels. When the filter is applied to the image, the bordering pixels specified by the threshold option get lighter and the darker pixels get darker. It's important to understand that the Unsharp Mask does not actually sharpen the image; it only attempts to create the illusion of sharpness. Be careful, an overapplication of this filter creates harsh images with ragged edges and shadows. Also, the effects of the Unsharp Mask filter appear more severe on a monitor with its low resolution, than when the document is output to a printer.

Use the Unsharp Mask Filter

1. In the Editor, open an image and display the **Layers** palette.

2. Select the layer you want to sharpen.

3. Click the **Enhance** menu, and then click **Unsharp Mask**.

4. Select from the following options:

   ◆ **Preview.** Select the option to view changes to the image directly in the active document window.

   ◆ **Amount.** Drag the slider or enter a value to determine how much to increase the contrast of pixels.

   ◆ **Radius.** Drag the slider or enter a value to determine the number of pixels surrounding the edge pixels that affect the sharpening.

   ◆ **Threshold.** Drag the slider or enter a value to determine how different the sharpened pixels must be from the surrounding area before they are considered edge pixels and sharpened by the filter.

5. Click **OK**.

Using the Blur Tool

The Blur tool allows you to manually soften hard edges or areas of an image. With the Blur tool, you can select the areas of the image where you want to reduce detail. It's best to make small adjustments with the Strength option, so you can see the changes as they take place and prevent blurring. If you want to use additional blurring options, you can use commands on the Blur submenu in the Filters menu.

Use the Blur Tool

1. In the Editor, open an image.

2. Select the **Blur** tool on the toolbox.

3. Select from the following Blur options on the Options bar:

   ◆ **Brushes menu.** Click the **Brushes** list arrow on the Options bar next to the brush sample, select a Brushes category, and then select the brush you want.

   ◆ **Size.** Click the **Size** list arrow on the Options bar, and then select the size you want in pixels.

   ◆ **Mode.** Click the **Mode** list arrow, and then select the blend mode you want.

   ◆ **Strength.** Click the **Strength** list arrow on the Options bar, and then select a sharpening percentage.

   ◆ **All Layers.** Select check box to sharpen all visible layers. Deselect check box to sharpen only the active layer.

4. Drag over the part of the image you want to blur.

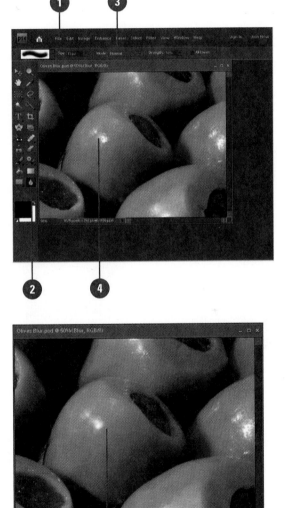

Blur applied

Using the Clone Stamp Tool

One of Photoshop Elements' most powerful features is its ability to retouch a photographic image. When you want to manipulate an image, you can apply the Clone Stamp tool. The Clone Stamp tool allows you to sample the image, and then apply that sample over another same image, or another open image. By selecting the Aligned check box on the Options bar, you can reuse the most current sampling point, no matter how many times you stop and resume painting. When Aligned is deselected, you'll reuse the same sampled pixels each time you paint. For example, you could use the Clone Stamp tool to repair damage to an image, remove a tree, even remove or add someone from an image.

Use the Clone Stamp Tool

1. In the Editor, open an image.

2. Select the **Clone Stamp** tool on the toolbox.

3. Select a brush tip, and then select brush options, such as blending mode, and opacity on the Options bar.

4. Select the **Aligned** check box on the Options bar to sample pixels continuously without losing the current sampling point. Deselect the check box to continue to use the sampled pixels from the initial sampling point each time you stop and resume painting.

5. Select the **All Layers** check box on the Options bar to copy all data from all visible layers. Deselect to copy data from only the active layer.

6. Click the **Clone Overlay** button on the Options bar, select the **Show Overlay** check box, and then select the options you want: **Opacity**, **Auto Hide**, or **Invert**.

7. Hold down the Alt key, and then click an area to sample the portion of the image you want to use for your sample.

8. Drag over the area of the image you want to restore or modify.

Joshua tree removed using the Clone Stamp tool.

Using the Dodge and Burn Tools

You can use the Dodge and Burn tools to lighten or darken specific areas of an image. If you wanted to lighten the shadow areas of an image, you would use the Dodge tool, and conversely, if you wanted to darken the highlight areas of an image, you would select the Burn tool. While there are other ways to control the highlights and shadows of an image, such as the Levels adjustment, the Dodge and Burn tools are controlled by using a brush and dragging in the image. That kind of control gives you the option to choose exactly what you want to modify.

Use the Dodge and Burn Tools

1. In the Editor, open an image.

2. Select the **Dodge** or **Burn** tool on the toolbox.

3. Select a brush tip, and then select brush options on the Options bar.

4. Click the **Range** list arrow on the Options bar, and then select from the following options:

   ◆ **Midtones.** Changes the middle range of grays.

   ◆ **Shadows.** Changes the dark areas.

   ◆ **Highlights.** Changes the light areas.

5. Specify the Exposure value for the stroke.

6. Drag over the part of the image you want to lighten or darken.

Dark areas restored using the Dodge tool

Using the Sponge Tool

The Sponge tool does not lighten or darken an image. You can use the Sponge tool to bring out or mute the color in a photo. It saturates or desaturates color values as you drag over portions of the image. Since over- or underexposed images have a tendency to lose some tonal values and appear flat, you can use the Sponge tool (with saturate) to return some of the color intensity back to the image.

Use the Sponge Tool

1. In the Editor, open an image.

2. Select the **Sponge** tool on the toolbox.

3. Select a brush tip, and then select brush options on the Options bar.

4. Click the **Mode** list arrow on the Options bar, and then select from the following options:

   ◆ **Saturate.** Changes colors to make them more vivid (less black or white added).

   ◆ **Desaturate.** Changes colors to make them muted (more black or white added).

5. Specify the **Flow** value for the strength of the tool for each stroke. In Saturate mode, a higher percentage increases the saturation, while in Desaturate mode, a higher percentage increases the desaturation.

6. Drag over the part of the image you want to lighten or darken.

Colors more vivid using the Sponge tool.

Using the Healing Brush Tool

These tools have become my favorite tools for working and correcting problems with digital images. The Healing Brush tool allows you to correct small imperfections, making them disappear into the surrounding image. This tool works from a sample of the original image, and then matches the texture, lighting, transparency, and shading of the sampled pixels into the source pixels. If an image contains a lot of random noise, before working with the Healing Brush try lowering the amount of noise with the Reduce Noise filter. Once applied you can use the Healing Brush to clean up the rest of the troubled areas. When you use healing operations in a separate layer, you gain control over the process; you can even use the opacity and blending mode settings to further control the healing process. Always use the Healing Brush in a separate layer... always.

Use the Healing Brush Tool

1. In the Editor, open an image.

2. Select the **Healing Brush** tool on the toolbox.

3. Select a soft round brush on the Options bar.

4. Select the **All Layers** check box on the Options bar to copy all data from all visible layers. Deselect to copy data from only the active layer.

5. Hold the Alt key, and then click on the area of the image for a sample.

   This area should represent both the texture and the color of the areas you want to heal.

6. Use small short strokes and carefully drag over the areas you want to change, and then release your mouse and move to the next area.

   The Healing Brush works to match the sample to the source.

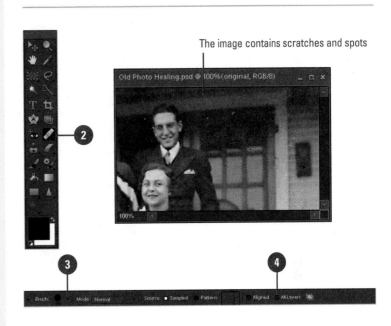

The image contains scratches and spots

6 The Healing Brush makes short work of correcting damaged images.

Working with the Spot Healing Brush

A tool in Photoshop Elements' formidable arsenal of restoration and correction tools is the Spot Healing Brush. With a name similar to the Healing Brush, you might expect that the tools have similar features, and you would be correct. The main difference between the two tools is that the Spot Healing Brush does not require you take a sample of the area to heal. The Spot Healing Brush tool takes the area sample as you work by sampling the surrounding pixels. The Spot Healing brush, as its name implies, works best on small spots and imperfections. To heal larger areas, the standard Healing Brush, and even the good old Clone Stamp tool are your best bets.

Use the Spot Healing Brush

1. In the Editor, open an image.

2. Select the **Spot Healing Brush** tool on the toolbox.

3. Select a soft round brush on the Options bar.

4. Select a Spot Healing Type option on the Options bar.

   ◆ **Proximity Match.** Uses the pixels around the edge of the selection to find an image area to use as a patch for the selected area.

   ◆ **Create Texture.** Uses all the pixels in the selection to create a texture to use as a patch to fix the selected area.

5. Select the **All Layers** check box on the Options button to copy all data from all visible layers. Deselect to copy data from only the active layer.

6. Using small short strokes, carefully drag over the areas you want to change, and then release your mouse and move to the next area.

   The Spot Healing brush works to match the sample to the source.

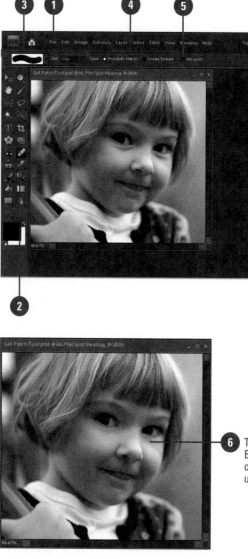

6. The Spot Healing Brush smoothed out the lines under the eyes.

Working with the Red Eye Tool

The Red Eye tool not only gives the digital restorer an excellent tool for removing pesky red eye, it will also remove the green and white reflections in pets' eyes. The biggest generator of red eye is the onboard flash on your camera. Actually, if they would simply rename a camera's built-in flash, red-eye generator, it might help amateur photographers pay more attention. However, until that day comes, designers will still have to deal with images that contain red eye. The Red Eye tool performs two operations: it desaturates the red values, and darkens the pupil. If you want Photoshop Elements to automatically fix red eye within an image, you can use the Auto Red Eye Fix command on the Enhance menu or the Quick Fix tab.

Use the Red Eye Tool

1 In the Editor, open an image.

2 Select the **Red Eye** tool on the toolbox.

> **TIMESAVER** *Click the Auto button on the Options bar to quickly remove red eye.*

3 Select from the following options on the Options bar:

◆ **Pupil Size.** Select the size of the pupil in relation to the amount of red eye.

◆ **Darken Amount.** Select how much you want to darken the pupil area of the eye.

4 Click in the middle of the red portion of the eye, and release.

The red is removed, and the pupil is darkened.

See Also

See "Using Full Edit and Quick Fix" on page 138 for information on using Auto Red Eye Fix.

4 The red eye is removed with the click of your mouse.

Retouching with the Smart Brush

Photoshop Elements has gotten to be very good at finding the edges of objects within images, and so the wizards at Adobe decided to apply this talent to making it easier to apply special effects. The Smart Brush (**New!**) can apply any of dozens of cool effects, some subtle and others not, with a single click to show Photoshop Elements where you want the effect. Special tools show up when you're using the Smart Brush so that you can remove the effect from places it's not supposed to go or add it in other locations throughout your image.

Colorize an Object

1 In the Editor, open an image.

2 Select the **Smart Brush** tool on the toolbox.

3 Specify a brush size on the Options bar.

4 If you don't see the **Smart Effects** list, click the thumbnail on the Options bar to display it. Choose an effect, such as Grape Expectations.

5 Click in the image to apply the effect; click again to add to the affected area.

6 Select the **Subtract from Selection** tool, and then click to remove the effect from an area. Select the **New Selection** tool if you want to apply the effect to a different area.

7 Select options on the Options bar:

  ◆ **Refine Edge.** Click to clean up the edges of the affected area.

  ◆ **Inverse.** Click to apply the effect to the unselected parts of the image and remove it from the selected area.

> ### See Also
>
> See "Refining a Selection Edge" on page 188 for information on using the Refine Selection Edge controls.

Make the Sky Bluer

① In the Editor, open an image.

② Select the **Smart Brush** tool on the toolbox.

③ Specify a brush size on the Options bar.

④ If you don't see the **Smart Effects** list, click the thumbnail on the Options bar to display it. Choose an effect, such as Blue Skies.

⑤ Click or drag in the image to apply the effect.

⑥ Select the **Subtract from Selection** tool, and then click to remove the effect from an area of the image.

Did You Know?

Photoshop Elements applies Smart Brush effects to a separate layer. This means you can always go back and modify them. To change a Smart Effect, click its layer in the Layers palette and select the Smart Brush tool. Then double-click the Smart Effect icon in the image window and choose a new effect from the Smart Effects list or change the affected area with the Subtract From Selection, Add To Selection, or New Selection tool.

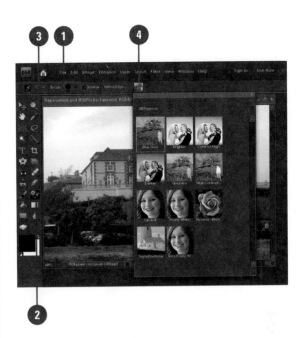

Working with the Detail Smart Brush

Related to the Smart Brush is the Detail Smart Brush (**New!**); with this new tool you can apply effects from the Smart Effects library anywhere in your image by painting them in. When you use the Detail Smart Brush, Photoshop Elements doesn't try to guess where you want an effect applied; it simply follows your lead and lays in the effect wherever you paint. The Detail Smart Brush is more useful than the Smart Brush when the edges of the area you want to affect aren't clearly defined.

Apply a Smart Effect by Painting

1. In the Editor, open an image.

2. Select the **Detail Smart Brush** tool on the toolbox.

3. Specify a brush size on the Options bar.

4. If you don't see the **Smart Effects** list, click the thumbnail on the Options bar to display it. Choose an effect, such as Lipstick.

5. Drag in the image to apply the effect.

6. To modify the effect, display the **Layers** palette, and then double-click the thumbnail for the effect layer.

7. Change the settings, such as choosing a new color.

Did You Know?

The Subtract from Selection, Add to Selection, and New Selection tools appear in the Options bar. You can choose these tools from the miniature toolbox that appears in the image window whenever you use the Smart Brush or the Smart Detail Brush, or you can choose them in the Options bar.

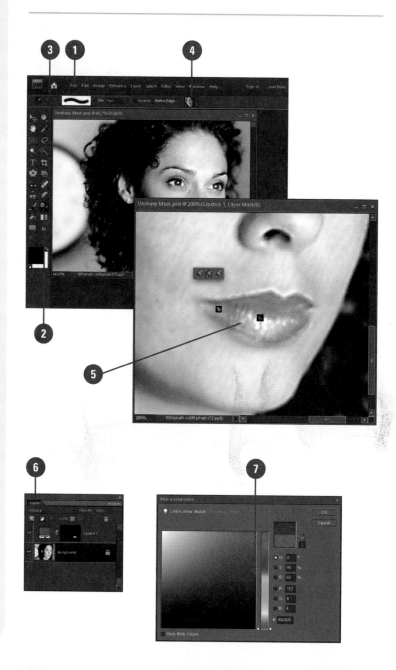

Using the Paint, Shape Drawing, and Eraser Tools

13

Introduction

Photoshop Elements supplies you with all types of adjustment and manipulation tools. In addition to image enhancement, Photoshop Elements can also be considered a powerful design from scratch application. With the vast array of brushes, tips, and shape drawing tools that are supplied, Photoshop Elements helps you produce the images, either enhanced or developed from scratch, which you might need for virtually any conceivable project.

Brushes come in all sizes and shapes, and can be controlled with a mouse or drawing tablet. Since the shape of the tip controls brushes, Photoshop Elements gives you access to several sets of pre-defined brush tip shapes, or you can create your own customized sets. As for shape drawing tools, Photoshop Elements doesn't limit your creativity to just drawing circles and squares; it gives you instant access to dozens of pre-defined shapes. When it comes to Editor's paint and drawing tools, your choices are limitless, based only on your knowledge of the available tools, and a creative imagination—the more you know, the more you can do with Photoshop Elements.

And, when all the drawing is said and done, there will be a need for cleaning up. With the various Eraser tools, you can make quick work of touching up those small problem areas. Photoshop Elements provides straight eraser tools, eraser tools that erase to a definable edge, and even eraser tools that target specific color values.

When enhancing an image, you might want to apply a gradient. Gradients can be something as simple as black and white, or as complex as one that contains the colors of the rainbow. Gradients can be applied to an image; completely covering the original image information, or they can be controlled through targeted selection, and creative uses of blending modes.

What You'll Do

Understand Foreground and Background Colors

View the Brushes Palette

Change the Brushes Palette View

Select and Create Brush Tips

Modify or Delete Brush Tips

Create Custom Brush Tip Sets

Work with the Brush, Airbrush, Pencil, Impressionist, and Smudge Tools

Set Dynamic Brush Options

Work with Auto Erase

Use the Paint Bucket and Pattern Stamp Tools

Work with the Eraser Tools

Work with the Magic Eraser Tool

Create and Apply Gradients

Use the Color Replacement Tool

Create Shapes in a Layer

Select and Move Shapes

Work with the Line and Standard Shape Tools

Work with the Custom Shape Tool

Understanding Foreground and Background Colors

The Foreground and Background colors, located near the bottom of the toolbox, are the way of identifying your primary painting color, as well as the color Photoshop Elements uses in conjunction with the Background layer. When you select any of the painting or drawing tools, the color applied to the image will be the foreground color—that's its purpose. Hence, it's sometimes referred to as the active color. The Background color serves several functions—its primary purpose is to instruct Photoshop Elements how to handle erasing on the Background layer. When you use an eraser tool on a layer, by default, the pixels are converted to transparent. However, when you use an eraser tool on the Background something different happens. Since the Background does not support transparency, it replaces the erased pixels with the current background color.

Change the Active Foreground and Background Colors

Use any of the following methods to change the active foreground or background colors:

◆ Select the **Eyedropper** tool on the toolbox, and then click anywhere in the active image to change the foreground color.

 Hold down the Alt key, and then click to change the background color.

◆ Click on a color swatch in the Swatches palette to change the foreground color.

 Hold down the Ctrl key, and then click to change the background color.

◆ Create a color in the Color palette. Click the **Foreground** or **Background** thumbnail to choose the color's destination.

◆ Click the **Foreground** or **Background** color box to open the Color Picker dialog box, select a color or enter color values, and then click **OK**.

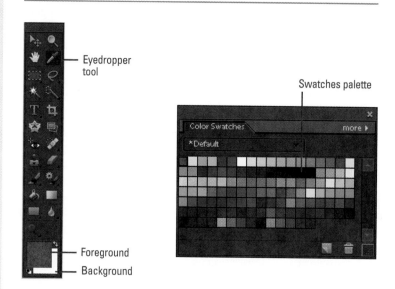

Eyedropper tool

Swatches palette

Foreground

Background

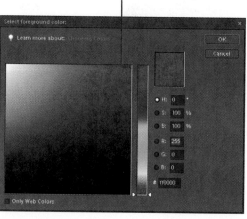

Color Picker dialog box

Default and Switch the Foreground and Background Colors

① Click the **Default Foreground And Background Colors** button to revert the foreground and background colors to their default values of black and white.

② Click the **Switch Foreground And Background Colors** button to switch current colors.

TIMESAVER *Press D to change the foreground and background colors to their default values of black and white, and press X to switch the current colors.*

Viewing the Brushes Palette

The Brushes palette provides access to brush tips you can use with brush and painting tools. The Brushes palette is, by default, located on the Options bar. You access the Brushes palette by selecting a brush tool, or a tool that requires the use of a brush, such as the Eraser tool, and then clicking the Brushes list arrow on the Options bar, which is next to the currently selected brush. The Brushes palette displays another list arrow at the top where you can select a brush set, also known as a library, and the current brush set at the bottom. The Brushes palette comes with 14 pre-defined brush sets.

View the Brushes Palette

1. In the Editor, select a Brush tool on the toolbox.

2. Click the **Brushes** list arrow on the Options bar.

3. Click the **Brushes** list arrow on the Brushes palette.

4. Select the set of brushes you want to use.

   ◆ Default Brushes.

   ◆ Assorted Brushes.

   ◆ Basic Brushes.

   ◆ Calligraphic Brushes.

   ◆ Drop Shadow Brushes.

   ◆ Dry Media Brushes.

   ◆ Faux Finish Brushes.

   ◆ Natural Brushes.

   ◆ Natural Brushes 2.

   ◆ Pen Pressure.

   ◆ Special Effects Brushes.

   ◆ Square Brushes.

   ◆ Thick Heavy Brushes.

   ◆ Wet Media Brushes.

5. To close the Brushes palette, click the **Close** button on the palette, or click outside the palette.

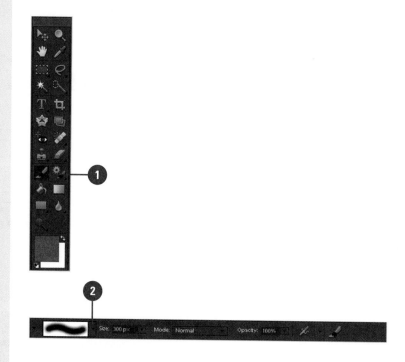

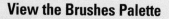

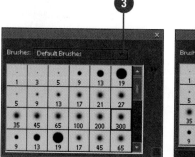

Changing the Brushes Palette View

The Brushes palette comes in many forms; you can view brushes as strokes, or you can choose thumbnails, or even text descriptions. The form of the Brushes palette does not impact its performance, only how you view the available brush tips. Choose the version that best suits your current design needs, and then change the view as needed. When you select a brush, it becomes the default for that tool only until you change it. This gives you the ability to choose a default brush for each of the brush-specific tools.

Change the Brushes Palette View

① In the Editor, select a Brush tool on the toolbox.

② Click the **Brushes** list arrow on the Options bar.

③ Click the **More Options** button, and then select from the available View options:

◆ **Text Only.** Select this option to display all brush tips by their names.

◆ **Small Thumbnail.** Select this option to display all brush tips using a small thumbnail.

◆ **Large Thumbnail.** Select this option to display all brush tips using a large thumbnail.

◆ **Small List.** Select this option to display all brush tips by their names and small thumbnail.

◆ **Large List.** Select this option to display all brush tips by their names and large thumbnail.

◆ **Stroke Thumbnail.** Select this option to display all brush tips with a stroke. (This is useful in determining how the brush will look when applied in the image).

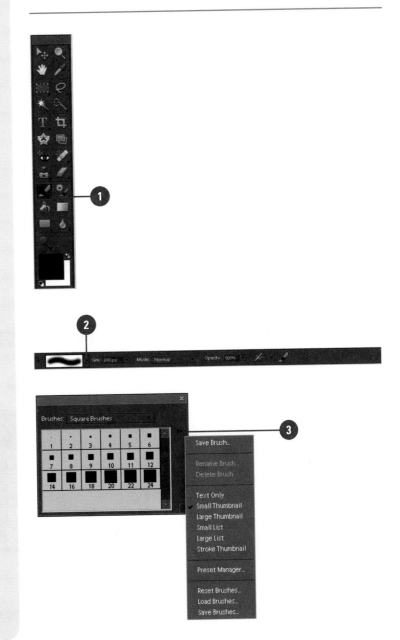

Selecting Brush Tips

The Brushes palette comes with 14 pre-defined sets. Each set organizes specific brush tips by name. Since more than the Brush tool uses brush tips, it's important to have the right tool (brush tip) for the right job. Using or making do with the wrong brush tip is akin to digging a swimming pool with a teaspoon. You wouldn't paint a portrait with a house-painting brush, so don't settle for anything less than the exact brush tip you need to get the job done.

Select a Brush Tip

1. In the Editor, select a Brush tool on the toolbox.

2. Click the **Brushes** list arrow on the Options bar.

3. Click the **Brushes** list arrow on the palette, and then select any of the pre-defined brush sets.

   This replaces the current brush tips with the selected set.

4. Select the brush tip you want to use.

   The brush tip on the Options bar changes to the one you selected.

   TIMESAVER *Click the brush sample on the Options bar to select the last brush tip.*

Did You Know?

You can resize the Brushes palette. If you're having a hard time viewing all the brushes in the Brushes palette, display the Brushes palette, point to the bottom right-corner of the palette (cursor changes to a diagonal double-arrow, and then drag to resize the palette.

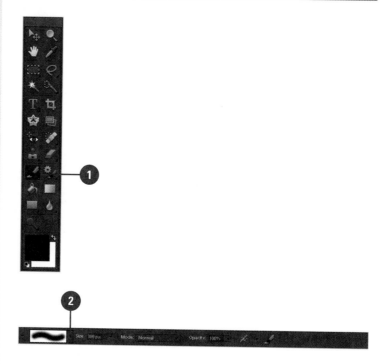

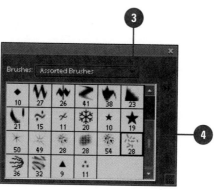

Selected brush tip

Creating Custom Brush Tips

The Brushes palette gives you many choices for brush tips. Any good designer will tell you that no matter how many brush tips you have, you'll always want more. For example, you're working on a 100-year-old photograph, and you need a specific brush to add hair details to the blown-out areas of the image. It's a special type of brush that literally creates the illusion of wavy hair. In an effort to help keep you organized, Photoshop Elements gives you the ability to create your very own customized brush tips, and then save them later in organized sets.

Create a New Brush Tip

1. In the Editor, open an image, scan an item, or select any of the painting tools and create a shape for a new brush tip.

   IMPORTANT *Since the color of a brush is determined when the brush tip is selected, create the brush tip using black or in shades of gray.*

2. Select the brush tip using any of the selection tools.

   IMPORTANT *Photoshop Elements picks up any pixel information in the underlying layers, even white. If you want the brush to have a transparent background, make sure the areas surrounding the image show as transparent.*

3. Click the **Edit** menu, and then click **Define Brush from Selection.**

4. Enter a name for the new brush preset.

5. Click **OK**.

6. Open the Brushes palette on the Options bar, and then scroll to the bottom of the list to access your newly created brush tip.

   Since the Define Brush Preset button picks up any background colors within the selection area, always create the brush tip in an otherwise empty layer.

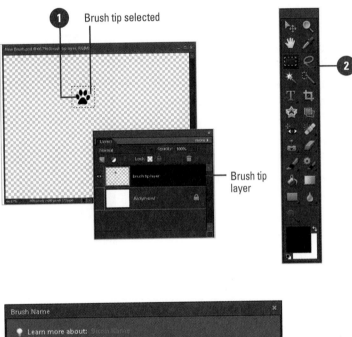

Brush tip selected

Brush tip layer

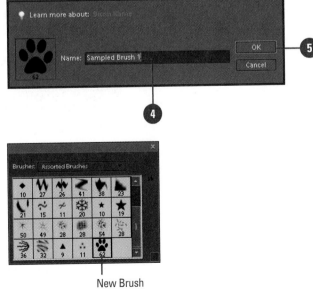

New Brush

Modifying or Deleting Brush Tips

After looking through the brush tip sets that come with Photoshop Elements, you don't see the one that suits your needs. You can modify an existing brush tip that is close to the one you want to create a new brush. Simply select the brush tip you want to modify on the Brushes palette, make the changes you want, and then save it as a new brush tip. If you no longer want to use a brush tip, you can quickly remove it from the Brush palette.

Modify an Existing Brush Tip

1. In the Editor, select a Brush tool on the toolbox.

2. Click the **Brushes** list arrow on the Options bar.

3. Click the **Brushes** list arrow on the palette, and then select any of the pre-defined brush sets.

   This replaces the current brush tips with the selected set.

4. Select the brush tip you want to use.

5. Change settings on the Options bar to modify the brush tip.

6. Click the **Brushes** list arrow, click the **More Options** button, and then click **Save Brush**.

7. Enter a name for the new brush preset.

8. Click **OK**.

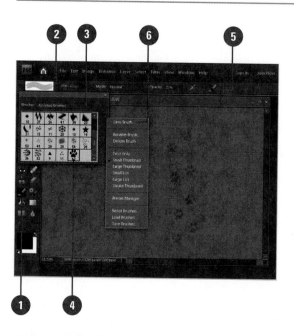

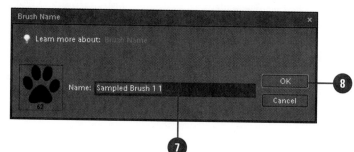

Delete an Existing Brush Tip

1. In the Editor, select a Brush tool on the toolbox.

2. Click the **Brushes** list arrow on the Options bar.

3. Click the **Brushes** list arrow on the palette, and then select any of the pre-defined brush sets.

   This replaces the current brush tips with the selected set.

4. Select the brush tip you want to use.

   TIMESAVER *Hold down the Alt key (cursor changes to scissors), and then click the brush you want to delete.*

5. Click the **Brushes** list arrow, click the **More Options** button, and then click **Delete Brush**.

6. Click **OK**.

Did You Know?

You can rename a brush. Select a brush tool on the toolbox, click the Brushes list arrow on the Options bar, select the brush you want to rename from a brush set, click the More Options button, click Rename Brush, enter a new name, and then click OK.

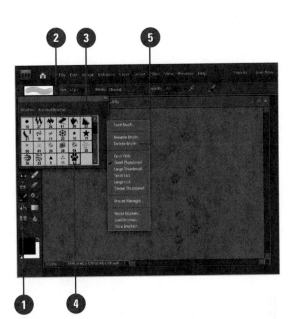

Creating Custom Brush Tip Sets

Once a brush tip is created, it becomes a part of the current set. However, the brush has not yet been permanently saved in Photoshop Elements. Although the new brush tip will reappear every time you access the Brushes palette, if you choose the option to reset the palette, the new brush will be lost. To keep brushes you must save them into customized sets.

Save a Customized Brush Set

1. In the Editor, select a Brush tool on the toolbox.

2. Click the **Brushes** list arrow on the Options bar.

3. Create a set of customized brushes.

4. Click the **More Options** button, and then click **Save Brushes**.

5. Enter a name for the set (with the .ABR extension) in the File name box.

    The default folder location appears, displaying Adobe/Photoshop Elements/7.0/Presets/Brushes.

    When you store a brush set in the default folder, it appears in the Brushes list arrow on the Brushes palette.

6. Click **Save**.

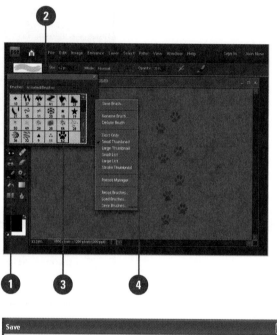

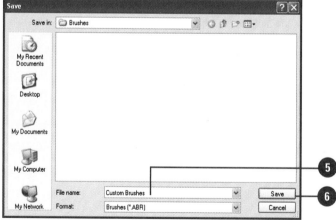

Load a Customized Brush Set

1. In the Editor, select a Brush tool on the toolbox.

2. Click the **Brushes** list arrow on the Options bar.

3. Click the **More Options** button, and then click **Load Brushes**.

   The default folder location appears, displaying Adobe/ Photoshop Elements/7.0/ Presets/Brushes.

4. Select the brush set file (.ABR extension) you want to load from the Brushes folder.

5. Click **Load**.

Did You Know?

You can reset a brush set back to its original state. If you modified a brush tip in a brush set and no longer want it, you can reset the brush set back to its original state. Select a brush tool on the toolbox, click the Brushes list arrow on the Options bar, click the Brushes list arrow on the Brushes palette, select the brush set you want to reset, click the More Options button, and then click Reset Brushes.

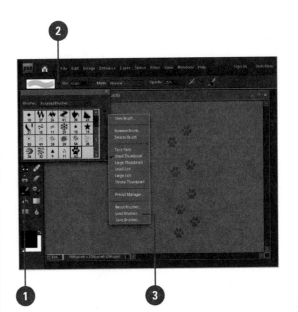

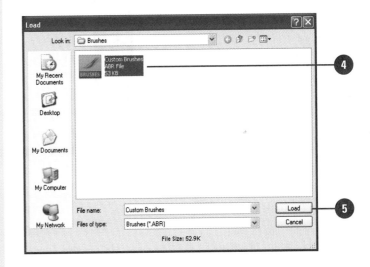

Working with the Brush and Airbrush Tools

The Brush and Airbrush tools were designed to reproduce the visual effect of applying paint to a canvas. You have full control over the brush tip, color, size, opacity, and even the brush's blending mode. Control over the image is achieved by using additional layers to hold the brush strokes (adding additional layers increases the file size of an image image). Since layers have their own control systems, such as opacity, fill, and blending modes, you achieve even greater control over the final design, and once the brush stroke is correct, you can always merge the brush-stroke layer into the image to conserve file size.

Work with the Brush and Airbrush Tools

1. In the Editor, select the **Brush** tool on the toolbox.

2. Click the **Brushes** list arrow on the Options bar, and then select a brush tip.

3. Select from the following Brush options on the Options bar:

   ◆ **Size.** Sets the size of the brush in pixels.

   ◆ **Mode.** Click the list arrow to choose from the available blending modes. The blending mode option controls how the active brush color blends with the colors in the active image.

   ◆ **Opacity.** Enter an opacity percent (1 to 100), or click the list arrow, and then drag the slider left or right.

   ◆ **Airbrush.** Click the button to change the Brush into an Airbrush.

   ◆ **Brush Tablet.** Sets the options to control with your stylus when you have a drawing tablet, such as a Wacom tablet, attached to your computer.

4. Drag within the image to paint.

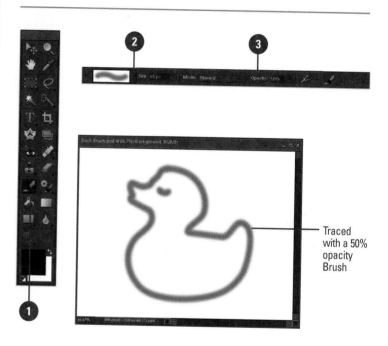

Traced with a 50% opacity Brush

For Your Information

Using the Brush and Airbrush Tools

The Brush and Airbrush tools look the same, but they perform quite differently. The Brush maintains a specific opacity; for example, if you choose 50 percent opacity, the Brush maintains that opacity no matter how many times you drag over an area. If you release and drag again, the Brush adds another 50 percent to the image. The Airbrush tool is an accumulating tool—dragging the image produces a brush stroke based on the opacity of the brush, and the speed you move the tool across the image. If you hold the Airbrush tool in one position, the ink color will slowly increase until it reaches 100 percent, just like a real airbrush.

Setting Dynamic Brush Options

The Brush tool also includes a set of controls, known as brush dynamics, that let you define how a brush tip is applied to the active image. Features, such as Scattering, Spacing, and Hardness let you further customize your brush tips so you can create that specialized brush for your image enhancement needs.

Set Dynamic Brush Options

1. In the Editor, select the **Brush** tool on the toolbox.

2. Click the **Brushes** list arrow on the Options bar, and then select a brush tip.

3. Click the **Brush Dynamics** button on the Options bar, and then specify the following options:

   ◆ **Fade.** Enter the number of steps (0 to 9999) until the paint flow fades to nothing. A low number fades quickly, while a high number fades later.

   ◆ **Hue Jitter.** Enter the rate at which the stroke color switches between the foreground and background color. A high value causes frequent switches.

   ◆ **Scatter.** Enter a value to create brush marks in a stroke. A low number creates a thicker stroke, while a high number creates a scattered effect.

   ◆ **Spacing.** Sets the distance between the brush marks in a stroke.

   ◆ **Hardness.** Enter a value to control the size of the brush's center.

   ◆ **Angle.** Enter an angle by which an elliptical brush's long axis is offset from horizontal.

   ◆ **Roundness.** Enter a value to set the ratio between the brush's short and long axes.

4. Drag within the image to paint.

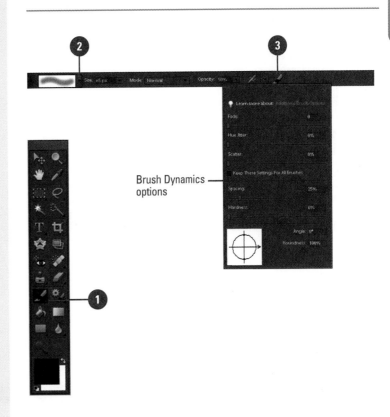

Brush Dynamics options

For Your Information

Setting Options for a Drawing Tablet

If you have a drawing tablet, such as a Wacom tablet, you can set brush tool options for the stylus. To set the pen pressure, open the Editor, select the Brush tool on the toolbox, click the Brush Tablet Options list arrow on the Options bar, select the check boxes next to the options you want (Size, Opacity, Hue Jitter, Scatter, and Roundness), and then click the Close button in the palette.

Working with the Pencil Tool

The Pencil tool is exactly what its name implies... a pencil. The Pencil tool is limited to hard brush tips of any size or shape, and creates freeform lines using the current foreground color. In fact, the major difference between the Pencil and Brush tools, is the Pencil tool's inability to draw anything but a hard edge line. A unique feature of the Pencil tool is its ability to switch between the current foreground and background colors using the Auto Erase feature.

Work with the Pencil Tool

1. In the Editor, select the **Pencil** tool on the toolbox.

2. Click the **Brushes** list arrow on the Options bar, and then select a brush tip.

3. Click the **Mode** list arrow on the Options bar, and then select a blending mode.

4. Enter an Opacity percentage value (1 to 100) on the Options bar.

5. Drag the **Pencil** tool across the image.

Did You Know?

You can use the Pencil tool to create calligraphy lettering. Select the Pencil tool, click black as your painting color, and then click one of the oblong brush tips on the Options bar. If you own a drawing tablet, use the tablet with the Pencil tool to create beautifully formed calligraphy letters.

You can draw straight lines using brush tools. Holding the Shift key while dragging, constrains the brush to a 90-degree line. To draw a straight line between two points, click once in the image window, move the mouse to another position, hold down the Shift key, and then click a second time. A straight line will be drawn between the first and last mouse clicks.

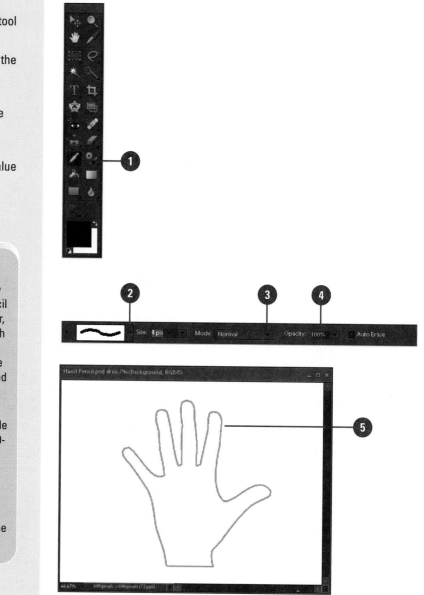

Working with Auto Erase

The Auto Erase feature lets you automatically switch the Pencil tool's painting color using the current foreground and background color swatches. The trick is where you start drawing the line. If you start dragging the brush tip from a new location in the image, the Pencil tool creates a line in the active foreground color. If you then place the brush tip on a previously drawn line and drag, the Pencil tool creates a new line in the active background color. Since the Auto Erase feature doesn't really erase anything, it will perform exactly the same way on a transparent layer as it does on the Background layer.

Work with Auto Erase

1. In the Editor, select the **Pencil** tool on the toolbox.

2. Select the **Auto Erase** check box on the Options bar.

3. Drag the **Pencil** tool across the active image to create a line in the active foreground color.

4. Click anywhere in the background and the Pencil tool will use the foreground color.

5. Move the brush tip over one of the previous lines, and then drag to create a line in the active background color.

Did You Know?

You can draw straight lines with the Pencil tool. Click once in the image to create a black dot, move to another position, hold down the Shift key, and then click again. When you hold down the Shift key, the Pencil tool creates a straight line between the two mouse clicks.

Working with the Impressionist and Smudge Tools

The Impressionist and Smudge tools were designed to reduce or blur the details in an image. The Impressionist Brush tool changes the existing colors and details in an image to look blurred, like it was painted with a stylized brush. The Smudge tool simulates dragging a finger through wet paint. You have full control over the brush tip, size, opacity, and even the brush's blending mode. The Impressionist Brush and Smudge tools also provide tool specific options. The Impressionist Brush includes tools that affect the style, area, and tolerance of the brush stroke, while the Smudge tool includes tools that affect the strength and color of the smear.

Work with the Impressionist Brush Tool

1. In the Editor, select the **Impressionist Brush** tool on the toolbox.

2. Click the **Brushes** list arrow on the Options bar, and then select a brush tip.

3. Select from the following Impressionist Brush options on the Options bar:

   ◆ **Size.** Specify a size of the brush in pixels.

   ◆ **Mode.** Click the list arrow to choose from the available blending modes. The blending mode option controls how the active brush color blends with the colors in the active image.

   ◆ **Opacity.** Enter an opacity percent (1 to 100), or click the list arrow, and then drag the slider left or right.

   ◆ **Style.** Specify a shape of the brush stroke.

   ◆ **Area.** Specify a size of the brush stroke.

   ◆ **Tolerance.** Select a Tolerance value (0 to 255). The Tolerance value influences the range of the brush stroke to fill a given area.

4. Drag within the image to paint.

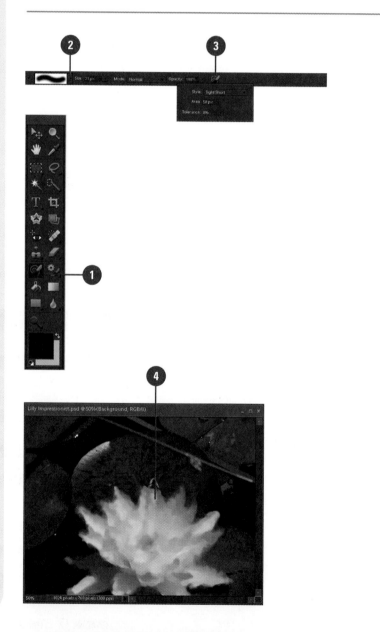

Work with the Smudge Tool

1. In the Editor, select the **Smudge** tool on the toolbox.

2. Click the **Brushes** list arrow on the Options bar, and then select a brush tip.

3. Select from the following Smudge options on the Options bar:

   ◆ **Size.** Specifies the size of the brush in pixels.

   ◆ **Mode.** Click the list arrow to choose from the available blending modes. The blending mode option controls how the active brush color blends with the colors in the active image.

   ◆ **Strength.** Specifies the amount of the smudge effect.

   ◆ **All Layers.** Select to smudge using color from all visible layers. Deselect to smudge using colors from only the active layer.

   ◆ **Finger Painting.** Select to smear using the foreground color at the beginning of each stroke. Deselect to smear using the color under the pointer at the beginning of each stroke.

4. Drag within the image to smudge color.

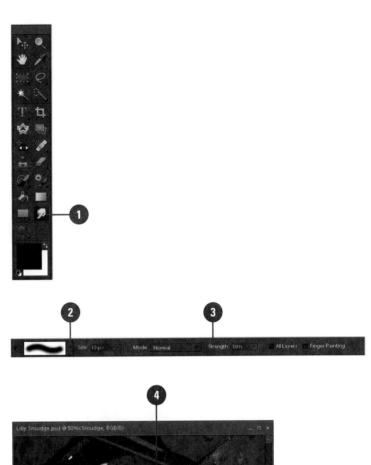

Using the Paint Bucket Tool

The Paint Bucket tool is not new, in fact it's been around almost as long as Photoshop Elements. The paint bucket's primary function is to fill an area with the active foreground color, but that's not all it's capable of doing. The Paint Bucket tool can fill areas with a selected pattern and, much in the same way that the Magic Wand tool selects image information, the fill area can be controlled by the shift in brightness of image pixels. Combine those features with the ability to change the paint bucket's blending mode, opacity, and you have a tool with a lot of horsepower.

Use the Paint Bucket Tool

1 In the Editor, select the **Paint Bucket** tool on the toolbox.

2 Select the **Pattern** check box to fill a selected area with a pattern. Deselect to fill a selected area with the current foreground color.

3 Click the **Pattern** list arrow, and then select a pre-defined fill pattern. This option is available if you select Pattern as a fill option.

4 Click the **Mode** list arrow, and then select a blending mode.

5 Enter an Opacity percentage value (1 to 100).

6 Select a Tolerance value (0 to 255). The Tolerance value influences the range of the Paint Bucket uses to fill a given area.

7 Select the **Anti-alias** check box to create a visually smoother line.

8 Select the **Contiguous** check box to restrict the fill to the selected area.

9 Select the **All Layers** check box to use color range information from all of the image's layers.

10 Click the **Paint Bucket** tool cursor on the area to be changed.

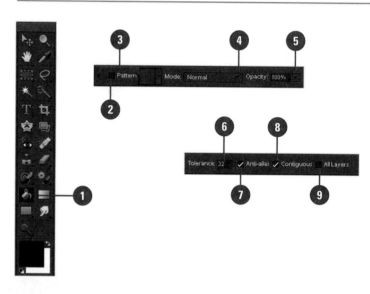

Using the Pattern Stamp Tool

The Pattern Stamp tool allows you to paint with a pattern from a predefined set on the Patterns palette or defined from your image, and then apply it over the same or another image. For example, you could use the Pattern Stamp tool to apply a pattern to an image or add something to an image. When you select the Aligned check box on the Options bar, you can reuse the most current sampling point, no matter how many times you stop and resume painting. When Aligned is deselected, you'll reuse the same sampled pixels each time you paint. When you select the Impressionist check box on the Options bar, you can paint the pattern using the paint daubs to create an impressionist effect.

Use the Pattern Stamp Tool

1. In the Editor, select the **Pattern Stamp** tool on the toolbox.

2. Select a brush tip, and then select brush options, such as size, blending mode, and opacity on the Options bar.

3. Click the **Pattern** list arrow on the Options bar, and then select a pattern.

4. To select another pattern set, click the **More Options** button on the Pattern palette, and then select the pattern set you want from the bottom of the list.

   ◆ **Create Custom Pattern.** Select the pattern in an image, click the **Edit** menu, click **Define Pattern from Selection**, type a name, and then click **OK**.

5. Select from the following Pattern Stamp options on the Options bar:

   ◆ **Aligned.** Select to repeat the pattern as a contiguous paint aligned from one paint stroke to the next. Deselect to center the pattern on each paint stroke.

   ◆ **Impressionist.** Select to paint the pattern using the paint daubs to create an impressionist effect.

6. Drag within the image to paint.

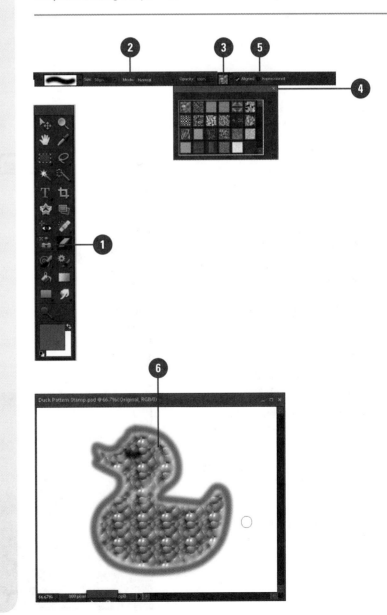

Working with the Eraser Tools

The basic Eraser tool converts image pixels in a layer to transparent pixels. While the primary function of the eraser tool has not changed, it has been greatly improved upon. For example, you can use the eraser tool to remove a specific color or to erase around the edge of an image object. You can instruct the Eraser tool to remove a specific color while protecting another color and at the same time, increase or decrease the tool's tolerance (the range of selection). If you use the Eraser tool on an image layer, the tool will erase to transparency. If the Eraser tool is used on a flattened image (flattened images do not support transparency), the active background color appears in erased areas. The Background Eraser tool lets you select specific colors within an image and erase just those colors. As you can see, the eraser tools do more than blindly erase image information. As you master the eraser tools, you just may find those complicated image eraser jobs becoming easier and easier.

Use the Basic Eraser Tool

1 In the Editor, select the **Eraser** tool on the toolbox.

2 Click the **Brush** list arrow on the Options bar, and then select a brush tip.

3 Click the **Size** list arrow on the Options bar, and then select a brush size.

4 Click the **Mode** list arrow on the Options bar, and then click **Brush**, **Pencil**, or **Block**. Options vary depending on the the brush tip.

5 Enter an Opacity percentage value (1 to 100) on the Options bar to determine how much the eraser removes from the image.

6 Drag the Eraser over an image layer to convert the image pixels to transparent.

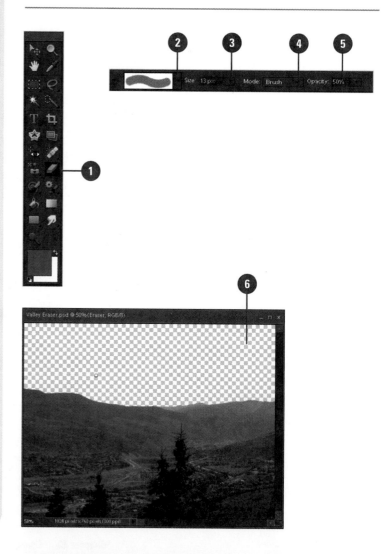

Use the Background Eraser Tool

1. In the Editor, select the **Background Eraser** tool on the toolbox.

2. Click the **Brush Preset Picker** list arrow on the Options bar, and then select from the following options:

   ◆ **Diameter.** Sets the brush size from the center to the edge in pixels.

   ◆ **Hardness.** Enter a value to control the size of the brush's center.

   ◆ **Spacing.** Sets the distance between the brush marks in a stroke.

   ◆ **Angle.** Enter an angle by which an elliptical brush's long axis is offset from horizontal.

   ◆ **Roundness.** Enter a value to set the ratio between the brush's short and long axes.

   ◆ **Size and Tolerance.** Select options for a drawing tablet: Off Pen Pressure, or Stylus Wheel.

3. Click the **Limits** list arrow, and then click how far you want the erasing to spread:

   ◆ **Discontiguous.** Lets the Eraser tool work with all similar color range pixels throughout the image.

   ◆ **Contiguous.** Restricts the Eraser tool to the selected color range, without moving outside the originally sampled area.

4. Select a Tolerance percentage value (1 to 100). The higher the tolerance, the greater the range of colors erased.

5. Drag the image to erase.

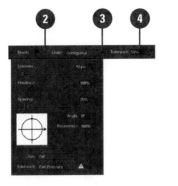

For Your Information

Using the Background Eraser Tool

The Background Eraser tool erases an image by converting the image pixels to transparent. If you attempt to use the Background Eraser tool on a flattened image, it automatically convert the flattened background into a layer. Photoshop Elements is actually making an assumption, that if you're using the Background Eraser tool, you obviously need the image to be on a layer, not a Background.

Working with the Magic Eraser Tool

The Magic Eraser tool functions the same way the Magic Wand selection tool functions, except instead of selecting an area it erases it. The Magic Eraser tool works on any traditional layer, including the Background. Clicking with the Magic Eraser tool converts image pixels into transparent pixels. Since the Background layer does not support transparency, using the Magic Eraser tool causes Photoshop Elements to convert the Background into a traditional layer.

Work with the Magic Eraser Tool

1. In the Editor, select the **Magic Eraser** tool on the toolbox.

2. Enter a Tolerance percentage value (0 to 255). The higher the value the greater the range the Magic Eraser erases.

3. Select the **Anti-alias** check box to create a visually softer eraser (useful when dealing with intensely rounded or curved selections).

4. Select the **Contiguous** check box to select adjacent pixels within the active image.

5. Select the **All Layers** check box to erase using color from all visible layers. Deselect to erase using colors from only the active layer.

6. Enter an Opacity percentage value (1 to 100) on the Options bar to determine how much the eraser removes from the image.

7. Click within the active image.

   The Magic Eraser tool, depending on options, samples the pixels directly under the tool and uses that to create a range for erasing image information.

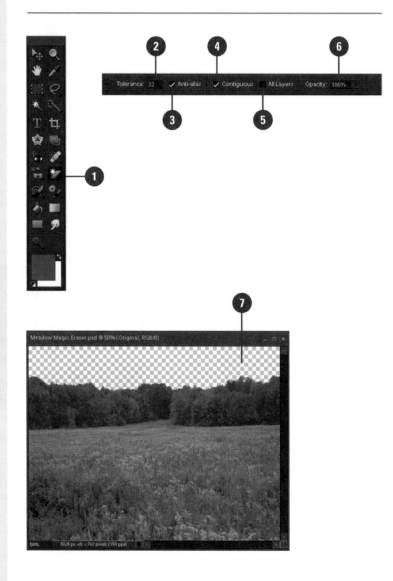

Creating and Applying Gradients

While most of the paint and drawing tools let you select and paint with a single color, the gradient tool lets you paint with a veritable rainbow of colors. The gradient tool comes packaged with several sets of pre-designed gradients, or you can create and save your own customized gradient sets. The process of creating a gradient is simple; you select a gradient along with a specific type, and then drag in the image window. The length and angle of the drag, determines how the gradient is applied. Since gradients, by default, overwrite the image, it's a good idea to create gradients in separate layers.

Create a Standard Gradient

1. In the Editor, select the **Gradient** tool on the toolbox.

2. Click the **Gradient** list arrow, and then select from the available gradients.

   ◆ To change the gradient set, click the **More Options** button, and then select a gradient set at the bottom of the menu.

3. Click one of the following gradient buttons: **Linear**, **Radial**, **Angle**, **Reflected** or **Diamond**.

4. Click the **Mode** list arrow, and then select a blending mode.

5. Enter an Opacity percentage value (1 to 100).

6. Select the **Reverse** check box to reverse the color order of the selected gradient.

7. Select the **Dither** check box to visually create a smoother transition between gradient colors.

8. Select the **Transparency** check box to create gradients using a gradient mask (allows for transparency in the gradient).

9. Drag in the image to create a gradient.

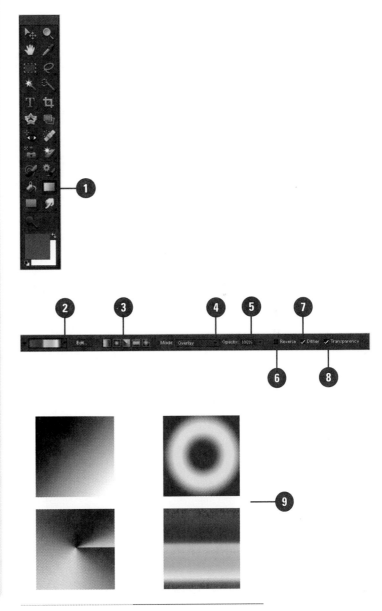

Creating Custom Gradients

Customized gradients are easy to create and essential when you just can't find what you want in the predefined sets. It doesn't matter how many gradients Photoshop Elements provides for you, there will always be that one instance where they just don't do the required job. With just a few clicks of your mouse, you can create your own customized gradients. You can start with one of the predefined gradients, and modify it to your needs. You can also start completely from scratch; the choice is yours, and so are the rewards of creating that one-of-a-kind stunning gradient you can use for your current project and in the future.

Create and Save a Customized Gradient

① In the Editor, select the **Gradient** tool on the toolbox.

② Click **Edit** or the current gradient on the Options bar to open the Gradient Editor dialog box.

③ Select a gradient from the available options that is close to what you want to create.

④ Enter a name for the new gradient.

⑤ Click **New**.

A thumbnail (copy of the selected gradient) appears at the bottom of the list.

⑥ Click the **Gradient Type** list arrow, and then select one of the following:

◆ **Solid.** Uses solid colors for the gradient.

◆ **Noise.** Uses randomly distributed colors within a range.

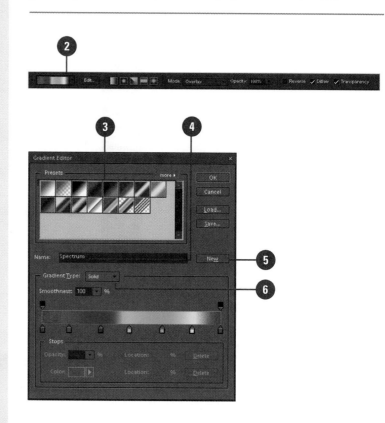

7 Click the **Smoothness** list arrow, and then select one of the following:

◆ **Smoothness.** A percentage value (0 to 100) that determines how smoothly the colors of the gradient blend together (available when the Solid option is selected).

◆ **Roughness.** A percentage value (0 to 100) that determines how much noise to introduce into the gradient colors (available when the Noise option is selected).

8 To add Opacity Stops, click above the gradient line; to remove Opacity Stops, drag a stop away from the line.

9 To add Color Stops, click below the gradient line; to remove Color Stops, drag a stop away from the line.

10 Click on an Opacity Stop, and then enter an Opacity percentage (0 to 100), and a Location percentage (0 to 100) for the stop to rest on the line.

11 Click on a Color stop, and then select a color, and a Location percentage (0 to 100) for the color stop to rest on the line.

12 Click **Delete** to delete the selected opacity or color stop.

13 Click **Save** to save the new gradient set.

The set will include the new gradients, and all the gradients that appear in the Presets panel.

14 Click **OK**.

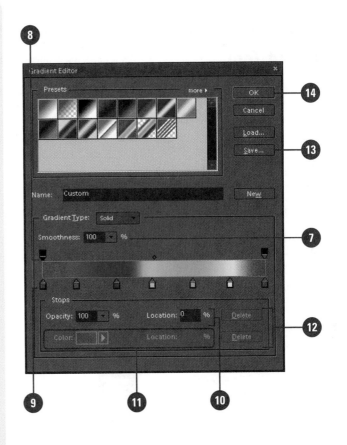

For Your Information

Creating a Customized Gradient

Gradients serve many purposes. They can be used to jazz up a shape drawn with the drawing tools or they can be applied to an entire image and used as a background on a web page, brochure or newsletter. Whatever you use gradients for, remember that they are powerful image elements. Use gradients to attract attention to a image, but don't use them if they draw people's eyes away from the main elements of the image. It will be a small consolation to know that your fantastic marketing graphic attracted attention, but everyone was so focused on your special effects and gradients, that they forgot to buy what you were selling. Remember, it's always about the message. An image is worth a thousand words... let the image tell its story.

Using the Color Replacement Tool

The Color Replacement tool lets you replace a specific color in your image. For best results use soft brushes with this tool, to help blend the colors into the original image. Have you ever captured that perfect picture of a family member or friend, only to realize that the person's sweater clashes horribly with the backdrop? Or maybe there's a part of your image where the color draws attention away from the focal point. Either way, the Color Replacement tool is a great feature that allows you to take control of the image output.

Use the Color Replacement Tool

1. In the Editor, select the **Color Replacement** tool on the toolbox.

2. Click the **Brush Preset Picker** list arrow on the Options bar, and then select from the available options.

3. Select from the available Limits options:

   ◆ **Discontiguous.** Replaces the sampled color under the pointer.

   ◆ **Contiguous.** Replaces connected areas containing the sampled color and preserves the sharpness of shape edges.

4. Enter a Tolerance percentage value (0 to 255).

5. Select the **Anti-alias** check box for a smoother edge on areas you correct.

6. Select a foreground color to use to replace the unwanted color.

7. Drag in the image over the color you want to replace.

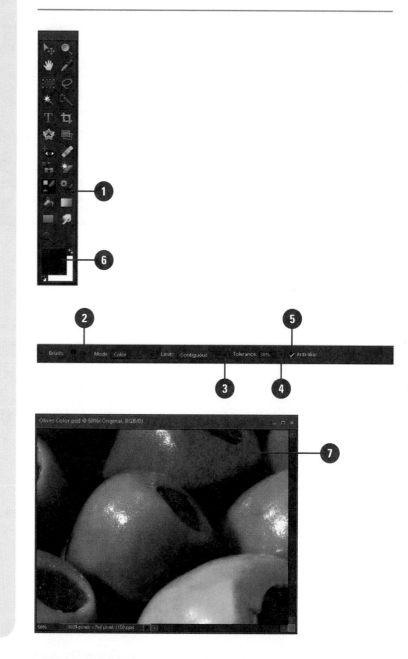

Creating Shapes in a Layer

Shape are created in shape layers. They are useful for creating buttons, navigation bars, frames, backgrounds, and other elements for web pages. You can add one or more shapes to a shape layer depending on the shape area you select. The shape area options allow you to add a shape, remove areas, show intersecting shapes, and remove overlapping areas. You can change shape color and apply effects, such as bevels and shadows, to all shapes on a layer.

Create Shapes in a Layer

1. Select a shape tool (Rectangle, Rounded Rectangle, etc.) on the toolbox.

2. Click one of the following shape area options on the Options bar:

   ◆ **Create New Layer.** Add a shape to a new shape layer.

   ◆ **Add.** Add a shape to the existing shape.

   ◆ **Subtract.** Removes the area where shapes overlap.

   ◆ **Intersect.** Shows only the area where shapes intersect.

   ◆ **Exclude.** Removes the overlapping areas in the new and existing shapes.

3. To change the shape color, click the **Color** list arrow on the Options bar, and then select a color.

   ◆ To change the color of all shapes in a layer, double-click the shape layer thumbnail in the Layers palette, and then use the Color Picker tool to select a new color.

4. To add a style to the shape, click the **Style** list arrow on the Options bar, and then select a style effect.

   ◆ To remove the style, click the **More Options** button, and then click **Remove Style**.

5. Drag in the image window to create the shape.

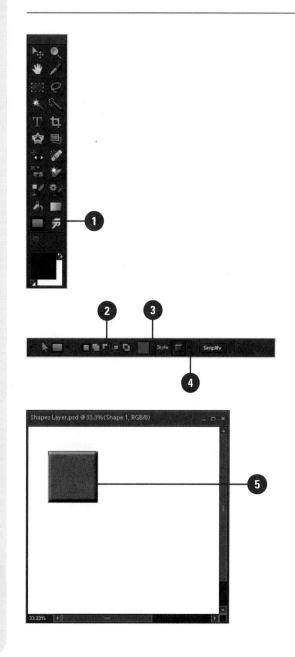

Selecting and Moving Shapes

After you create shapes in a layer, you can use the Shape Selection tool to select one or more of them by clicking each one. After you select one or more shapes on the same layer, you can move or modify them. To a move a selected shape, you simply drag it to a new location. If you simplify a shape (covert it into a bitmap element) using the Simplify button on the Options bar, you can no longer use the Shape Selection tool. You need to use the Move tool instead, which you can also use to move all the shapes on the same shape layer at the same time.

Select and Move Shapes on a Layer '

① In the Editor, select the layer with the shapes you want to use in the Layers palette.

② Select the **Shape Selection** tool on the toolbox.

◆ If another shape is selected, click the **Shape Selection** tool on the Options bar.

③ Select or deselect the **Show Bounding Box** check box to show or hide the selection border.

④ Click one of the following shape area options on the Options bar:

◆ **Add.** Adds to the shape area.

◆ **Subtract.** Removes the area where shapes overlap.

◆ **Intersect.** Shows only the area where shapes intersect.

◆ **Exclude.** Removes the overlapping areas in shapes.

⑤ To select a shape, click it or drag a selection box around the shapes to select them.

⑥ To add or remove shapes to the selection, hold down the Ctrl key, and then click the shapes you want to add or remove.

⑦ To combine two or more shapes, select the shapes on the same layer, and then click **Combine** on the Options bar.

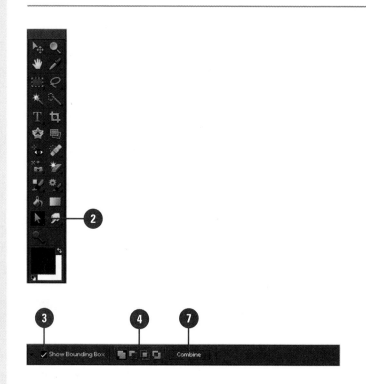

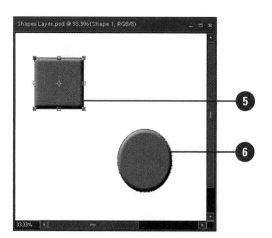

Working with the Line Tool

The Line tool lets you draw lines by dragging from one point in the active image and releasing in another. Lines drawn at precise 90- or 45-degree angles are achieved by holding down the Shift key as you drag. Select the Line tool, or if you have any drawing tool selected, you can choose the Line tool from the Options bar. Then configure the Line tool, using the Options bar. It's also a good idea to create the lines in a separate layer. That way once the line has been drawn, it's as easy as selecting the Move tool, and repositioning the line to the desired position.

Work with the Line Tool

1. In the Editor, select the **Line** tool on the toolbox.

2. Click the **Geometry** list arrow, and then select from the following options:

   ◆ **Arrowheads.** Select the Start and/or End check boxes to create arrowheads on the line.

   ◆ **Width.** Enter a percentage (10 to 1000), to determine the width of the arrowhead in relation to the width of the line.

   ◆ **Length.** Enter a percentage (10 to 5000), to determine the length of the arrowhead.

   ◆ **Concavity.** Enter a percentage (-50 to +50) to determine the concavity of the arrowhead.

3. Enter a value (1 to 1000 pixels) to determine the weight of the line.

4. Click one of the following shape area options on the Options bar: **Create New Layer**, **Add**, **Subtract**, **Intersect**, or **Exclude**.

5. To change the shape color, click the **Color** list arrow on the Options bar, and then select a color.

6. To add a style to the shape, click the **Style** list arrow on the Options bar, and then select a style effect.

7. Drag in the image window to create the line.

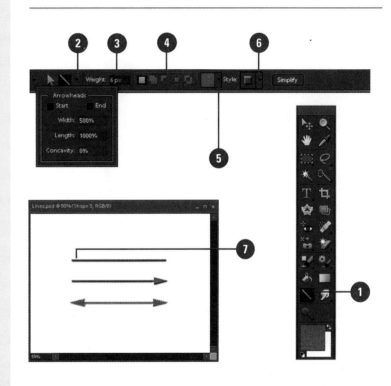

For Your Information

Using the Line Tool

The Line tool can be used to create customized guidelines for those projects that require something other than guidelines that are vertical or horizontal. Just create a new layer, and then select the line tool. Choose a line width of one or two pixels, select a drawing color that contrasts with the image, and then draw the required guides. When you're finished, lock the layer, and use the visual guides to complete your project. Hide the layer when it's not needed, and finally, delete the layer when you're done with the job. One more thing— remember to turn off the arrowhead option.

Using the Standard Shape Tool

Creating standard shapes, such as polygons or rectangles with rounded corners is a simple matter of selecting a shape tool, choosing a color, and then drawing the shape. A shape is a **vector graphic** made up of lines and curves instead of pixels, which allows you to move, resize, and change it without losing quality. As with any of the drawing functions, control is maintained with the use of additional layers. The standard shapes consist of rectangles, rounded rectangles, ellipses, polygons; and each one of the shape tools comes with additional options to control exactly how the shape appears when drawn, including extensive layer effects to colorize the shape, add a drop shadow or bevel, even apply a gradient or pattern to the shape.

Work with the Standard Shape Tool

1. In the Editor, select the **Rectangle**, **Rounded Rectangle**, **Ellipse**, or **Polygon** tool on the toolbox.

2. Click the **Geometry** list arrow, and then select from the following drawing options or check boxes:

   ◆ **Unconstrained.** (Rectangle, Rounded Rectangle, Ellipse) Draws to any size.

   ◆ **Square.** (Rectangle, Rounded Rectangle) Draws a perfect square.

   ◆ **Circle.** (Ellipse) Draws a perfect circle.

   ◆ **Fixed Size.** (Rectangle, Rounded Rectangle, Ellipse) Draws to a specific size.

   ◆ **Proportional.** (Rectangle, Rounded Rectangle, Ellipse) Draws to proportional width and height.

   ◆ **From Center.** (Rectangle, Rounded Rectangle, Ellipse) Draws from center.

   ◆ **Snap to Pixels.** (Rectangle, Rounded Rectangle) Snaps edges to the pixel boundaries.

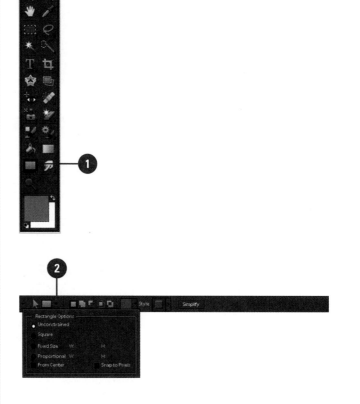

- ◆ **Radius.** (Polygon) Specify the distance from the center to the outer points.

- ◆ **Smooth Corners.** (Polygon) Select to smooth corners.

- ◆ **Star.** (Polygon) Select to turn a polygon into a star.

- ◆ **Indent Sides By.** (Polygon) Specify a depth for the star's indentations.

- ◆ **Smooth Indents.** (Polygon) Select to display a star with smooth edges.

3 Click one of the following shape area options on the Options bar:

- ◆ **Create New Layer.** Add a shape to a new shape layer.

- ◆ **Add.** Add a shape to the existing shape layer.

- ◆ **Subtract.** Remove the area where shapes overlap.

- ◆ **Intersect.** Show only the area where shapes intersect.

- ◆ **Exclude.** Remove the overlapping areas in the new and existing shapes.

4 To change the shape color, click the **Color** list arrow on the Options bar, and then select a color.

5 To add a style to the shape, click the **Style** list arrow on the Options bar, and then select a style effect.

- ◆ To remove the style, click the **More Options** button, and then click **Remove Style**.

6 Drag in the image window to create the shape.

IMPORTANT *Maintain control over your design by drawing shapes in separate layers.*

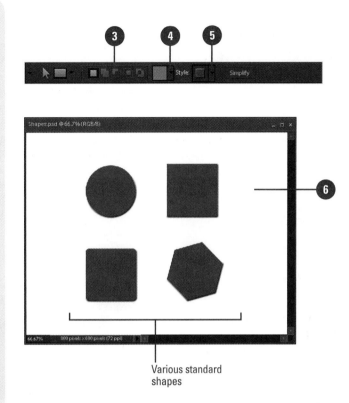

Various standard shapes

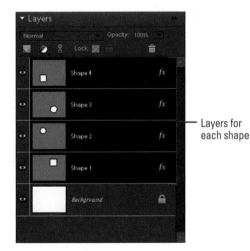

Layers for each shape

Working with the Custom Shape Tool

Having the ability to draw a perfect polygon or rounded-corner rectangle is nice, however, Photoshop Elements went way beyond standard shapes when it introduced the Custom Shape tool. Photoshop now comes packaged with dozens of pre-designed shapes, or you can even create your own. User-defined shapes can be literally any vector objects. For example, a company logo can be converted to a custom shape. Custom shapes have many timesaving applications. As previously mentioned, a company logo, if used frequently, is only a mouse click away. Any vector form, outline, or shape used on a recurring basis, can be converted to a custom shape and saved for future use. Select the Custom Shape tool or, if you have any shape drawing tool selected, click the Custom Shape button from the Options bar, and then configure the shape using the options on the Option bar.

Work with the Custom Shape Tool

1. In the Editor, select the **Custom Shape** tool on the toolbox.

2. Click the **Fill Pixels** button to create raster shapes using the active foreground color.

3. Click the **Geometry** list arrow, and then select from the available options: **Unconstrained, Defined Proportions, Defined Size, Fixed Size,** or **From Center**.

4. Click the **Shape** list arrow, and then select a shape from the available options.

5. Click one of the following shape area options on the Options bar: **Create New Layer, Add, Subtract, Intersect,** or **Exclude**.

6. To change the shape color, click the **Color** list arrow on the Options bar, and then select a color.

7. To add a style to the shape, click the **Style** list arrow on the Options bar, and then select a style effect.

   ◆ To remove the style, click the **More Options** button, and then click **Remove Style**.

8. Drag in the image window to create the customized shape.

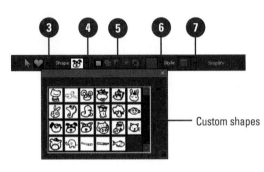

Custom shapes

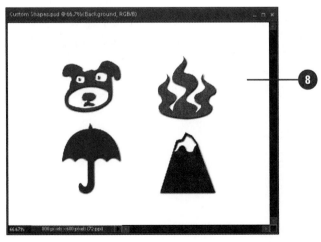

Working with Layer Styles and Photo Effects

14

Introduction

Layer styles are the very definition of creativity and control when using Photoshop Elements. Using styles, such as Bevel or Drop Shadow, you can move from two-dimensional into the world of three-dimensional. You can effortlessly change the look of an image, and you can do it all without ever changing the original image. That means you can apply a style to an image, and at any time in the creative process, change your mind. This level of control gives you the power you need to take your designs to the creative edge and beyond.

A photo effect is a photographic technique applied to all or part of an image. Photoshop Elements comes with 6 pre-defined sets of photo effects, which includes Faded Photo, Frame, Misc. Effects, Monotone Color, Old Photo, and Vintage Photo. You can display the different photo effect types in the Effects palette using the Photo Effects button and the Type list arrow.

In addition to layer styles and photo effects, you can also apply a variety of artwork, themes, and text styles to images or projects using the Content palette. Photoshop Elements comes with 6 pre-defined content sets, which includes Backgrounds, Frames, Graphics, Shapes, Text, and Themes. Each one of the style sets displays thumbnail examples you can add or apply to an image.

What You'll Do

Explore Layer Styles

Apply Layer Styles

Work with Layer Styles

Change Drop Shadow Style Settings

Change Bevel Style Settings

Change Inner and Outer Glow Style Settings

Change Stroke Style Settings

Explore Photo Effects

Apply Photo Effects

Use the Content Palette

Add Stylized Shapes or Graphics

Add a Stylized Frame or Theme

Add Stylized Text

Add Styles and Effects to Favorites

Exploring Layer Styles

Photoshop Elements comes with 14 pre-defined sets of layer styles, and new styles are made available automatically via Photoshop.com (**New!**). You can display the different layer style types in the Effects palette using the Layer Styles button and the Type list arrow. The layer style types include Bevels, Complex, Drop Shadows, Glass Buttons, Image Effects, Inner Glows, Inner Shadows, Outer Glows, Patterns, Photographic Effects, Strokes, Visibility, Wow Chrome, Wow Neon, and Wow Plastic. Each of the layer style types displays thumbnail examples you can add or apply to an image.

Layer styles are applied to the layers in the active document. When you add a style to a layer, the results of the style are only displayed in that layer and a effects icon (fx) appears to the right of the layer's name in the Layers palette. You can apply more than one style to a layer, where each style is applied to the others, to create a complex effect. Layer styles can be applied to any layer, except the Background.

In addition to applying the pre-defined layer styles, you can also use the Style Settings dialog box to edit the settings of a layer's style or apply other available style options, which includes Lighting Angle, Shadow Distance, Outer or Inner Glow Size, Bevel Size or Direction, and Stroke Size or Opacity.

Layer Styles

Drop Shadows

Bevel

Complex

Glass Buttons

Inner Glows

Outer Glows

Patterns

Image Effects

Photo Effects

Wow Chrome

Wow Neon

Wow Plastic

Applying Layer Styles

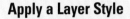

To add a layer style to the active layer, select the layer, and apply one or more of the styles by using the Layer Styles button in the Effects palette. Once applied, layer styles are easy to modify. Each of the layer styles has options to control exactly how the style appears in the active document. If you don't like the results of the layer style, you can undo it. If you want to hide all the layer style effects to view the original image, you can use the Hide All Effects command, which toggles to the Show All Effects command.

Apply a Layer Style

1. In the Editor, display the **Layers** palette and **Effects** palette.

2. Select a layer.

3. Click the **Layer Styles** button in the Effects palette.

4. Click the **Type** list arrow, and then click **Show All** or select the layer style type you want.

5. Select the style you want in the Effects palette.

   TIMESAVER *Double-click a style or drag it onto the layer, or drag it onto the active window.*

6. Click **Apply**.

   ◆ To undo the results, click the **Undo** button on the Shortcuts bar.

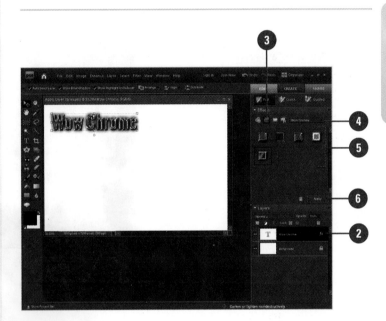

Did You Know?

You can show or hide all layer styles in an image. In the Editor, click the Layer menu, point to Layer Style, and then click Show All Effects or Hide All Effects.

Working with Layer Styles

Once applied, layer styles are easy to modify. Each of the layer styles has options to control exactly how the style appears in the active document. To modify a style, just open the Layer Style dialog box, and make your changes. If the size of a layer style is too big or small, you can change the scale to decrease or increase the effect. Once you like a layer style, you can copy the style settings between layers.

Modify an Existing Layer Style

1. In the Editor, display the **Layers** palette.

2. Double-click the effects icon (fx) in the Layers palette containing the layer style you want to change.

3. To preview the changes in your image, select the **Preview** check box.

4. Make changes to the layer style using the options; options vary depending on the layer style.

5. Click **OK**.

Did You Know?

You can remove a layer style. In the Editor, select the layer you want to remove the style in the Layers palette, click the Layer menu, point to Layer Style, and then click Clear Layer Style.

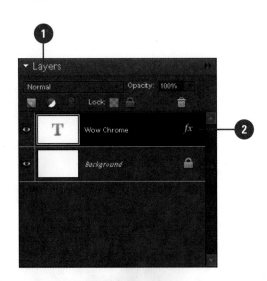

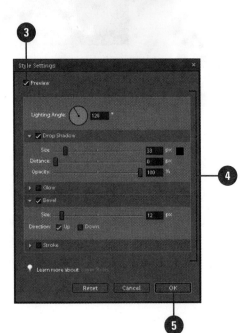

Change the Scale of a Layer Style

1. In the Editor, display the **Layers** palette.

2. Select the layer in the Layers palette containing the layer style you want to change.

3. Click the **Layer** menu, point to **Layer Style**, and then click **Scale Effects**.

4. To preview the changes in your image, select the **Preview** check box.

5. Enter the scale percentage you want based on the current one. If 100% appears, 200% doubles it.

6. Click **OK**.

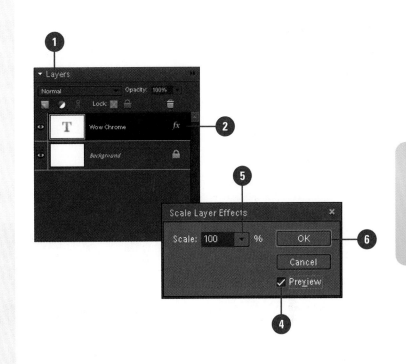

Copy Layer Style Settings Between Layers

1. In the Editor, display the **Layers** palette.

2. Select the source layer in the Layers palette containing the layer style you want to copy.

3. Click the **Layer** menu, point to **Layer Style**, and then click **Copy Layer Style**.

4. Select the destination layer in the Layers palette.

5. Click the **Layer** menu, point to **Layer Style**, and then click **Paste Layer Style**.

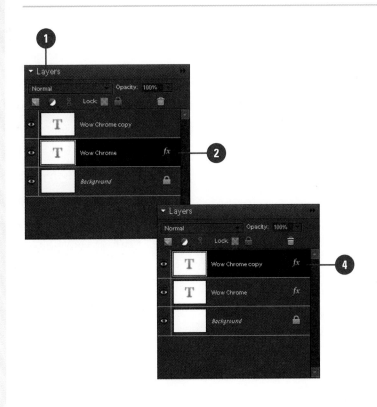

Changing Drop Shadow Style Settings

The Drop Shadow style is probably the most common layer style used (next to Bevel and Glow). Since Photoshop Elements needs somewhere to apply the drop shadow, you will need a layer that contains an object surrounded by a transparent Background. For example, you can create a type layer or use the shape drawing tools to create a unique object, add a drop shadow with the click of the mouse, and then use the layer style options to controls the color, shape, and direction of the shadow. Once the shadow is created, it can be transferred to other objects in other layers—not only making the process easy, but consistent.

Change Drop Shadow Style Settings

1. In the Editor, display the **Layers** palette and **Effects** palette.

2. Select a layer with a drop shadow or apply one to a layer.

   ◆ **Create.** Click the **Layer Styles** button in the Effects palette, Click the **Type** list arrow, and then click **Drop Shadows**, and then double-click the style you want.

3. Double-click the effects icon (fx) in the Layers palette containing the layer style you want to change.

4. To preview the changes in your image, select the **Preview** check box.

5. To adjust the lighting angle, enter a value from 0 to 360 degrees, or drag the Radius slider left or right to set the angle of the lighting.

6. Click the triangle to expand the Drop Shadow settings, if necessary, and then select the **Drop Shadow** check box.

7. Select from the following Drop Shadow style settings:

   ◆ **Opacity.** Specify an Opacity percentage value for the shadow, or drag the slider left or right (default: 75 percent).

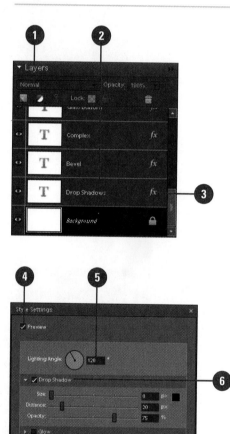

- **Size.** Enter a value from 0 to 250 pixels, or drag the slider left or right. Size determines the amount of blur applied to the shadow.

- **Distance.** Enter a value from 0 to 30000 pixels, or drag the slider left or right. Distance determines the amount the shadow is offset from the original image.

- **Color.** Click the Color Swatch, and then select a color for the shadow (default: Black).

8 Click **OK**.

Drop Shadow style applied

For Your Information

Using the Lighting Angle

You can control the direction of a light source across multiple layers. The Lighting Angle option is very important because it ties the light sources used in multiple layers together. For example, if you create multiple layers with drop shadows, and you change the direction of the shadow in one of the layers, the Lighting Angle option will ensure that all the layers maintain the same direction. The most common shadow angle used is 125 degrees; called the comfortable angle, it directs the shadow down and to the right. Studies show that most people expect the light source to be in the upper-right portion of the image.

Changing Bevel Style Settings

The Bevel style, second only to Drop Shadow in popularity, creates the 3-D illusion of roundness to a flat surface. You can apply the Bevel layer style to text, to get the impression of 3-D text. If the layer you're applying the Bevel to has no transparent areas, the style will be applied to the outer edge of the image, and if you want to move away from the standard rounded bevel, you can now use a Chisel Hard Technique, that makes a bevel appear as if it's carved out of stone.

Change Bevel Style Settings

1. In the Editor, display the **Layers** palette and **Effects** palette.

2. Select a layer with a bevel or apply one to a layer.

   ◆ **Create.** Click the **Layer Styles** button in the Effects palette, click the **Type** list arrow, click **Bevel**, and then double-click the style you want.

3. Double-click the effects icon (fx) in the Layers palette containing the layer style you want to change.

4. To preview the changes in your image, select the **Preview** check box.

5. To adjust the lighting angle, enter a value from 0 to 360 degrees, or drag the Radius slider left or right to set the angle of the lighting.

6. Click the triangle to expand the Bevel settings, if necessary, and then select the **Bevel** check box.

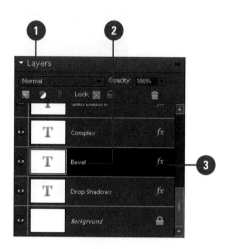

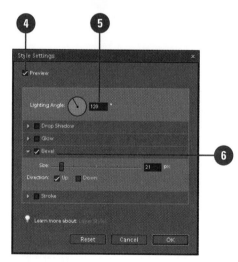

7 Select from the following Bevel style settings:

◆ **Size.** Enter a value from 0 to 250 pixels, or drag the slider left or right. Size determines the width of the beveled edge.

◆ **Distance.** Select the Up or Down check box to reverse the highlights and shadows of the Bevel.

8 Click **OK**.

Bevel style applied

Changing Inner and Outer Glow Style Settings

The Outer Glow style applies a glow in any color you choose to all objects within the active layer, while the Inner Glow style creates the appearance of a glow on the inside of a layer object. For example, creating black text and applying an inner glow style, changes the object by lightening the edges of the text. When you apply the Inner Shadow style, the shadow effect appears on the inside edges of the image—like a reverse drop shadow. When applying an outer glow style, the glow effect spreads out into the surrounding transparent areas of the layer. Once you apply the inner or outer glow, you can control the color size and intensity of the glow style to create the exact special effect you're after.

Change Inner and Outer Glow Style Settings

1. In the Editor, display the **Layers** palette and **Effects** palette.

2. Select a layer with an outer glow or apply one to a layer.

   ◆ **Create.** Click the **Layer Styles** button in the Effects palette, click the **Type** list arrow, click **Outer Glows**, and then double-click the style you want.

3. Double-click the effects icon (fx) in the Layers palette containing the layer style you want to change.

4. To preview the changes in your image, select the **Preview** check box.

5. To adjust the lighting angle, enter a value from 0 to 360 degrees, or drag the Radius slider left or right to set the angle of the lighting.

6. Click the triangle to expand the Glow settings, if necessary, and then select the **Glow** check box.

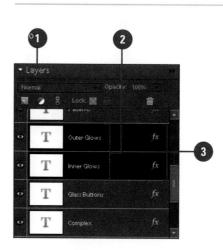

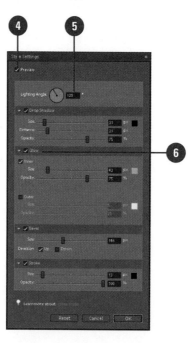

7. To set inner glow options, select the **Inner** check box, and then select from the following Inner Glow style settings:

- ◆ **Size.** Enter 1 to 250 pixels to define the width of the inner glow.

- ◆ **Opacity.** Enter an amount, or drag the slider left or right. Opacity determines how much of the inner glow masks the original image pixels (default: 100).

- ◆ **Color.** Click the color box, and then select a color.

8. To set outer glow options, select the **Outer** check box, and then select from the following Outer Glow style settings:

- ◆ **Size.** Enter 1 to 250 pixels to define the width of the outer glow.

- ◆ **Opacity.** Enter an amount, or drag the slider left or right. Opacity determines how much of the outer glow masks the original image pixels (default: 100).

- ◆ **Color.** Click the color box, and then select a color.

9. Click **OK**.

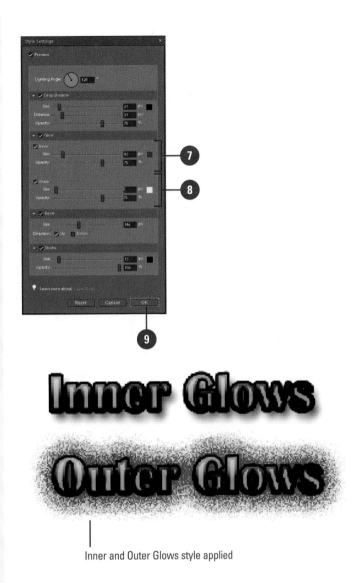

Inner and Outer Glows style applied

For Your Information

Creating Chiseled Text with Inner Glow

You can create realistic chiseled text using the Inner Glow style. Just create some white text, and apply an inner glow using a dark gray inner glow color. Add a dark Background layer, and the text appears as if it's chiseled into the background.

Changing Stroke Style Settings

The Stroke style lets you apply a stroke around any layer object. Since the stroke will be applied to the edge of the object, it must be surrounded by transparent pixels. For example, you could use the stroke feature to apply a solid color or gradient stroke to a group of text, or apply a stroke around an image. Strokes are not limited to solid colors, you can also use gradients, and even patterns as a stroke. The Stroke style can provide you with many interesting styles.

Change Stroke Style Settings

1 In the Editor, display the **Layers** palette and **Effects** palette.

2 Select a layer with the stroke you want to change.

3 Double-click the effects icon (fx) in the Layers palette containing the layer style you want to change.

4 To preview the changes in your image, select the **Preview** check box.

5 To adjust the lighting angle, enter a value from 0 to 360 degrees, or drag the Radius slider left or right to set the angle of the lighting.

6 Click the triangle to expand the Stroke settings, if necessary, and then select the **Stroke** check box.

7 Select from the following Stroke style settings:

◆ **Size.** Enter 1 to 250 pixels to define the width of the stroke.

◆ **Opacity.** Enter an amount, or drag the slider left or right. Opacity determines how much of the stroke masks the original image pixels (default: 100).

◆ **Color.** Click the color box, and then select a color.

8 Click **OK**.

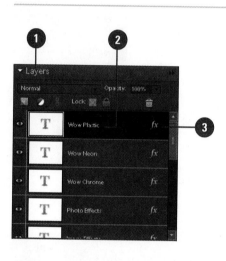

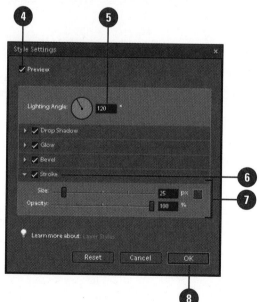

Exploring Photo Effects

A photo effect is a photographic technique applied to all or part of an image. Photoshop Elements comes with 6 pre-defined sets of photo effects, which includes Faded Photo, Frame, Misc. Effects, Monotone Color, Old Photo, and Vintage Photo, and new effects are made available automatically via Photoshop.com (**New!**). Each one of the style sets displays thumbnail examples you can add or apply to an image. You can display the different photo effect types in the Effects palette using the Photo Effects button and the Type list arrow.

The photo effects are grouped into three categories: Frame, Image Effects, and Textures. Frame photo effects, such as Drop Shadow, are applied to the edges of the selection. Image photo effects, such as Neon Glow or Blizzard, are applied to the selection. Texture photo effects are applied to the selection, which includes a new image as a background or an existing image.

Photo effects are applied to an entire layer or a selection portion of an image in the active document. By applying different photo effects to different layers, you can create interesting images.

Faded Photo

Frame

Misc. Effects

Monochrome Color

Old Photo

Vintage Photo

Applying Photo Effects

A photo effect is a photographic technique applied to all or part of an image. Photoshop Elements comes with 6 pre-defined sets of photo effects, which includes Faded Photo, Frame, Misc. Effects, Monotone Color, Old Photo, and Vintage Photo. You can display the different photo effect types in the Effects palette using the Photo Effects button and the Type list arrow.

Apply a Photo Effect

1. In the Editor, display the **Layers** palette and **Effects** palette.

2. Select the part of the image you want to apply the photo effect.

   ◆ **Entire Layer.** Select the layer in the Layers palette.

   ◆ **Layer Portion.** Select the layer in the Layers palette, and then use the selection tool to select the area you want.

   IMPORTANT *To preserve the original image, make a duplicate layer. Click the Layer menu, and then click Duplicate Layer.*

3. Click the **Photo Effects** button in the Effects palette.

4. Click the **Type** list arrow, and then click **Show All** or select the photo effect type you want.

5. Select the effect you want in the Effects palette.

   TIMESAVER *Double-click a style or drag an effect onto the layer.*

6. Click **Apply**.

   ◆ To undo the results, click the **Undo** button on the Shortcuts bar.

7. If prompted, flatten the image with multiple layers.

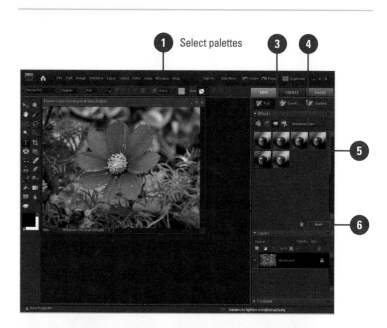
Select palettes

Photo Effect applied

Using the Content Palette

The Content palette provides easy access to a variety of artwork, themes, and text styles you can apply to images or projects. Photoshop Elements comes with 6 pre-defined sets of styles, which includes Background, Frames, Graphics, Shapes, Text Effects, and Themes, and new styles are made available via Photoshop.com (**New!**). Each one of the style sets displays thumbnail examples you can add or apply to an image.

You can display the different style types in the Content palette using sort and category options. The Sort list arrow allows you to sort the content in a variety of ways, including by Type, Activity, Color, Event, Mood, Object, Seasons, Style, and Word. After you select a sort option, you can use the Category list arrow to further filter the styles.

Background **Text** **Themes** **Graphics**

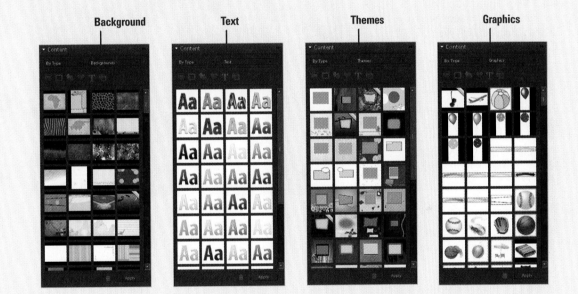

Adding Stylized Shapes or Graphics

The Content palette includes a variety shapes and graphics you can quickly add to your images. When you add a shape—such as an arrow or icon—or graphic—such as a banner—to an image, the item is placed in a new layer, which doesn't affect the original image. After you place a shape or graphic, you can use the Move tool to move or resize the object. In addition to adding shapes and graphics, you can also add a stylized background to replace the existing background layer.

Add Stylized Shapes or Graphics to an Image

1 In the Editor, display the **Content** palette.

2 Click the **Filter for Graphics** or **Filter for Shapes** button in the Content palette, or use the list arrows to select **By Type** and **Graphics** or **Shapes**.

3 For a shape, click a color in the toolbox.

4 Select the shape or graphic you want in the Content palette.

> **TIMESAVER** *Double-click a shape or graphic or drag it onto the image.*

5 Click **Apply**.

◆ To undo the results, click the **Undo** button on the Shortcuts bar.

6 To move or resize the shape or graphic, use the **Move** tool, and then click **Commit** or **Cancel**.

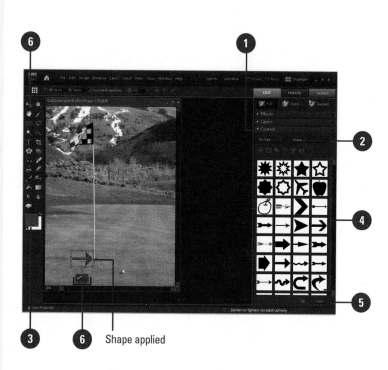

Shape applied

Add Stylized Background to an Image

1 In the Editor, display the **Content** palette and **Layers** palette.

2 Select the Background layer in the Layers palette.

> **IMPORTANT** *To preserve the original image background, make a duplicate layer. Click the Layer menu, and then click Duplicate Layer.*

3 Click the **Filter for Background** button in the Content palette, or use the list arrows to select **By Type** and **Background**.

4 Select the background you want in the Content palette.

> **TIMESAVER** *Double-click a background or drag it onto the image.*

5 Click **Apply**.

◆ To undo the results, click the **Undo** button on the Shortcuts bar.

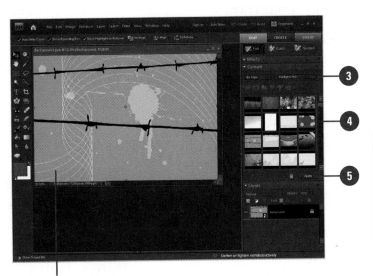

Background applied

Adding a Stylized Frame or Theme

If you have a photo project in Photoshop Elements, you can add a frame or theme to an image. The frames and themes are available in the Contents palette. If you apply a frame to a blank layer, you need to drag the photo project image from the Project Bin to the frame, which appears with a blank gray area for the image. If the active layer contains an image, it's placed within the frame.

Add a Stylized Frame or Theme to an Image

1. In the Editor, display the **Content** palette.

2. Click the **Filter for Themes** or **Filter for Frames** button in the Content palette, or use the list arrows to select **By Type** and **Themes** or **Frames**.

3. Select the theme or frame you want in the Content palette.

   TIMESAVER *Double-click a theme or frame or drag it onto the image.*

4. Click **Apply**.

   ◆ To undo the results, click the **Undo** button on the Shortcuts bar.

   A frame appears with a blank gray area for the image.

5. Drag the image from the Project Bin to the frame.

6. Use the slider to resize the image in the frame or theme border.

7. Click the **Commit** (green check mark) or **Cancel** (red circle with a line through it) button under the bounding box.

8. To center the image, use the Move tool, and then click **Commit** or **Cancel**.

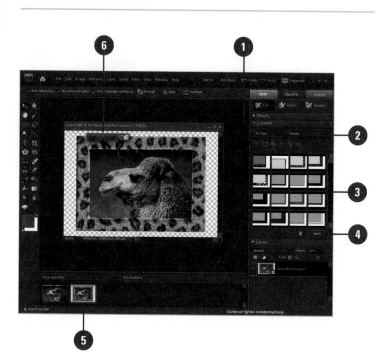

Adding Stylized Text

If you want to add text to an image, you can stylize it using text style effects in the Content palette. When you add text to an image, Photoshop Elements automatically creates a new text layer and adds the text to it, so the text doesn't affect the original image. When you select and apply a text style, a text frame appears over the image with the Text tool on the toolbox selected. You can type the text you want and make any changes you want using options on the toolbox or Options bar.

Add Stylized Text to an Image

1. In the Editor, display the **Content** palette.

2. Click the **Filter for Text** button in the Content palette, or use the list arrows to select **By Type** and **Type**.

3. Select the text style you want in the Content palette.

   TIMESAVER *Double-click a text style or drag it onto the image.*

4. Click **Apply**.

   ◆ To undo the results, click the **Undo** button on the Shortcuts bar.

   A text frame appears over the image with the Text tool on the toolbox selected.

5. Type in the new text, make any changes within the text box, and then click outside the text to deselect it.

6. Use the **Move** tool on the toolbox to move or resize the text box, or use the Color palette on the Options bar to add color to the text, and then click **Commit** or **Cancel**.

5. Text applied

Adding Styles and Effects to Favorites

If you use the same layer style, photo effect, or filter in the Effects palette or the same filter in the Content palette, you can add them to the Favorites palette for quick and easy access later. If your favorites list gets too long or you no longer use a favorite, you can remove it from the Favorites palette.

Add Styles and Effects to the Favorites List

1. In the Editor, display the **Effects** palette and/or **Content** palette.

2. Display the effect or artwork thumbnail you want to add to the favorites list.

3. Right-click the thumbnail, and then click **Add to Favorites**.

   The effect or artwork is added to the Favorites palette.

4. To display the Favorites palette, click the **Window** menu, and then click **Favorites**.

5. To use the effects in the Favorites palette, double-click a style or drag an effect onto the layer.

   ◆ To undo the results, click the **Undo** button on the Shortcuts bar.

6. To remove a thumbnail from the Favorites palette, select the thumbnail, and then click the **Delete Favorite** button.

7. When you're done, click the **Close** button in the Favorites palette.

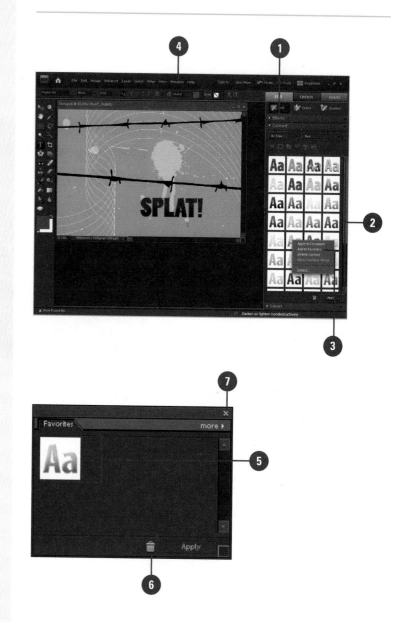

Manipulating Images with Filters

15

Introduction

One of the most powerful features in Photoshop Elements is its ability to manipulate a photographic image with filters. Photographers use the term photographic restoration to describe image retouching. Photo restoration describes the process of returning an image to its original state. For example, removing dust and scratches from an old image, using the Dust and Scratches filter, or repairing all the problems associated with working with old images. Since there are the same tools and filters that can be used to restore an image, you can use the various filters and tools to find out which ones will help you with your image restoration.

Photoshop Elements filters are a designer's dream come true. With filters you can turn a photograph into an oil painting or a watercolor; even change night into day. The Filter menu includes no fewer than 105 highly creative filters, which can be applied once, reapplied, or combined with other filters to create any effect your imagination can dream up.

The possible combination of filters and images literally runs into the millions. This means that Photoshop Elements filters are truly an undiscovered territory. As a matter of fact, the Filter Gallery lets you view the effects of one or more filters on the active image. This level of power gives you unbelievable creative control over your images.

Take a moment to view some of the various filter effects that Photoshop Elements offers. Because there are 105 filters available, we can't show you all of them, but I think you'll enjoy viewing the selection at the end of the chapter.

What You'll Do

Work with the Filter Gallery

Apply Multiple Filters to an Image

Control Filters Using a Selection

Blend Modes and Filter Effects

Use the Color Halftone Pixelate Filter

Modify Images with the Liquify Filter

Work with Liquify Filter Options

Use the Lighting Effects Filter

Use Blur Filters

Use the Gaussian Blur Filter

Apply the Surface Blue Filter

Use the Add Noise Filter

Use the Reduce Noise Filter

View Various Filter Effects

Working with the Filter Gallery

The Filter Gallery maintains complete and total control over the filters. In essence, the Filter Gallery gives you access to all of the filters and lets you apply the filters to any raster image, while viewing a large preview of the results. The Filter Gallery dialog box is composed of three sections—Image Preview, Filter Selection, and Filter Controls. When you use the Filter Gallery to modify the image, you see exactly how the image will look; there is no guesswork involved. When you apply a filter to an image you are physically remapping the pixel information within the image. Photoshop Elements contains 105 filters and the combinations of those filters are astronomical. If you are a math wizard, there are over 100 million combinations available, and that means that no one has discovered all the ways you can manipulate an image in Photoshop Elements... have fun trying.

Work with the Filter Gallery

1. In the Editor, open an image.

2. Display the **Layers** palette, and then select the layer you want to modify with a filter effect.

3. Click the **Filter** menu, and then click **Filter Gallery**.

4. Change the image preview by clicking the plus or minus zoom buttons, or by clicking the black triangle and selecting from the pre-set zoom sizes.

5. If necessary, drag the lower-right corner in or out to resize the Filter Gallery dialog box.

6. Click the **expand triangle**, located to the left of the individual categories, to expand a filter category. Filter categories include:

   ◆ Artistic

   ◆ Brush Strokes

   ◆ Distort

   ◆ Sketch

   ◆ Stylize

   ◆ Texture

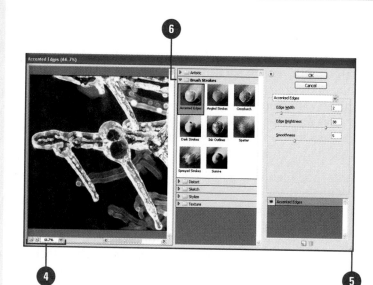

7 Click a filter from the expanded list to view its default effects to the image.

8 Modify the effects of the filter using the filter controls.

9 To temporarily hide the Filter Selections, click the **Hide Filter Section** button.

10 Click **OK**.

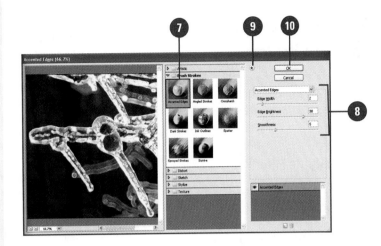

Did You Know?

You can reapply the last filter effect using a shortcut. Press Ctrl+F to reapply the last filter to the image.

For Your Information

Reading Imaging with Watermarks

Digital watermarks are designed to protect your intellectual property. When you embed a digital watermark, it actually inserts the watermark information as visible noise into the image. This means that someone can copy your image, scan it, and the watermark is still part of the image. You cannot embed a watermark in Photoshop Elements; you need a program like Photoshop CS4. However, you can read a watermark from a Photoshop image in Photoshop Elements. To embed a digital watermark, you must first register with Digimarc Corporation; which maintains a database of artists, designers, and photographers and their contact information. You can then embed the Digimarc ID in your images, along with information such as the copyright year or a restricted-use identifier, using Photoshop CS4. If you want to read a watermark, you can view it in Photoshop Elements. Open the image with the watermark in Photoshop Elements, click the Filter menu, point to Digimarc, and then click Read Watermark.

Applying Multiple Filters to an Image

Not only does the Filter Gallery let you apply and view a filter effect, it lets you view the multiple effects of two or more filters. The Filter Gallery has its own Layers palette, and can have a lot of effect layers. The order of the filters influences their impact on the image. When you create a filter effect using more than one filter, drag the filter effect up or down in the effects stack. Changing the order of the filters changes their impact on the image, so experiment with different stacking orders to create eye-popping special effects.

Apply Multiple Filters to an Image

① In the Editor, open an image.

② Display the **Layers** palette, and then select the layer you want to modify with a filter effect.

③ Click the **Filter** menu, and then click **Filter Gallery**.

④ Select the filter you want.

⑤ Adjust the filter as necessary.

⑥ Click the **New Effect Layer** button, located at the bottom of the Filter Adjustments section. You can add as many effect layers as needed.

⑦ Select and adjust a second filter (repeat steps 4 and 5).

⑧ Adjust each individual effect by clicking on the effect layer you want to change.

⑨ To change filter influence on the image, drag an effect layer to another position in the stack.

⑩ To temporarily show or hide the effect on the image, click the **Show/Hide** button.

⑪ To delete a selected effect layer, click the **Delete** button.

⑫ Click **OK**.

IMPORTANT *Once you click the OK button, the effects are permanently applied to the active image.*

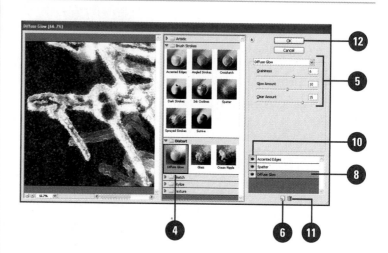

Controlling Filters Using a Selection

When you apply a filter to an image, Photoshop Elements applies the filter equally to the entire image. Unfortunately, that might not be what you had in mind. For example, you might want to apply the Gaussian Blur filter to a portion of the image. In that case, the selection tools come to the rescue. The primary purpose of selection is to define a work area, and when you select an area before applying a filter, the only area impacted by the filter will be the selected area.

Control Filters Using a Selection

1. In the Editor, open an image.

2. Display the **Layers** palette, and then select the layer you want to apply a filter.

3. Click one of the selection tools on the toolbox, and then create a selection in the image window.

4. Click the **Filter** menu, and then click **Filter Gallery**.

5. Click any of the filters.

6. Adjust the filter options until you see the image you want.

7. Click **OK**.

   The filter is only applied to the selected areas of the image.

See Also

See Chapter 9, "Mastering the Art of Selection," on page 175 for more information on creating selections.

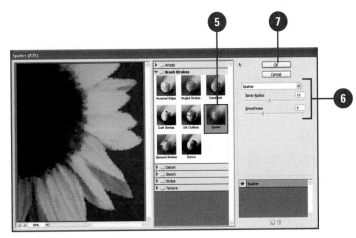

Blending Modes and Filter Effects

The Filter Gallery gives designers the ability to view the effects of multiple filters applied to a single image. While this changed forever how we apply filters to an image, there is one more creative way to work: Blending Modes. For example, make a copy of an image, then apply a separate filter effect to each layer, and then use the Blending Modes option to create a totally different image. While this is not a new technique, the results of combining two or more layers together, each with a different filter effect can produce quite stunning results.

Work with Blending Modes and Filter Effects

1. In the Editor, open an image.

2. Select the layer containing the image you want to modify.

3. Click the **Layer** menu, point to **New**, and then click **Layer Via Copy** or press Ctrl+J to create a copy of the selected layer.

4. Select the layers one at a time and apply a different filter to each layer.

5. Click the **Blending Modes** list arrow and experiment with the various blending options.

In this example, the Cutout and Find Edges filters were used on the separate layers, and then combined with the Linear Light Blending Mode.

Did You Know?

You can use the Opacity option to further control the final image. If the blending effect appears a bit too intense, simply lower the opacity of the top, or bottom layer to change the intensity of the filter effects.

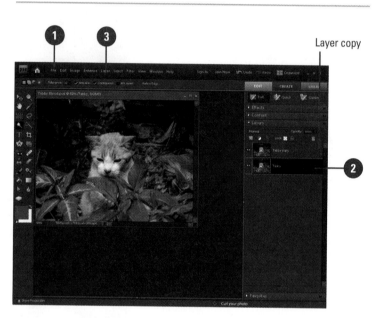

Layer copy

Final image with blending modes

348

Using the Color Halftone Pixelate Filter

The Color Halftone filter, one of the Pixelate group, simulates using a halftone screen on a layer. Halftones are created through a process called dithering, in which the density and pattern of the dots are varied to simulate different color shades. The filter divides the image into rectangles and replaces each rectangle with a circle, which is proportional in size to the brightness of the rectangle.

Use the Color Halftone Pixelate Filter

① In the Editor, open an image.

② Select the portions of the image you want to pixelate or leave the image unselected to apply the filter to the entire image.

③ Click the **Filter** menu, point to **Pixelate**, and then click **Color Halftone**.

④ Enter a value (4 to 127) for the maximum radius of a halftone in pixels

⑤ Enter a screen-angle value (between -360 and 360) for one or more channels.

◆ **Grayscale Image.** Enter a value in channel 1.

◆ **Color Image.** Enter a value in channel 1, 2, 3, and 4 for the CMYK (cyan, magenta, yellow, and black) channels.

⑥ To return all the screen angles to default settings, click **Default**.

⑦ Click **OK**.

Final image with Halftone pixelate filter

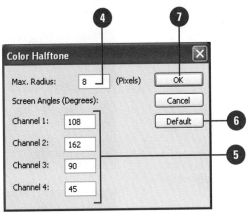

Modifying Images with the Liquify Filter

The Liquify filter gives you amazing control over an image. For example, you can distort the image pixels almost as if the image were an oil painting that had yet to dry. In addition, you can magnify specific areas of an image or reduce them in size. The Liquify filter lets you push, pull, rotate, reflect, pucker, and bloat any area of an image. The distortions you create can be subtle or drastic, which makes the Liquify command a powerful tool for retouching images as well as creating artistic effects.

Modify Images with the Liquify Filter

1. In the Editor, open an image.

2. Display the **Layers** palette, and then select the layer you want to liquify.

3. Click the **Filter** menu, point to **Distort**, and then click **Liquify**.

4. Select from the following Liquify tools:

   ◆ **Warp.** Pushes pixels in front of the brush as you drag.

   ◆ **Turbulence.** Smoothly scrambles the pixels in an image. Creates realistic waves or fire.

   ◆ **Twirl Clockwise.** Click in an area to twirl the pixels (contained inside the brush tip) clockwise.

   ◆ **Twirl Counter Clockwise.** Click in an area to twirl the pixels (contained inside the brush tip) counter clockwise.

   ◆ **Pucker.** Click and hold to move pixels towards the center of the brush tip.

Warp

Turbulence

- **Bloat.** Click and hold to move pixels away from the center of the brush tip.

- **Shift Pixels.** Drag to push pixels to the left of the brush tip and Alt-drag to push to the right. For example, dragging straight up pushes pixels to the left, and moving to the right pushes pixels up.

- **Reflection.** Drag to copy pixels to the left of the stroke.

- **Reconstruct.** Drag the image, using a specific brush size to restore previously modified areas of the image.

- **Zoom.** Click to zoom in on a specific area of the image. Click and drag to define an area to zoom in on. Hold down the Alt key and click to zoom out.

- **Hand.** Drag to move the visible image. Useful if the image is larger than the physical image window.

5 Click **OK**.

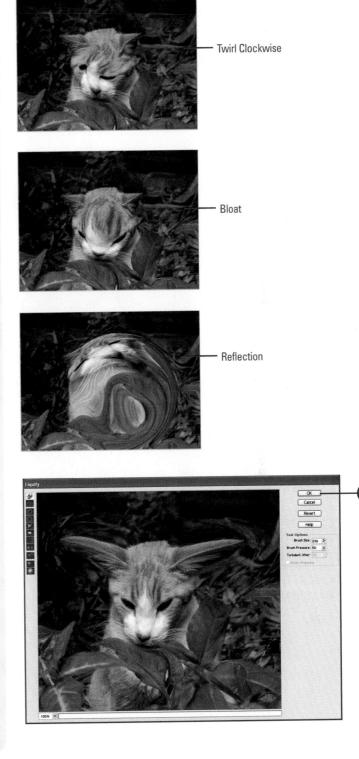

Twirl Clockwise

Bloat

Reflection

Working with Liquify Filter Options

The Liquify Tool options control the brush tip. Since all the Liquify commands are executed with a brush, it's important to understand how you control the brush tip. When you apply the brush stroke, the faster you drag the mouse the less effect is applied to the image; if you drag slowly, you gain more control and the effect is more intense. Practice dragging the cursor over the image to produce different effects, and if you make a mistake, don't forget the undo key—Ctrl+Z.

Work with Liquify Filter Options

1. In the Editor, open an image.

2. Display the **Layers** palette, and then select the layer you want to liquify.

3. Click the **Filter** menu, point to **Distort**, and then click **Liquify**.

4. Select from the following Liquify Tool options:

   ◆ **Brush Size.** Select a value (1 to 600).

   ◆ **Brush Pressure.** Select a value (1 to 100). Determines how quickly a liquify effect is applied to the image, when the brush is moving. The lower the value, the slower the effect.

   ◆ **Turbulent Jitter.** Select a value (1 to 100). Controls how tightly the Turbulent Jitter tool distorts the image. The higher the value, the more distortion.

   ◆ **Stylus Pressure.** Select the check box if you're using a drawing tablet to allow pressure on the tablet to control pressure applied with the Liquify brush.

5. Click **OK**.

Using the Lighting Effects Filter

If you want to add professional lighting effects to an RGB image, the Lighting Effects filter provides everything you need. You can set up multiple lights with unique light properties, and move them around to achieve the results you want. In addition, you can also use textures from grayscale files called texture maps to create 3D effects. If you like your results, you can save your own styles for use later.

Use the Lighting Effects Filter

1. In the Editor, open an image.

2. Display the **Layers** palette.

3. Select the image, layer, or area you want to apply the filter.

4. Click the **Filter** menu, point to **Render**, and then click **Lighting Effects**.

5. Select the **Preview** check box to view the results.

6. Click the **Style** list arrow, and then select a preset lighting effect.

7. To adjust the light type, intensity, and focus, click the **Light Type** list arrow, select a light type (Directional, Omni, or Spotlight), and then use the sliders: **Intensity** and **Focus**.

8. To adjust any of the property settings, use the sliders: **Gloss**, **Material**, **Exposure**, and **Ambience**.

9. To add a texture for the image, select a color channel, and adjust the height (depth) of the texture (0 to 100).

10. Click **OK**.

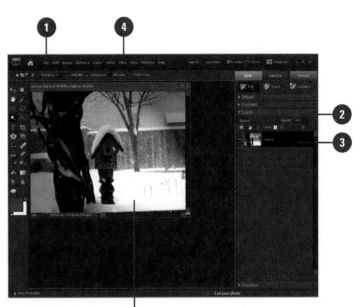

Final image with
Lighting Effects filter

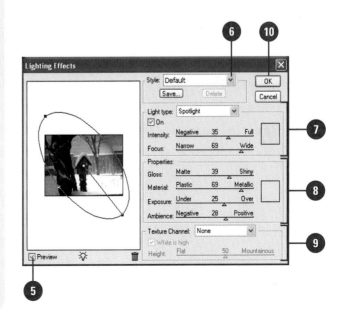

Using Blur Filters

Photoshop Elements includes several blur filters: Average, Blur, Blur More, Gaussian, Motion, Radial, Smart, and Surface (**New!**). The Average, Blur, and Blur More filters soften color pixels next to hard edges using different degrees of smoothing without any user interaction. These blur filters blurs an image based on the average color value of neighboring pixels. The other blur filters (Gaussian, Motion, Radial, Smart, and Surface) allow you to set blur options. The Motion Blur filter blurs in a specific direction and at a certain distance to simulate a moving object. The Radial Blur filter uses a spin or zoom blur method along with a radius amount to simulate a zooming or rotating camera. The Smart Blur filter uses radius, threshold, quality, and mode options to precisely blur an image. The Radius option specifies the size of the area sampled for the blur, while the Threshold option controls how much the tonal values of neighboring pixels must diverge before being part of the blur. Surface Blur affects surfaces and leaves edges alone.

Use the Smart Blur Filter

1 In the Editor, open an image.

2 Click the **Filter** menu, point to **Blur**, and then click **Smart Blur**.

3 Drag the **Radius** slider left or right to decrease or increase the amount of blur applied to the image.

4 Drag the **Threshold** slider left or right to decrease or increase the acceptance of the shift in brightness of the image information (the edges).

5 Click the **Quality** list arrow, and then select the quality level you want: **Low**, **Medium**, or **High**.

6 Click the **Mode** list arrow, and then select the mode level you want: **Normal** (entire selection), **Edge Only** (edges of color transitions), or **Overlay Edge** (edges of color transitions).

7 Click **OK**.

Final image with Smart Blur filter

Use the Radial Blur Filter

1. In the Editor, open an image.

2. Click the **Filter** menu, point to **Blur**, and then click **Radial Blur**.

3. Drag the **Amount** slider left or right to decrease or increase the amount of blur applied to the image.

4. Click the **Spin** or **Zoom** option as the blur method.

5. Click the **Draft**, **Good**, or **Best** option for blur quality.

6. Click **OK**.

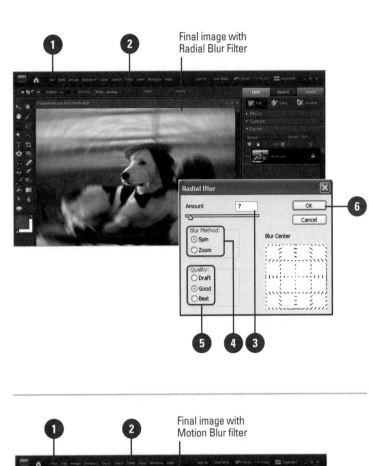

Final image with Radial Blur Filter

Use the Motion Blur Filter

1. In the Editor, open an image.

2. Click the **Filter** menu, point to **Blur**, and then click **Motion Blur**.

3. Enter the angle you want for the motion blur.

4. Drag the **Distance** slider to set the distance amount of blur applied to the image.

5. Click **OK**.

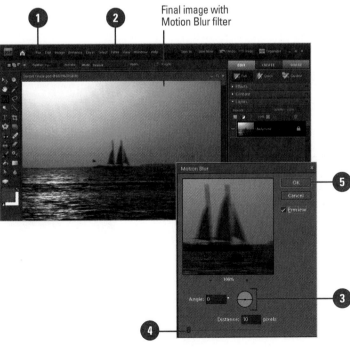

Final image with Motion Blur filter

Using the Gaussian Blur Filter

You can also apply the Gaussian Blur filter which blurs an image, or a selection by a controllable amount. While not strictly a restoration tool, the Gaussian Blur filter can be used to add a sense of depth to the image. For example, you could select and blur the background of an image, while leaving the foreground object in focus. The outcome of the filter is to create a hazy, out-of-focus effect to the image.

Use the Gaussian Blur Filter

① In the Editor, open an image.

② Select the portions of the image you want to blur or leave the image unselected to apply the filter to the entire image.

③ Click the **Filter** menu, point to **Blur**, and then click **Gaussian Blur**.

④ Select the **Preview** check box to view the results.

⑤ Drag the **Radius** slider or enter a pixel value to increase or decrease the amount of Gaussian blur applied to the image.

⑥ Click **OK**.

Final image with Gaussian Blur filter

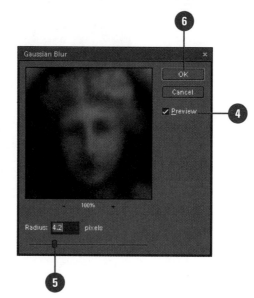

Using the Surface Blur Filter

The Surface Blur filter (**New!**) softens the appearance of surfaces while maintaining sharp edges and details. This filter is intended to be used on portrait shots to give a soft focus effect, but it also comes in handy for smoothing out rough, grainy surfaces without blurring corners and edges. It has both a Radius slider and a Threshold slider, so you can control its application very precisely.

Use the Surface Blur Filter

1. In the Editor, open an image.

2. Select the portions of the image you want to blur or leave the image unselected to apply the filter to the entire image.

3. Click the **Filter** menu, point to **Blur**, and then click **Surface Blur**.

4. Select the **Preview** check box to view the results.

5. Drag the **Radius** slider or enter a pixel value to increase or decrease the amount of blur applied to the image.

6. Drag the **Threshold** slider left or right to decrease or increase the acceptance of the shift in brightness of the image information (the edges).

7. Click **OK**.

Final image with Surface Blur filter

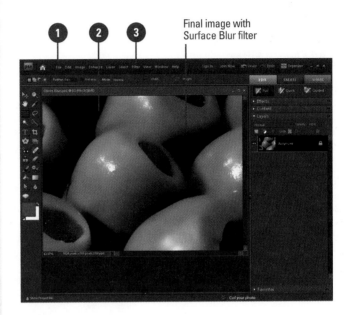

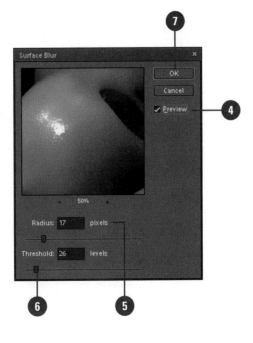

Using the Add Noise Filter

When wanting to retouch an image, you can apply the Add Noise filter. The Add Noise filter applies random pixels to an image, simulating a grainy effect. For example, you would use the Add Noise filter to make an image look like it was taken using high-speed film. In addition, the Add Noise filter can be used to reduce banding in feathered selections or graduated fills or even give a more realistic look to heavily retouched areas. Experiment with the Add Noise filter in combination with other filters, such as Motion Blur filters, to create eye-catching special effects.

Use the Add Noise Filter

1. In the Editor, open an image.

2. Display the **Layers** palette.

3. Select the layer in which you want to apply the Add Noise filter.

4. Click the **Filter** menu, point to **Noise**, and then click **Add Noise**.

5. Select from the following options:

   ◆ **Amount.** Drag the slider, or enter a value (0.10 to 400) to increase or decrease the amount of noise added to the image.

   ◆ **Distribution.** Click the Uniform option to created a more ordered appearance, or click the Gaussian option to create a more random noise pattern.

   ◆ **Monochromatic.** Select this check box to apply the filter to the tonal elements in the image without changing the colors.

   TIMESAVER *The plus and minus signs, located directly under the image preview, let you increase or decrease the viewable area of the image.*

6. Click **OK**.

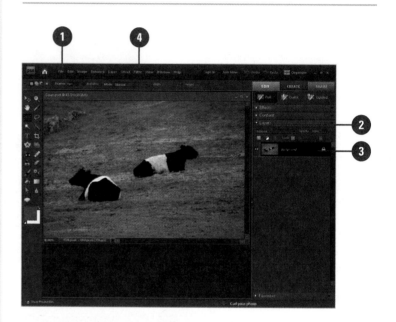

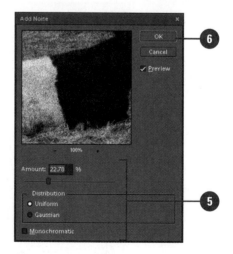

Using the Reduce Noise Filter

The Reduce Noise Filter helps to remove the random noise that crops up in digital images. It's called noise, but in reality is a pattern of distracting color or grayscale information that lays on the original image information. Noise can be generated by the Add Noise filter, but it typically comes from scanners and even digital cameras. Since there is a mathematical pattern to most noise, the Reduce Noise filter is designed to seek out and reduce the amount of noise in an image. The Reduce Noise filter works on individual layers, not the entire image. After applying the filter, you can use other restoration tools, such as the Healing Brush and Patch tool, to further clean up image problem areas.

Use the Reduce Noise Filter

1. In the Editor, open an image.

2. Click the **Filter** menu, point to **Noise**, and then click **Reduce Noise**.

3. Select the **Preview** check box to view the changes to the image.

4. Select from the following options:

   - **Strength.** Drag the slider to determine how strong to apply the Reduce Noise filter.

   - **Preserve Details.** Drag the slider to determine a balance between blurring the noise and preserving details.

   - **Reduce Color Noise.** Drag the slider to convert noise composed of colors into shades of gray (this may desaturate other areas of the image).

   - **Sharpen Details.** Drag the slider to determine where the details of the image exist, in terms of shift of brightness.

   - **Remove JPEG Artifact.** Check to help remove artifacts (typically noise within shadows) from severely compressed JPEG images.

5. Click **OK**.

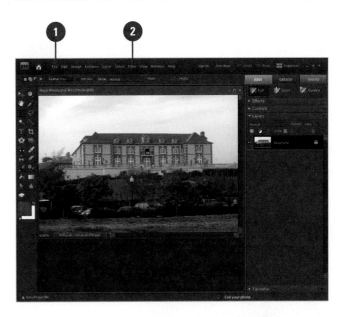

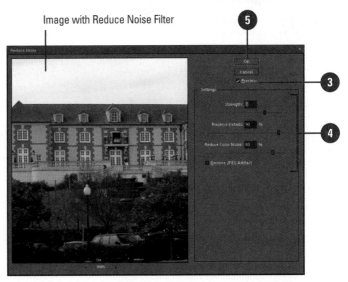

Image with Reduce Noise Filter

Viewing Various Filter Effects

Photoshop Elements provides a bountiful selection of filters, 105 to be exact. Take a moment to view some of the various filter effects that Photoshop Elements offers. The original image is shown to the right, and we've displayed some common filters on the following pages. A good thing to think about when using filters is your original image. Look at the background colors, and see if they will look good with some of the filters. The best thing to do is open an image that has a lot of various details, and then apply some filters to see what you like.

Various Filter Effects

Cutout

Dry Brush

Fresco

Palette Knife

Accented Edges

Glass

Diffuse Glow

Note Paper

Stamp

Glowing Edges

Grain

Spatter

Mosaic Tiles

Stained Glass

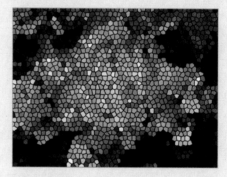

Graphic Pen

Plastic Wrap

Getting Creative with Type

16

Introduction

The Type tool in Photoshop Elements has advanced far beyond its humble beginnings. When Photoshop Elements first appeared, the most you could expect from the Type tool was to enter text. Today it's a powerful and creative tool. Not only can you place text into any open Photoshop Elements image, you can also use text as a mask, path, or even warp text into any shape you desire. In addition, Photoshop Elements now preserves type without rasterizing. That means, that type created in Photoshop Elements will print out as fine as type created in Adobe Illustrator, or InDesign; regardless of the image's resolution. When you work, type becomes as creative a design element as any other available feature.

Working with the Options bar for a text tool gives you the ability to select a specific font, style, and size, as well as expand or contract the space between letters with leading and kerning; or you could simply increase or decrease the physical width of the text. Baseline shifting even gives you the ability to raise or lower text off the original line.

You can isolate image pixels with a type mask to create words out of pictures. For example, you could type the phrase *Fall Is Coming,* and use the image of leaves. The type mask would make the words appear as if they were spelled out in colorful fall leaves. In addition, you could use a type mask in combination with the layer styles to create text that almost leaps off the page. Working with text is more than typing words on paper, it's a process every bit as creative as working with graphic images.

Using Standard Type Tools

Photoshop Elements comes with a set of standard typing tools, which are controlled in much the same way as typing tools in any program that uses text. However, the creative possibilities go far beyond those of a standard typing program. When you work with the Type tools, you begin by typing some text, and then controlling the text, through the toolbox and the Options bar. Photoshop Elements helps you maintain control over the text by automatically placing it in a separate text layer.

Use Standard Type Tools

① In the Editor, select the **Horizontal Type** or **Vertical Type** tool.

② Click in the image window to create a single line of text, or drag a rectangle to create a text box.

③ Begin typing.

Photoshop Elements creates a text layer, and places the text in the layer. A line appears through the text and a small line appears through the I-beam cursor to mark the position of the text baseline.

◆ If you did not create a text box, you can press Enter to create a new line.

IMPORTANT *When you work with the Type tools, the normal shortcut functions of the keyboard will not work. For example, holding down the Spacebar to access the Hand tool will only create a space at the insertion point of the text.*

④ Move your cursor to a point away from the text (which displays the move cursor), and then drag to move the text.

⑤ Double-click to select a specific word, or drag across the text to select groups of words.

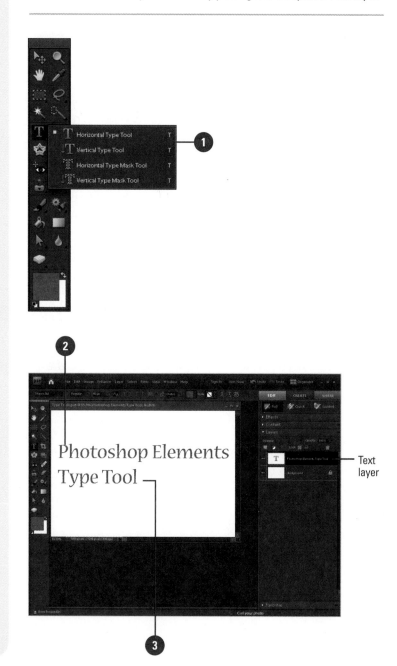

Text layer

6 Change the text color by clicking the Color list arrow on the Options bar, and then choosing a new color from the Color Swatches palette or clicking **More Colors** to select a new color from the Color Picker dialog box.

7 Delete the text by clicking within the text and pressing the Backspace key to erase one letter at a time, or select a group of text and press the Backspace key.

8 Insert text by clicking within the text to create an insertion point, and then typing.

9 Click the **Commit** button on the Options bar or click outside the text box to accept the text, or click **Cancel** to ignore the changes.

TIMESAVER *Press the Enter key on the numeric keypad to accept the text.*

See Also

See "Creating a New Layer" on page 204 for more information on creating layers.

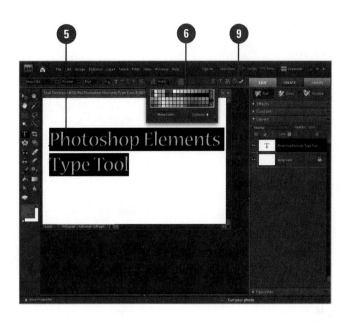

For Your Information

Preserving Text to Print

Photoshop Elements lets you preserve text to print. The type options give you control over text in much the same way as high-end layout programs, and even allow you to save the vector nature of text. This allows you to print images with crisp text that's not dependent on the resolution of the image.

To save an image file and preserve the text, click the File menu, point to Save As, and then choose the EPS (Encapsulated PostScript) format. Click the Include Vector Data option, and then save the file. The EPS file holds the type information and lets you print the image from any program including layout programs like InDesign, and QuarkXPress.

Editing Type

When you add text to an image, Photoshop Elements automatically places it in a separate text layer. To edit type in a text layer, select the text layer in the Layers palette, select a standard type tool on the toolbox, place the insertion point or select the text with the I-beam cursor, and then edit the text you want. As you edit the text, a line appears through the text and a small line appears through the I-beam cursor to mark the position of the text baseline. For horizontal type, the baseline marks the line on which the type rests, while for vertical type, the baseline marks the center axis of the type characters.

Edit Type in a Text Layer

① In the Editor, select the **Horizontal Type** or **Vertical Type** tool.

   ◆ You can also select the **Move** tool and then double-click the text.

② Select the text layer in the Layers palette.

③ Edit the text using any of the following:

   ◆ Click to place the insertion point.

   ◆ Select one or more characters you want to edit.

④ Type to insert or replace text.

⑤ Click the **Commit** button on the Options bar or click outside the text box to accept the text, or click **Cancel** to ignore the changes.

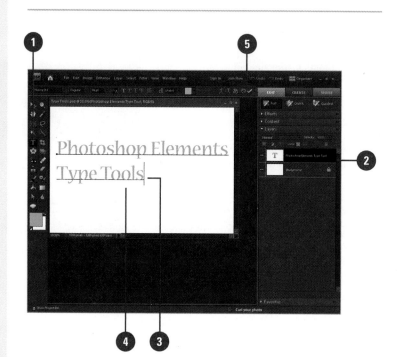

Working with Asian Type

If you work with Asian type, such as Chinese, Japanese, or Korean, you can set options in Photoshop Elements to use double-byte fonts, also known as CJK fonts. Before you can set Asian type options, you need to enable the Show Asian Text Options check box in Type Preferences. You can set several Asian type options: (1) reduce spacing between Asian characters known as Tsume, (2) turn on or off Tate-chuu-yoko, also called kumimoji or renmoji, and (3) turn on or off Mojikumi, which is the spacing between punctuations, symbols, number and other characters in Japanese type.

Show Asian Type Options

1. In the Editor, click the **Edit** menu, point to **Preferences**, and then click **Type**.

2. Select the **Show Asian Text Options** check box.

3. Select the **Show Font Names in English** check box.

4. Click **OK**.

   The Asian Type Option button appears on the Options bar.

5. Select a **Type** tool on the toolbox, and then select a text layer in the Layers palette or create a new type.

6. Click the **Asian Text Option** button on the Options bar, and then specify the following options:

   - **Tsume.** Reduces the space around a character by the specified percentage value. The greater the percentage, the tighter the spacing.

   - **Tate-Chuu-Yoko.** Select to display a block of horizontal type within a vertical type line.

   - **Mojikumi.** Determine spacing between punctuation, symbols, numbers, and other characters in Japanese type. Select to use half-width spacing. Deselect to use full-width spacing.

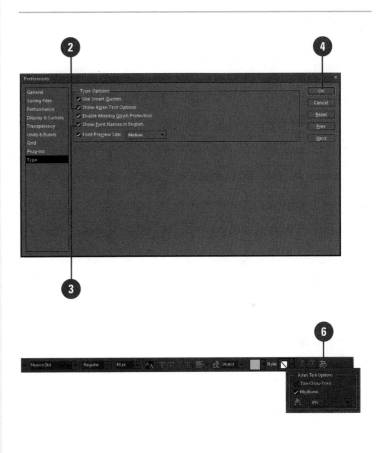

Working with Type Options

Photoshop Elements lets you control text through the type options, located on the Options bar. To access the Type options you must have one of the Type tools selected. It is not necessary to change type options after typing. If you know what you're after, you can set the options, and then commence typing. However, if the need arises to change the text, Photoshop Elements comes to the rescue with a host of type options, such as font family, size, color, justification, even high-end type processing controls like leading and kerning. You can preview font families and font styles directly in the Font menu. Font names appear in the regular system font, and a sample word ("Sample") appears next to each font name, displayed in the font itself.

Work with Type Options

1. In the Editor, open an image.

2. Select a **Type** tool on the toolbox, and then select a text layer in the Layers palette or create a new type.

3. Click the **Font Family** list arrow, and then select from the fonts available on your computer.

4. Click the **Font Style** list arrow, and then select from the font styles available on your computer.

5. Click the **Font Size** list arrow, and then select from the pre-set font sizes, measured in points (6 to 72).

   Photoshop Elements uses a standard Postscript measuring system of 72 points to the inch.

6. Click the **Anti-aliasing** button to turn anti-aliasing on and off.

   Anti-aliasing creates text that is visually smoother to the eye.

7. Click the **Faux Bold, Faux Italic, Underline**, or **Strikethrough** button.

   Use the faux option if your font doesn't have a true bold or italic style under Font Style.

8. Click the **Align** button, and then click **Left Align Text, Center Text**, or **Right Align Text** button.

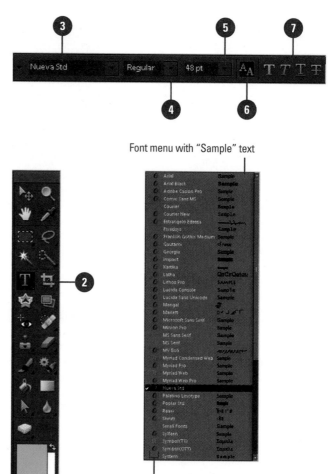

Font menu with "Sample" text

Indicates font type

9 Click the **Leading** list arrow, and then select from the pre-set values for leading. Leading adds or subtracts space vertically between lines of text.

10 Click the **Color Swatch** button, and then select a color from the Color Picker dialog box.

11 Click the **Warped Text** button to apply special warped text effects to text.

12 To toggle between horizontal and vertical type, click the **Text Orientation** button on the Options bar.

If this option is selected on a pre-existing text layer, the text switches between horizontal and vertical.

13 Click the **Commit** button on the Options bar or click outside the text box to accept the text, or **Cancel** to ignore the changes.

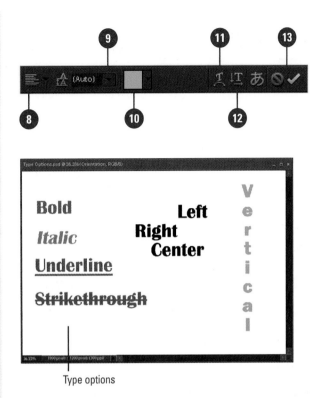

Type options

Did You Know?

You can use non pre-set font sizes from the Options bar. Select the current point size on the Options bar, type a point size, and then press Enter.

See Also

See "Using the Warp Text Option" on page 370 for information on warping text in your image.

For Your Information

What's the Difference Between the Fonts?

Everything you type appears in a font, a particular typeface design and size for letters, numbers, and other characters. Usually, each typeface, such as Times New Roman, is made available in four variations: normal, bold, italic, and bold italic. There are two basic types of fonts: scalable and bitmapped. A **scalable font** (also known as **outline font**) is based on a mathematical equation that creates character outlines to form letters and numbers of any size. The two major scalable fonts are Adobe's Type 1 PostScript and Apple/Microsoft's TrueType or OpenType. Scalable fonts are generated in any point size on the fly and require only four variations for each typeface. A **bitmapped font** consists of a set of dot patterns for each letter and number in a typeface for a specified type size. Bitmapped fonts are created or prepackaged ahead of time and require four variations for each point size used in each typeface. Although a bitmapped font designed for a particular font size will always look the best onscreen, scalable fonts eliminate storing hundreds of different sizes of fonts on a disk.

Using the Warp Text Option

The Warp Text option gives you creative control over the look of text. No longer are you confined to straight vertical or horizontal text. In the Photoshop Elements world, text can be created in almost any size and shape. As an additional bonus, warping text does not require converting the text into a raster. So days later, you can access the warped text, change its font family, size, and color. It's all about control... in this case, controlling text.

Use Warp Text

1. In the Editor, open an image.

2. Select a **Type** tool on the toolbox, and then select a text layer in the Layers palette or create a new type.

3. Click the **Warp Text** button on the Options bar.

4. Click the **Styles** list arrow, and then select from the following style options:

   - Arc
   - Arc Lower
   - Arc Upper
   - Arch
   - Bulge
   - Shell Lower
   - Shell Upper
   - Flag
   - Wave
   - Fish
   - Rise
   - Fisheye
   - Inflate
   - Squeeze
   - Twist

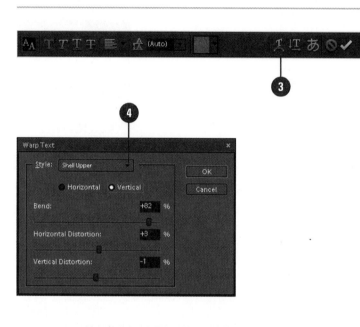

Samples of Warped Text

5 Click the **Horizontal** or **Vertical** option to warp the text in a horizontal or vertical direction.

6 Enter a percentage value in the Bend box, or drag the slider left or right (-100 to 100). Bend controls the physical amount of bend applied to the text, based on warp style.

7 Enter a percentage value in the Horizontal Distortion box, or drag the slider left or right (-100 to 100). Horizontal Distortion controls the amount of distortion on the horizontal axis applied to the text, based on warp style.

8 Enter a percentage value in the Vertical Distortion box, or drag the slider left or right (-100 to 100). Vertical Distortion controls the amount of distortion on the vertical axis applied to the text, based on warp style.

9 Click **OK**.

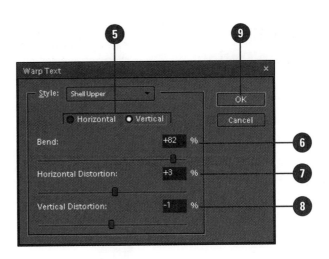

For Your Information

Designing with Warp Text

The Warp Text option is a great way to draw attention to a heading or word within an image file. However, warped text can be extremely hard to read, so use it sparingly. Think of the overall design of the image, and then ask yourself if the warped text supports the mood and message of the image. If it doesn't, then don't use it. Don't fall into the designer's trap of using every new feature you come across. If it doesn't support the message, use something else, like a layer style gradient, or bevel and emboss.

Setting the Anti-Aliasing Type Option

The Anti-aliasing option helps to make text appear smoother by painting the edges of the text with semi-transparent colors. When text is displayed on a raster monitor, the text is built using pixels, and since pixels are essentially bricks, the edges of curved type have a tendency to look ragged. By painting the edges of the text with semi-transparent pixels, the type blends into the background, creating a smoother look. Unless you apply a gradient or mask, text is typically one color; activating anti-aliasing can increase the number of colors (at the edge) to 6 to 10. While this works to make the text smoother, it will also make small text (under 12 points) harder to read. The trick with anti-aliasing is to experiment with the various options to determine which one works the best, and that means occasionally turning anti-aliasing off.

Set the Anti-Aliasing Type Option

1. In the Editor, open an image that contains a text layer.

2. Select a **Type** tool on the toolbox.

3. Select the layer containing the text in the Layers palette.

4. Click the **Anti-aliasing** button to turn anti-aliasing on and off.

   IMPORTANT *The anti-aliasing option is only applied to the type in the active text layer.*

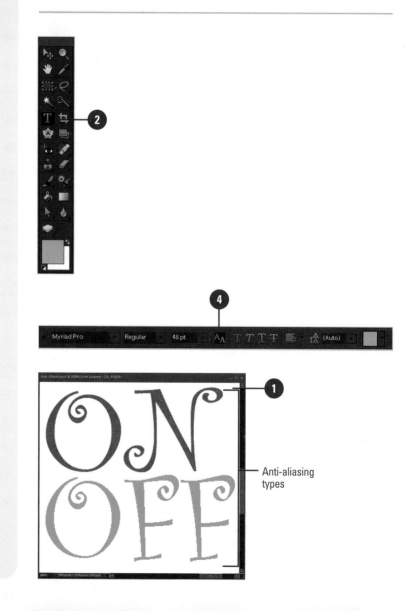

Anti-aliasing types

Creating a Type Mask

Photoshop Elements has two type tools—the Horizontal or Vertical type tools and the Horizontal or Vertical Type Mask tools. The former create regular type, using the fonts available on your computer system, and when you add type to the screen, the color of the font defaults to the current foreground color. The latter are masking tools. When you use one of the type mask tools, Photoshop Elements creates a mask in the size and shape of the selected font with the mask appearing as a red overlay. Once the mask is created, you can modify it just like any normal text layer, by changing the font, size, or even use the Warp feature. Unlike the normal type tools, Photoshop Elements does not create a text layer for the mask; the mask simply appears in the active layer. Being able to create a mask from a font opens up all kinds of creative possibilities. For example, you could use a mask in conjunction with a photograph to create a unique fill or you could use a mask to create a chiseled look to text.

Create a Type Mask

1. In the Editor, open an image.

2. Select the **Horizontal Type Mask** or **Vertical Type Mask** tool on the toolbox.

3. Click in the image window to create a single line of text, or drag a rectangle to create a text box, and then type.

    As you type, Photoshop Elements creates a mask in the size and shape of the current font.

4. Use the type tools on the Options bar to change its font family, style, and size.

5. Click the background color box on the toolbox to select the background color of the mask if it is on the Background layer.

6. Select the **Marquee** tool on the toolbox, or any other of the selection tools.

    The mask converts from a red overlay into a traditional selection.

7. Select the **Move** tool, and then point into the interior of one of the letters, and then drag to move the selection.

More mask text

Isolating Image Pixels Using a Type Mask

One of the advantages to a mask is you can create type using any fill you desire. For example, you're doing an advertising piece for a real estate company in California, and you want something unique for the text, so you get an image of the plains, create a type mask with the words SUNSET and then use the image and mask to create a unique fill.

Isolate Image Pixels

① In the Editor, open an image containing the image you want to mask.

② Select the layer containing the image in the Layers palette.

③ Select the **Horizontal Type Mask** or **Vertical Type Mask** tool on the toolbox.

④ Click in the image window to create a single line of text, or drag a rectangle to create a text box, and then type.

As you type, Photoshop Elements creates a mask in the size and shape of the current font.

IMPORTANT *If you want a lot of the image to show through the mask, use a large, thick mono-weight font, like Impact.*

⑤ Use the type tools on the Options bar to change its font family, style, and size.

Did You Know?

You can move the mask after you've converted it into a selection. Click any selection tool, and then drag from inside the selection. The selection area will move without modifying the actual image. In addition, you can use your arrow keys to gently nudge the selection left, right, up, or down.

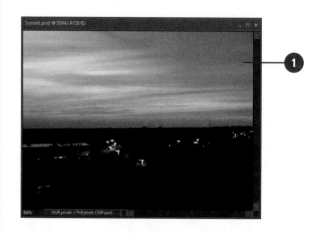

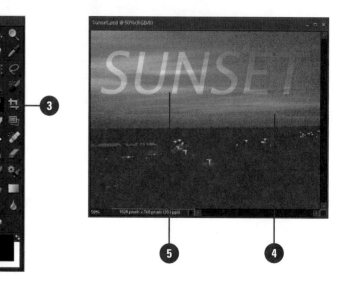

6 Select the **Marquee** tool on the toolbox, and then position the mask directly over the portion of the image you want inside the text.

7 Click the **Select** menu, and then click **Inverse**.

8 Press the Backspace key to delete the inverse selection.

The Invert command reverses the selection and the deletion removes all the pixels outside the mask.

Did You Know?

You can use the adjustment tools to control the selection. Instead of deleting the surrounding image, click the Image menu, point to Adjustments, and then click Levels. Move the middle gray slider left or right to increase or decrease the brightness of the surrounding pixels. That way the text will stand out against the original image background.

Inverted Type Mask

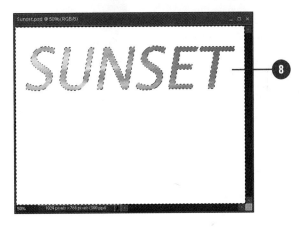

8

Creating Chiseled Type with a Type Mask

This technique is great for creating three-dimensional text on any image. For example, you can use this technique to create the extended text on a plastic credit card, or words chiseled in marble. The technique is simple, but the results are impressive. Using the Bevel and Emboss layer style generates the effect, and the trick is it darkens the upper-left portions of the selection, while lightening the lower-right portions. This creates the illusion of a light source falling across a concave or chiseled surface.

Create Chiseled Type

1. In the Editor, open an image containing the image you want to use for the chisel effect.

2. Select the layer containing the image in the Layers palette.

3. Select the **Horizontal Type Mask** or **Vertical Type Mask** tool on the toolbox.

4. Click in the image window to create a single line of text, or drag a rectangle to create a text box, and then type.

   As you type, Photoshop Elements creates a mask in the size and shape of the current font.

5. Use the editing tools on the mask to change its font, style, and size.

   IMPORTANT *This trick works best with a thick sans serif font, like Arial Black, or Impact.*

6. Select the **Marquee** tool on the toolbox, and then position the mask directly over the portion of the image you want the words to appear.

7. Press Ctrl+J to create a new layer via a copy.

   Photoshop Elements creates a copy of the image pixels inside the type mask, and then places them in a layer directly above the active layer.

Type Mask

8 Click the layer containing the copied image pixels.

9 Select a bevel layer style from the Effects palette, and then click **Apply**.

10 To edit the layer style, click the effects icon (fx) in the Layers palette containing the bevel layer style, make the changes you want, and then click **OK**.

See Also

See Chapter 14, "Working with Layer Styles and Photo Effects," on page 323 for more information on using layer styles.

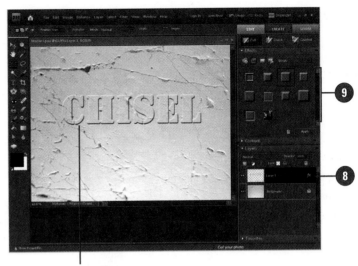

Chisel Type

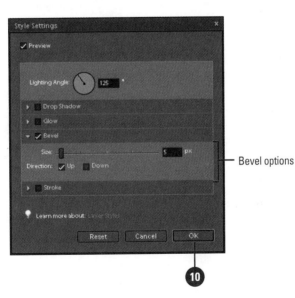

Bevel options

Applying a Gradient Fill to Text

After you create the text you want, you can apply a gradient fill to the text. A gradient fill lets you paint with a rainbow of colors. The gradient tool comes packaged with several sets of pre-designed gradients, or you can create and save your own customized gradient sets. Before you can apply a gradient fill to text, you need to convert the text layer with vector to a traditional bitmap layer, which means you cannot edit the text anymore. Since gradients, by default, overwrite the image, it's a good idea to create gradients in separate layers.

Apply a Gradient Fill to Text

1. In the Editor, open an image that contains a text layer.

2. Select a **Type** tool on the toolbox.

3. Display the **Layers** palette.

4. Select the layer containing the text.

5. Click the **Layer** menu, and then click **Simplify Layer** to convert the vector text to a bitmap.

   You won't be able to edit the text after you simplify it.

6. Ctrl-click the thumbnail for the text layer in the Layers palette.

7. Select the **Gradient** tool on the toolbox.

8. Click the **Gradient Type** list arrow on the Options bar, and then select the gradient you want.

9. To adjust the gradient, click **Edit** on the Options bar, make the changes you want, and then click **OK**.

10. Click to set the starting point of the gradient and drag to define the ending point.

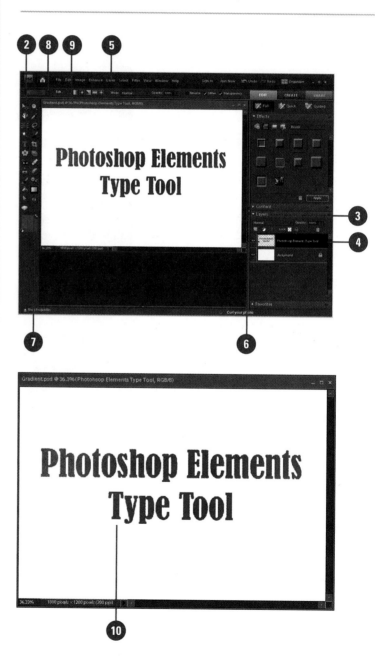

Saving Photos for the Web and Other Devices

17

Introduction

If you need to manipulate a photographic image, there's not a better program on the market than Photoshop Elements that will do the job for you.

Photoshop Elements uses various file formats such as JPEG, GIF, and PNG, to save images for the web. For example, the JPEG format is used primarily for compressing photographic images, while the GIF format is used for compressing clip art and text. Each format is designed to serve a purpose, and knowing when to use a specific format will help you design fast-loading, dynamic web documents.

When preparing images for the web, it's important to understand that file size and format are important considerations. People aren't very patient when it comes time to downloading web pages. Creating good-looking, yet fast-loading images keeps visitors on your web site, waiting for more. Photoshop Elements gives you the ability to perform image compression using formats such as the JPEG (Joint Photographers Expert Group), and GIF (Graphics Interchange File) formats. That will make your images as small as possible, while still retaining great image quality. In image preparation it's all about control, and Photoshop Elements gives you the tools to make the job easy.

What You'll Do

Save for the Web

Work with Save for Web Options

Work with Transparency and Mattes

Work with Dithering

Work with Web File Formats

Optimize a JPEG File

Optimize a GIF File

Optimize a PNG-8 File

Optimize a PNG-24 File

Optimize an Image to File Size

Create an Animated GIF

Preview an Image in a Web Browser

Prepare Clip Art for the Web

Prepare a Photo for the Web

Prepare an Image for the Inkjet or Laser Printer

Understand Monitor, Image, and Device Resolution

Saving for the Web

The Save for Web command is a dream come true for prepping images for the Internet, or even for saving images in a quick-loading format for PowerPoint slide presentations, and you don't even have to leave Photoshop Elements. The Save for Web command lets you open any Photoshop Elements file, and convert it into a web friendly format using the GIF, JPEG, PNG-8, or PNG-24 formats. You can even try different optimization settings or compare different optimizations viewing the original image (on the left) and the preview image (on the right). In addition, the dialog area below each image provides optimization information on the size and download time of the file.

Save for the Web

① In the Editor, open an image.

② Click the **File** menu, and then click **Save for Web**.

③ Click the **Preset** list arrow, and then select a new format from the available options.

④ Click the **Format** list arrow, and then select from the following options:

- ◆ **GIF.** The Graphic Interchange File format is useful for clip art, text, or images that contain a large amount of solid color. GIF uses lossless compression.

- ◆ **JPEG.** The Joint Photographers Expert Group format is useful for images that contain a lot of soft colors, like photographs. JPEG uses lossy compression.

- ◆ **PNG-8.** The Portable Network Graphic 8-bit functions in a manner similar to the GIF format. PNG uses lossless compression.

- ◆ **PNG-24.** The Portable Network Graphic 24-bit functions in a manner similar to the JPEG format. PNG-24 uses lossless compression.

5 Select from the various options that change based on your Format selection.

6 Select from the various options that change the image's width and height, and then click **Apply**.

7 Select from the various options that view and change GIF animations.

8 Click **OK**.

9 Enter a name, and then select a location to save the image file.

10 Click **Save**.

Photoshop Elements saves the modified file, and returns you to the original image.

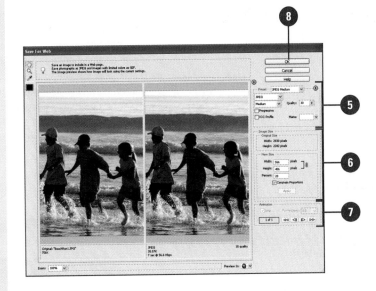

Working with Save for Web Options

When you work with Save for Web, the intention is to prepare the image in one of three web formats: GIF, JPEG, or PNG. Save for Web comes with options, which will help you through the process. For example, if you choose the JPEG format, you can select the amount of compression applied to the image or if you select the GIF format, you can choose how many colors are preserved with the image. The PNG format lets you save images in an 8-bit (256 colors) or a 24-bit (millions of color) format. The options available with Save for Web give you the control you need to produce small image files with quality.

Work with Save for Web Options

1. In the Editor, open an image.

2. Click the **File** menu, and then click **Save for Web**.

3. Select from the various Save for Web tools:

   ◆ **Hand Tool.** Drag the image to change the view of a document.

   ◆ **Zoom Tool.** Click on the image to expand the view size.

   ◆ **Eyedropper Tool.** Drag the image to perform a live sampling of the image.

4. Click the **Thumbnail Options** button (triangle to the upper right of the optimized image), and then select color profile and bandwidth options for the image.

5. Click the **Zoom** list arrow, and then select a view size for the preview images.

6. Click the **Preview In Default Browser** list arrow, and then select the image.

7. Click **OK** to save the current image using the Save Optimized As dialog box.

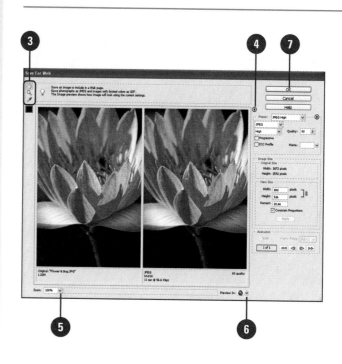

Change Image Size Settings with Save for Web Options

 In the Editor, open an image.

 Click the **File** menu, and then click **Save for Web**.

 Select the options you want to change the image size options.

◆ **Width.** Enter a width in pixels.

◆ **Height.** Enter a height in pixels.

◆ **Percent.** Enter a percentage to scale the image larger or smaller.

◆ **Constrain Proportions.** Select to constrain the width and height to maintain the original proportions. When you change the width, the height changes and vice versa.

 Click **Apply** to make the image size change.

 Click **OK** to save the current image using the Save Optimized As dialog box.

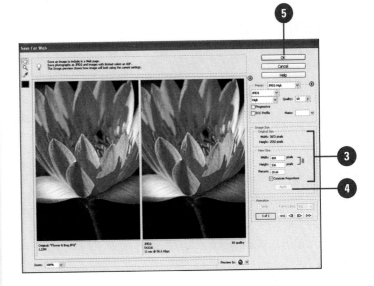

Working with Transparency and Mattes

Transparency in an image allows the background where you place it, such as a web page, to show through. The GIF and PNG formats support transparency, while the JPEG format doesn't. However, you can specify a matte color to simulate the appearance of transparency. Matting works best when the background is a solid color. The Matte option specifies the background color used to fill anti-aliased edges that lie adjacent to transparent areas of the image. The image must have transparency for the Matte options to be available. When the Transparency option is selected, the matte is applied to edge areas to help blend the edges with a web background of the same color. When the Transparency option is not selected, the matte is applied to transparent areas. Choosing the None option for the matte creates hard-edged transparency if Transparency is selected; otherwise, all transparent areas are filled with 100% white. Hard-edged transparency appears jagged and useful when a background is a texture or pattern.

Preserve Transparency

1. In the Editor, open an image that contains transparency.

2. Click the **File** menu, and then click **Save for Web**.

3. Click the **Format** list arrow, and then click **GIF**, **PNG-8**, or **PNG-24**.

4. Select the **Transparency** check box.

5. Click the **Matte** list arrow, and then select a color: **None**, **Eyedropper**, **White**, **Black**, or **Other** (to use the Color Picker).

   ◆ For GIF and PNG-8, select **None** from the Matte menu to create a hard-edged transparency.

6. Click **OK** to save the current image using the Save Optimized As dialog box.

Did You Know?

You can create transparency in a layer. In the Editor, you can create transparency when you create a new layer or use the Background Eraser, Magic Eraser, or Magic Extractor tools.

Create a Matted Image

 In the Editor, open an image that contains transparency.

 Click the **File** menu, and then click **Save for Web**.

 Click the **Format** list arrow, and then click **GIF**, **PNG-8**, **PNG-24**, or **JPEG**.

 For GIF and PNG-8, select from the following options:

♦ **Full and Blend Transparency.** Select the **Transparency** check box to keep fully transparent pixels transparent and blend partially transparent pixels with the matte color. This prevents the halo effect and the jagged edges of hard-edged transparency.

♦ **Fill Transparency.** Deselect the **Transparency** check box to fill transparent pixels with the matte color and blend partially transparent pixels with the matte color.

 Click the **Matte** list arrow, and then select a color: **None**, **Eyedropper**, **White**, **Black**, or **Other** (to use the Color Picker).

When you select None for the JPEG format, white is used as the matte color.

 Click **OK** to save the current image using the Save Optimized As dialog box.

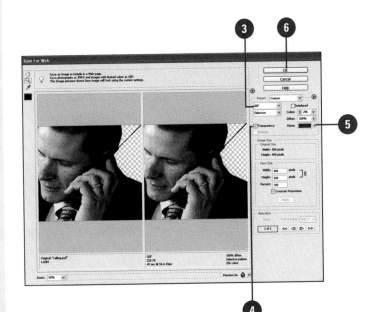

Working with Dithering

If a web user displays a 24-bit image on a computer with an 8-bit color display, the computer uses a technique called dithering to simulate colors it can't display to avoid color banding. Dithering uses adjacent pixels of different colors to give the appearance of a third color. There are two different kinds of dithering depending on where you display an image: Application and Browser. Application dither uses a dithering pattern in GIF and PNG-8 images to simulate colors, while Browser dither shifts selected colors in GIF, PNG, and JPEG images using an 8-bit color display to web-safe colors. In the Save for Web dialog box you can adjust the percentage level you want for dithering.

Adjust Dither in Images

1 In the Editor, open an image.

2 Click the **File** menu, and then click **Save for Web**.

3 Click the **Format** list arrow, and then click **GIF** or **PNG-8**.

4 Click the **Dither** list arrow, and then drag the slider to the percentage you want.

◆ A higher percentage creates the appearance of more colors and more detail, which also increases the size of the image file.

5 Click **OK** to save the current image using the Save Optimized As dialog box.

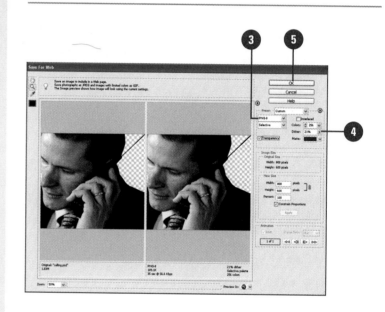

Preview Dither in Photoshop Elements

1 In the Editor, open an image.

2 Click the **File** menu, and then click **Save for Web**.

3 Specify the optimization settings you want.

4 Click the **Thumbnail Options** button (triangle to the upper right of the optimized image), and then click **Browser Dither**.

The optimized image (on the right) appears with the browser dither color display.

5 Click **OK**.

Did You Know?

You can preview dither in a browser set to 8-bit color. In Windows, open the Display Properties dialog box using the Control Panel, set the Color Quality to 8-bit, and then click OK. In the Editor (in Photoshop Elements), open the image file, click the File menu, click Save For Web, click the Preview In list arrow, and then select a browser.

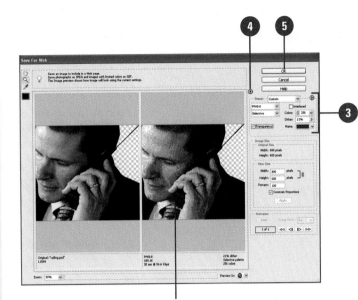

Dither preview

Working with Web File Formats

If you design web documents, you know that the size of your files is very important. Photoshop Elements gives you the option of compressing images in one of three Internet formats: GIF, JPEG, and PNG. The GIF format compresses images that contain solid colors with sharp, definable edges, such as clip art, and text. The JPEG format reduces the size of image files that contain a lot of soft transitional colors, such as photographs. The PNG format is a hybrid format designed to take the place of the GIF and JPEG formats. The PNG format lets you save images in an 8-bit (256 colors) or a 24-bit (millions of color) format. Whatever format you need to create stunning web images, Photoshop Elements helps you get there.

Work with Web File Formats

1. In the Editor, open an image.

2. Click the **File** menu, and then click **Save for Web**.

3. Click the **Format** list arrow, and then select a format from the available options.

4. Select the options you want to change the image's compression, and color options.

5. Click **OK**.

   The Save Optimized As dialog box appears.

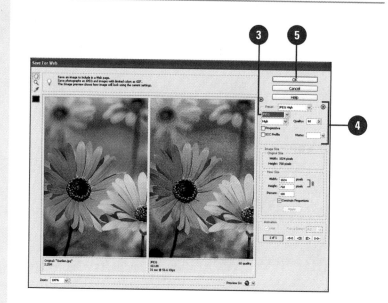

6 Enter a file name in the File name box.

7 Click the **Save as type** list arrow, and then select to save the image in HTML and Images, Images Only, or HTML Only.

8 Click the **Save in** list arrow, and then select the location to save the file.

9 Click **Save**.

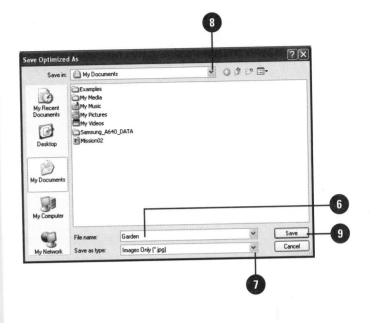

For Your Information

Creating an HTML File for an Image

When you save an optimized file using the Save Optimized As command, you can choose to generate an HTML file for the image. This file contains all the necessary information to display your image in a web browser.

Optimizing a JPEG File

Photoshop Elements comes complete with everything you will need to properly compress any JPEG file. The Internet is typically a slow device, and your visitors typically do not have much patience. When you compress a JPEG image, you're essentially removing information from the image to reduce its file size. The unfortunate results of that reduction is loss of image quality. Internet graphics are not always the best for quality; however, reducing file size is a necessary evil, to keep visitors from clicking off your site, and moving to another. To keep the visitors happy, your JPEG images must load fast, and Photoshop Elements is just the application to help you accomplish that goal.

Optimize a JPEG Document

1. In the Editor, open an image.

2. Click the **File** menu, and then click **Save for Web**.

3. Click the **Format** list arrow, and then click **JPEG**.

4. Select from the following Quality options:

   ◆ **Quality.** Click the list arrow, and then select a preset JPEG quality from Low (poor quality) to Maximum (best quality).

   ◆ **Amount.** Enter a JPEG quality compression value (0 to 100). The lower the value, the more information (color) is sacrificed for image size.

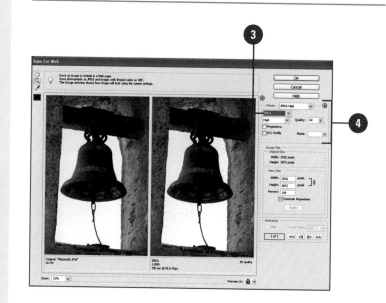

5 Click the **Matte** list arrow, and then select from the available options.

JPEG images do not support transparency. If your image contains transparent areas, use the Matte option to fill them in using a specific color.

6 Select from the following options:

♦ **Progressive.** Select the check box to load a JPEG in three progressive scans. Not supported by all browsers.

♦ **ICC Profile.** Select the check box to embed an ICC color profile into the JPEG image. This increases file size but helps maintain color consistency between monitors, and operating systems.

7 Click **OK** to save the current image using the Save Optimized As dialog box.

Optimizing a GIF File

The GIF file format is used primarily for images that contain solid colors with sharp edges, such as clip art, text, line art, and logos. Since the Internet is a slow device, using the GIF format on images significantly reduces their file size, and will create fast-loading graphics. The GIF format utilizes an 8-bit pixel, and creates a document with a maximum of 256 colors (the less colors the smaller the file size). The GIF format has been around long enough for it to be considered an Internet "native" format. A native format is one that does not require a specific plug-in for the browser to display the file.

Optimize a GIF Document

1. In the Editor, open an image.

2. Click the **File** menu, and then click **Save for Web**.

3. Click the **Format** list arrow, and then click **GIF**.

4. Click the **Reduction** list arrow to select a visual reduction method for the image colors.

   ◆ **Perceptual.** Creates a custom color table using color for which the human eye has greater sensitivity.

   ◆ **Selective.** Creates a color table close to perceptual that provides greater range of colors and preserves web color.

   ◆ **Adaptive.** Creates a color table using color samplings from the common spectrum.

   ◆ **Restrictive (Web).** Uses the web-safe color table (216-color) common for Windows and Mac OS.

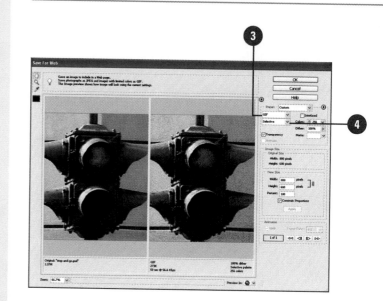

5 Select from the following options:

Color Option:

◆ **Colors.** Enter or select a value from 2 to 256 maximum colors.

Transparency Options:

◆ **Transparency.** Select to make the transparent areas of a GIF image transparent.

◆ **Matte.** Click to fill the transparent areas of a GIF image.

◆ **Dither.** Click to select a dithering scheme, and enter an amount for the mixing of the matte color.

Other Options:

◆ **Interlaced.** Select to have the GIF image load in three scans.

◆ **Animate.** Select to create a GIF animation.

6 Click **Save** to save the current image using the Save Optimized As dialog box.

See Also

See "Creating an Animated GIF" on page 398 for information on creating an animated GIF.

Optimizing a PNG-8 File

The PNG-8 file format is used primarily for images that contain solid colors with sharp edges—clip art, text, line art, and logos—and was designed as an alternative to the GIF file format. Since the PNG-8 format generates an image with a maximum of 256 colors, it significantly reduces an images file size. While similar to the GIF file format, the PNG-8 format is not completely supported by older browsers. However, it is considered a native format to the creation of Flash animation movies.

Optimize a PNG-8 Document

1. In the Editor, open an image.

2. Click the **File** menu, and then click **Save for Web**.

3. Click the **Format** list arrow, and then click **PNG-8**.

4. Click the **Reduction** list arrow to select a visual reduction method for the image colors.

   ◆ **Perceptual.** Creates a custom color table using color for which the human eye has greater sensitivity.

   ◆ **Selective.** Creates a color table close to perceptual that provides greater range of colors and preserves web color.

   ◆ **Adaptive.** Creates a color table using color samplings from the common spectrum.

   ◆ **Restrictive (Web).** Uses the web-safe color table (216-color) common for Windows and Mac OS.

5 Select from the following options:

Color Option:

◆ **Colors.** Enter or select a value from 2 to 256 maximum colors.

Transparency Options:

◆ **Transparency.** Select to make the transparent areas of a PNG-8 image transparent.

◆ **Matte.** Click to fill the transparent areas of a PNG-8 image.

◆ **Dither.** Click to select a dithering scheme, and then enter an amount for the mixing of the matte color.

Other Options:

◆ **Interlaced.** Select to have the PNG image load in three scans.

6 Click **Save** to save the current image using the Save Optimized As dialog box.

Optimizing a PNG-24 File

The PNG-24 file format is used primarily for images that contain lots of colors with soft transitional edges, such as photographs, and was designed as an alternative to the JPEG file format. The PNG-24 format generates an image with millions of colors, and still manages to reduce the size of a file. While similar to the JPEG file format, the PNG-24 uses lossless compression, and does not compress files as small as the JPEG format. So for the time being, most designers are still using the JPEG format for creating fast-loading web graphics.

Optimize a PNG-24 Document

1. In the Editor, open an image.

2. Click the **File** menu, and then click **Save for Web**.

3. Click the **Format** list arrow, and then click **PNG-24**.

4. Select from the following options:

   Transparency Options:

   ◆ **Transparency.** Check to make the transparent areas of a PNG-24 image transparent.

   ◆ **Matte.** Click to fill the transparent areas of a PNG-24 image.

   Other Options:

   ◆ **Interlaced.** Check to have the PNG-24 image load in three scans.

5. Click **Save** to save the current image using the Save Optimized As dialog box.

Optimizing an Image to File Size

The Save for Web dialog box has many options to help you create the exact image you need—including helping you compress an image down to a specific file size. For example, you've just created an image you want to display on the web, but the maximum file size you can use is 35k. You could open the image, and experiment with Save for Web's compression options, or you could use the Optimize To File Size option.

Optimize an Image to File Size

1. In the Editor, open an image.

2. Click the **File** menu, and then click **Save for Web**.

3. Click the **Format Options** button, and then click **Optimize to File Size**.

4. Enter a file size in the Desired File Size data box.

5. Click the **Current Settings** option or the **Auto Select GIF/JPEG** option to let Photoshop Elements choose between the JPEG or GIF format.

6. Click **OK**.

Photoshop Elements compresses the image.

7. Click **OK** to save the compressed image using the Save Optimized As dialog box.

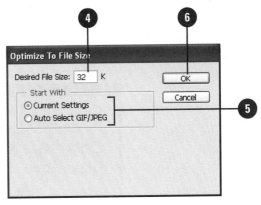

Creating an Animated GIF

An **animation** is a sequence of images, or frames, that vary slightly to create the illusion of movement over time. One of the most Internet compatible ways is the animated GIF. The original designation, GIF89a, gives you an idea of how long this format has been around. The GIF file format (Graphics Interchange Format) is used primarily for clip art, text, and line art, or for images that contain areas of solid color. Once the image is created, you can open and use it in any application that supports the GIF file format. To create an animated GIF, you work with layers, where each layer becomes a frame in the animated GIF. You can create an animated GIF from scratch or open an existing image document with layers. Photoshop Elements creates a RGB color image document in the Editor.

Create an Animated GIF from Scratch

1. In the Editor, click the **File** menu, point to **New**, and then click **Blank File**.

2. Enter a name in the Name box.

3. Click the **Preset** list arrow, and then select from the available presets, or enter in a customized Width and Height, and Resolution.

4. Click the **Color Mode** list arrow, and then select a color mode for the image.

5. Click the **Background Contents**, and then click **White, Background Color**, or **Transparent** (animated GIF files look best using transparency).

6. Click **OK**.

7. Create the first image for the animated GIF.

8. Press Ctrl+J to create a copy of your first animation in a separate layer.

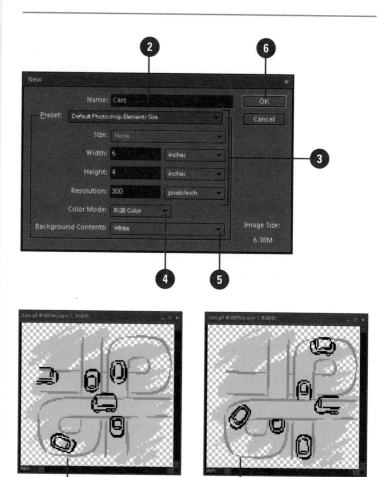

7. First image

Copied layers for the animation

9 Modify the second image (animations are essentially the same image, modified slightly between each animation frame or, in this case each layer).

10 Repeat steps 8 and 9 until you have enough cells for the animation.

11 Click the **File** menu, and then click **Save As** to save the file for editing purposes in the future.

12 Click the **File** menu, and then click **Save for Web**.

13 Click the **Format** list arrow, and then click **GIF**.

14 Select the **Animate** check box.

15 Select from the following options:

◆ **Loop.** Select to repeat the animation when it reaches the end.

◆ **Frame Delay.** Enter the number of seconds that each frame is displayed in a web browser. Use a decimal value to specify fractions of a second.

◆ **Display Frames.** Click the First Frame, Previous Frame, Next Frame, or Last Frame buttons to display the frames you want.

16 Click **OK** to save the current image using the Save Optimized As dialog box.

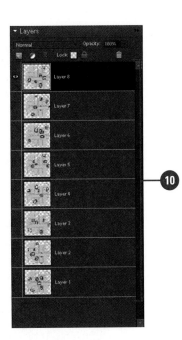

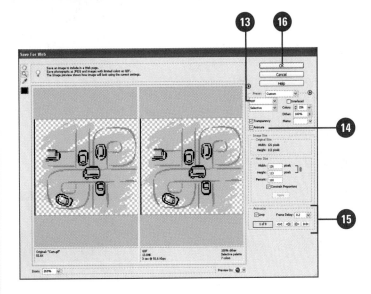

Did You Know?

You can open an animated GIF. In the Editor, click the File menu, click Open, select the animated GIF file, and then click Open. Each frame in the animation appears as a layer in Photoshop Elements.

Previewing an Image in a Web Browser

You can preview an image or animated GIF optimized for the web in any web browser you have installed on your computer. The browser preview displays the image or animated GIF with a caption listing the image's file type, pixel dimensions, file size, compression information, and other HTML information. If you want to preview the image or animated GIF on a different monitor, you can change the display to simulate another color display in the Save for Web dialog box. The preview options don't change color in the original or optimized image.

Preview an Image or Animated GIF in a Web Browser

1. In the Editor, open an image or animated GIF.

2. Click the **File** menu, and then click **Save for Web**.

3. Specify the optimization settings you want.

4. Click the **Preview In** list arrow, and then select a browser name.

   Your web browser opens, displaying the image or animated GIF along with information about the image or animated GIF.

   TIMESAVER *Click the browser icon to launch your default web browser.*

5. For an animated GIF, use your browser's Stop, Refresh, or Reload commands to stop or replay the animation, and then click the **Close** button.

6. Click **OK**.

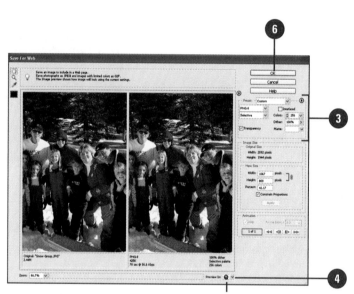

Click to open default browser

Reload and Stop buttons

Did You Know?

You can add a browser to the Preview In menu. In the Editor, click the File menu, click Save For Web, click the Preview In list arrow, click Edit List, click Add, select a browser, click Open, select the browser, and then click OK.

Preview on Different Color Monitors

1 In the Editor, open an image or animated GIF.

2 Click the **File** menu, and then click **Save for Web**.

3 Specify the optimization settings you want.

4 Click the **Thumbnail Options** button (triangle to the upper right of the optimized image).

5 Select from the following color monitor displays:

◆ **Uncompensated Color.** Displays with no color adjustment (default).

◆ **Standard Windows Color.** Displays with color to simulate a standard Windows monitor.

◆ **Standard Macintosh Color.** Displays with color to simulate a standard Macintosh monitor.

◆ **Use Document Color Profile.** Displays with color from the image color profile, if available.

The optimized image (on the right) appears with the color display.

6 Click **OK**.

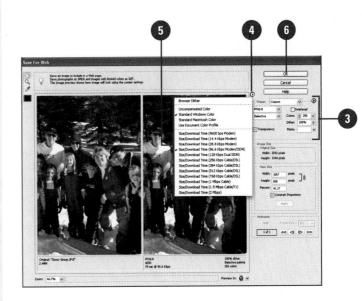

Did You Know?

You can view estimated download time. In the Editor, click the File menu, click Save For Web, click the triangle in the upper right of the optimized image, and then select an Internet access speed. The estimated download time appears under the preview of the optimized image.

Preparing Clip Art for the Web

Clip art is defined as non-photographic image information, with a lot of solid-color areas. For this process the GIF or PNG-8 formats would serve best. The GIF (Graphics Interchange File) and PNG (Portable Network Graphics) formats use an RLE (Run Length Encoding) scheme. When the file is saved, areas of solid color are compressed into small units and then restored to the file when it is opened. The GIF format supports a maximum of 256 colors. While that may not seem like much, most GIF images, such as clip art and text, contain far less color information. By reducing the number of colors available for the GIF color table, you can significantly reduce the image's file size. For example, a GIF image of black text might only require a maximum of 2 colors (black and white). Experiment with the GIF Colors option to produce small, fast-loading image files. Since the GIF format has been around for a long time, using it almost guarantees the image will open on a visitor's browser. The PNG format is newer, and has some new encoding schemes that make even smaller files, but it is not supported by all web browsers.

Prepare Clip Art for the Web

1. In the Editor, open a clip art document.

2. Click the **File** menu, and then click **Save As**.

3. Enter a name for the file in the File name box.

4. Click the **Save in** list arrow, and then select a location to save the file.

5. Click the **Format** list arrow, and then click **CompuServe GIF**.

6. Click **Save**.

   ◆ If the Save In Version Set dialog box appears, click **OK** to continue.

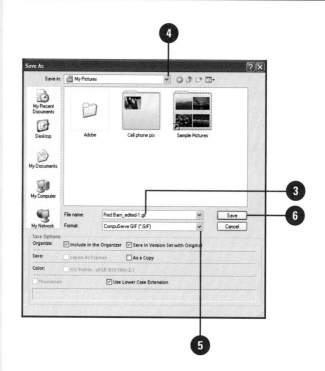

7 Select from the following Indexed Color options:

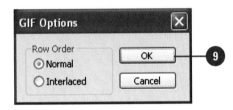

- ◆ **Palette.** Click the list arrow, and then select from the available color palette options, including Web (Safe), Mac, and Win System palettes.

- ◆ **Colors.** If you selected a local color, or custom palette, click to select the number of colors saved with the image. The maximum number of colors is 256.

- ◆ **Forced.** Click the list arrow, and then select what colors will be forced to remain in the image.

- ◆ **Transparency.** Select the check box to preserve any transparent areas.

- ◆ **Matte.** If the image contains transparent areas, clicking this list arrow lets you select a color to fill the areas. For example, you could fill all transparent areas of the image with black to match the black of a web document.

- ◆ **Dither.** Click the list arrow, and then select how you want the remaining image colors to mix.

- ◆ **Amount.** Enter an Amount percentage to instruct the GIF format how aggressively to dither the image colors.

- ◆ **Preserve Exact Colors.** Select the check box to force the preservation of the original image colors (based on how many colors were chosen using the Palette option).

8 Click **OK**.

9 If prompted, click the **Normal** or **Interlaced** option, and then click **OK**.

Preparing a Photo for the Web

Reducing the size of a photograph presents its own particular set of problems, and Photoshop Elements comes to the rescue with the solution. For photographic images, the best format to use is the JPEG (Joint Photographic Experts Group) format. This format reduces file size by removing image information (lossy compression). For example, a 1MB uncompressed TIFF file, can be reduced to 20 or 30K using JPEG compression. That reduces the download time of the image on a 33K modem from 15 minutes, to 10 seconds. While that is quite a reduction, it also means most of the image colors have been removed and the remaining color are used in a dithering scheme to fool the eyes into seeing colors that are no longer in the image. Highly compressed JPEG images look good on a monitor, but fair poorly when sent to a printer.

Prepare a Photograph for the Web

1. In the Editor, open a photo document.

2. Click the **File** menu, and then click **Save As**.

3. Enter a name for the file in the File name box.

4. Click the **Save in** list arrow, and then select a location to save the file.

5. Click the **Format** list arrow, and then click **JPEG**.

6. Click **Save**.

   ◆ If the Save In Version Set dialog box appears, click **OK** to continue.

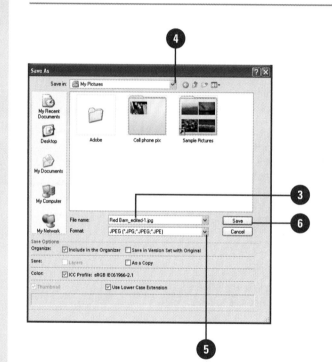

7 Select from the following JPEG Options:

◆ **Matte.** The JPEG format does not support transparency. Click the Matte list arrow, and then select what color to fill transparent areas within the active document.

◆ **Quality.** The Quality option determines the amount of image information loss. Enter a value from 1 to 12; the higher the value the more information is retained, thus creating a larger file.

◆ **Baseline (Standard).** The format is recognized by most browsers.

◆ **Baseline Optimized.** Produces optimized color, and a slightly smaller file size, but is not supported by older browsers.

◆ **Progressive.** Displays a series of increasingly detailed scans as the image downloads. The visual impression is of a blurred image, slowly coming into focus (not supported by older browsers).

◆ **Scans.** If Progressive is selected, select the number of scan passes for the image.

◆ **Size.** Allows you to view the download time of the image, based on standard Internet bandwidths.

8 Click **OK**.

For Your Information

Using the JPEG 2000 Format

The JPEG 2000 is a file format that provides more options and greater flexibility than the standard JPEG format. It produces images with better compression and quality for both web and print publishing.

Preparing an Image for the Inkjet or Laser Printer

While not everyone has access to a 4-color press, even casual computer users have or have access to an inkjet or laser printer. Inkjet and laser printers apply ink to the paper using dots of color. In fact, one of the measurements of quality for this type of output is its printing resolution. For example, a photo-quality inkjet or laser printer can run with a resolution of 1,400dpi and higher, or one thousand four hundred dots of color information per linear inch. There are several file format options for output to print, however none is so versatile as the TIFF format. The Tagged Image File Format, uses lossy or lossless compression, and lets you save multiple layers, as well as alpha channel information. In addition, there is hardly a layout application in the marketplace, Macintosh or Windows, that will not open a TIFF saved image.

Prepare an Image for the Inkjet or Laser Printer

① In the Editor, open an image document.

② Click the **File** menu, and then click **Save As**.

③ Enter a name for the file in the File name box.

④ Click the **Save in** list arrow, and then select a location to save the file.

⑤ Click the **Format** list arrow, and then click **TIFF**.

⑥ Click **Save**.

◆ If the Save In Version Set dialog box appears, click **OK** to continue.

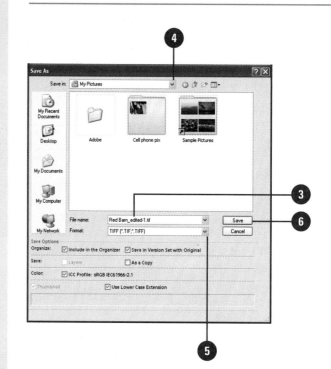

7 Select from the following TIFF Options:

- **None.** No compression is performed to the image.

- **LZW.** Performs lossless compression to the image. When used, the receiving application must have the corresponding LZW option or they will not be able to uncompress the file.

- **Zip.** Performs a standard Zip (lossless) compression to the image. Receiving application must have an unzip utility.

- **JPEG.** Performs lossy (image loss) compression to the image.

- **IBM PC.** Select PC if the image is to be used on a Windows system.

- **Macintosh.** Select Macintosh if the image is to be used on a Macintosh system.

- **Save Image Pyramid.** Check to save the image using several image resolutions, and lets you decide, when reopening the image, what resolution to use.

- **Save Transparency.** Check to preserves any transparent areas in the active image.

- **RLE.** Run Length Encoding (RLE) helps to compress solid areas of color across multiple layers.

- **ZIP.** Uses the Zip format to compress multiple layers.

- **Discard Layers And Save A Copy.** Creates a copy of the file without the layers, essentially saves a composite image file.

8 Click **OK**.

For Your Information

Getting the Best Results on an Inkjet or Laser Printer

Since your monitor displays an image using light and a desktop printer reproduces an image using inks, dyes, or pigments, it is impossible for a desktop printer to reproduce all the colors that can be displayed on a monitor. However, by incorporating certain procedures (such as color management) into your workflow, you can achieve predictable results when printing your images to a desktop printer. For more information on getting the best color results, see Chapter 19, "Printing and Sharing Photos."

Understanding Monitor, Image, and Device Resolution

Remember that raster images are all about resolution. Images have a specific scanned resolution (spi, samples per inch), your monitor has a resolution (ppi, pixels per inch), and output devices such as inkjet printers (dpi, dots per inch), and high-end presses (lpi, lines per inch). While all these terms may seem a bit complicated, they're not; they simply explain how much resolution, or information is contained within the image.

Most computer monitors are set to a fixed resolution of 72 or 96 ppi. Say you scan an image a 4 by 4 inch image at 288spi (that's 4 times the resolution of a 72ppi monitor). If you attempted to display the image at 100 percent view, the monitor would take the image pixels and adjust the width and height to match its resolution, so the image would be 16 by 16 inches (288 divided by 72 = 4). With monitors 16 inches is not an exact number, but it's close enough for this example. If you attempt to reduce the zoom size of the image to make it fit the monitor size, Photoshop Elements will have to remove pixels from the image to make it fit. This typically causes the image to generate jagged lines; especially around angles lines. The moral of this story is when adjusting an image for viewing on a monitor, for example a slide presentation, never change the zoom of the image to fit the monitor, always adjust the resolution by selecting the Image menu, pointing to Resize, and then clicking Image Size.

When it comes to output, such as to an inkjet print, the rules are a bit more forgiving. Many output devices have print resolutions of 1,440 or higher. However, we're not talking about fixed monitor pixels (ppi), we're talking about dot of ink hitting a piece of paper (dpi). Most inkjet printer, because of the dot gain of the inks (that's the amount of space a dot of ink spreads when it hits the paper), does not need image resolution greater than 300spi. Unlike a monitor, if you use higher resolutions than needed, the image typically will not suffer, quality wise, you'll just be printing an image with a larger file size. However, that can be a time-wasting problem. For example, a 300spi 8 by 10 image will have a file size of about 20MB, the same image scanned at 1200spi will produce a 329MB file size. When you print the two images, you will probably not notice any quality difference; however, it will take, on average, 6 minutes longer to print the 1200spi document on most mid-range printers.

The bottom line is that resolution represents the amount of information contained within a linear inch; however, various devices handle that same resolution number differently. The good news is that understanding those differences helps you to create a useable workflow. Knowledge is power.

Making Specialty Projects

18

Introduction

After you finish working with your photos, you can use them to make specialty projects in Photoshop Elements. You can create print-oriented **photo projects**, such as photo books, photo calendars, photo collages, scrapbooks, CD/DVD labels and jackets, and greeting cards, or **digital projects**, such as flipbooks, slide shows and online albums.

In Photoshop Elements, you can create a photo or digital project starting from the Organizer or Editor using the Create tab. For photo projects, you use the Projects panel in the Palette Bin (in the Editor) to specify a size, layout, and theme for the project type. However, in some cases, such as a photo book, Photoshop Elements uses an outside service through Adobe Photoshop Services. For digital projects, you specify settings in a dialog box or use a wizard to guide you through a series of prompts to select a page design, layout, and other options for the project type.

All photo and digital projects are stored in the Photo Browser as projects, so you can quickly find and open them as needed. However, Photoshop Elements saves them in different formats depending on the number of pages in the file. When a project has only a single page, Photoshop Elements saves it in the Photoshop format (PSD). When a project has multiple pages (up to 30 at a time), it saves the project in the Photo Projects format (PSE).

Have you ever taken a series of pictures trying to get the perfect shot, but can never quite get it? One person either has their eyes closed or doesn't look right. You can use Photomerge Group Shot to combine a person in one photo with another photo to create the perfect photo. If your camera doesn't take panoramas, you can use Photomerge Panorama to create one. And you can use Photomerge Scene Cleaner (**New!**) to remove intrusive objects from your photos if you have more than one photo of the same scene.

What You'll Do

Find, Open, and Save Projects

Make a Photo Book, Photo Calendar, or Photo Collage

Create Labels, Jackets, and Greeting Cards

Create an Online Album

Create a Flipbook

Create a Slide Show

Set Slide Show Preferences

Work with Content in a Slide Show

Edit a Slide Show

Add Effects and Extras to a Slide Show

Publish a Slide Show

Create a VCD with a Menu of Slide Shows

Use Photomerge Faces, Group Shot, Panorama, or Scene Cleaner

Keep Proper Perspective with Vanishing Point

Resize and Rotate Project Photos

Edit Photo Projects in Photoshop CS4

409

Finding and Opening Projects

After you have completed and saved a project, you can open it to make changes. By default, projects appear in the Photo Browser along with all your photos and other media files with the exception of projects ordered through Adobe Photoshop Services. If you have trouble finding a project, you can use the Projects command on the By Media Type submenu on the Find menu to locate all the projects in the catalog.

Find and Open Projects

1. In the Organizer (in Photo Browser view), click the **Find** menu, point to **By Media Type**, and then click **Projects**.

   ◆ To show only projects, uncheck all the other items on the By Media Type submenu.

2. Double-click the project you want to open.

Did You Know?

You can add and remove pages in a photo project. Open the photo project. To add a page, select the page before where you want to insert a new one in the Project Bin, click the Edit menu, and then click Add Blank Page, or Add Page Using Current Layout. To remove a page, select the page, click the Edit menu, and then click Delete Current Page.

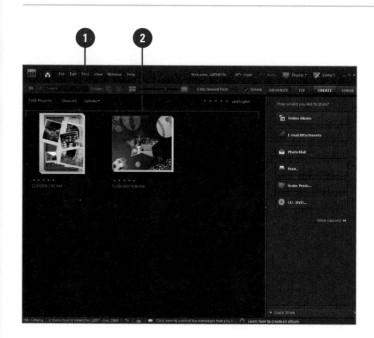

Saving a Project

Photoshop Elements saves photo and digital projects in different formats depending on the number of pages in the file. When a project has only a single page, Photoshop Elements saves it in the Photoshop format (PSD). When a project has multiple pages (up to 30 at a time), it saves the project in the Photo Projects format (PSE).

Save a Project

1. Click the **File** menu, and then click **Save**.

2. Enter a name for the file in the File Name box.

3. Click the **Format** list arrow, and then click **Photo Project Format (*PSE)** for multiple page projects or **Photoshop (*PSD, *PDD)** for single page projects.

    Photoshop Elements sets the appropriate format for the selected project.

4. Click the **Save in** list arrow, and then choose where to store the image.

5. Select from the available Save options (settings vary depending on the project):

    ◆ **Include in the Organizer.** Includes the project in the Organizer.

    ◆ **Layers.** Maintains all layers in the image.

    ◆ **As A Copy.** Saves a copy of the file while keeping the current file open on your screen.

    ◆ **ICC Profile.** Embeds proof profile information in an untagged document. If the document is tagged, the profile is embedded by default.

    ◆ **Use Lower Case Extension.** Makes the file extension lowercase.

6. Click **Save**.

Making a Photo Book

A photo book makes it easy to create a professional designed book of photos that you can print on your home printer or order a bound version from Adobe Photoshop Services. You can select from a variety of creative designs available on the Content palette in the Editor.

Make a Photo Book

1. Select (in the Organizer) or open (in the Editor) the photos you want to use in your project.

2. Click the **Create** tab.

3. Click **Photo Book** on the Create tab.

   The Projects panel in the Palette Bin in the Editor appears.

4. Drag the photo you want in the Project Bin for the title place photo to the first position on the left.

5. Click **Next**.

6. Click the **Random Photo Layout** or **Choose Photo Layout** option.

7. Select a photo layout or theme.

8. Select the additional options you want, if available:

   - **Auto-Fill with Project Bin Photos.** Automatically uses photos in the Project Bin.

   - **Include Captions.** Adds captions on or below the image.

   - **Number of Pages.** Specifies the number of pages for the project.

9. Click **Create**.

10. Click the **File** menu, click **Save As**, type a name, specify a location, and then click **Save**.

    Continue on the next page to modify the photo book.

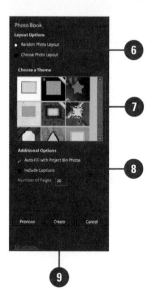

Modify a Photo Book

1. Double-click (in Organizer) or open (in Editor) the project you want to edit.

2. Click the page you want to modify in the Project Bin.

3. Use the Photo Book Editing toolbar to navigate between pages and add or remove pages.

4. To move a page, drag the photo page you want in the Project Bin to a new location.

5. Click a photo placeholder or drag a photo to a placeholder in the photo book.

6. Click the **Artwork** tab under the Create tab.

7. Display the Content palette, and then use the first pop-up menu to select a content type, such as By Activity, By Style, and Show All.

   ◆ **Pop-up.** Use the second pop-up to select different content designs, if available.

   ◆ **Filter buttons.** Use the filter buttons to select different content designs, if available.

8. Drag a design or item onto a photo book page. You can also select a design or item, and then click **Apply**.

9. Click the **File** menu, and then click **Save**.

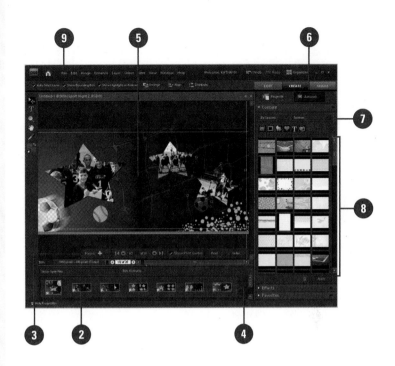

Making a Photo Calendar

In Photoshop Elements, you can use your photos to create a photo calendar. Photo Calendars are designed to be ordered online using Adobe Photoshop Services provided by Kodak EasyShare Gallery. The Photo Calendar wizard steps you through the process to select a professional layout and creative design and then order the calendar.

Make a Photo Calendar

① In the Organizer (in Photo Browser view) or Editor, click the **Create** tab. If you want, you can select 1 to 12 photos to get started.

② Click **Photo Calendar** on the Create tab.

The Photo Calendar wizard dialog box appears, displaying options provided by Kodak EasyShare Gallery.

③ Click **Select More Photos**, and then do the following:

◆ Select options to display the photos you want to add.

◆ Select the check boxes next to the photos.

◆ Click **Add Selected Photos.**

◆ Click **Done**.

④ Click **Next** to continue.

⑤ Specify login information or click the **Join Now** link, and then click **Next** to continue.

Your photos are uploaded to the web for use in the Kodak Gallery.

⑥ Click **Next**.

The Kodak Gallery web site appears in your browser.

⑦ Follow the online instructions to select a page design, layout, and other options to create your photo calendar.

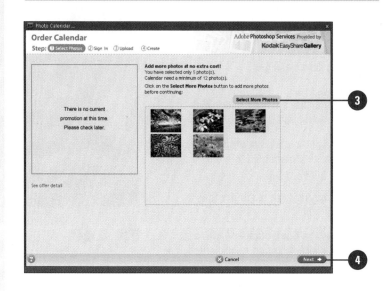

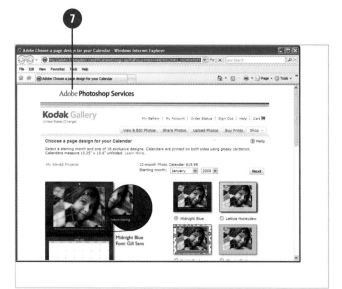

Making a Photo Collage

Photo collages are large photo print projects, such as a scrapbook. You can select from a variety of themes and layouts on the Content palette in the Editor. After you finish your photo collage, you can print it from your home printer, order a professionally printed version online, or send it by e-mail.

Make a Photo Collage

1. Select (in the Organizer) or open (in the Editor) the photos you want to use in your project.

2. Click the **Create** tab.

3. Click **Photo Collage** on the Create tab.

4. Click the **Page Size** list arrow, and then select a page size.

5. Select a photo theme (optional) and a layout.

6. Select the additional options you want, if available:

   ◆ **Auto-Fill with Project Bin Photos.** Automatically uses photos in the Project Bin.

   ◆ **Include Captions.** Adds captions on or below the image.

   ◆ **Number of Pages.** Specifies the number of pages for the project.

7. Click **Done**.

8. Click the **File** menu, click **Save As**, type a name, specify a location, and then click **Save**.

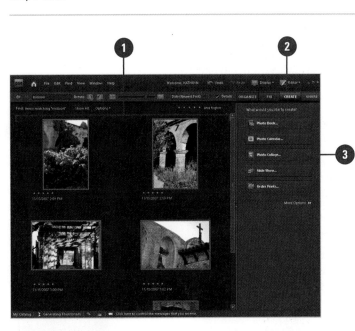

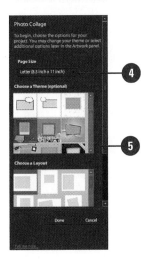

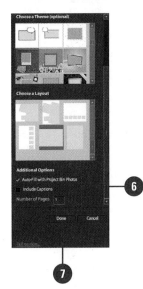

Creating Labels and Jackets

With Photoshop Elements, you can create disc labels for CDs and DVDs and cover jackets for CD and DVD cases. You don't need to be a designer, Photoshop Elements provides professionally designed themes and layouts from which you can choose. When you're done, you can save your results and then print the adhesive disc labels or cover jackets on your home printer.

Create Labels and Jackets

1. Select (in the Organizer) or open (in the Editor) the photos you want to use in your project.

2. Click the **Create** tab.

3. Click the **More Options** button on the Create tab, and then click **CD/DVD Label**, **CD Jacket**, or **DVD Jacket**.

4. Select a photo theme and a layout.

5. Select the **Auto-Fill with Project Bin Photos** check box to automatically use photos in the Project Bin.

6. Click **Done**.

7. Click the **File** menu, click **Save As**, type a name, specify a location, and then click **Save**.

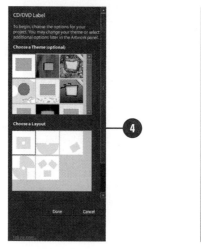

Creating Greeting Cards

Greeting cards are great way to let people know how you feel. Instead of buying them at the store, you can create your own with Photoshop Elements. You don't need to be a designer, Photoshop Elements provides professionally designed themes and layouts from which you can choose. Within the designs, you can add up to 22 photos on a page; however, it's not recommended. When you're done, you can save your results and then print your greeting card on your home printer. If you prefer, you can order a greeting card online from Adobe Photoshop Services.

Create Greeting Cards

1. Select (in the Organizer) or open (in the Editor) the photos you want to use in your project.

2. Click the **Create** tab.

3. Click the **More Options** button on the Create tab, and then click **Greeting Card**.

4. Click the **Page Size** list arrow, and then select a page size.

5. Select a photo theme (optional) and a layout.

6. Select the additional options you want, if available:

   ◆ **Auto-Fill with Project Bin Photos.** Automatically uses photos in the Project Bin.

   ◆ **Include Captions.** Adds captions on or below the image.

7. Click **Done**.

8. Click the **File** menu, click **Save As**, type a name, specify a location, and then click **Save**.

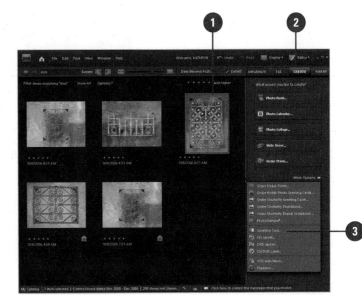

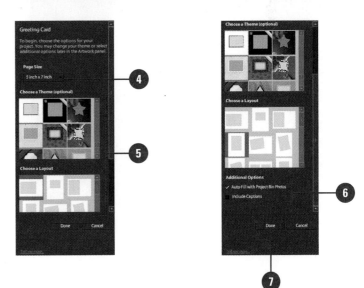

Creating an Online Album

An online album is a way to present your photos on a web page where other can access them. You can choose from a variety of layouts and designs (**New!**) including interactive, animated, transitions, or slide show, so it doesn't take a lot of work. The layout categories include Classic, Family, Fun, Occasions, Seasons, and Travel. The Online Album wizard walks you through the entire process step by step. You can publish the online album on the Photoshop Showcase (**New!**) on the Photoshop.com web site, or export it to CD/DVD or FTP site.

Create an Online Album

1. Select (in the Organizer) or open (in the Editor) the photos you want to use in your project.

2. Click the **Share** tab.

3. Click the **Online Album** button on the Share tab.

4. Give your album a filename. (This text won't appear on the album's pages.)

5. Add or remove photos in the Items area, then drag the photo thumbnails in the order you want them to appear in the online album.

6. Click **Share**.

7. Choose how you will share your album.

   ◆ **Photoshop Showcase.** Publishes the online album on the Photoshop.com web site (**New!**).

   ◆ **Export to CD/DVD.** Burns the online album files onto a CD or DVD disc for full-screen playback.

   ◆ **Export to FTP.** Uploads the online album files to a web server.

8. Click **Change Template**.

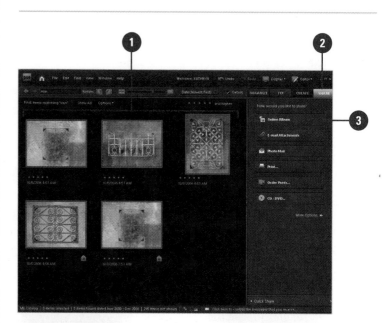

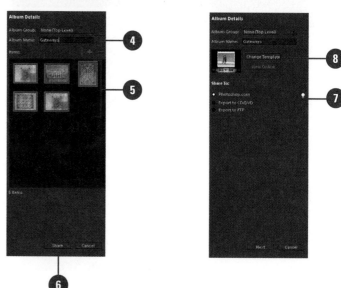

9 Click the **Select a Category** list arrow, and then select a category:

- ◆ **Classic**
- ◆ **Family**
- ◆ **Fun**
- ◆ **Occasions**
- ◆ **Seasons**
- ◆ **Travel**
- ◆ **Show All**

10 Select a template.

11 Click **Apply**. If you like what you see, click **Next**.

12 Enter a title and subtitle to appear on the album's pages.

13 Click **Next**.

14 Click **Next** again.

15 Enter the necessary details for the sharing method you selected in Step 7:

- ◆ **Photoshop Showcase.** Sign-in, choose whether you will make the album public or share it only with friends; if the latter, then enter your friends' email addresses. Click **Next** to continue through the wizard, view the gallery (if you want), and then click **Done**.

- ◆ **Export to CD/DVD.** Choose a destination drive and give the disc a name, then click **Export**.

- ◆ **Export to FTP.** Enter the server address, username, password, and folder name, then click **Export**.

Online album

Creating a Flipbook

If you have taken photos using the burst mode on your camera, you can use Photoshop Elements to animate the photos in a flipbook. A flipbook is a stop-motion video of your photos. It's a series of still images that looks like a video when you flip through them. When you create a flipbook, the project is saved in the WMV format, which you can view on your computer, a TV using Windows Media Center Edition, the web, or in e-mail. You can even export a flipbook to your mobile phone.

Create a Flipbook

1. Select (in the Organizer) or open (in the Editor) the photos you want to use in your project.

2. Click the **Create** tab.

3. Click the **More Options** button on the Create tab, and then click **Flipbook**.

4. Select the additional options you want, if available:

   ◆ **Speed.** Specifies the frames per second (FPS) for the flipbook.

   ◆ **Reverse Order.** Select to start showing photos from the end.

   ◆ **Output Settings.** Specifies the output type and screen size. Select a movie size and then click **Details** to find out information about your choice.

   ◆ **Loop Preview.** Select to play the flipbook again when it reaches the end.

5. Click **Output**.

6. Type a name, specify a location, and then click **Save**.

7. Upon completion, click **OK**.

Creating a Slide Show

With Photoshop Elements, you can collect and present your photos in a slide show using Slide Show preferences and the Slide Show Editor. Slide Show preferences allow you to set default settings for all of your slide shows, while the Slide Show Editor allows you to edit and customize individual slide shows. When you're done with a slide show, you can preview, save, and share it with others.

Create a Slide Show

1. Select (in the Organizer) or open (in the Editor) the photos you want to use in your project.

2. Click the **Create** tab.

3. Click the **Slide Show** button on the Create tab.

4. If the slide Show Preferences dialog box appears, select the options you want, and then click **OK**.

5. Edit the slide show using the options available in the Slide Show Editor.

6. To preview the slide show, click the **Full Screen Preview** button.

7. Click the **Save Project** button, enter a name for the project, and then click **Save** to save the slide show.

See Also

See "Setting Slide Show Preferences" on page 422 for information on selecting the preferences options.

Setting Slide Show Preferences

Slide Show preferences allow you to set default settings for all of your slide shows. When you create a new slide show, Photoshop Elements opens the Slide Show Preferences dialog box by default so you can set slide show settings for the new project. If you prefer not to display the Slide Show Preferences dialog box when you create a new slide show, you can deselect the option in the dialog box. In Slide Show preferences, you can set options for slide duration, transition effect and duration, background color, panning and zooming, captions, soundtracks, and audio captions.

Set Slide Show Preferences

1. In the Organizer or Editor, use either of the following methods:

   ◆ **New.** Click the **Slide Show** button on the Create tab.

   The Slide Show Preferences dialog box appears when the option in Step 5 is selected.

   ◆ **Open Existing.** Double-click (in the Organizer) or open (in the Editor) the slide show project. In the Slide Show Editor, click the **Edit** menu, and then click **Slide Show Preferences.**

2. Select the options you want:

   ◆ **Static Duration.** Select the default time for every slide.

   ◆ **Transition.** Select how slides change from one slide to the next.

   ◆ **Transition Duration.** Select the time for each transition.

   ◆ **Background Color.** Select the default color that appear behind each slide.

   ◆ **Apply Pan & Zoom to All Slides.** Select to apply a random pan and zoom to all slides.

- **Include Photo Captions as Text.**
  Select to add the caption
  attached to a photo in the slide
  show.

- **Include Audio Captions as
  Narration.** Select to add the
  audio caption attached to a
  photo in the slide show.

- **Repeat Soundtrack Until Last
  Slide.** Select to loop the
  soundtrack until the slide show
  ends.

- **Crop To Fit Slide.** Select the
  Portrait Photos or Landscape
  Photos check boxes to crop the
  photos to fit on a slide,
  removing any black bars due to
  different aspect ratios.

③ Click the **Preview Quality** list
  arrow, and then select a quality
  level. The higher the quality level,
  the larger the file size.

④ Select the **Show this dialog each
  time a new Slide Show is created**
  check box to open the slide show
  preferences dialog box when you
  click the Slide Show button on the
  Create tab.

⑤ Click **OK**.

Working with Content in a Slide Show

When you create or open an existing slide show, you can modify it by using the Slide Show Editor. In the Slide Show Editor, you can work with existing content and add new content. You can use the Add Media button to add photos, videos, and audio from the Organizer or from a folder on your computer. If you no longer want to use the content in a slide show, you can quickly remove it using the Slide Show Editor.

Work with Slide Show Content

1. Double-click (in the Organizer) or open (in the Editor) the slide show project you want to change.

2. To add a blank slide, click the **Add Blank Slide** button.

3. Select the slide in the storyboard, where you want to add content.

4. Click the **Add Media** button, and then click one of the following:

   ◆ **Photos and Videos from Organizer.** Click an option to display the photos you want to add, select the check boxes next to the photos you want, click **Add Selected Photos**, and then click **Done**.

   ◆ **Photos and Videos from Folder.** Select a file from your computer, and then click **Open**.

   ◆ **Audio from Organizer.** Select music from your catalog, and then click **OK**.

   ◆ **Audio from Folder.** Select music file from your computer, and then click **Open**.

5. To remove a slide, select the slide in the storyboard, and then press the Delete key.

6. To move a slide, drag it to a new location.

7. Click the **Save Project** button to save the slide show.

8. Click the **File** menu, and then click **Exit Slide Show Editor**.

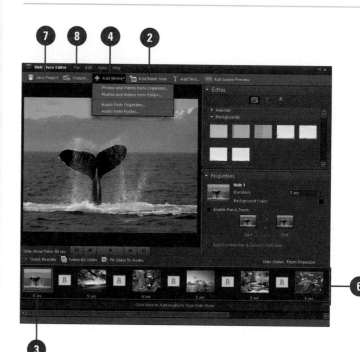

Editing a Slide Show

After you create a slide show, you can use the Slide Show Editor to edit individual photos. In the Properties palette of the Slide Show Editor, you can use options to edit and fix photos, resize and crop images, and rotate slides. Before you can use these options, you need to select the slide you want to change in the storyboard at the bottom of the Editor, and then select the photo in the main preview window. When you see a bounding box with square resize handles, you're ready to edit.

Edit a Slide Show

1. Double-click (in the Organizer) or open (in the Editor) the slide show project you want to change.

2. Select a slide in the storyboard you want to edit.

3. Click the photo in the main preview window.

4. Select from the available options from the Properties palette:

   ◆ **Edit and Adjust Slides.** Click **Auto Smart Fix** to perform a quick fix, **Auto Red Eye Fix** to remove photo red eye, or **More Editing** to edit the photo in the Editor.

   ◆ **Resize Slides.** Drag the **Size** slider, or click the **Crop to Fit** or **Fit on Slide** buttons.

   ◆ **Rotate Slides.** Click the **Rotate Left 90°** or **Rotate Right 90°** buttons.

5. Click the **Save Project** button to save the slide show.

6. Click the **File** menu, and then click **Exit Slide Show Editor**.

Adding Effects to a Slide Show

With the Slide Show Editor, you can add some special effects—such as transitions, pans, and zooms—to your slide show to add motion and interest. Transitions are effects that appear when you change from one slide to the next, while pans and zooms are effects that add motion to a still image. A transition effect is useful for moving from one photo subject to another, while a pan and zoom effect is useful for changing the focus on a photo from one area to another area.

Work with Transitions

1 Double-click (in the Organizer) or open (in the Editor) the slide show project you want to change.

2 Select the slides you want to add or change a slide transition:

◆ **All Transitions.** Click the **Edit** menu (Slide Show Editor), and then click **Select All Transitions**.

◆ **Single Transition.** Click the transition icon (between slides) in the storyboard.

3 In the Properties palette, click the **Transition** list arrow, and then select a transition.

◆ **Remove.** Click **None** from the list to remove a transition.

4 In the Properties palette, click the **Duration** list arrow, and then select a time duration.

5 Click the **Save Project** button to save the slide show.

6 Click the **File** menu, and then click **Exit Slide Show Editor.**

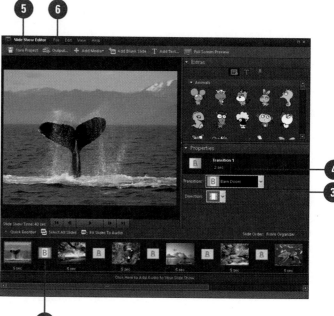

2 Transition icon

Did You Know?

You can apply a color effect to a slide show. In the storyboard, select a slide, click the slide in the main preview window, and then click the Black And White or Sepia button in the Properties palette. Click the Normal button to restore colors.

Set Pan and Zoom

1. Double-click (in the Organizer) or open (in the Editor) the slide show project you want to change.

2. Select the slide you want to change in the storyboard.

3. In the Properties palette, select the **Enable Pan & Zoom** check box.

   The Start bounding box has a green outline.

4. In the main preview window, drag a corner of the bounding box to resize it, if you want.

5. Drag the Start box to the area of the photo where you want panning and zooming to start. Resize the box until it surrounds the area you want to focus on.

6. Click the thumbnail marked End.

   The End bounding box has a red outline.

7. In the main preview window, resize and move the box until it surrounds the area where you want the additional pan and zoom to end.

8. To add an additional area to the pan and zoom, click **Add Another Pan & Zoom to this slide** button, and then drag the new End bounding box until it surrounds the area where you want it.

9. To swap start and end points, select the point, and then click the **Swap** button.

10. Click the **Save Project** button to save the slide show.

11. Click the **File** menu, and then click **Exit Slide Show Editor**.

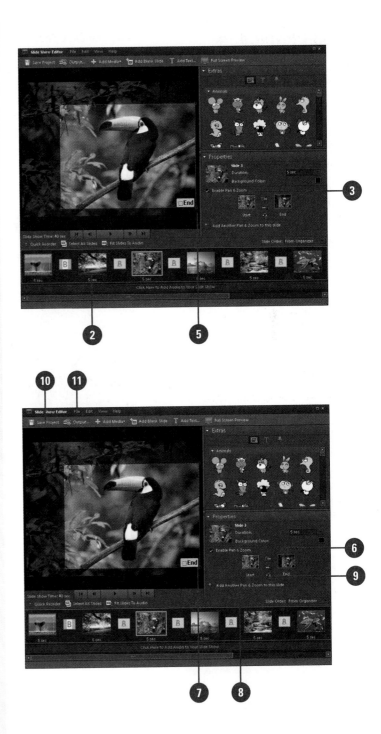

Adding Extras to a Slide Show

With the Slide Show Editor, you can add clip art graphics and text to your slide shows. In the Extras palette, you can scroll through a wide variety of clip art graphics—such as animals, background, costumes, flowers, food, frames, holiday & special occasions, and home items, and thought & speech bubbles—that you can quickly add to a photo. If you want to add text, you can use the Extras palette to select the right style to fit the photo image.

Add Clip Art to a Slide Show

1 Double-click (in the Organizer) or open (in the Editor) the slide show project you want to change.

2 Display the **Extras** palette, and then click the **Graphics** button.

3 Scroll down the list to browser through the clip art graphics.

4 Drag the clip art graphic onto the slide you want.

5 Use any of the following options to edit or modify the graphics:

◆ Resize. Drag a corner resize handle.

◆ Move. Click the center and drag it to a new location.

◆ Stacking Order. Click a graphic, click the **Edit** menu (Slide Show Editor), point to **Arrange**, and then select an arrange option.

6 Click the **Save Project** button to save the slide show.

7 Click the **File** menu, and then click **Exit Slide Show Editor**.

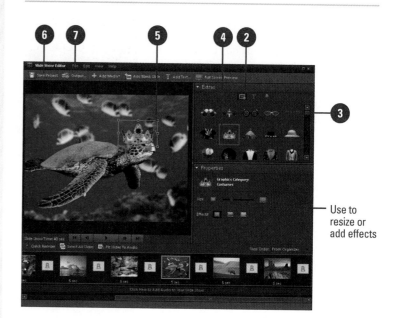

Use to resize or add effects

Did You Know?

You can adjust slide time and audio. Click the current time under the slide in the storyboard, and then select the time you want. To synchronize the slide show with a music clip, click the Fit Slides To Audio button.

Add Text to a Slide Show

1. Double-click (in the Organizer) or open (in the Editor) the slide show project you want to change.

2. Display the **Extras** palette, and then click the **Text** button.

3. Drag the text sample icon onto the slide you want.

4. Double-click the text placeholder, replace the sample text with the text you want, and then click **OK**.

5. Select from the available options from the Properties palette:

   ◆ **Font and Font Size.** Click to select a font family and size.

   ◆ **Color and Opacity.** Click to select a text color from the Color Picker dialog box, and a opacity (transparency) level.

   ◆ **Alignment.** Click to select an alignment: Left, Center, or Right.

   ◆ **Font Style.** Click to select a style: Bold, Italic, Underline, or Strikethrough.

   ◆ **Drop Shadow and Color.** Click to add a drop shadow (3D text appearance), and a color.

6. Click the **Save Project** button to save the slide show.

7. Click the **File** menu, and then click **Exit Slide Show Editor**.

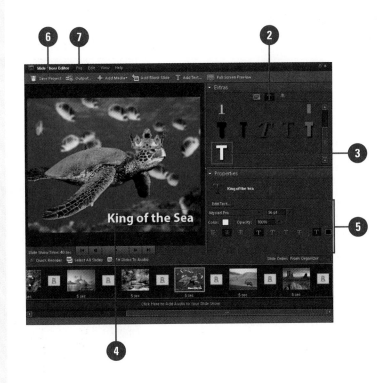

For Your Information

Adding Narration to a Slide Show

If you have a microphone attached to your computer, you can record a voice narration for a slide in a slide show. Double-click (in the Organizer) or open (in the Editor) the slide show project you want to change, click the Narration button in the Extras palette, select the slide you want, click the Record button, record the voice narration, and then click the Stop button. To hear the narration, click the Play button. To delete it, click the Delete button, and then click Delete This Narration or Delete All Narrations. To use an existing narration, click the Open button, and then click Use Existing Audio Caption to use the currently attached audio caption or Browse to select one.

Publishing a Slide Show

When you're done with a slide show, you can use the Output button in the Slide Show Editor to publish it as a file (either WMV or PDF), as a video CD (VCD) or DVD, on TV using a Windows Media Center Edition computer, or in a video project using Adobe Premiere Elements. With the Slide Show Output dialog box, you can select all the options you need to publish a slide show with the output you want.

Publish a Slide Show as a File

① Double-click (in the Organizer) or open (in the Editor) the slide show project you want to publish.

② Click the **Output** button.

③ Click **Save As a File**.

④ Click the **Movie File (WMV)** or **PDF File (PDF)** option.

⑤ Click the **Slide Size** list arrow, and then select the size you want.

⑥ If you selected the PDF File option, select from the following options:

◆ **Loop.** Select to replay the slide show when it reaches the end.

◆ **Manual Advance.** Select to not automatically play the slide show.

◆ **View Slide Show after Saving.** Select to view the slide show after you created it.

⑦ Click **OK**, enter a file name, specify a location, and then click **Save**.

⑧ Click the **File** menu, and then click **Exit Slide Show Editor**.

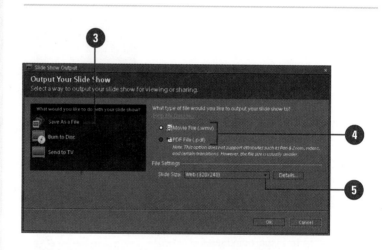

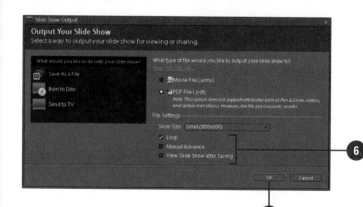

Did You Know?

You can publish a slide show to Premiere Elements. In the Slide Show Editor, click the Output button, click Send To Premiere Elements, and then click OK. If requested, save your project. In the Premiere Elements Organizer, drag the project into the Sceneline or Timeline.

Publish a Slide Show as a CD or DVD Disc

1. Double-click (in the Organizer) or open (in the Editor) the slide show project you want to publish.

2. Click the **Output** button.

3. Click **Burn to Disc**.

4. Select the **Include additional slide shows I've made on this disc** check box to publish multiple slide shows on a disc.

5. Click **OK**.

6. If you selected the option to include additional slide shows, click the **Add Slide Shows** button, select the check boxes next to the slide shows you want to add, and then click **OK**.

   ◆ To rearrange the slide show, drag the shows around.

7. Select a destination drive.

8. Click the **NTSC** or **PAL** option, and then click **Burn**, if necessary.

9. If available, click the **Select Drive Speed** list arrow, and then select the speed you want.

10. Insert a writable CD into your CD-RW or DVD-RW drive, and then click **OK**.

11. Click the **File** menu, and then click **Exit Slide Show Editor**.

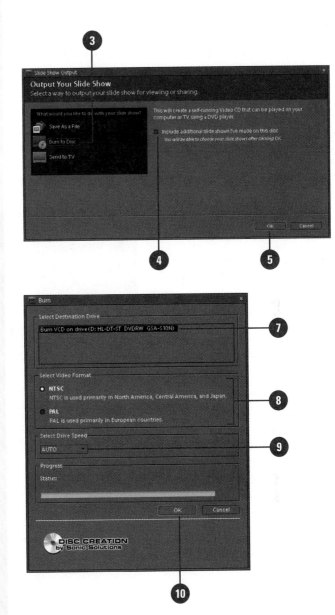

Did You Know?

You can publish a slide show to your TV using Windows Media Center Edition. In the Slide Show Editor, click the Output button, click Send To TV, enter a title, specify a screen size, click OK, enter a file name, specify a folder location, and then click Save.

Creating a VCD with a Menu of Slide Shows

If you have more than one slide show, you can burn them on a video CD (VCD) with a menu for easy access and viewing. In order to burn a VCD, you need a CD-RW or DVD-RW drive on your computer and blank CD-RW or DVD-RW discs. You can view a VCD on your TV using a DVD player or on your computer using a CD/DVD drive and software that supports the VCD format. Photoshop Elements creates a VCD by saving a WMV file for each slide show to your computer, converting the WMV files to VCD, and burning them to a disc.

Create a VCD with a Menu of Slide Shows

1. Select (in the Organizer) or open (in the Editor) the slide show projects or WMV files you want to use in your VCD project.

2. Click the **Create** tab.

3. Click the **More Options** button on the Create tab, and then click **VCD with Menu**.

4. Arrange and manage the slide shows in your VCD.

   ◆ **Add.** Click **Add Slide Shows**, select the slide shows, and then click **OK**.

   ◆ **Move.** Drag a slide show to a new location in the slide show pane.

   ◆ **Remove.** Select a slide show, and then click **Remove Slide Show**.

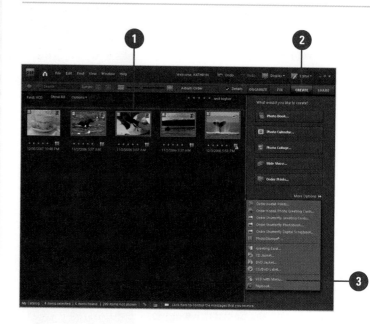

Add slide show

5 Click the **NTSC** or **PAL** option.

6 Insert a writable CD into your CD-RW or DVD-RW drive, and then click **Burn**.

Photoshop Elements saves the project to your computer and then starts the burn process.

7 Select the burn options you want.

8 Click **OK**.

9 Upon completion, click **OK**.

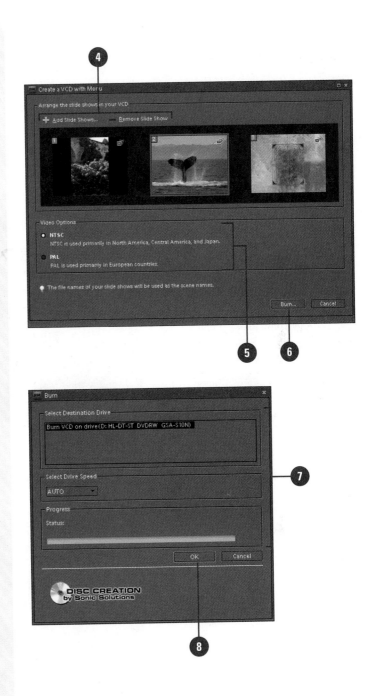

Using Photomerge Faces

Have you ever taken a series of pictures trying to get the perfect portrait, but can never quite get it. Either the person has their eyes closed or doesn't look right. If you can't get the perfect shot the natural way using a camera, you can use Photomerge Faces to combine multiple facial features from multiple photos to create the perfect portrait.

Use Photomerge Faces

1 Select (in the Organizer) or open (in the Editor) the photos you want to use in your project.

2 Click the **File** menu, point to **New**, and then click **Photomerge Faces**.

> **TIMESAVER** *In the Editor, click the Edit tab, click the Guided button, and then click Faces.*

3 Drag the photo with the face you want as your base image from the Project Bin to the Final window.

4 Click another image in the Project Bin.

5 Click the **Alignment** tool, and then place the three alignment markers on the eyes and mouth on the source image and the final image, and then click **Align Photos**.

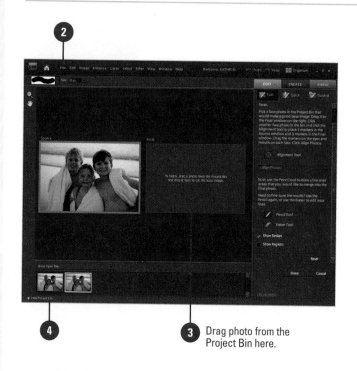

3 Drag photo from the Project Bin here.

Alignment markers

6 Click other photos in the Project Bin (color-coded) to help you keep track), and then use the **Pencil** tool to draw a line over the areas that you want to merge into the final photo.

7 To fine-tune the final image, use the **Pencil** tool to add additional content or the **Eraser** tool to remove content.

8 Select the options you want:

◆ **Show Strokes.** Select to show your Pencil strokes in the source image.

◆ **Show Regions.** Select to display the selected regions in the final image.

9 To reset the process and start over, click **Reset**.

10 When you're finished, click **Done**.

11 Click the **File** menu, click **Save As**, type a name, specify a location, and then click **Save**.

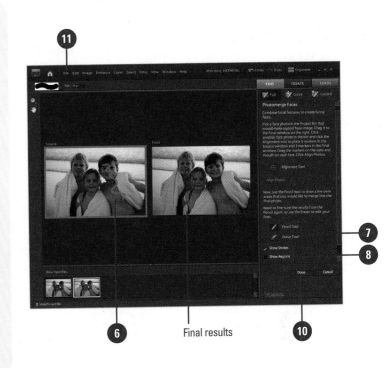

Final results

Using Photomerge Group Shot

Have you ever taken a series of pictures trying to get the perfect group shot, but can never quite get it? One person either has their eyes closed or doesn't look right. If you have a good shot of a person on one photo and a good shot of the other people on another photo, you can use Photomerge Group Shot to combine the single person in one photo with the other people in the other photo to instantly create the perfect group photo.

Use Photomerge Group Shot

1. Select (in the Organizer) or open (in the Editor) the photos you want to use in your project.

2. Click the **File** menu, point to **New**, and then click **Photomerge Group Shot**.

   TIMESAVER *In the Editor, click the Edit tab, click the Guided button, and then click Group Shot.*

3. Drag the photo with the best group shot you want to use from the Project Bin to the Final window.

4. Click other photos in the Project Bin (color-coded to help you keep track) to position them in the Source window, and then use the **Pencil** tool to draw a line over the areas that you want to merge into the final photo.

5. To fine-tune the final image, use the **Pencil** tool to add additional content or the **Eraser** tool to remove content.

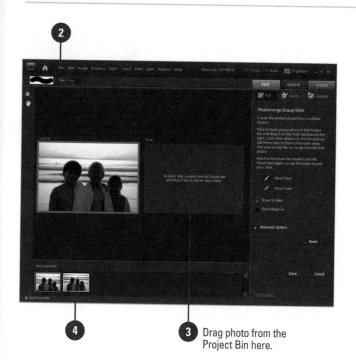

Drag photo from the Project Bin here.

6 Select the options you want:

◆ **Show Strokes.** Select to show your Pencil strokes in the source image.

◆ **Show Regions.** Select to display the selected regions in the final image.

7 Click the triangle next to Advanced Options to display additional options, and then use the ones you want:

◆ **Alignment Tool.** Click the Alignment tool, and then place the three alignment markers on the eyes and mouth on the source image and the final image, and then click Align Photos.

◆ **Pixel Blending.** Select to blend pixels.

8 To reset the process and start over, click **Reset**.

9 When you're finished, click **Done**.

10 Click the **File** menu, click **Save As**, type a name, specify a location, and then click **Save**.

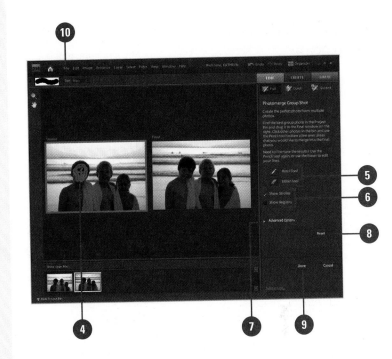

Using Photomerge Panorama

Ever wanted to create a panoramic photograph? Panoramas are those great looking images that encompass a wide area into one photograph. For example, you want to create a single photograph of the Grand Canyon, but the lens on your camera doesn't go that wide. So you start at the left of the canyon wall, and take a photo. Then you move slightly to the right and take another photo, and another, until you have reached the far right canyon wall. So, now you have four or five separate images on the Grand Canyon, and you want to stitch them together into a single panoramic view. If you have Photoshop Elements, you have what you need to make it happen.

Use Photomerge Panorama

1. In the Organizer or Editor, click the **File** menu, point to **New**, and then click **Photomerge Panorama**.

2. Click the **Use** list arrow, and then select from the following options:

    ◆ **Files.** Select the files to include in the merge document. Click the Browse button, and then select the images.

    ◆ **Folder.** Select a folder that contains all the images. Click the Browse button, and then select the folder containing all the images.

    ◆ **Open Files.** Selects the currently open Photoshop images.

3. To quickly add currently opened files to the list, click **Add Open Files**.

4. To remove any images from the list, click the file name, and then click **Remove**.

5. Click one of the layout options:

    ◆ **Auto.** Analyzes the images and uses the Perspective or Cylindrical layout.

    ◆ **Perspective.** Creates a stretched or skewed effect on the side images.

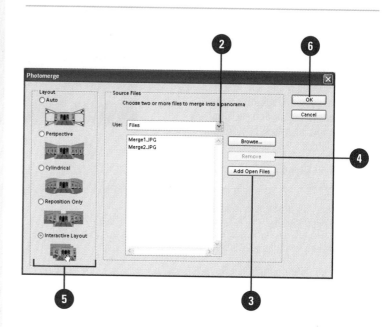

- **Cylindrical.** Creates a bow-tie effect like an unfolded cylinder.

- **Reposition Only.** Aligns the layers and matches overlapping content.

- **Interactive Layout.** Allows you to manually rearrange the images to create a panorama.

⑥ Click **OK**.

⑦ If you selected the Interactive Layout option in step 5, use the Toolbox to arrange the images, and then click **OK**.

Photoshop merges the images into a single panoramic document file.

⑧ Click the **File** menu, click **Save As**, type a name, specify a location, and then click **Save**.

Did You Know?

You can use the following hints for the best results with Photomerge. For the best results, use the following rules of thumb when you take pictures. Overlap images by approximately 25% to 40%, don't change the zoom depth, keep the camera level, stay in the same position, maintain the same exposure, and avoid using distortion lenses.

You can preserve alignment in Interactive Layout. Select the Reposition Only and Snap To Image options to preserve alignment at overlapping image areas and apply blending to even out differences of exposure between images.

Toolbox   Lightbox   Navigator view box   ⑦

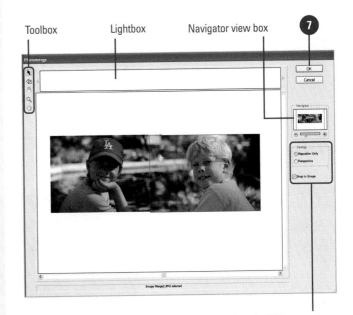

Select options to set and preview the Photomerge

Single panoramic document

Using Photomerge Scene Cleaner

Have you ever tried repeatedly to get the right shot of a moving scene? In one photo, the background is clear but the subject isn't quite right; in another, the subject's perfect but there's an intrusive passer-by in the background. Now, you can use Photomerge Scene Cleaner (**New!**) to copy scenery in one photo into another photo to cover up what you want to hide and create the perfect composite image with just a few clicks.

Use Photomerge Scene Cleaner

① Select (in the Organizer) or open (in the Editor) the photos you want to use in your project.

② Click the **File** menu, point to **New**, and then click **Photomerge Scene Cleaner**.

TIMESAVER *In the Editor, click the Edit tab, click the Guided button, and then click Group Shot.*

③ Drag the photo with the best group shot you want to use from the Project Bin to the Final window.

④ Click other photos in the Project Bin (color-coded to help you keep track) to position them in the Source window, and then use the **Pencil** tool to draw a line over the areas that you want to merge into the final photo.

⑤ To fine-tune the final image, use the **Pencil** tool to add additional content or the **Eraser** tool to remove content.

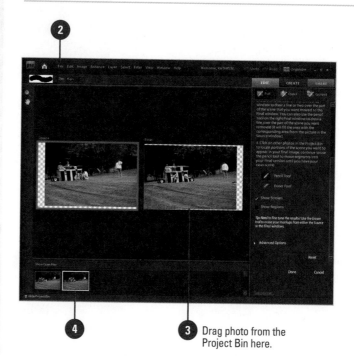

③ Drag photo from the Project Bin here.

6. Select the options you want:

◆ **Show Strokes.** Select to show your Pencil strokes in the source image.

◆ **Show Regions.** Select to display the selected regions in the final image.

7. Click the triangle next to Advanced Options to display additional options, and then use the ones you want:

◆ **Alignment Tool.** Click the Alignment tool, and then place the three alignment markers on the eyes and mouth on the source image and the final image, and then click Align Photos.

◆ **Pixel Blending.** Select to blend pixels.

8. To reset the process and start over, click **Reset**.

9. When you're finished, click **Done**.

10. Click the **File** menu, click **Save As**, type a name, specify a location, and then click **Save**.

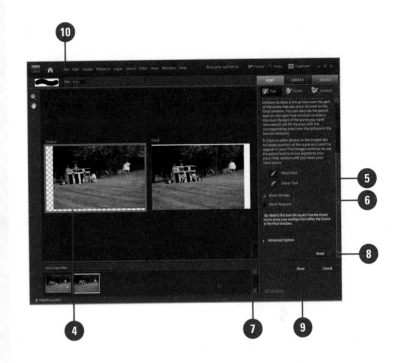

Keeping Proper Perspective with Vanishing Point

Vanishing Point gives you the ability to move and/or copy objects and still maintain the same visual perspective of the original. Let's say that you shoot an image of a roadway disappearing into the distance, and along the road there's a billboard. Unfortunately, you want the billboard to appear as if it's further away. With Vanishing Point, you can create a stretched or skewed effect on the side images that displays the depth of the image. Wherever you move the sign, it will appear within the proper perspective.

Use the Vanishing Point Tool

1. In the Organizer or Editor, click the **File** menu, point to **New**, and then click **Photomerge Panorama**.

2. Click the **Use** list arrow, and then select from the following options:

   - **Files.** Select the files to include in the merge document. Click the Browse button, and then select the images.

   - **Folder.** Select a folder that contains all the images. Click the Browse button, and then select the folder containing all the images.

   - **Open Files.** Selects the currently open Photoshop images.

3. To quickly add currently opened files to the list, click **Add Open Files**.

4. To remove any images from the list, click the file name, and then click **Remove**.

5. Click the **Interactive Layout** option.

6. Click **OK**.

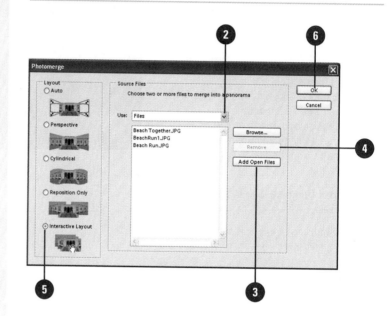

Select the **Vanishing Point** tool in the Toolbox.

Click the **Perspective** option.

Click on an image to make it the vanishing point image. There can only be one vanishing point image in a panorama.

◆ Hold down the Alt key when you point to an image to show the selection border of the photo.

Click the **Select Image** tool on the Toolbox, and then adjust the position of the non-vanishing point images as necessary.

A non-vanishing point image appears with a red border around it when selected.

◆ The non-vanishing point images are linked to the vanishing point image. To remove vanishing point, click the **Reposition Only** button to break the links.

Click **OK**.

Click the **File** menu, click **Save As**, type a name, specify a location, and then click **Save**.

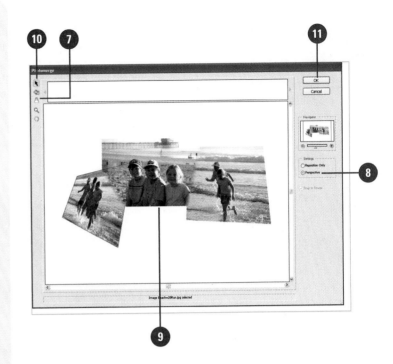

Resizing and Rotating Project Photos

If you have a photo project that needs some work, you can use some of the on-screen editing tools to directly resize, rotate, and move photos. When you work with photo projects, you have the option to change the photo and its frame or just the photo itself. After you select the part of the photo you want to change, you can use the bounding box with square resize handles and a circle rotate handle to make the photo adjustments you want.

Resize and Rotate Photos in a Photo Project

1 Open (in the Editor) the photo project you want to change.

2 Click the photo once to reposition the photo and its frame, or double-click the photo to change the size, position, or angle of a photo within a frame.

A bounding box appears showing the edges of the photo.

3 Use any of the following options to edit the photo:

◆ **Resize Photo.** Drag the slider, or drag a corner resize handle (square). Click the **Commit** button (green check mark) to accept it.

◆ **Rotate Photo.** Position the cursor over the circle handle, and then drag to rotate the photo. Click the **Commit** button (green check mark) to accept it.

◆ **Move Photo.** Click within the bounding box, and then drag the photo.

◆ **Replace Photo.** Right-click the photo, and then click **Replace Photo**.

◆ **Remove Photo.** Right-click the photo, and then click **Clear Photo**.

4 Click the **File** menu, and then click **Save**.

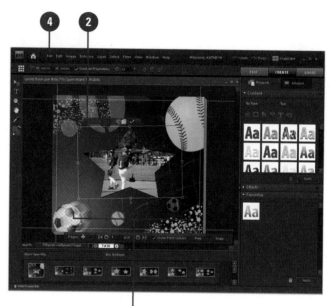

Editing Photo Projects in Photoshop CS4

When a project only has a single page, Photoshop Elements saves it in the Photoshop format (PSD). When a project has multiple pages (up to 30 at a time), it saves the project in the Photo Projects format (PSE). If you have Photoshop CS4 and Photoshop Elements 7 installed on the same computer, you can use Photoshop CS4 to edit single page projects and files using the Photoshop PSD file format. You can launch Photoshop CS4 directly from Photoshop Elements in the Organizer or from Windows Explorer using the Open with command.

Edit Photo Projects in Photoshop CS4

1. Use either of the following methods:

   ◆ **In the Organizer.** Select the photo project with a single page, click the **Edit** menu, and then click **Edit with Photoshop**.

   ◆ **In Windows Explorer.** Right-click the photo project with the Photoshop format (PSD), point to **Open with**, and then click **Adobe Photoshop CS4**

   Photoshop CS4 opens and displays the photo project from Photoshop Elements.

2. In Photoshop CS4, make the editing changes you want.

3. Click the **File** menu, and then click **Save**.

4. If Photoshop asks you to replace the existing file, click **Yes**.

1 In the Organizer

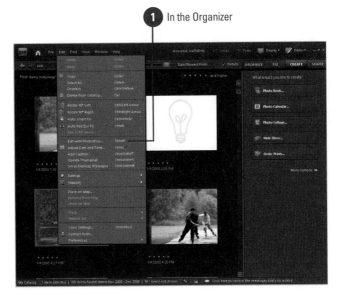

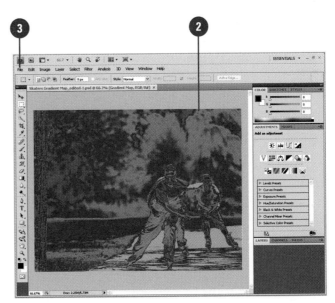

Printing and Sharing Photos

19

Introduction

Once you create your Photoshop Elements masterpiece, you will have to decide the output for the image file, and how the image will be printed. These are not easy considerations. For example, an image created with a resolution of 72ppi, might be fine if output to the web, but would not be of sufficient quality for output to a high-quality laser printer.

Raster images (Photoshop documents) do not handle change very well, so it's important to design with a goal in mind. Designers call this process a workflow. When you start a Photoshop Elements project you should have a good idea whether the project is headed to a press or inkjet printer, a copy machine, or a monitor. Knowing this information helps you design with the end in mind. That's not to say you can't make changes to a Photoshop document; however, when it comes to color space and resolution, the less change the better the output quality.

Color management has changed a lot in the last few years, standards have been set up, and Adobe is at the forefront of this new technology. No longer do you have to fear color management, because Photoshop Elements has taken all (or at least most) of the guesswork out of the equation. Adobe's color management system translates, using "rendering, intents, color discrepancies between the input device and the output device using color profiles to avoid color-matching problems.

Working with Page Setup

You can use the Page Setup dialog box to select the size and location in the printer of the paper you want to use. You can also select the page orientation (portrait or landscape) that best fits the entire document or any selection. **Portrait** orients the page vertically (taller than it is wide) and **landscape** orients the page horizontally (wider than it is tall). When you shift between the two, the margin settings automatically change. **Margins** are the blank space between the edge of a page and the image. The printer only prints within these margins. Different printer models support different options and features; the available options depend on your printer and print drivers.

Work with Page Setup

1. In the Organizer or Editor, display a a document.

2. Click the **File** menu, and then click **Page Setup**.

   TIMESAVER *Press Ctrl+Shift+P to open the Page Setup dialog box.*

3. Select from the various Page Setup options:

   ◆ **Size.** Click the list arrow, and then select from the available options. The default printer will determine the available paper sizes.

   ◆ **Source.** Click the list arrow, and then select from the available options.

   ◆ **Orientation.** Click the Portrait or Landscape option.

   ◆ **Margins.** Enter Top, Bottom, Left, and Right paper margins for the custom item.

4. Click **OK**.

Setting Measurement Units for Printing

When you print a photo, you can set options to print image sizes and other measurement information. In General preferences for the Organizer, you can set the unit of measurement you want to use for printing. The two available options include Inches (in) and centimeters (cm)/millimeters (mm).

Set Measurement Units for Printing

1. In the Organizer, display the Photo Browser or Date view.

2. Click the **Edit** menu, point to **Preferences**, and then click **General**.

   TIMESAVER *Press Ctrl+K to open General preferences.*

3. Click the **Print Sizes** list arrow, and then click **Inches** or **Centimeters/ Millimeters**.

4. Click **OK**.

Printing in the Organizer

When you're working in the Organizer, you can print one or more photos and other media files. If you select a video to print, only the first frame of the video prints. When you select the Print command in the Organizer, Photoshop Elements displays the Print Photos dialog box, where you can preview and print one or more photos. You can print your photos as individual prints, in a contact sheet (photo thumbnails), in a picture package (multiple photos on a single sheet), or as labels. When you print a picture package or labels, you can add an artistic frame around the photos. For labels, you can select a layout from some common Avery label sheets.

Print in the Organizer

1. In the Organizer, select the photos and other files you want to print.

2. Click the **File** menu, and then click **Print**.

3. To add photos to the list, click **Add**, and then do the following:

   ◆ Select options to display the photos you want to add.

   ◆ Select the check boxes next to the photos.

   ◆ Click **Add Selected Photos.**

   ◆ Click **Done.**

4. To remove a photo from the list, select the photo, and then click **Remove**.

5. Click the **Select Printer** list arrow to select a printer.

   ◆ If available, click the **Show Printer Preferences** button (next to the list arrow) to set printer specific options.

   ◆ If available, select the **PRINT Image Matching (PIM)** or **Exif Print** option.

6. Click the **Select Type of Print** list arrow, and then select a print type:

   ◆ **Individual Prints.**

   ◆ **Contact Sheet.**

   ◆ **Picture Package.**

   ◆ **Labels.**

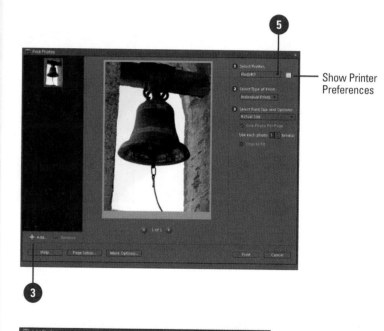

Show Printer Preferences

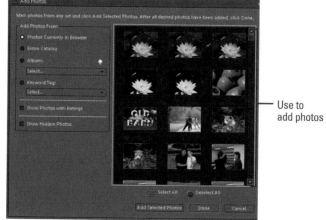

Use to add photos

7 If you selected **Individual Prints**, select from the following options:

- ◆ **Select Print Size.** Click the list arrow to select a print size.

- ◆ **Options.** Select or deselect the **One Photo Per Page** check box, specify the number of times to use each photos, and select or deselect the **Crop to Fit** check box.

8 If you selected **Contact Sheet**, select from the following options:

- ◆ **Columns.** Enter the numbers of columns (1-9).

- ◆ **Add a Text Label.** Select or deselect the Date, Caption, Filename, or Page Number check boxes.

9 If you selected **Picture Package** or **Labels**, select from the following options:

- ◆ **Layout.** Click the list arrow to select a print size.

- ◆ **Frame.** Click the list arrow to select a frame.

- ◆ **Options.** Select or deselect the **Fill Page with First Photo** check box, and select or deselect the **Crop to Fit** check box.

- ◆ **Offset Print Area.** For Labels, enter an offset print area to align print labels. Check your label sheets for numbers.

10 To preview your photos, click the **Previous** and **Next** buttons under the Preview pane.

11 Click **Print**.

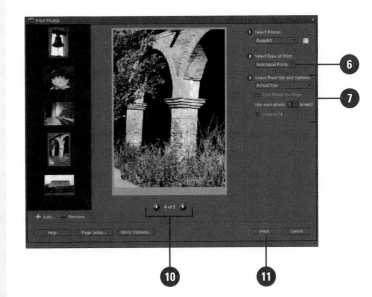

For Your Information

Understanding PIM and Exif Print

Photoshop Elements provides options to use **PRINT Image Matching** (PIM) and **Exif Print** to produce the best possible photos prints. PIM uses print specific information from PIM enabled digital cameras to print improved color, quality and details in supported Epson printers. Exif Print uses Exif tag information embedded in photos from Exif enabled digital cameras to optimize and enhance print quality on supported Epson printers. Exif Print is a subset of PIM that is supported by Epson devices. In some cases, you can select both the PIM and Exif Print options for a more improved print. The PIM and Exif print options in the Print dialog box are only available for supported Epson printers. Check your printer's documentation for details.

Using More Print Options in the Organizer

When you print from the Organizer, Photoshop Elements provides more print options. The options available depending on the type of print job you want to perform. If you want to print a contact sheet, picture package, or labels, you can select a print profile to use the right colors for the print job. If you want to print individual prints, you can add information labels under the photos, add a border, invert the image for transfer printing, print crop marks for alignment purposes, and set print resolution in addition to selecting a print profile.

Use More Print Options in the Organizer

1. In the Organizer, select the photos and other files you want to print.

2. Click the **File** menu, and then click **Print**.

3. Click the **Select Printer** list arrow to select a printer.

4. Click the **Select Type of Print** list arrow, and then one of the following:

   ◆ **Contact Sheet**.

   ◆ **Picture Package**.

   ◆ **Labels**.

5. Click **More Options**.

6. Click the **Print Space** list arrow, and then select a print profile.

7. Click **OK**.

8. Click **Print**.

Select More Individual Print Options in the Organizer

1 In the Organizer, select the photos and other files you want to print.

2 Click the **File** menu, and then click **Print**.

3 Click the **Select Printer** list arrow to select a printer.

4 Click the **Select Type of Print** list arrow, and then click **Individual Prints**.

5 Click **More Options**.

6 Select from the following options:

◆ **Label.** Select the **Date**, **Caption**, or **File Name** check boxes to display the information below each photo.

◆ **Invert Image (Transfer printing).** Select to print T-shirt transfers with an inverted image.

◆ **Print Crop Marks.** Select to print guide lines on all four edges to make it easier to trim a photo.

◆ **Max Print Resolution.** Enter the maximum resolution needed to print a photo (220 to 600 ppi). The default is 220 ppi.

◆ **Add a Border.** Select to add a border, and then enter a value for a border's thickness in inches (in), centimeters (cm), or millimeters (mm). Click the color box to select a color. If you want to print guides around the image, select the **Include Trim Guideline** check box.

◆ **Color Management.** Click the **Print Space** list arrow, and then select a print profile.

7 Click **OK**.

8 Click **Print**.

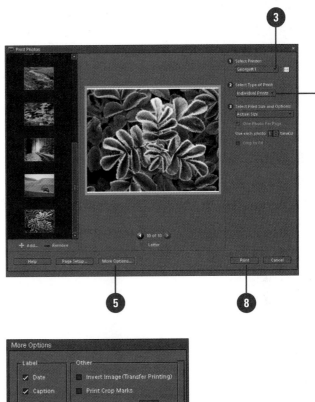

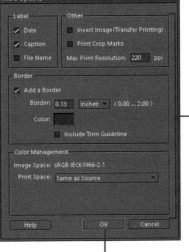

Printing in the Editor

When you select the Print command in the Editor, Photoshop Elements displays a preview dialog box, which gives you the opportunity to view the image (on screen), and decide whether to print or return to the drawing board. The white area in the image preview is the printable area, while the shaded border at the edge is the paper margins. You can adjust the position and scale of the image and see the results. The size of the image is determined by the document size settings in the Image Size dialog box. When you scale an image in the Print dialog box, the changes only affect the printed image, not the actual image.

Print in the Editor

1. In the Editor, open a document.

2. Click the **File** menu, and then click **Print**.

3. Click the **Printer** list arrow to select a printer.

4. Click the **Print Size** list arrow, and then select a print size.

5. Select from the Preview options:

   ◆ **Orientation.** Click the **Portrait** or **Landscape** button.

   ◆ **Preview.** Click the **Previous** or **Next** button.

   ◆ **Rotate.** Click the **Rotate 90° Left** or **Rotate 90° Right** button.

6. Select the **Crop to Fit Print Proportions** check box to make sure the photo prints at the size chosen from the Print Size.

7. Select from the Position options:

   ◆ **Center Image.** Select to center the image on the paper.

   ◆ **Top.** Select to print the image from the top of the page.

   ◆ **Left.** Select to print the image from the left of the page.

   ◆ **Units.** Specify the measurement units.

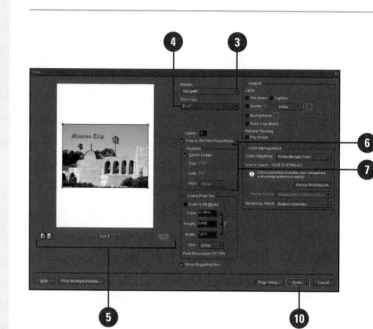

8 Select from the various Scaled Print Size options:

- **Scale to Fit Media.** Select the check box to scale the image to the selected paper size.

- **Scale.** Enter a percentage value.

- **Height.** Enter a specific height for the image.

- **Width.** Enter a specific width for the image.

- **Show Bounding Box.** Select the check box to create a viewable bounding box around the image.

9 To print multiple photos, click **Print Multiple Photos**, and then do the following:

- Select options to display the photos you want to add.

- Select the check boxes next to the photos.

- Click **Add Selected Photos.**

- Click **Done.**

TIMESAVER *Press Alt+Ctrl+P or click the File menu, and then click Print Multiple Photos to print multiple photos from the Editor.*

10 Click **Print** to open the Print dialog box, or click **Cancel** to return to your document without printing.

11 To access other print buttons, do any of the following:

- **Reset.** Hold down Alt, and then click Reset to reset print options.

- **Print One.** Hold down Alt, and then click Print One to print without displaying a dialog box.

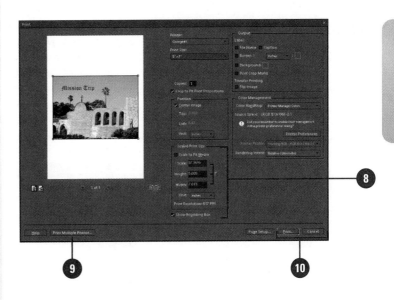

For Your Information

Scaling and Positioning an Image

You can scale an image if it's larger than the printable area of the paper. If a warning appears, indicating your image is larger than the printable area, click Cancel, click the File menu, click Print, select the Scale To Fit Media check box, then click Print. You can also click the File menu, and then click Page Setup to change your paper size. You can manually scale and position an image. Select the Show Bounding Box check box, and then deselect the Scale To Fit Media, and Center Image check boxes. Then simply drag the image in the View window to reposition, and then click and drag a corner to resize.

Setting Print Output Options

On the right side of the Print dialog box from the Editor, Photoshop Elements not only gives you access to its powerful color management tools, it also lets you print file name labels or captions, print crop marks, print T-shirt transfers with an inverted image, add a background color outside the image area, and even place a custom border around the image. It's just one more way that Photoshop Elements gives you control over document output.

Set Print Output Options in the Editor

1. In the Editor, open a document.

2. Click the **File** menu, and then click **Print**.

3. Select from the various Output options:

   ◆ **File Name.** Select to print the image file name.

   ◆ **Caption.** Select to print the image caption in 9-point Helvetica plain type.

   ◆ **Border.** Select to print a border around the image. Specify the size of the border and select a color.

   ◆ **Background.** Select to use a background color to be printed outside the image area. Select a color.

   ◆ **Print Crop Marks.** Select to print marks where the page is to be trimmed.

   ◆ **Flip Image.** Select to print T-shirt transfers with an inverted image.

4. Click **Print** to open the Print dialog box.

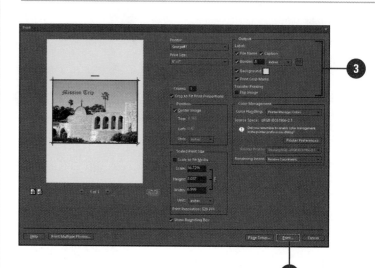

Choosing Color Settings

Colors in an image many times will appear different when you view them using different monitors. They may also look very different when printed on your desktop printer or when printed on a professional printing press. If your work in Photoshop Elements requires you to produce consistent color across different devices, managing color should be an essential part of your workflow. Photoshop Elements gives you a group of pre-defined color management systems, which are designed to help you produce consistent color. In most cases, the predefined sets are all you will need to manage color workflow. The power of color management lies in its ability to produce consistent colors with a system that reconciles differences between the color spaces of each device.

Choose Color Settings

1 Open Photoshop Elements (it is not necessary to open a document).

2 In the Organizer or Editor, click the **Edit** menu, and then click **Color Settings**.

3 Select from the available options:

◆ **No Color Management.** Select to use your monitor profile and removes any embedded profiles and leaves the image untagged.

◆ **Always Optimize Colors for Computer Screens.** Select to use sRGB as the RGB working space or the Gray Gamma 2.2 as the Grayscale working space and maintains any embedded profiles.

◆ **Always Optimize for Printing.** Select to use Adobe RGB as the RGB working space or Dot Gain 20% as the Grayscale working space and maintains any embedded profiles.

◆ **Allow Me to Choose.** Select sRGB or Adobe RGB when opening untagged files.

4 Click **OK**.

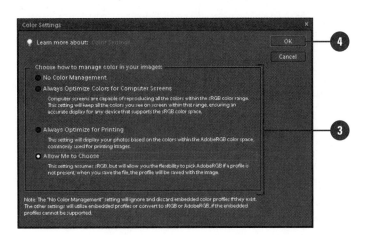

Setting Print Color Management Options

Photoshop Elements' color management system must know the color space of the image so it can decipher the meaning of the color values in the image. When assigning a profile to an image, the image will be in the color space described by the particular profile. For example, a document's profile can be assigned by a source device, like a printer, or assigned directly in Photoshop Elements. When using the Assign Profile command, color values are mapped directly into the new profile space. Rendering intent deals with how the color profile selected is converted from one color space into another. When you define rendering intent you are specifying how the colors should be displayed, even at the expense of the original gamut (colors) within the active document. The rendering intent you choose depends on whether colors are critical in an image and on your preference of what the overall color appearance of an image should be. Many times the intent of the images color gamut is different than how the original image was shot.

Set Print Color Management Options in the Editor

1. In the Editor, open a document.

2. Click the **File** menu, and then click **Print**.

3. Click the **Color Handling** list arrow, and then select from the following options:

   ◆ **Printer Manages Colors.** Select to let the printer specify the color profile.

   ◆ **Photoshop Elements Manages Colors.** Select to choose the profile you want.

   ◆ **No Color Management.** Select to use your monitor profile and removes any embedded profiles and leaves the image untagged.

4. To change printer specific options, click **Printer Preferences**. Options vary depending on the printer.

5. If you selected the Photoshop Elements Manages Colors option, click the **Printer Profile** list arrow, and then select a profile.

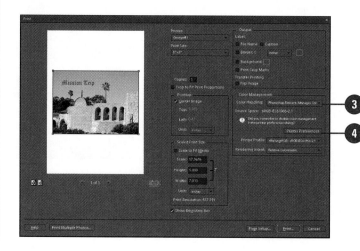

6 Click the **Rendering Intent** list arrow, and then select from the following options:

◆ **Perceptual.** Preserves the natural colors of an image, as viewed by the human eye, sometimes at the expense of the true color values. Good for photographic images.

◆ **Saturation.** Produces vivid colors in an image, without paying attention to the original color values of the image. Good for business graphics, and charts where you want the colors to pop.

◆ **Relative Colorimetric.** Shifts the color space of the document to that of the maximum highlight values of the destination. Useful for photographic images, and preserves more of the original color than Perceptual.

◆ **Absolute Colorimetric.** Clips any colors in the destination image that do not fall into the color gamut of the destination. Use to proof images sent to devices, such as 4-color presses.

7 Click **Print** to open the Print dialog box.

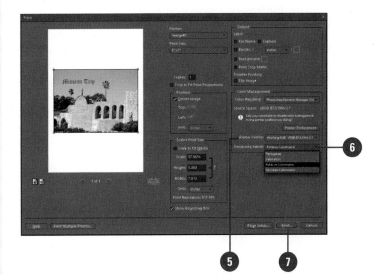

Printing a Document

Printing a paper copy is the most common way to preview and share your documents. You can use the Print dialog box to set how many copies to print, specify a range of pages to print, and print your document. Understand that the options available for the Print command will be determined by the default printer, and operating system. Different printers will display different options; there are some options that are fairly universal, and these options are covered here.

Print a Document

1. In the Editor, open a document.

2. Click the **File** menu, and then click **Print**.

   A print preview dialog box opens.

3. Specify the print options you want, and then click **Print**.

4. If necessary, click the **Name** list arrow, and then click the printer you want.

5. Type the number of copies you want to print.

6. Specify the pages to print:

   ◆ **All.** Prints the entire document.

   ◆ **Pages.** Prints the specified pages.

   ◆ **Selection.** Prints the selected item.

   ◆ **Current Page.** Prints the currently selected page.

7. Click **Print**.

Printing Multiple Layers

If you have an image document with multiple layers, such as a Photoshop document with the PSD format or an image file with the TIFF format, Photoshop Elements prints the layers that are visible in the Editor. Use the eye icon in the Layers palette to make the layers visible, and then print the document.

Print Multiple Layers

1. In the Editor (in Full Edit), open a document (PSD) or image (TIFF) with multiple layers.

2. Display the **Layers** palette.

3. Click the eye icon in the Layers palette to make the layers you want to print visible.

4. Click the **File** menu, and then click **Print** to view the visible layers in the preview.

5. Specify the print options you want.

6. Click **Print**.

Using the Sharing Center

In Photoshop Elements, you can use the Sharing Center to share and send your photos and projects to others as e-mail, as PDFs, on CD/DVD, and online using Photoshop.com and other online services. You can access the Sharing Center on the Share tab from either the Organizer or the Editor.

Use the Sharing Center

1. Select (in the Organizer) or open (in the Editor) the photos you want to use in your project.

2. Click the **Share** tab.

3. Select any of the sharing options:

   ◆ **Online Gallery.** Presents your photos on a web page.

   ◆ **E-mail Attachments.** Sends photos and projects in as an e-mail attachment.

   ◆ **Photo Mail.** Sends photos as an e-mail.

   ◆ **Order Prints.** Orders prints online using Adobe Photoshop Services.

   ◆ **CD/DVD.** Creates a CD/DVD with your photos and projects.

   ◆ **PDF Slide Show.** Creates a PDF Slide Show with your photos and projects.

   ◆ **Share and Send to Adobe Photoshop Services.** Shares photos and projects with Kodak Easyshare Gallery, or sends them to SmugMug Gallery, a CEIVA Digital Photo Frame, or Flickr.

See Also

See "Creating an Online Gallery" on page 418 for information on creating an online gallery.

For Your Information

Using the Quick Share Palette

The Quick Share Palette in the Organizer is a quick and easy way to order prints online. Click the Window menu, and then click Quick Share, drag the photos you want to the Quick Share palette, fill out the target form information (first time only) or click the New Order Prints Recipient button to create a new recipient or click the Edit Recipient button to modify the current recipient information, and then follow the onscreen instructions to complete the order.

Sending Files in E-Mail

In Photoshop Elements, you can send photos and other media files to other recipient as attachments in an e-mail message. You can use the Share tab to start the process, select file options, type a message, and select recipients before Photoshop Elements creates an e-mail message using the e-mail application you specified in Sharing Preferences in the Organizer.

Send Files in E-mail

1. Select (in the Organizer) or open (in the Editor) the photos you want to use in your project.

2. Click the **Share** tab.

3. Click **E-mail Attachments** on the Share tab.

4. To add photos to the list, click **Add**, select options to display the photos you want, select photo check boxes, click **Add Selected Photos**, and then click **Done**.

5. To remove a photo, select the photo, and then click **Remove**.

6. Select from the following options:

   ◆ **Convert Photos to JPEGs.** Select to convert to JPEG.

   ◆ **Maximum Photo Size.** Select a resolution size; larger the size, the larger the file size.

   ◆ **Quality.** Select a image quality setting; higher the setting, the larger the file size.

7. Click **Next**.

8. Type a message.

9. Select or enter the recipients you want to send the e-mail.

10. To save and name these settings for future use as a Quick Share Flow, click the **Yes** option and name it.

11. Click **Next**.

12. Complete and send the e-mail from your e-mail program.

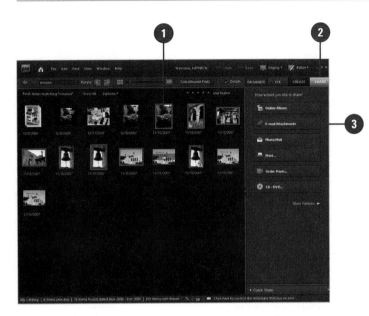

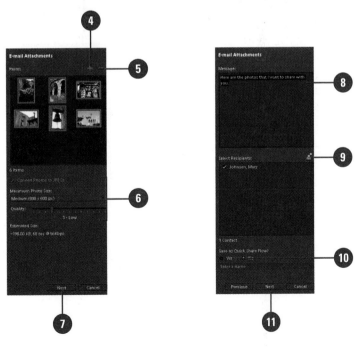

Sending Files in Photo Mail

Instead of sending photos and other media files as e-mail attachments, you can send them in a photo e-mail as an embedded message using colorful stationery, which you can customize with different backgrounds, layouts, text, and borders. You can use the Share tab to start the process, type a message, select recipients and select stationery options before Photoshop Elements creates an e-mail message using the e-mail application you specified in Sharing Preferences in the Organizer.

Send Files in Photo Mail

1. Select (in the Organizer) or open (in the Editor) the photos you want to use in your project.

2. Click the **Share** tab.

3. Click **Photo Mail** on the Share tab.

4. To add photos to the list, click **Add**, select options to display the photos you want, select photo check boxes, click **Add Selected Photos**, and then click **Done**.

5. To remove a photo, select the photo, and then click **Remove**.

6. Select the **Include caption** check box to add the photo caption to the photo mail.

7. Click **Next**.

8. Type a message.

9. Select or enter the recipients you want to send the e-mail.

10. To save and name these settings for future use as a Quick Share Flow, click the **Yes** option and name it.

11. Click **Next**.

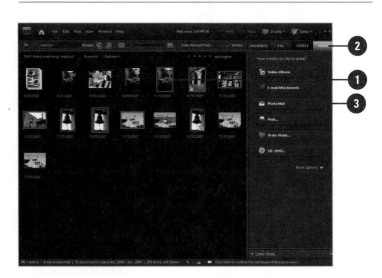

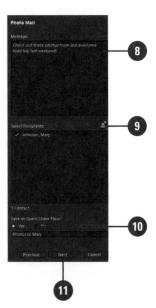

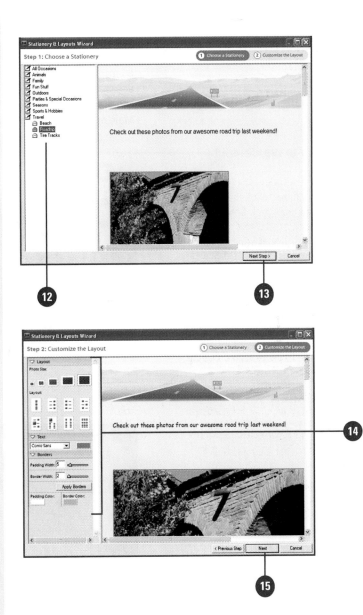

12 In the Stationery & Layouts Wizard dialog box, select a stationery template.

13 Click **Next Step**.

14 Select a photo size, layout format, text specifications, and border settings.

15 Click **Next**.

16 Complete and send the e-mail from your e-mail program.

Using the Contact Book

The contact book allows you to store, edit, group, and manage e-mail addresses for use in Photoshop Elements. Instead of typing an e-mail address every time you want to send a photo or project in as an e-mail attachment, you can quickly select an address from the contact book. You can import addresses from Outlook, Outlook Express/Windows Mail, or a vCard file, and export them as a vCard file.

Add an Entry to the Contact Book

1. In the Organizer, click the **Edit** menu, and then click **Contact Book**.

2. Click the **New Contact** button.

3. Type a name, e-mail address, and other information.

4. Click **OK**.

5. Click **OK**.

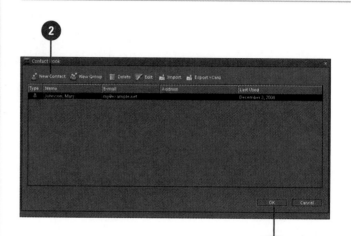

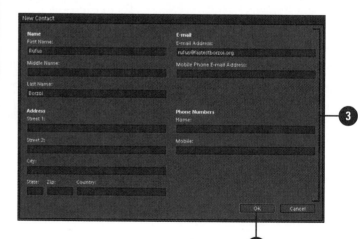

Did You Know?

You can delete a contact. In the Organizer, click the Edit menu, click Contact Book, select a contact, click the Delete button, and then click OK.

You can import addresses into the contact book. In the Organizer, click the Edit menu, click Contact Book, click the Import button, select the application where you want to get contacts from, and then click OK.

You can export contact information to vCard files. In the Organizer, click the Edit menu, click Contact Book, select the contacts you want to export (use Ctrl-click to select multiple contacts) click the Export vCard button, select a destination for the vCard file, and then click OK.

Edit an Entry to the Contact Book

1. In the Organizer, click the **Edit** menu, and then click **Contact Book**.

2. Select the contact you want to edit.

3. Click the **Edit** button.

4. Edit the contact information.

5. Click **OK**.

6. Click **OK**.

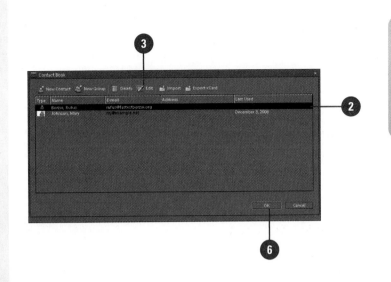

Create a New Group in the Contact Book

1. In the Organizer, click the **Edit** menu, and then click **Contact Book**.

2. Click the **New Group** button.

3. Type a name for the group.

4. Select the contact you want to add to the group, and then click the **Add** button.

   ◆ Use the Shift-click to add adjacent contacts, or Ctrl-click to add nonadjacent ones.

5. To remove a contact, select it, and then click the **Remove** button.

6. Click **OK**.

7. Click **OK**.

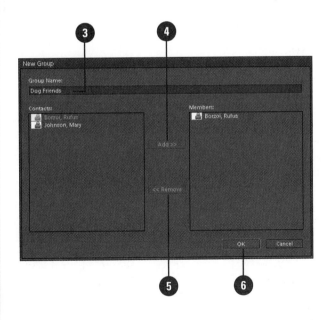

Making a CD or DVD with Files

If you want to share a large number of files with someone or you simply want to back them up for safe keeping, you can create a CD or DVD with the files you have stored in Photoshop Elements. You don't need an external program to make a CD or DVD. You can write, also known as burn, a CD or DVD directly from Photoshop Elements in the Organizer.

Make a CD or DVD with Files

1. Select (in the Organizer) or open (in the Editor) the photos you want to use in your project.

2. Click the **Share** tab.

3. Click **CD/DVD** on the Share tab.

   TIMESAVER *Press Ctrl+Alt+C to make a CD or DVD.*

4. Select the destination drive.

5. Enter a name for the CD or DVD.

6. Click the **Write Speed** list arrow, and then select a write speed that works with your CD or DVD drive.

7. Click **OK**.

   A progress dialog box appears during the burning process.

8. Click **Verify** or **Don't Verify**.

9. If prompted upon completion, click **OK**.

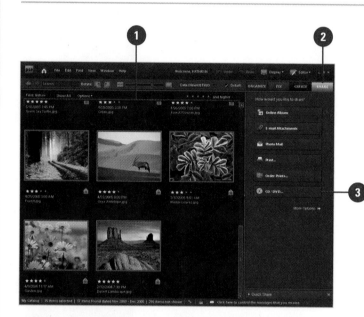

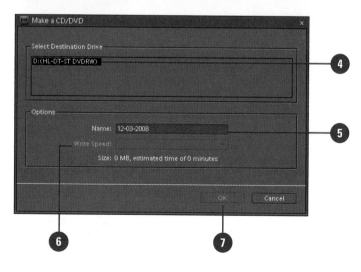

Making a PDF Slide Show

A PDF (Portable Document Format) is a common file type that allows anyone with the Adobe Reader software (available free at *www.adobe.com*) to open and view the file contents. In Photoshop Elements, you can select a number of photos to create a slide show in the PDF format, which makes it accessible to almost everyone.

Make a PDF Slide Show

① Select (in the Organizer) or open (in the Editor) the photos you want to use in your slide show project.

② Click the **Share** tab.

③ Click the **More Options** button on the Share tab, and then click **PDF Slide Show**.

④ To add photos to the list, click **Add**, select options to display the photos you want, select photo check boxes, click **Add Selected Photos**, and then click **Done**.

⑤ To remove a photo, select the photo, and then click **Remove**.

⑥ Select from the following options:

♦ **Maximum Photo Size.** Select a resolution size; larger the size, the larger the file size.

♦ **Quality.** Select a image quality setting; higher the setting, the larger the file size.

⑦ Enter a name for the PDF file.

⑧ Click **Next**.

⑨ Type a message.

⑩ Select or enter the recipients you want to send the e-mail.

⑪ To save and name these setting for future use as a Quick Share Flow, click the **Yes** option and name it.

⑫ Click **Next**.

⑬ Click **OK** or **Cancel** to attach the PDF to an e-mail message.

⑭ Complete and send the e-mail from your e-mail program.

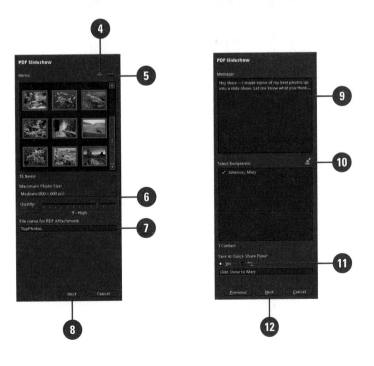

Exporting Files

After correcting and fixing files in Photoshop Elements, you can export them as files to use in other applications or share with others, or export them to a mobile phone. When you export photos as files, you can export them with the original file format or select a different file format, such as PSD Photoshop, and rename them in a sequence.

Export Files

1 In the Organizer, select the photos and other media you want to export.

2 Click the **File** menu, and then click **Export As New File(s)**.

TIMESAVER *Press Ctrl+E to export photos and media to files.*

3 To add photos to the list, click **Add**, select options to display the photos you want, select photo check boxes, click **Add Selected Photos**, and then click **Done**.

4 To remove a photo, select the photo, and then click **Remove**.

5 Select a file type option: **Use Original Format**, **JPEG**, **PNG**, **TIFF**, or **PSD** (Photoshop).

6 Click the **Photo Size** list arrow, select a size, and then drag the **Quality** slider; higher the setting, the larger the file size.

7 Click **Browse**, select an export location, and then click **OK.**

8 Click the **Original Names** option to use existing file names or click the **Common Base Name** option, and then enter a name to export files with the same name plus a sequential number.

9 Click **Export**.

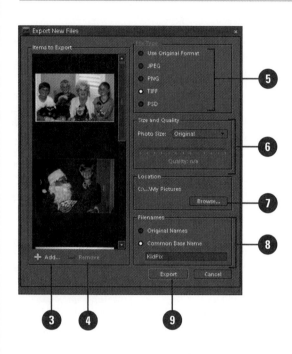

Copying or Moving Files to a Disk

If you want to share files in Photoshop Elements with others or you simply want to back them up for safe keeping, you can copy or move them to a removable disk or create a CD or DVD. You can copy or move them to a removable disk or CD/DVD directly from Photoshop Elements in the Organizer.

Copy or Move Files to a Removable Disk

1. In the Organizer, select the photos and other media you want to copy or move to a removable disk.

2. Click the **File** menu, and then click **Copy/Move to Removable Disk**.

   TIMESAVER *Press Ctrl+Shift+O to copy or move files to a disk.*

3. Select from the following options:

   ◆ **Move Files.** Select to move files from your computer; not available for projects and audio clips.

   ◆ **Include All Files in Selected Collapsed Stacks.** Select to include all files in a selected collapsed stack.

   ◆ **Include All Files in the Selected Collapsed Version Sets.** Select to include all files in a selected collapsed version set.

4. Click **Next**.

5. If missing files are detected, click **Reconnect** to automatically connect, **Browse** to manually select, or **Cancel**.

6. Select the destination drive.

7. For a CD or DVD, enter a name, click the **Write Speed** list arrow, and then select a write speed.

8. For a removable disk, specify a destination path; click **Browse** to select a folder.

9. Click **Done**, and then complete the process for a CD or DVD, if necessary.

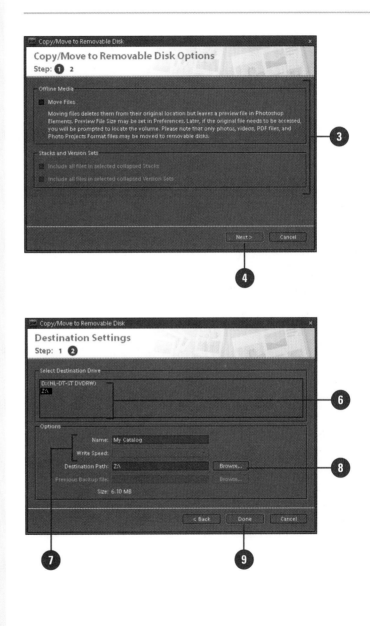

Customizing the Way You Work in the Editor

Introduction

No description of Photoshop Elements would be complete without that well known, but little utilized area called Preferences. Photoshop Elements preferences for the Editor serve several purposes. They help customize the program to your particular designing style, and they help you utilize available computer resources to increase the overall performance of the program.

As you use Photoshop Elements, you'll come to realize the importance of working with units and rulers. Precision is the name of the game when you are working with images. What about the color of your grids? No big deal, you say. Well, if you've ever tried viewing a blue guide against a blue-sky image, you know exactly why color is important. By working through preferences such as Image Cache, Scratch Disks, and RAM Memory, speed increases of up to 20 percent can be achieved.

In addition, customizing the program, helps make you more comfortable, and studies show that the more comfortable you are as a designer the better your designs. What does setting up preferences do for you? They make Photoshop Elements run faster (up to 20 percent), you work more efficiently, and your designs are better. That's a pretty good combination. Photoshop Elements doesn't give you preferences to confuse you, but to give you choices, and those choices give you control.

What You'll Do

Optimize Photoshop Elements

Set General Preferences

Modify Saving Files Preferences

Set File Associations

Select Scratch Disks

Allocate Memory & Image Cache

Set Undo History Preferences

Set Display & Cursors Preferences

Set Units & Rulers Preferences

Work with the Grid

Control Transparency Preferences

Set Type Preferences

Select Plug-Ins

Manage Libraries with the Preset Manager

Use Drawing Tablets

Optimizing Photoshop Elements

Photoshop Elements is a powerful program, and as such, requires a tremendous amount of computing power. When working on large documents, a poorly optimized Photoshop will translate into long wait times. That's the bad news if you have a deadline to meet. The good news is that Photoshop Elements can be configured to run more efficiently. To optimize Photoshop Elements, click the Edit menu, point to Preferences, and then click Performance. The Performance preferences dialog box contain options that will help increase the performance of Photoshop Elements.

History States

History States controls the number of undos available. In fact, you can have up to 1000 undos (ever wonder who would make so many mistakes that they would need 1000 undos?). Unfortunately, increasing the number of History States will ultimately increase the amount of RAM Photoshop Elements uses to manage the Undo History palette. Assigning more RAM memory to manage History means less memory for Photoshop Elements to perform normal operations, and will reduce the performance of the program. If you are experiencing slow performance problems, lowering the number of History States frees up more RAM, and permits Photoshop Elements to operate more efficiently.

Scratch Disk

When your computer doesn't have enough RAM to perform an operation, Photoshop Elements uses free space on any available drive, known as a **Scratch Disk**. Photoshop Elements requires 5 times the working size of the file in contiguous hard drive space. For example, if the working size of your file

History States

is 100MB, you will need 500MB of contiguous hard drive space, or you will receive an error message: Out of Scratch Disk Space (I hate it when that happens). Using additional hard drives gives Photoshop Elements the ability to divide the processing load and increase performance. Photoshop Elements detects and displays all available internal disks in the Preferences dialog box. Scratch disks must be physically attached to your computer (avoid networks and removable media, such as removable drives, or rewriteable CDs or DVDs). For maximum speed, avoid USB, and use 4 or 6-pin Firewire drives. Benchmark tests show Firewire drives provide up to a 20 percent speed improvement when used as scratch disks. Think of saving one hour out of every five, or one full day out of every five. That's not too bad. For best results, select a scratch disk on a different drive than the one used for virtual memory or any large files you're editing.

Memory & Image Cache

Photoshop Elements functions in RAM memory (actually all applications work within RAM). To run efficiently, Photoshop Elements requires five times the working size of the open document in available memory (some tests indicate 6 to 8 times). Strictly speaking, the more RAM memory you can assign to Photoshop Elements, the more efficiently the program operates, especially when opening large documents.

RAM memory usage is determined by the working size of the document, not its open size. As you work on a document, you will eventually add additional layers to separate and control elements of the image. As you add these new layers, the working size of the file increases.

RAM memory allocation

Available Scratch Disks

Setting General Preferences

Photoshop Elements' General preferences in the Editor help you configure some of the more common features of the program, including changing the appearance of the user interface (**New!**). Selecting a color picker dialog box, as well as the shortcut keys for using Undo and Redo are available in General preferences. Other options, such as showing tool tips, beeping when an operation is finished, centering document windows when an image opens, and saving palette locations, can all be turned on or off in the options area. If you have hidden a dialog box by selecting the Don't Show Again check box, you can reset all the warning dialog boxes so they appear again.

Set General Options

1 In the Editor, click the **Edit** menu, and then point to **Preferences**.

2 Click **General**.

3 Click the **Color Picker** list arrow, and then select Adobe or the Windows operating system.

4 Click the **Step Back/Fwd** list arrow, and then select the keyboard shortcuts you want to use to step backward and forwards in the Undo History palette with the Undo and Redo commands.

5 Select the various options you want to use:

- ◆ **Export Clipboard.** Transfers a copied image to the operating systems clipboard.

- ◆ **Show ToolTips.** Displays a screen tip when you point to buttons and options in the Photoshop Elements window or dialog boxes.

- ◆ **Zoom Resizes Windows.** Forces the image window to resize when zoom is selected.

- ◆ **Beep When Done.** Sounds when an operation is complete.

- ◆ **Select Move tool after committing text.** Changes from the Text tool to the Move tool after you create a text box.

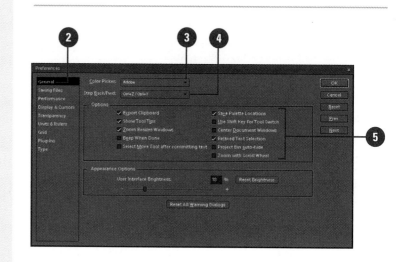

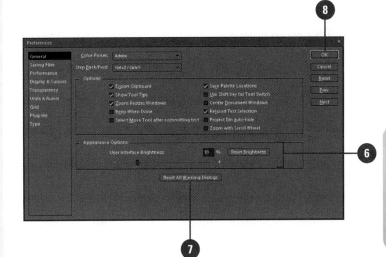

- ◆ **Save Palette Locations.** Saves and restores the current palette locations when you exit/launch Photoshop Elements.

- ◆ **Use Shift Key For Tool Switch.** Allows you to use the Shift key plus the keyboard shortcut to switch among tools that share the same slot in the toolbox.

- ◆ **Center Document Windows.** Determines whether to center document windows when you open an image.

- ◆ **Relaxed Text Selection.** Allows you to select text by clicking near it.

- ◆ **Project Bin Auto-Hide.** Displays the Project Bin closed until you point to the bin border edge.

- ◆ **Zoom With Scroll Wheel.** Determines whether scroll wheels zoom or scroll.

6 To adjust the brightness of Photoshop Elements' gray background, drag the **User Interface Brightness** slider (**New!**). Click **Reset Brightness** to restore the default value.

7 To display all warning dialog boxes hidden by selecting the Don't Show Again check box, click **Reset All Warning Dialogs**.

8 Click **OK**.

- ◆ **Prev and Next.** Click to display the previous or next preference section. When you reach the last section, it cycles back to the first section.

Did You Know?

You can access Editor preferences from the Organizer. In the Organizer, click the Edit menu, point to Preferences, and then click Editor Preferences.

For Your Information

Restoring Default Preferences

If you want to reset all the preferences settings in Photoshop Elements back to their original settings, you can use the Reset button in the Preferences dialog box. Click the Edit menu, point to Preferences, click General, click Reset, and then click OK. If Photoshop Elements crashes or starts to act differently than normal, the preferences file may be damaged. If you think this might be the case, you can restore all the preferences to their default settings. Close Photoshop Elements, if necessary, and then relaunch Photoshop Elements. Immediately after you launch Photoshop Elements, press and hold Alt+Ctrl+Shift. When a warning dialog box alert appears, click Yes to delete the Adobe Photoshop Elements settings file. The next time you launch Photoshop Elements, a new preferences file is created.

Modifying Saving Files Preferences

Sooner or later, you'll have to save the file (document) you've created in Photoshop Elements. The final output of any document is contained within a specific file format such as TIFF, EPS, JPEG, or even BMP. In fact, Photoshop Elements lets you save files using over 18 different formats. The Saving Files preferences in the Editor provide several options that modify what information is saved with a file. Image previews are typically very small and add very little to the file size of the saved document. Once saved you will want to open, print, and possibly even modify the document using other image-editing applications. The File Compatibility options help you save a file that will be transportable to other applications.

Modify Saving Files Options

1. In the Editor, click the **Edit** menu, and then point to **Preferences**.

2. Click **Saving Files**.

3. Select the File Saving options you want to use:

   ◆ **On First Save.** Select Always Ask, Ask If Original, or Save Over Current File.

   ◆ **Image Previews.** Select Always Save, Never Save, or Ask When Saving.

   ◆ **File Extension.** Choose to have upper or lower case extensions.

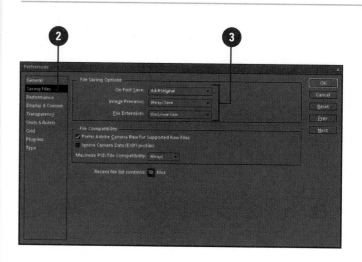

4 Select the File Compatibility options you want to use:

- **Prefer Adobe Camera Raw for Supported Raw Files**. Open Raw supported files in Camera Raw.

- **Ignore Camera Data (EXIF) Profiles.** Ignores color space metadata attached to digital camera images.

- **Maximize PSD File Compatibility.** Lets you save PSD files that can be opened in earlier versions of the program.

5 Enter the number of files (up to 30) to keep in the Open Recent menu available on the File menu.

6 Click **OK**.

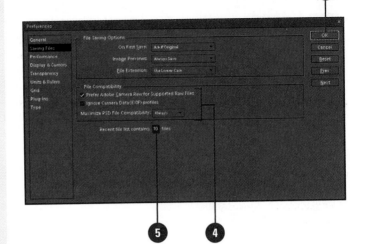

See Also

See "Understanding File Formats" on page 147 for information on some of the various file formats available in Photoshop Elements.

Allocating Memory & Image Cache

The Performance preferences in the Editor give you control over how much RAM memory is assigned to Photoshop Elements, and how much memory is allocated to screen draws (Image Cache). Photoshop Elements, being a high-performance application, requires a fairly large amount of RAM memory. Adjusting these options can help increase Photoshop Elements' overall speed performance. Photoshop Elements uses many things that effect RAM memory: History States, Undo, Clipboard, and Cache. When you modify the cache settings, you are increasing or decreasing the amount of RAM Photoshop Elements uses for various tasks. Experimentation is the key here. Try different settings and record Photoshop Elements' performance. By fine-tuning Photoshop Elements' engine, you increase its overall speed, and you'll get more design miles to the gallon.

Allocate Memory & Image Cache Options

① In the Editor, click the **Edit** menu, and then point to **Preferences**.

② Click **Performance**.

③ Select the History & Cache options you want to use:

◆ **History States.** Enter the amount of History States steps you want to keep as undos; you can enter up to 1,000.

◆ **Cache Levels.** Select a number from 1 to 8.

IMPORTANT *History States impact Photoshop Elements' performance by holding the History States using a combination of RAM and Scratch Disk space. The more History States used, the more RAM memory is required. Using an extensive number of History States can impact Photoshop Elements' performance.*

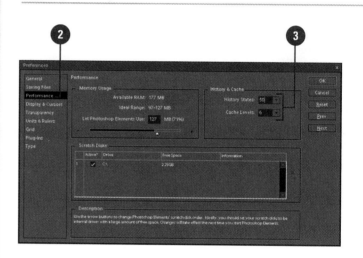

See Also

See "Installing Photoshop Elements" on page 2 for information on RAM and other system needs.

For Your Information

Setting the Cache Levels

Cache levels are screen redraws. It's how many versions of the current active document Photoshop Elements saves. When you're working on large documents, cache levels help speed up the redraw function, and makes image manipulation proceed faster. However, they are held primarily in RAM memory, so the higher your Cache Levels setting is, the less RAM memory is available for other Photoshop Elements functions.

Enter the percentage of RAM used in the Let Photoshop Elements Use box.

Photoshop Elements needs RAM memory to work efficiently (5 times the size of the open document).

IMPORTANT *Any setting changes made for allocating memory and image caching will take place the next time you start Photoshop Elements. Please see the message at the bottom of the dialog box.*

Click **OK**.

IMPORTANT *Never select 100 percent Memory Usage. Selecting 100 percent gives Photoshop Elements your entire available RAM, leaving nothing for the operating system or any other open programs. If you are experiencing more than your usual share of Photoshop Elements crashes, experiment with reducing memory usage.*

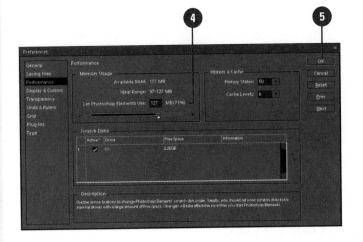

Selecting Scratch Disks

The Performance preferences in the Editor are available to help you get the best performance out of your computer, by letting you choose one or more hard drives for scratch operations. When your computer doesn't have enough RAM to perform an operation, Photoshop Elements uses free space on any available drive, known as a scratch disk. Photoshop runs faster when you divide the scratch disk workload. Scratch operations are performed on your hard drive, and take place when Photoshop Elements is using one of its many filters and adjustments. Photoshop Elements detects and displays all available internal disks in the Performance preferences dialog box, where you can select the disks you want. By assigning additional hard drives to the task, you speed up Photoshop Elements' overall performance. Scratch Disk changes take effect the next time you start Photoshop Elements.

Set Scratch Disks Options

1. In the Editor, click the **Edit** menu, and then point to **Preferences**.

2. Click **Performance**.

3. Select the check box next to the scratch disk you want to use or clear the check box to remove it.

   IMPORTANT *Photoshop Elements holds scratch disk space as long as the application is open. To free up scratch disk space for other uses you must close Photoshop Elements.*

4. Click **OK**.

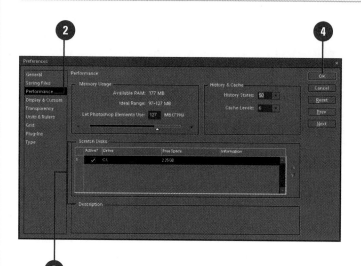

Using Drawing Tablets

When you design on a computer, you're leaving the natural world of oil, watercolor, and canvas, for the electronic world of computer monitors and pixels (don't worry, it's a relatively painless transition). Without a doubt there are many differences between traditional and digital design; however, it's not necessary to abandon all aspects of the natural media world. For example, the computer mouse has always been a problem with designers who miss the feel and control of a brush in their hands. Fortunately, technology came to the rescue several years ago, with the invention of the drawing tablet. Drawing tablets incorporate a drawing surface, and a brush-like drawing tool. A designer picks up the brush and moves it across the drawing tablet surface. In turn, the drawing tablet interprets those movements as brush strokes. Not only does Photoshop Elements fully support drawing tablet technology, it also interprets the particular drawing style of the designer. For example, pushing harder with the brush against the drawing tablet, instructs Photoshop Elements to create a wider stroke, or even to apply more color. Drawing tablets have helped to translate the control of working with real art brushes against canvas, into the world of the digital designer. Of all the manufacturers, Wacom stands out as the leader in drawing tablet technology. Wacom returns the feel of designing with a brush to the digital designer's world, and the software required to power the tablet works seamlessly with Photoshop Elements and the Windows operating systems. To check out what tablet might be right for your needs, point your browser to *www.wacom.com* and check out the available options.

Wacom tablet

Drawing pen

Setting Undo History Preferences

Working with the Undo History palette in the Editor requires a firm understanding of how the palette functions, and what you can and cannot do with History. The Undo History palette records your steps as you work through a document. A step is defined as a specific action, such as creating a layer, or adding a brush stroke. Every time you perform an action, a step is recorded in the Undo History palette. The Undo History palette gives you the ability to go back to a previous history state, which is the same as performing an undo command. You can perform multiple undo commands up to the number set in Photoshop Elements preferences for the History States.

Set Number of History States

① In the Editor, click the **Edit** menu, and then point to **Preferences**.

② Click **Performance**.

③ Enter a value from 0 to 1000 for the number of steps recorded in the History States box.

④ Click **OK**.

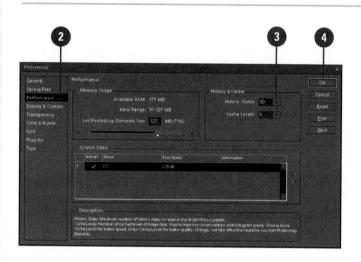

Change the Undo/Redo Keyboard Shortcut Command

① In the Editor, click the **Edit** menu, and then point to **Preferences**.

② Click **General**.

③ Click the **Step Back/Fwd** list arrow, and then select one of the following keyboard shortcuts to step backward and forward through the Undo History palette:

◆ **Ctrl+Z / Shift+Ctrl+Z.** Ctrl+Z executes the Undo command, while the Shift+Ctrl+Z executes the Redo command.

◆ **Alt+Ctrl+Z / Shift+Ctrl+Z.** Alt+Ctrl+Z executes the Undo command, while the Shift+Ctrl+Z executes the Redo command.

◆ **Ctrl+Z / Ctrl+Y.** Ctrl+Z executes the Undo command, while the Ctrl+Y executes the Redo command (default).

④ Click **OK**.

For Your Information

Resetting Palettes

You can reset all Photoshop Elements palettes back to their original configuration. Click the Window menu, and then click Reset Palette Location. Photoshop Elements resets all palettes, regardless of current settings.

Setting Display & Cursors Preferences

We communicate with Photoshop Elements using various devices, such as a drawing table, mouse, touch screen, track pad, and a keyboard. Photoshop Elements communicates with us using visual cues, the most prominent one being the shape of the cursor. For example, when a cursor looks like an I-beam, this typically means it's time to enter text, or when the cursor looks like a magnifying glass, clicking on the image expands the view size. Photoshop Elements also displays visual cues, such as transition effects and color shields for cropped areas of an image. Working with the Display & Cursors preferences in the Editor gives you control over how Photoshop Elements communicates with you.

Set Display Options

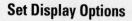

1 In the Editor, click the **Edit** menu, and then point to **Preferences**.

2 Click **Display & Cursors**.

3 Select the **Show Transition Effects** check box to show transition effects.

4 Select the **Use Shield** check box to display a color in the cropped area, and then select a shield color and opacity.

◆ **Shield Color.** Displays the selected color in the cropped area. Click the list arrow to select a color or click **Options** to select another color palette.

◆ **Opacity.** Displays the transparency level for the shield color. The lower the number, the higher the transparency.

5 Click **OK**.

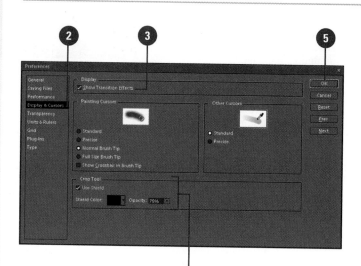

See Also

See "Using the Color Swatches Palette" on page 242 for information on using color.

Set Cursors Options

① In the Editor, click the **Edit** menu, and then point to **Preferences**.

② Click **Display & Cursors**.

③ Select the Painting Cursors options you want to use:

◆ **Standard.** Painting cursors appear as their toolbox buttons.

◆ **Precise.** Painting cursors appear as cross-hairs.

◆ **Normal Brush Tip.** Painting cursors appear with the shape of the active brush tip.

◆ **Full Size Brush Tip.** Shows the full size of the brush tip, including feathered edges.

◆ **Show Crosshair in Brush Tip.** Displays a crosshair in the center of the brush tip.

④ Select the Other Cursors options you want to use:

◆ **Standard.** Painting cursors appear as their toolbox buttons.

◆ **Precise.** Painting cursors appear as cross-hairs.

⑤ Click **OK**.

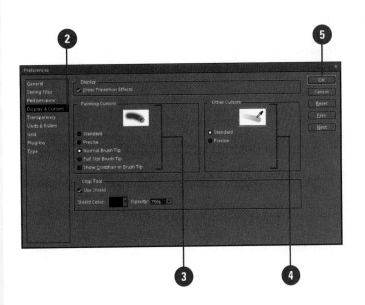

For Your Information

Toggling Between Precise and Standard Tools

Pressing the Caps Lock key while using a painting cursor, toggles the tool between the precise and brush size options, and pressing the Caps Lock key when using any other cursor, toggles between standard and precise.

Setting Units & Rulers Preferences

While changing the measurable units and rulers do not affect output quality, it does help you to measure information in a document consistent with the specific output device. Ruler units give you precise information on the width and height of the active document. The column size measurements provide information that Photoshop Elements needs to create documents in the column and width of newspapers, magazines, brochures, etc. The Preset Resolutions lets you select specific resolution values for creating new documents. Insert the values you'll use most often in the creation of a new document.

Set Units & Rulers Options

1. In the Editor, click the **Edit** menu, and then point to **Preferences**.

2. Click **Units & Rulers**.

   TIMESAVER *Double-click the ruler to display the Units & Rulers Preference dialog box.*

3. Select the Units options you want to use:

   ◆ **Rulers.** Sets a default measuring system for the Ruler bar.

   For example, pixels would be most common for images displayed on a monitor, and pica or inches most common for output to press or printer.

   ◆ **Type.** Sets to measure type with a default value of pixels, points, or millimeters.

   ◆ **Print Sizes.** Sets to measure print with a default value of inches or centimeter/millimeters (cc/mm).

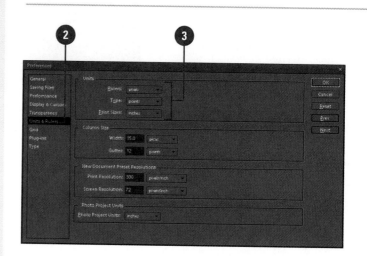

4 Select the Column Size settings you want to use:

- ◆ **Width.** Choose a measurement system and numerical value for column width.

- ◆ **Gutter.** Choose a measurement system and numerical value for gutter (the space between the columns).

  When you choose a measurement system (points, inches, or cm), Photoshop Elements changes the value to correspond to the type of measurement system.

5 Select the New Document Preset Resolutions settings you want to use:

- ◆ **Print Resolution.** Select a print resolution and measurement value for default printing.

- ◆ **Screen Resolution.** Select a print resolution and measurement value for default screen display.

6 Click the **Photo Project Units** list arrow, and then select a measurement system (inches or cm/mm).

7 Click **OK**.

Did You Know?

You can switch between ruler measurements without going to preferences. To change the default measurement system of the rulers, simply right-click your mouse on either ruler. A list of available measurement options will be instantly available.

Working with the Grid

The Grid preferences in the Editor help keep a multi-layered document in proper order. For example, lining up buttons on a web interface, or making sure specific design elements are exactly in place within the document window. The Grid options let you decide on a color, style, and layout for Photoshop Elements' grid system. A grid is a series of crisscrossed lines that aid in aligning objects in the document window. The grid is useful in designing a layout that is proportional and balanced. You can also use the Snap To option with the grid to enable objects to snap to a grid line when they get close to it.

Set Grid Options

1. In the Editor, click the **Edit** menu, and then point to **Preferences**.

2. Click **Grid**.

3. Select the Grid options you want to use:

    ◆ **Color.** Select a default color for displaying grids.

    ◆ **Style.** Select a default style (Lines, Dashed Lines, or Dots) for displaying the grid.

    ◆ **Gridline Every.** Enter a value for how often the grid lines appear within the active document.

    ◆ **Subdivisions.** Enter a value for how many subdivisions (lines) appear between each main gridline.

4. Click **OK**.

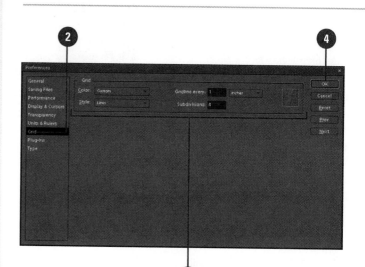

Did You Know?

You can change color choices for the grid. Not satisfied with the color choices offered by the color and style menus? Click on the Color box located on the Preferences dialog box, and then select any color from the Color Picker.

Use the Grid Along with the Snap To Option

1 In the Editor, click the **View** menu, and then click **Grid** to show the grid lines.

The grid appears in the Document window with the color and size you selected in the Grid preferences dialog box.

2 Select an object.

3 Select the **Move** tool on the toolbox.

4 Drag the object in the Document window to line it up along the grid line.

5 To have the object snap to a grid line, click the **View** menu, point to **Snap To**, and then click **Grid**.

As you drag close to a grid line, the object snaps to the grid line.

◆ A check mark appears next to the Grid option when enabled, while no check mark appears when the option is disabled.

6 Click the **View** menu, and then click **Grid** to hide the grid lines.

Grid in red

Controlling Transparency Preferences

The Transparency preferences in the Editor control how Photoshop Elements displays transparent areas of a document (commonly called the tablecloth), as well as the color and opacity of areas of an image that fall outside of the CMYK (Cyan, Magenta, Yellow, Black), color mode. It's important to understand that transparency in Photoshop Elements does not always translate into transparency, after you save the file. For example, the JPEG format is used primarily for images saved for the Internet, and does not support transparency. When you save the file, Photoshop Elements will fill the transparent areas of the image with a matte color (default white).

Control Transparency Options

1. In the Editor, click the **Edit** menu, and then point to **Preferences**.

2. Click **Transparency**.

3. Select the Transparency Settings options you want to use:

   ◆ **Grid Size.** Allows you to select a transparency grid size.

   ◆ **Grid Colors.** Allows you to choose the color scheme for the transparency grid.

4. Click **OK**.

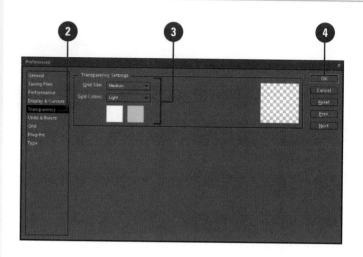

Setting Type Preferences

Although Photoshop Elements is not by definition a type setting application, such as Adobe InDesign, it does have some very powerful type features. For example, Photoshop Elements allows you to output PostScript text to a printer with a PostScript option. This way you will not need to place images into type intensive applications, such as InDesign or Illustrator, just to create a few lines of text. In addition, type font menu on the Options bar (with the Text tool selected) lets you see fonts as they will print or display. For designers that use a lot of fonts, this WYSIWYG (What You See Is What You Get) type font menu is a timesaver. You can use Type preferences in the Editor to help you select the type and font options you want to use.

Set Type Options

1. In the Editor, click the **Edit** menu, and then point to **Preferences**.

2. Click **Type**.

3. Select the Type options you want to use:

   ◆ **Use Smart Quotes.** Select to use left and right quotations.

   ◆ **Show Asian Text Options.** Select to display Japanese, Chinese, and Korean type options in the Character and Paragraph palettes.

   ◆ **Enable Missing Glyph Protection.** Select to automatically select incorrect, unreadable characters between Roman and non-Roman (Japanese or Cyrillic) text.

   ◆ **Show Font Names In English.** Select to display non-Roman fonts using their Roman names.

   ◆ **Font Preview Size.** Select to display fonts on the menu in small, medium, or large size.

4. Click **OK**.

   IMPORTANT *Photoshop Elements uses PostScript measuring systems to size fonts. Therefore a 72 point font will print 1 inch tall. Knowing this lets you know how big the fonts will appear when output to print.*

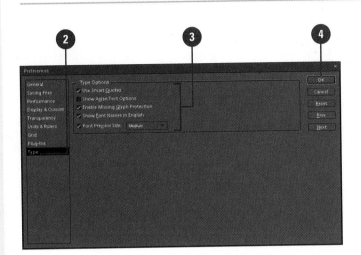

Selecting Plug-Ins

The Plug-Ins preferences in the Editor give you the ability to organize your plug-ins by saving them in one or more folders. These additional folders are typically used to hold additional third-party plug-ins. When selected, plug-ins contained within the folder will be available from Photoshop Elements' Filters menu. Organizing your plug-ins into folders helps keep your project focused and reduces the clutter of plug-ins when you select the Filter menu. After an plug-in is installed and ready to use, you can use the Help menu to open an About box for the plug-in to find basic information about it.

Set Plug-Ins Options

1. In the Editor, click the **Edit** menu, and then point to **Preferences**.

2. Click **Plug-Ins**.

3. Select the **Additional Plug-Ins Folder** check box to store additional plug-in.

   IMPORTANT *The first time you select this option, Photoshop asks you where to store the plug-ins. The next time you want to store plug-ins or add additional plug-ins, click Choose.*

4. If necessary, click **Choose** to identify the folder where you want to store plug-ins, and then click **OK**.

5. Click **OK**.

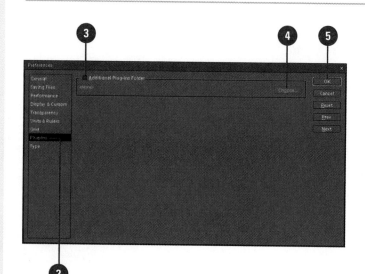

Find Out About a Plug-In

1. In the Editor, click the **Help** menu, and then point to **About Plug-in**.

2. Click the plug-in you want to find out about.

3. Click the About window or click **OK**.

DIGIMARC

ImageBridge(TM) Reader v 1.70.3
Protected by U.S. Patents 5,636,292; 5,710,834; 5,721,788;
5,745,604; 5,748,763; 5,768,426; 5,809,160; 5,832,119;
5,841,886; 5,841,978; 5,850,481; 5,930,377; 6,072,888;
6,122,392; 6,122,403; and 6,137,892 . Patents pending.
Copyright 1996-2002, Digimarc Corporation.
All rights reserved.

Managing Libraries with the Preset Manager

The Preset Manager gives you one place to manage brushes, swatches, gradients, and patterns. The Preset Manager can be used to change the current set of preset items and create new libraries of customized sets. Once a library is loaded in the Preset Manager, you can access the library's items in all locations the preset is available. Changes made in the Preset Manager are global, and are applied every time you open Photoshop Elements. When you save a new preset, the name appears in the dialog box for the specific option you selected. If you change a preset type, you can reset it to the original default or replace it with another preset.

Create a New Preset

1. In the Editor, click the **Edit** menu, and then click **Preset Manager**.

2. Click the **Preset Type** list arrow, and then select a preset type, such as Patterns.

3. Click the **More Options** button, and then select from the available presets to add them to the list.

4. To remove any items in a new preset, click a thumbnail, and then click **Delete**.

5. To reorganize their order, click and drag the thumbnails to new positions within the view window.

6. To change a preset name, click a thumbnail, click **Rename**, change the name, and then click **OK**.

7. Click a thumbnail, and then click **Save Set**.

8. Enter a new set name, and then use the default location (Patterns folder) to store the set, which is stored as a Patterns file with an .PAT extension.

9. Click **Save**.

10. Click **Done**.

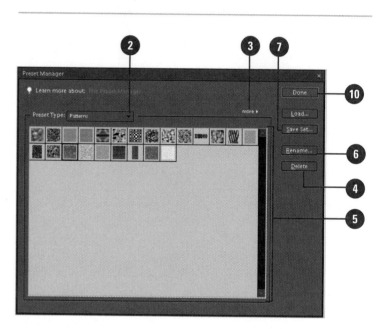

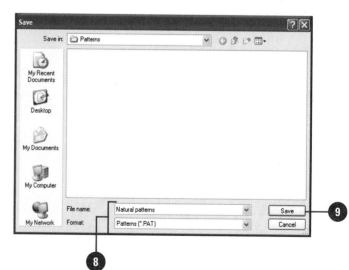

Reset or Replace a Preset

1. In the Editor, click the **Edit** menu, and then click **Preset Manager**.

2. Click the **Preset Type** list arrow, and then select the options.

3. Click the **More** button, and then select the reset or replace command you want:

   ◆ **Reset Brushes** or **Replace Brushes**.

   ◆ **Reset Swatches** or **Replace Swatches**.

   ◆ **Reset Gradients** or **Replace Gradients**.

   ◆ **Reset Patterns** or **Replace Patterns**.

4. To replace a preset, select the preset file, and then click **Load**.

   ◆ **Brushes.** Uses the .ABR extension.

   ◆ **Swatches.** Uses the .ACO extension.

   ◆ **Gradients.** Uses the .GRD extension.

   ◆ **Patterns.** Uses the .PAT extension.

5. Click **Done**.

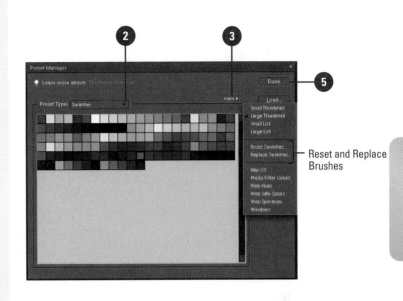

Reset and Replace Brushes

Swatches file

Swatches .ACO extension

Did You Know?

You can save specific items in the view window as a preset. Press Ctrl+click on only those items you want in the new set, and then click Save Set.

Workshops

Introduction

The Workshop is all about being creative and thinking outside of the box. These workshops will help your right-brain soar, while making your left-brain happy; by explaining why things work the way they do. Exploring the possibilities is great fun; however, always stay grounded with knowledge of how things work. Knowledge is power.

Getting and Using the Project Files

Each project in the Workshop includes a start file to help you get started with the project, and a final file to provide you with the results so you can see how well you accomplished the task.

Before you can use the project files, you need to download them from the web. You can access the files at *www.perspection.com*. After you download the files from the web, uncompress the files into a folder on your hard drive to which you have easy access from Photoshop Elements.

Project 1: Creating a Sketch from Scratch

Skills and Tools: Multiple Layers, Gaussian Blur, and Blending Modes

Photoshop Elements has a ton of filters. In fact, there are 105 filters located under the Filters menu. Filters perform a wealth of special-effects operations; everything from artistic, distort, and even sketch effects, and while filters are very creative, and fun to use, there is a limit to what they can do. For example, Photoshop Elements has no less than 14 Sketch filters, and while they do creative things to an image they can't do everything. What if you want to create what looks like a sketch effect and none of the sketch filters do what you want? If you don't know how to do things from scratch, you're stuck with the limitations of the filters. The technique you are about to learn will not only let you create an awesome sketch effect, but will give you a better understanding of how blending modes work with multiple layers. There are a lot of steps to this process; however, the end result is more than worth the effort. In addition, if this process seems familiar, they are; many of the steps used in the sharpening workshop are similar to this effect, until you get to the end.

The Project

In this project, you'll take a photograph and through the judicious use of multiple layers, and blending modes convert in into a beautiful colorized sketch. There are a lot of steps in this workshop, but the final results are more than worth the journey.

The Process

1. Open the file sketch_start.psd in Editor, and then save it as **my_sketch.psd**.

2. Create a duplicate of the image by dragging the layer over the Create New icon.

3. Click the **Enhance** menu, point to **Adjust Color**, and then click **Remove Color**. The copied layer is converted (desaturated) into shades of gray.

4. Create a copy of the desaturated layer, and then select it.

5. Click the **Filter** menu, point to **Adjustments**, and then click **Invert**. The image layer becomes a grayscale negative (leave the negative image selected).

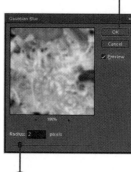

6. Click the **Blending Mode** list arrow on the Layers palette, and then click **Color Dodge**. The image appears to change to white.

   Note: If you see areas of the image that do not change to white, but are pure black, don't worry, those areas of the image were originally pure black, and they will never convert to white.

7. Click the **Filter** menu, point to **Blur**, and then click **Gaussian Blur**.

8. Very slightly blur the image (just a few radius pixels) until you see a soft-ghosted outline of the image.

9. Click **OK**.

10. Select the top layer in the Layers palette, click the **More Options** button, and then click **Merge Down**.

    You should now be left with the original image (the bottom layer), and the softly ghosted image (the top layer), which I've named, Sketch Effect.

Softly-ghosted image

11 Create a copy of the layer named Sketch Effect, and select it.

12 Click the **Blending Mode** list arrow on the Layers palette, and then click **Multiply**. The two copies combine to create a darker image.

13 Continue to make copies of the Sketch Effect layer until the image darkens to your taste (this might be 3 or 10 layers).

14 Merge all the Sketch Effect layers together, but do not merge the original image layer into the Sketch Effect layers.

Note: You can quickly merge layers by using the Merge Down shortcut. Select the top layer, and then press Ctrl+E. This merges the top layer into the layer directly underneath. Continue using the Merge Down shortcut until all the Sketch layers are merged.

15 Create another copy of the merged Sketch Effect layer, and select it.

16 Click the **Blending Mode** list arrow on the Layers palette, and then click **Multiply**.

17 Click the **Filter** menu, point to **Blur**, and then click **Gaussian Blur**.

18 Add a small amount of Gaussian Blur to taste (1 or 2 Radius). This will soften the edges of the image and create softer sketch lines.

19 Click **OK**.

20 Merge the two Sketch Effects layers together.

21 To colorize the image, select the top layer (Sketch Effect), click the **Blending Mode** list arrow, and then click **Luminosity**.

The Results

Finish: Compare your completed project file with the image in **sketch_fnl.psd**.

Tweaking the Image

The subjective items that will influence the final sketch image are how much you Gaussian Blur the image, and how many additional copy layers you create. Creating more blur enhances the sketch lines, and adding more copy layers, increases the overall density of the final sketch image.

Project 2: Creating a Sharper Image

Skills and Tools: Multiple Layers, Blending Modes, Layer Opacity, and Paint Brush

In the world of photography, not everything has to be in focus. In fact, smart photographers know that placing image elements out of focus will help to draw the eye to the focused areas. However, there are times when you will take a photograph and the image was accidentally, not intentionally, out of focus (I hate it when that happens). Photoshop Elements has several filters that help you create a sharper image. As a matter of fact, Photoshop Elements has four sharpen filters and tools: Sharpen tool, Auto Sharpen, Adjust Sharpen, and Unsharp Mask. Of these filters, Auto Sharpen, and Unsharp Mask are considered the two most powerful sharpening filters. Unfortunately, all the sharpen tools have one major flaw; they do not separate the sharpening effects from the image, as in an adjustment layer. So, when you click OK, you're stuck with the results. That's not necessarily a bad thing; however, there is another way. The technique you're about to learn for sharpening an image does not require any of the sharpening filters, its effect on the image creates a more believable sharpening effect, and the changes to the image are contained within a separate layer. That gives you the control you need to be creative, and get the pleasing sharpening results possible.

The Project

In this project, you'll take an out-of-focus image and sharpen it by creating an editable sharpening layer. Separating the sharpening adjustments from the image, gives you creative control over the entire process.

The Process

① Open the file lighthouse_start.psd in Editor, and then save it as **my_lighthouse.psd**.

② Create a duplicate of the image by dragging the layer over the **Create New Layer** button, or by selecting the layer and pressing Ctrl+J.

③ Click the **Enhance** menu, point to **Adjust Color**, and then click **Remove Color**. The copied layer is converted into shades of gray.

Note: If the image is originally a grayscale image, you can skip step 3.

④ Create a copy of the desaturated layer and select it.

⑤ Click the **Filter** menu, point to **Adjustments**, and then click **Invert**. The image layer becomes a grayscale negative (leave the negative image selected).

⑥ Click the **Blending Mode** list arrow on the Layers palette, and then click **Color Dodge**. The image appears to change to white.

Note: If you see areas of the image that do not change to white, but are pure black, don't worry, those areas of the image were originally pure black, and they will never convert to white.

7 Click the **Filter** menu, point to **Blur**, and then click **Gaussian Blur**.

8 Very slightly blur the image (just a few radius pixels) until you see a soft-ghosted outline of the image.

9 Click **OK**.

10 Select the top layer in the Layers palette, click the **More Options** button, and then click **Merge Down**, or press Ctrl+E.

You should now be left with the original image (the bottom layer), and the softly ghosted image (the top layer), which I've named, Unsharp Mask.

11 Click the **Blending Mode** list arrow on the Layers palette, and then click **Multiply**. The white areas of the ghosted image change to transparent, and the darker lines are blended in with the original image, creating the illusion of sharpness.

The Results

Finish: Compare your completed project file with the image in **lighthouse_fnl.psd**. ☞

Tweaking the Image

It's possible that the sharpening effect is too intense. If that's the case, simply reduce the opacity of the top layer to reduce its effect on the image. If, however, the effect is less than you hoped for, simply create a copy of the top layer to double the effect. Additionally, if you want to remove some of the sharpening effects from portions of the image, just select your Paintbrush tool, and paint the top layer using white, in the areas you want removed.

Good to Know: What happens in this technique is that the unsharp mask layer actually creates visible lines of force around the out-of-focus areas of the image, and the mind interprets those lines as being a sharper image.

Project 3: Restoring Life to Heirloom Images

Skills and Tools: Levels Adjustment Layer

There is nothing more important to a family than its history. History is found in many ways, places, and formats. For example, you may have historical documents that relate to who you are, or you might have physical artifacts from your ancestors. However, nothing strikes an emotional cord more than a photograph. A picture is indeed worth a thousand words. Yet even while an image freezes a moment in time, the actual photograph is traveling through time and unfortunately, Father Time can do major damage to a photographic image. Fortunately for us we have Photoshop Elements. Photoshop Elements is your time machine for restoring old images. While there are many methods for restoring an old grayscale image, one of the most consistently successful methods is through the use of a Levels Adjustment layer.

The Project

In this project, you'll take an old image, and through the use of the amazing Adjustment layers, restore the image. It's not that difficult, and the final results are awesome.

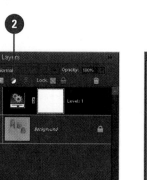

The Process

① Open the file three_girls_start.psd in Editor, and then save it as **my_three_girls.psd**.

Important: Always scan old grayscale images as RGB, not Grayscale. Most old images begin taking on a color as they age, such as: brown, sepia, or yellow. Although you will want to remove that color, it is information that Photoshop Elements can use to correct the image.

② Click the **Create New Fill or Adjustment Layer** button (half-moon icon), and then click **Levels**.

The Levels dialog box represents the brightness values of the pixels within the image. The data is called a Histogram, and is similar to a bar chart.

③ Click the **RGB Channel** list arrow, and then click the **Red** channel.

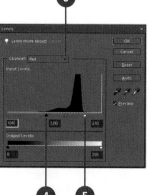

4 Drag the **black input** slider to just below the visible rise of the histogram.

5 Drag the **white input** slider to just below the visible rise of the histogram (that's where white has moved to after all those years).

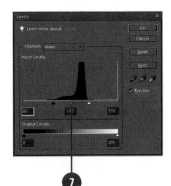

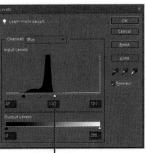

6 Once you have established the position of black and white, increase the input value of the white slider by 4, and decrease the value of the black slider by 4.

The value of 4 is an average, and based on the image; however, backing down both sliders, you help keep the light and dark areas of the image from blowing out (going pure white or black).

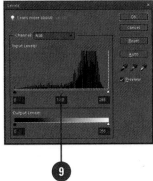

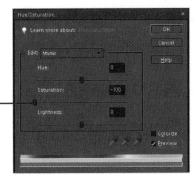

7 Click the **RGB Channel** selector, click the **Green** channel, and then repeat steps 4 thru 6.

8 Click the **RGB Channel** selector, click the **Blue** channel, and then repeat steps 4 thru 6.

9 If the image still appears a bit too dark or light, return the **RGB Channel** selection to the RGB option, then drag the middle gray slider to correspondingly lighten or darken the image in the mid-tones.

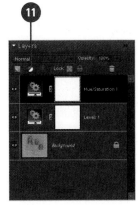

10 Click **OK**.

11 Click the **Create New Fill or Adjustment Layer** button (half-moon icon), located on the Layers palette, and then click **Hue/Saturation**.

12 Drag the **Saturation** slider to the far left.

13 Click **OK**.

This has the effect of removing any unwanted colorcasts from the image.

The Results

Finish: Compare your completed project file with the image in three_girls_fnl.psd.
👉

Tweaking the Image

It's possible that the sharpening effect is too intense. If that's the case, simply reduce the opacity of the top layer to reduce its effect on the image. If, however, the effect is less than you hoped for, simply create a copy of the top layer to double the effect. Additionally, if you want to remove some of the sharpening effects from portions of the image, just select your Paintbrush tool, and paint the top layer using white, in the areas you want removed.

Good to Know: The brightness levels of a pixel range from 0 (black) to 255 (white). When you move the input sliders, you're redefining where black and white are within the active image. As an image ages the original values of black and white shift. The purpose of Levels is to reestablish those positions. Once that's completed, Levels can approximate the positions of all the other remaining pixels, and balance the image.

Project 4: Colorizing a Grayscale Image

Skills and Tools: Multiple Layers, Blending Modes, Layer Opacity, and Paintbrush

Have you ever wanted to colorize an old grayscale image? Well, if you've ever wanted to add color to an old image, or ever change the colors within a new color image, then you've come to the right place. There are a lot of ways to colorize an image, and Photoshop Elements knows them all. The technique you are about to learn will help you control the colorization process through the use of layers, blending modes and opacity. As a matter of fact, you will be able to control each color within the image and, later change those colors with the click of a button. This method is so powerful that with a little bit of patience and care, the image won't just look colorized; it will look like an original color image. Just remember this simple item: every time you add a new color to the image, you will add a new layer. This means that a single image may contain twenty or more layers; however the final results are worth it.

The Project

In this project, you'll take a old, or new grayscale image, and through the use of multiple layers and blending modes create a colorized image that looks like it was taken with color film.

The Process

① Open the file colorization_start.psd in Editor, and then save it as **my_colorization.psd**.

② Click the **Create New Layer** button, located on the Layers palette, and name the layer to correspond to the area of the image you're coloring.

③ Click the **Blending Mode** list arrow, and then click **Color**.

④ Select the **Paintbrush** tool.

⑤ Select the color you want to use to paint a specific area of the image within the new layer.

⑥ Use the **Paintbrush** tool to paint an area of the image.

Note: Since you changed the blending mode of the layer to Color, the image retains its details, and only the color (Hue) of the information changes.

⑦ Depending on the color you chose, slightly lower the opacity of the layer to make it appear natural.

Note: Different colors require different opacity settings to appear natural. This occurs because of the saturation of the color, and the detail within the areas you are painting. Experiment with opacity settings until the image looks correct.

⑧ Repeat steps 2 thru 7 for each individual color within the image.

Name changed

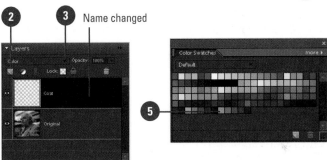

Multiple layer control color information

The Results

Finish: Compare your completed project file with the image in colorization_fnl.psd.

☞

Tweaking the Image

Since you are using individual layers to control the colorization process, if you over paint an area, it's a simple matter to use your eraser tool and remove the offending color information.

Smart Tip: When you change the opacity of a layer, it's not necessary to click the triangle button, located to the right of the Opacity input box, to access the triangular slider. All you have to do is click the word, Opacity, and drag left or right. It's that simple.

Project 5: Getting Creative with Adjustment Layers

Skills and Tools: Adjustment Layers, Layer Masks, and Paintbrush

Adjustment layers are thought of mostly for image enhancement. For example, the Levels and Curves adjustment layers are excellent tools for restoring lost contrast, or rebalancing out the colors in an old photograph. The technique you are about to learn will give you a greater understanding of how adjustment layers can be used to not only correct image problems, but to generate special effects. The key is in understanding that an adjustment layer can be controlled using its built-in layer mask. The adjustment layer mask functions similar to a normal layer mask; in other words, you can paint the mask with black, white, or shades of gray. However, the results are different. In a normal layer mask, areas of the mask painted black make the corresponding areas of the image transparent, when you paint with black on an adjustment layer mask, you mask out the effects of the adjustment. That means you can create a mask, and isolate its effects on the image by using the mask. While this is a powerful way to control image enhancement, it's also a great way to use adjustment layers to produce special effect. In addition, when you use an adjustment layer, the changes to the image are contained with the adjustment layer, and never change the original images. This gives you the ability to precisely control the creative process. In this example, you will completely change the mood of an image; using an adjustment layer and mask to create the illusion of looking through blinds.

The Project

In this project, you'll learn how to use Adjustment layers to precisely control the restoration, and enhancement of any Photoshop Elements image.

The Process

① Open the file **mystery_woman_start.psd** in Editor, and then save it as **my_mystery_woman.psd**.

② Select the **Rectangular Marquee** tool.

③ Create a long rectangular selection from left to right, across the image (like a window blind).

④ Hold the Shift key, and proceed to draw several more rectangular selections underneath the first.

Note: Holding the Shift key lets you create two or three additional selections within the document window.

①

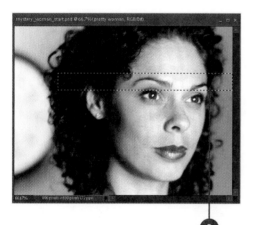

③

④

⑤ Click the **Select** menu, and then click **Inverse** (this reverses the selection).

⑥ Click the **Create New Fill or Adjustment Layer** button (half-moon icon), located on the Layers palette, and then click **Hue/Saturation**.

Photoshop Elements creates the adjustment layer, and the mask is created based on the selected areas of the image.

⑦ Drag the **Lightness** slider to the left until the non-masked areas of the image have significantly darkened.

⑧ Drag the **Saturation** slider to the left and lower the saturation value to -20 percent.

⑨ Click **OK**.

10 Select the **Hue/Saturation** adjustment layer.

11 Click the **Filter** menu, point to **Blur**, and then click **Gaussian Blur**.

12 Drag the **Radius** slider to the right to slightly blur the adjustment layer mask (you're looking for the light areas of the mask to resemble sunlight streaming through window blinds).

13 Click **OK**.

14 Use the **Paintbrush** tool with white (in this example) to paint out the blinds on the right side where they expose the back wall.

The image has now completely changed, and even the mood of the woman seems to be more serious. This is an example of how you can use adjustment layers to change the very mood of a digital image.

The Results

Finish: Compare your completed project file with the image in **mystery_woman_fnl.psd**.

Tweaking the Image

The realism in this effect is all in the Gaussian Blur. Light streaming through blinds, and falling on someone's face (in this example) would create a soft transition between dark and light. However the amount of blur would be determined by the image, and the resolution of the image. Therefore, don't look for a specific Radius, just look at the image and stop when you like what you see. Remember, being creative is not about a mathematical equation, it's about a certain look that you want to create.

Good to Know: The reason we slightly lowered the saturation value of the image is to make it appear more natural. In the real world, when images darken, they have a tendency to loose some of their tonal values, and that effect can be replicated by slightly lowering the saturation of the darker areas.

Project 6: Creating the Illusion of Depth

Skills and Tools: Multiple Documents, Selection, Adjustment Layers, and Blur Filters

When we look at an image in the Editor, the photograph is obviously flat. Computers lack one important thing, the third-dimension. Yet, although we know logically that the image is flat, our minds still persist in see the image as three-dimensional. For example, you're looking at an image of a landscape with mountains in the background, white puffy clouds in the sky, and your Uncle Charley waving in the foreground. The depth you perceive within the image is based on how our mind perceives three-dimensional objects, on a two-dimensional monitor, or page. The technique you are about to learn will give you a visible demonstration of how the illusion of depth can be achieved within a digital image. In this workshop, you will open two images, move one into the other, and using a few simple techniques, create the visual illusion of depth.

The Project

In this project, you'll learn how to blur selective areas of an image to focus the viewer's eye to specific portions of the image, and to create a feeling of depth within the image.

The Process

1. Open the file lincoln_monument_start.psd in Editor, save it as **my_lincoln_monument**, and then open soldier.psd.

2. Click in the document window of the image you want to move (in this example, soldier.psd).

3. Drag the layer from the Layers palette into the document window of the receiving document.

4. Close the document (solder.psd).

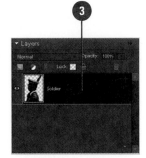

5 Move to the Layers palette and select the bottom layer.

6 Click the **Filter** menu, point to **Blur**, and then click **Motion Blur**.

7 Adjust the motion blur options until you create a soft blur (about 5 pixels).

8 Click **OK**.

9 Select the bottom layer in the Layers palette.

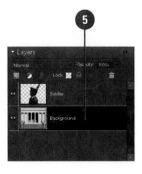

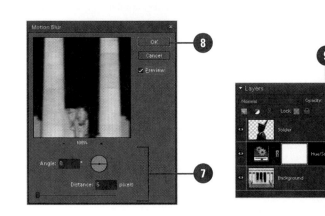

10 Click the **Add Fill or Adjustment Layer** button (half-moon icon), and then click **Hue/Saturation**.

11 Drag the **Saturation** slider to the left and reduce the saturation value to -20 percent.

12 Click **OK**.

With the background blurred and partially desaturated, the mind maps a greater distance between the foreground objects and the background, creating the illusion of depth.

The Results

Finish: Compare your completed project file with the image in lincoln_monument_fnl.psd.

Tweaking the Image

Blurring the background using the Lens blur filter, as opposed to the Gaussian Blur filter, creates a bit more realism within the image. You can vary the amount of Lens Blur to increase or decrease the effect depth. The human eye does not like to look at blurred objects. Therefore, when you blur specific areas of an image, not only are you generating the illusion of depth within the image, you're helping to direct the viewer's eyes to the focused areas.

Project 7: Using Your Free Photoshop.com Membership

Skills and Tools: Photoshop.com

Completing this project won't test your Photoshop Elements skills, but it will start you on the road to getting more from the program as you extend its capabilities to the Web, enabling you to manage your photo collection from anywhere with a web connection. Using Photoshop.com, you can add images, download them, and even create new albums to organize them. Photoshop.com also offers you a handy place to store online albums for your friends and family members to enjoy, and you can backup and sync your albums to Photoshop.com (**New!**) automatically so that there's always a safe copy of your photo collection online in case you run into computer trouble.

The Project

In this project, you'll learn how to sign up for your free Photoshop.com account and use Photoshop.com to manage your images and share them with friends.

The Process

1. To sign up for a membership, click **Join Now** at the top of the window (Organizer and Editor) or at the left side of the Welcome screen.

2. Enter your name, email address, and password, then choose a personal URL for your individual Photoshop.com page.

3. Specify your country and type in the security code, then click **Create Account**.

   Note: If you've made purchases or participated in message forums at Adobe.com, you can sign in using your existing Adobe ID without creating a new account.

4. On the Choose Your Membership Level screen, click **Basic**.

   Note: If you want to upgrade to a Plus membership, choose your membership level from the pop-up menu and click Plus. Benefits include new templates and artwork automatically added to Photoshop Elements and much more storage space for your images.

5. Click **Done** on the next screen, then check your email for a verification message. Follow the instructions in the email to verify your email address and activate your account.

6. To sign in to your Photoshop.com account, click **Sign In** at the top of the window (Organizer and Editor) or at the left side of the Welcome screen.

7. Enter your email address and password and click **Sign In**.

   When you're signed into your account, the Sign In and Join In links at the top of the Editor and Organizer screens change to "Welcome" and your first name.

8. In the Organizer, click the **Edit** menu, point to **Preferences**, and then click **Backup/Synchronization**.

9. Click **Backup/Sync** is On to activate Photoshop Elements' connection to Photoshop.com.

10. Set options for when and how albums will sync to Photoshop.com.

⑪ Click the check boxes to choose which albums to sync.

⑫ Click **OK**.

You can now use the Photoshop.com option in the Sharing Center, whenever you create online projects, to store those projects on Photoshop.com. Also, whenever you create a new album in the Organizer, you can choose have it automatically back up to Photoshop.com so that you always have a remote copy of your photos.

⑬ Go to *www.photoshop.com* in your web browser, and then click **Sign In**.

⑭ Enter your email address and password, and then click **Sign In**.

⑮ On your Photoshop.com page, choose one of the following: Click **My Photos** to see all the photos you've stored on Photoshop.com; click **My Gallery** to see a list of your shared albums; click **Browse** to look at other people's public photos; or click **Upload Photos** to add photos to your collection from Photoshop.com (this comes in handy when you're away from your computer and want to offload pictures from your camera).

The Results

Finish: Your personal page at Photoshop.com offers access to your online albums and as much of your photo collection as you choose to store there. ☞

Want More Projects

You can access and download more workshop projects and related files at *www.perspection.com*. After you download the files from the web, uncompress the files into a folder on your hard drive to which you have easy access from Photoshop Elements.

Get Everything on DVD

Instead of downloading everything from the web, which can take a while depending on your Internet connection speed, you can get all the files used in this book and much more on a Photoshop Elements 7 On Demand DVD. The DVD contains task and workshop files, tips and tricks, keyboard shortcuts, and other goodies from the author.

To get the Photoshop Elements 7 On Demand DVD, go to *www.perspection.com*.

New! Features

Adobe Photoshop Elements 7

Adobe Photoshop Elements means superior results faster with new features and enhancements that help you create and manage your images more easily and efficiently. The new and improved features help graphic web designers and photographers create the highest quality images with the control, flexibility, and capabilities that you expect from the professional standards in desktop digital imaging.

Only New Features

If you're already familiar with Photoshop Elements 6, you can access and download all the tasks in this book with Adobe Photoshop Elements 7 New Features to help make your transition to the new version simple and smooth. The Photoshop Elements 7 New Features as well as other Photoshop Elements 6 to Photoshop Elements 7 transition helpers are available on the web at *www.perspection.com.*

What's New

If you're searching for what's new in Photoshop Elements 7, just look for the icon: **New!**. The new icon appears in the table of contents and throughout this book so you can quickly and easily identify a new or improved feature in Photoshop Elements 7. The following is a brief description of each new feature and it's location in this book.

Photoshop Elements 7

◆ **Text Search box (p. 6, 96)** Type a word or two to locate your photos instantly—you can search on tags, dates, and any other file information using the new text search box that's always available in the Organizer's Thumbnail view.

◆ **Adjustable workspace brightness (p. 26–27, 476-477)** Drag a slider in the Preferences to adjust the Organizer's and Editor's background color to exactly the gray shade you prefer.

◆ **Improved Auto Red Eye detection (p. 48–53)** Photoshop Elements has gotten much better at automatically detected and removing red eye when you're importing new images.

- **Quick Fix Touch Up tools (p. 139)** Instantly remove red eye, whiten teeth, make skies bluer, or turn a color photo into a high-contrast black and white image using these new tools in the Editor's Quick Fix mode.

- **New Guided Edits (p. 140–141)** Try out several new adjustments and effects, such as Sketch and Saturated Slide.

- **Action Player (p. 141)** Execute automated Actions recorded in Photoshop to streamline your workflow.

- **Expanded Camera Raw import (p. 130–131)** Camera Raw now supports more camera formats and can automatically apply default conversion settings when you use raw images in a photo project.

- **Smart Brush tool (p. 288–289)** Select a specific photo area and apply special effects or standard photo improvements to the selection with a single click or a simple brushstroke.

- **Detail Smart Brush tool (p. 290)** Apply instant Smart Effects with incredible precision by painting them in exactly where you want them.

- **Photoshop.com/Photoshop Showcase (p. 324, 335, 337, 513–514)** Share your photos online directly from Photoshop Elements, access your photo collection from any Web browser, and back up your photo albums automatically.

- **Surface Blur filter (p. 357)** Apply this new Blur filter to remove grainy surface textures while preserving edge detail. Try it on portraits for a smooth, glamorous look.

- **New templates and content (p. 412–429)** You'll enjoy the expanded selection of templates, backgrounds, themes, and incidental art for use in your photo projects.

- **Online Album (p. 418–419)** Formerly called Online Gallery, this revamped project feature includes much more animation and interactive ability in its templates for an incredibly sophisticated look with minimal effort.

- **Photomerge Scene Cleaner (p. 440–441)** Remove unwanted objects from your scenic photos by combining the best background from one or more photos with the best foreground shot, using Photomerge's automatic image alignment and blending power.

Keyboard Shortcuts

Adobe Photoshop Elements 7

Adobe Photoshop Elements is a powerful program with many commands, which sometimes can be time consuming to access. Most menu commands have a keyboard equivalent, known as a **keyboard shortcut**, as a quicker alternative to using the mouse. For example, if you want to open a new document in the Editor in Photoshop Elements, you click the File menu, point to New, and then click Blank File, or you can abandon the mouse and press Ctrl+N to use shortcut keys. Using shortcut keys reduces the use of the mouse and speeds up operations. If a command on a menu includes a keyboard reference, known as a keyboard shortcut, to the right of the command name, you can perform the action by pressing and holding the first key, and then pressing the second key to perform the command quickly. In some cases, a keyboard shortcut uses three keys. Simply press and hold the first two keys, and then press the third key. Keyboard shortcuts provide an alternative to using the mouse and make it easy to perform repetitive commands.

Keyboard Shortcuts

Command	Shortcut
PHOTOSHOP ELEMENTS 7	
Shortcuts for the Organizer	
Navigating	
Move selection up/down/left/right	Up Arrow/Down Arrow/Left Arrow/Right Arrow
Move up without changing selection	Page Up
Move down without changing selection	Page Down
Select first item and scroll view to it. (In Date view, selects first item in Year, Month, or Day view	Home
Select last item and scroll view to it. (In Date view, selects last item in Year, Month, or Day view.	End
Select multiple contiguous items	Shift + Up Arrow/Down Arrow/Left Arrow/Right Arrow
Show full-sized thumbnail of selected photo	Enter

Keyboard Shortcuts *(continued)*

Command	Shortcut
Move through controls	Tab
Select control	Spacebar
Viewing Photos (Photo Browser)	
Full Screen view	F11
Side by side view	F12
Exit Full Screen or Side by Side view	Esc
View/hide details	Ctrl + D
View/hide Timeline	Ctrl + L
Collapse all tags	Ctrl + Alt +T
Expand all tags	Ctrl + Alt + X
Expand photos in stack	Ctrl + Alt + R
Viewing The Calendar (Date View)	
Go to subset View (year > month > day)	+ or =
Go to Superset view (day > month > year)	- or _
Move to previous photo on a selected day	,
Move to next photo on a selected day	.
Start automatic sequencing in Day view	Enter
Go to Day view when in Month/year view	Enter
Move to next day/month/year in calendar	]
Move to previous day/month/year in calendar	[
Editing Photos (Photo Browser)	
Undo last operation	Ctrl = Z
Redo last operation	Ctrl + Y
Copy	Ctrl + C
Select all	Ctrl + A
Deselect	Ctrl + Shift + A
Rotate 90 degrees left	Ctrl + Left Arrow
Rotate 90 degrees right	Ctrl + right Arrow
Edit in the Editor (Full Edit)	Ctrl + I
Display Properties palette	Alt + Enter
Adjust date and time of photo	Ctrl + J

Command	Shortcut
Add caption	Ctrl + Shift + T
Update thumbnails	Ctrl + Shift + U
Set photo as desktop wallpaper	Ctrl + Shift + W
Open Color Settings dialog box	Ctrl + Alt + G
Zoom in	Ctrl + + (plus sign)
Zoom out	Ctrl + - (minus sign)
OK	Enter
Cancel	Esc

Finding Photos

Command	Shortcut
Set data range	Ctrl + Alt + F
Clear date range	Ctrl + Shift + F
Find by caption or note	Ctrl + Shift + J
Find by filename	Ctrl + Shift + K
Find photos with unknown	Ctrl + Shift + X
Find untagged items	Ctrl + Shift + Q

Shortcuts for the Editor

Viewing Images (Full Edit)

Command	Shortcut
Cycle forward through open documents	Ctrl + Tab
Cycle backward through open documents	Ctrl + Shift + Tab
Fit image in window	Ctrl + 0 (or double-click hand tool)
Magnify 100%	Ctrl + Alt + 0 (or double-click the zoom tool)
Switch to Hand tool (when not in text-edit mode)	Spacebar
Switch to Zoom In tool	Ctrl + Spacebar
Switch to Zoom Out tool	Spacebar + Alt
Response zoom marquee while dragging	Spacebar-drag
Zoom in on specified area of an image	Ctrl-drag over preview in Navigator palette
Scroll up or down 1 screen	Page Up or Page Down
Scroll up or down 10 units	Shift + Page Up or Page Down
Scroll left or right 1 screen	Ctrl + Page Up or Page Down
Scroll left or right 10 units	Ctrl+Shift + Page Up or Page Down
Move view to upper-left corner or lower-right corner	Home or End

Command	Shortcut
Selecting Tools	
Cycle through tools that have the same keyboard shortcut	Shift-press keyboard shortcut (preference setting, Use Shift Key for Tool Switch, must be enabled)
Cycle through nested tools	Alt-click tool
Move tool	V
Zoom tool	Z
Hand tool	H
Eyedropper tool	I
Rectangular Marquee tool Elliptical Marquee tool	M
Lasso tool Magnetic Lasso tool Polygonal Lasso tool	L
Magic wand tool	W
Selection Brush tool (or Quick Selection tool)	A
Horizontal Type tool Vertical Type tool Horizontal Type Mask tool Vertical Type Mask tool	T
Crop tool	C
Cookie Cutter tool	Q
Straighten tool	P
Red Eye Removal tool	Y
Spot Healing Brush tool Healing Brush tool	J
Clone Stamp tool Pattern Stamp tool	S
Pencil tool	N
Eraser tool Background Eraser tool Magic tool	E
Brush tool Impressionist Brush Color Replacement tool	B
Paint Bucket tool	K
Gradient tool	G

Keyboard Shortcuts *(continued)*

Command	Shortcut
Rectangle tool Rounded Rectangle tool Ellipse tool Polygon tool Line tool Custom Shape tool Shape Selection tool	U
Blur tool Dodge tool Burn tool	O
Show/hide all palettes (not including Artwork and affects, and Layers palette)	Tab
Default foreground and background colors	D
Switch foreground and background colors	X

Selecting and Moving Objects

Command	Shortcut
Deselect a selection	Ctrl + D
Reposition marquee while selecting	Spacebar-drag
Add to or subtract from a selection	Any selection tool + Shift or Alt-drag
Intersect a selection	Any selection tool + Shift or Alt-drag
Constrain marquee to square or circle (if no other selections are active)	Shift-drag
Draw marquee from center (if no other selections are active)	Alt-drag
Constrain shape and draw marquee from center	Shift + Alt-drag
Switch to move tool	Ctrl (except when Hand or any shape tool is selected)
Switch from magnetic Lasso to Polygonal Lasso tool	Alt-click and drag
Delete last anchor point for Magnetic or Polygonal Lasso tool	Delete
Apply/cancel an operation of the Magnetic Lasso tool	Enter/Esc
Move copy of selection	Move tool + Alt-drag selection
Move selection area 1 pixel	Any selection + Right Arrow, Left Arrow, Up Arrow, or Down Arrow
Move selection 1 pixel	Move selection + Right Arrow, Left Arrow, Up arrow, or Down Arrow
Move layer 1 pixel when nothing selected on layer	Ctrl = Right Arrow, Left Arrow, Up Arrow, or Down Arrow
Increase/decrease detection width	Magnet Lasso tool + [or]

Keyboard Shortcuts *(continued)*

Command	Shortcut
Accept cropping or exit cropping	Crop tool + Enter or Esc
Toggle crop shield off and on	/ (forward slash)
Magic Extractor dialog box	
Foreground brush	B
Straighten tool	P
Point Eraser	E
Add To Selection tool	A
Remove From Selection tool	D
Healing brush tool	J
Zoom tool	Z
Hand tool	H
Transforming Selections	
Transforming from center of reflect	Alt
Constrain	Shift
Distort	Ctrl
Skew	Ctrl + Shift
Changing perspective	Ctrl + Shift + Alt
Apply	Enter
Cancel	Esc or Ctrl + . (period)
Painting and Brushes	
Switch to eyedropper tool	Any painting or editing tool + Alt (except Impressionist Brush)
Select background color	Eyedropper tool + Alt-click
Set opacity, tolerance, or exposure for painting	Any painting or editing tool + number keys (for example 0 = 100%, 1 = 10%, 4 & 5 in succession = 45%)
Cycle through blends modes	Shift + + (plus) or - (minus)
Fill selection/layer with foreground or background color	Alt + Backspace, or Ctrl + Backspace
Display Fill dialog box	Shift + Backspace
Lock transparent pixels on/off	/ (forward)
Connect points with a straight line (draw a straight line)	Any painting tool + Shift-click
Delete brush	Alt-click brush
Decrease/increase brush size	[or]

Keyboard Shortcuts *(continued)*

Command	Shortcut
Decrease/increase brush softness/hardness in 25% increments	Shift + [or]
Select previous/next brush size	, (comma) or . (period)
Select first/last brush	Shift + , (comma) or . (period)
Display precise cross hair for brushes	CAPS LOCK

Using Text

Command	Shortcut
Move type in image	Ctrl-drag type when Type layer is selected
Select 1 character left/right or 1 line down/up, or 1 word left/right	Shift + Left Arrow/Right Arrow or Down Arrow/Up Arrow, or Ctrl + Shift + Left Arrow/Right Arrow
Select character from insertion point to mouse click point	Shift-click
Move 1 character left/right, 1 line down/up, or 1 word left/right	Left Arrow/Right Arrow, Down Arrow/Up Arrow, or Ctrl +Left Arrow/Right Arrow
Select word, line, or paragraph	Double-click, triple-click, or quadruple-click
Scale and skew text within a bounding box when resizing	Ctrl-drag a bounding box handle
Align left, center, or right	Horizontal Type tool or Horizontal Type Mask tool + Ctrl + Shift + L, C, or R
Align top, center, or bottom	Vertical Type tool or Vertical Type Mask tool + Ctrl + Shift + L, C, or R
Return to default font style	Ctrl + Shift + Y
Turn Underlining on/off	Ctrl + Shift + U
Turn Strikethrough on/off	Ctrl + Shift + / (forward slash)
Decrease or increase type size of selected text pts/px	Ctrl + Shift + < or >

Layers Palette

Command	Shortcut
Set layer options	Alt-click New button
Delete without confirmation	Alt-click Trash button
Apply value and keep text box active	Shift + Enter
Load layer transparency as a selection	Ctrl-click layer thumbnail
Add to current selection	Ctrl + Shift-click layer
Subtract from current selection	Ctrl + Alt-click layer thumbnail
Intersect with current selection	Ctrl + Shift + Alt-click layer thumbnail
Merge visible layers	Ctrl + Shift + E

Keyboard Shortcuts (continued)

Command	Shortcut
Create new empty layer with dialog	Alt-click New Layer button
Create new layer below target layer	Ctrl-click New Layer button
Activate bottom/top layer	Shift + Alt + [or]
Select next layer down/up	Alt + [or]
Move target layer down/up	Ctrl + [or]
Merge a copy of all visible layers into target layer	Ctrl + Shift + Alt + E
Merge down	Ctrl + E
Copy current layer to layer below	Alt + Merge Down command from the palette pop-up menu
Copy all visible layers to active layer	Alt + Merge Visible command from the palette pop-up menu
Copy visible linked layers to active layer	Alt + Merge Linked command from the palette pop-up menu
Show/hide all other currently visible layers	Alt-click the eye icon
Toggle lock transparency for target layer, or last applied lock	/ (forward slash)
Edit layer properties	Double-click layer thumbnail
Select all text; temporarily select Type tool	Double-click text layer thumbnail
Create a clipping mask	Alt-click the line dividing two layers
Rename layer	Double-click the layer name
Blending Modes	
Cycle through blending modes	Shift + + (plus) or - (minus)
Normal	Shift + Alt + N
Dissolve	Shift + Alt + I
Behind	Shift + Alt + Q
Clear	Shift + Alt + R
Darken	Shift + Alt + K
Multiply	Shift + Alt + M
Color Burn	Shift + Alt + B
Linear Burn	Shift + Alt + A
Lighten	Shift + Alt + G
Screen	Shift + Alt + S
Color Dodge	Shift + Alt + D
Linear Dodge	Shift + Alt + W

Keyboard Shortcuts *(continued)*

Command	Shortcut
Overlay	Shift + Alt + O
Soft Light	Shift + Alt + F
Hard Light	Shift + Alt + H
Vivid Light	Shift + Alt + V
Linear Light	Shift + Alt + J
Pin Light	Shift + Alt + Z
Hard Mix	Shift + Alt + L
Difference	Shift + Alt + E
Exclusion	Shift + Alt + X
Hue	Shift + Alt + U
Saturation	Shift + Alt + T
Color	Shift + Alt + C
Luminosity	Shift + Alt + Y
Info Palette	
Change color readout modes	Click eyedropper icon
Change measurement	Click cross-hair icon
Color Swatches Palette	
Create new swatch from foreground color	Click in empty area of palette
Select background color	Control-click swatch
Delete color	Alt-click swatch
Showing or Hiding Palettes (Full Edit)	
Open Help	F1
Show/Hide Content palette	F7
Show/Hide Info palette	F8
Show/Hide Histogram palette	F9
Show/Hide Undo History palette	F10
Show/Hide Layers palette	F11
Show/Hide Navigator palette	F12
Filter Gallery	
Apply a new filter on top of selected	Alt-click on a filter
Open/close all disclosure triangles	Alt-click on a disclosure triangle
Change Cancel button to Default	Ctrl

Command	Shortcut
Change Cancel button to Reset	Alt
Undo/redo	Ctrl + Z
Step forward	Ctrl + Shift + Z
Step backward	Ctrl + Alt + Z
Liquify	
Warp tool	W
Turbulence tool	A
Twirl Clockwise tool	R
Twirl Counter Clockwise tool	L
Pucker tool	P
Bloat tool	B
Shift Pixels tool	S
Reflection tool	M
Reconstruct tool	E
Zoom tool	Z
Hand tool	H
Photomerge Panorama	
Select Image tool	A
Rotate Image tool	R
Set Vanishing Point tool (Perspective option selected)	V
Zoom tool	Z
Switch to Hand tool	Spacebar
Step backward	Ctrl + Z
Step forward	Ctrl + Shift + Z
Move selected image 1 pixel	Right Arrow, Left Arrow, Up Arrow, or Down Arrow
Change Cancel button to Reset	Alt
Show individual image border	Alt-move pointer over image
Camera Raw Dialog Box	
Display highlights that will be clipped in Preview	Alt-drag Exposure or Blacks sliders
Enable Open Copy button in the Camera Raw dialog box	Alt

Index

O

offset print area for labels, 451
Old Photo effect, 335, 336
online gallery, 418-419
    animated gallery, creating, 418
    interactive gallery, creating, 418
Online Learning Resources command, 19
online support. *See* Adobe web site
Online Support command, 19
opacity, 202, 205
    for adjustment layers, 228-229
    with basic Eraser tool, 310
    and blending modes, 348
    with Brush tool, 302
    display options, setting, 486
    for Drop Shadow layer style, 328
    for gradients, 313, 315
    with Impressionist tool, 306
    Inner Glow layer style settings, 333
    with Magic Eraser tool, 312
    Outer Glow layer style settings, 333
    with Paint Bucket tool, 308
    with Pencil tool, 304
    for slide show text, 429
    Stroke layer styles settings, 334
Open As command, 127
Open dialog box, 127
opening
    camera raw images, 130-131
    catalogs, 56-57
    non-supported files, 237
    other formats, files as, 127
    PDF files, 128
    Undo History palette, 166
OpenType font, 369
optimizing
    catalogs, 58
    JPEG document, 390-391
    Photoshop Elements, 474-475
    PNG-8 format, 394-395
    PNG-24 format, 396
Options bar, Editor, 7, 17
Ordered Online, finding photos by, 93
Organizer. *See also* albums; catalogs; Date
    view; Folder Location view; Map
    view; palettes; Photo Browser;

    printing
        adding photos from Editor, 56
        commands in, 8
        customizing work in, 25
        docking/undocking Properties
            palette, 14-15
        Editor, switching to, 9
        exiting, 24
        Files preferences in, 28-29
        fixing images in, 7
        general preferences, setting, 26-27
        larger work space, creating, 10
        saving files for, 144
        scanner preferences, setting, 34
        Sharing Center, accessing, 462
        slide shows, adding content to, 424
        task pane, working with, 10
        viewing workspace, 6
        watched folders, specifying, 42-43
orientation, 454
    Page Setup options, 448
    of text, 369
Orientation Metadata, 29
Other category, Keyword Tags palette, 82
Outer Glow layer style, 324
    changing settings, 332-333
outline fonts, 369
Outlook/Outlook Express. *See* Microsoft
    Outlook/Outlook Express
Out of Scratch Disk Space message, 475
ovals with Elliptical Marquee tool, 177
overexposed photos, correcting, 110
oversharpening, 279

P

page duration, Full Screen View Options
    dialog box options, 73
Page setup dialog box, 448
Paintbrush tool with adjustment layers, 232
Paint Bucket tool, 308
    shortcut key for, 16
Palette Bin, 7, 11
    attaching/detaching palettes, 14
Palette Knife filter, 360
palettes, 7. *See also* specific palettes
    attaching/detaching, 14